Roswitha Hecke   LOVE LIFE

R&B/Grove

LOVE LIFE

I have found the definition of beauty, of my sense of beauty. It is something both ardent and sad, something a little vague, leaving room for conjecture. Allow me to apply my ideas to the most interesting object in society, to a woman's face. An attractive and beautiful face is a face which induces simultaneous, though somewhat confused, visions of sensuality and sadness, a face which reveals a certain melancholy, weariness, even tedium. That is, an antithesis. An ardor, a passionate desire to live as well as a bitterness which seems to stem from deprivation or desperation.

    Baudelaire

The first time I saw Irene I thought of Baudelaire. She reminded me of his sardonic epigrams on the depravity, shamelessness, and beauty of women that I always felt tried to conceal a certain longing.
Baudelaire didn't want to believe in love. He was far too sceptical. He wanted to outsmart it with sarcasm and wit. But behind each barb, I can sense a wound.
To me, Irene is the very embodiment of his aggressive fantasy. She would have been a perfect target for him. Irene is not the kind of woman to be offended by his cutting remarks. She feels challenged by them.

<u>L'amour, c'est le goût de la prostitution.</u>

Baudelaire's definition of love has appealed to me since I was a teenager. It is as suggestive and voluptuous as Irene. She not only makes the difference between man and woman obvious, but thrilling, erotic. She wants to be beautiful, feminine, free. She is as straightforward and capricious as a child. She prefers flirts to marriage, excitement to harmony, desire to gratification, aloofness to familiarity. She lives her own life and accepts the consequences.
Someone as desirable as Irene usually doesn't stay on the street for long; she is lured away by some movie director ("Hey, baby, I'll make you a star!") or the promises of wealthy men. In Irene's case, they don't have a chance. She needs the click-clack of her high heels on the pavement as much as she needs her heartbeat. She would rather be a streetwalker than a call girl because she loves the street, her freedom, and the luxury of being a star, every day, every night, accountable to no one but herself.

Roswitha Hecke

Love may have its origin in a generous passion: in the pleasure of prostitution; but it is immediately corrupted by the pleasure of possession.

    Baudelaire

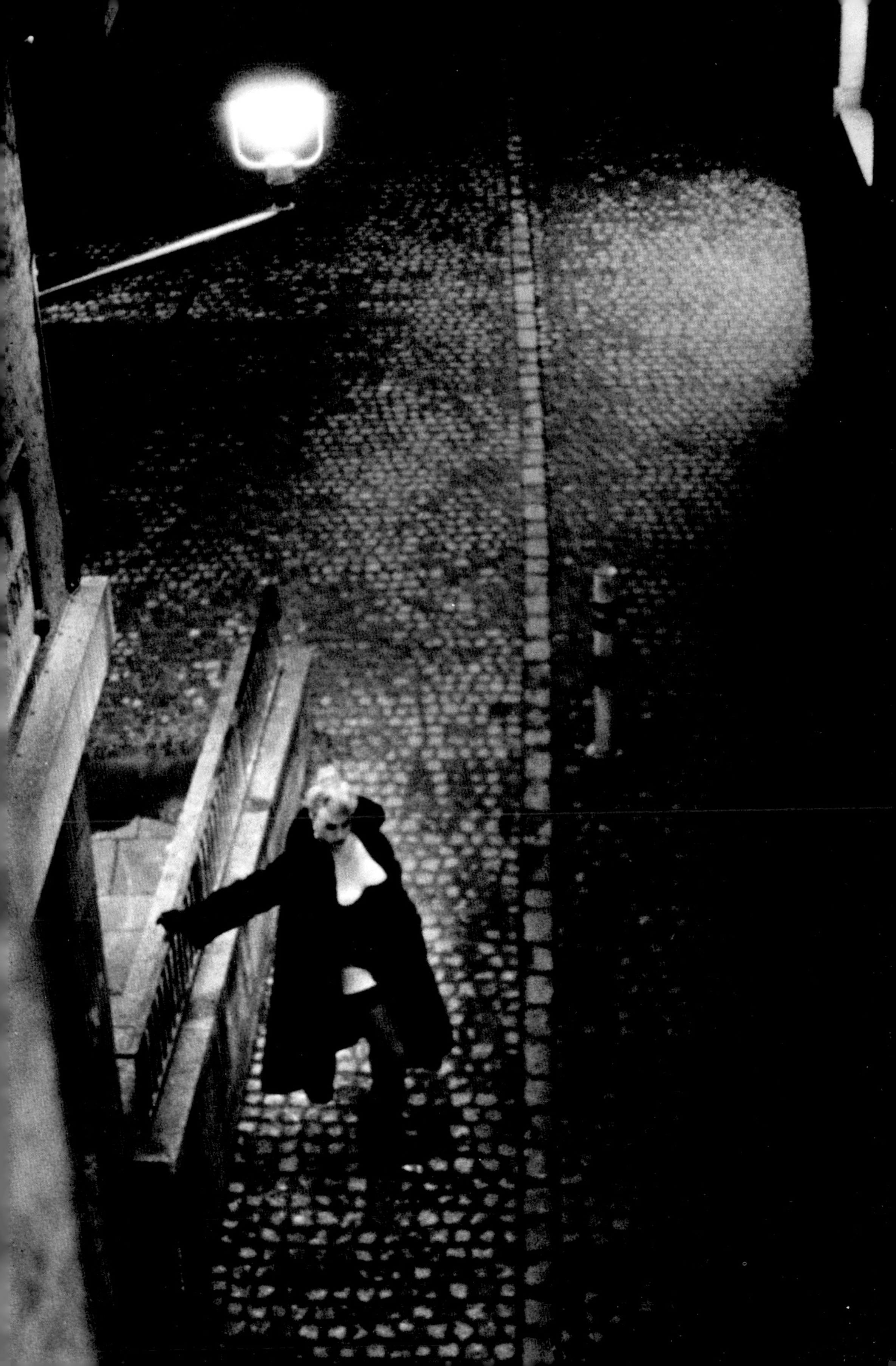

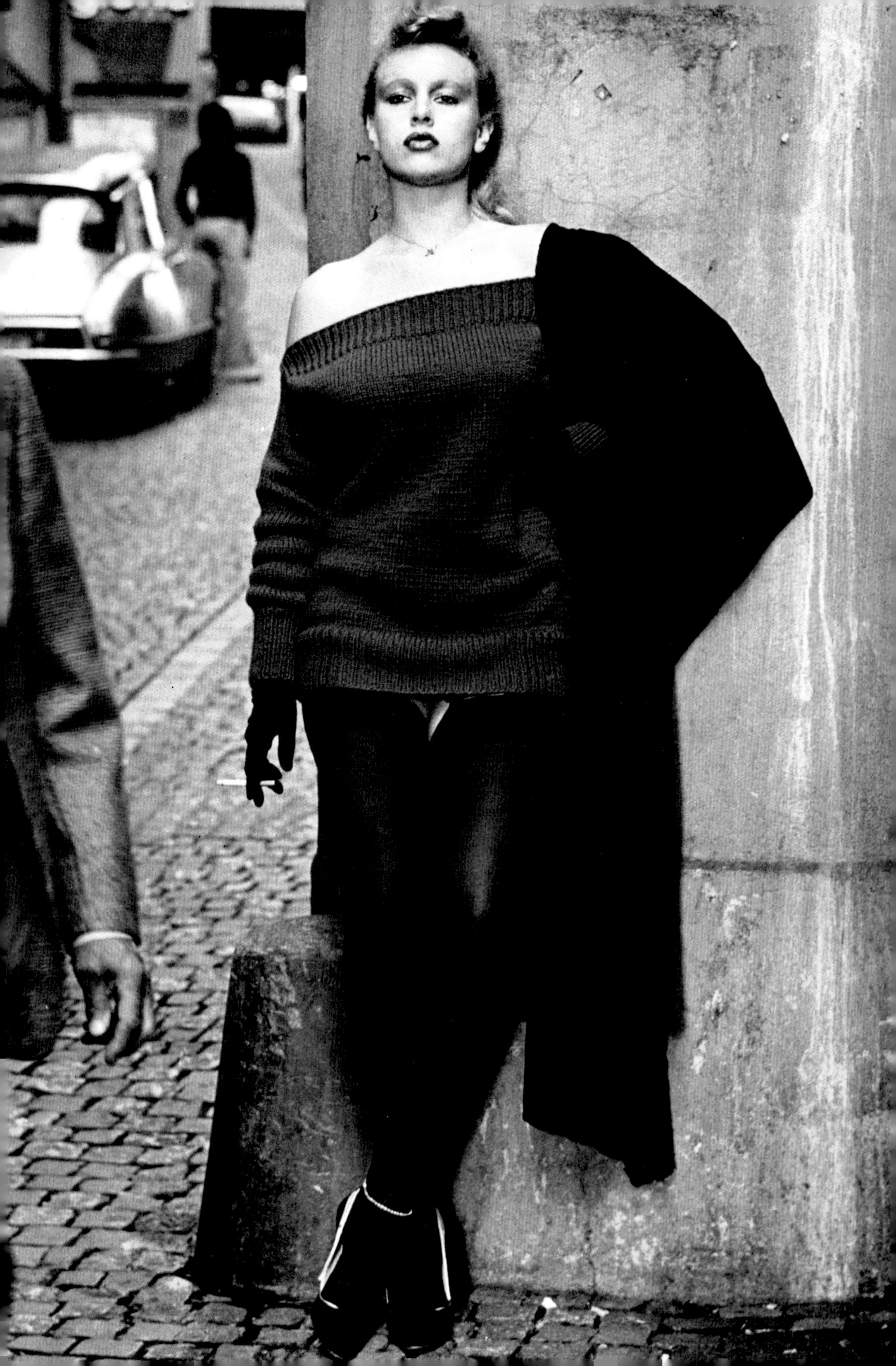

The qualities that determine a woman's beauty and make her attractive: indifference, boredom, licentiousness, impudence, introspection, lust for power, strength of will, malevolence, fragility, a feline air, childishness, nonchalance, and mockery.

    Baudelaire

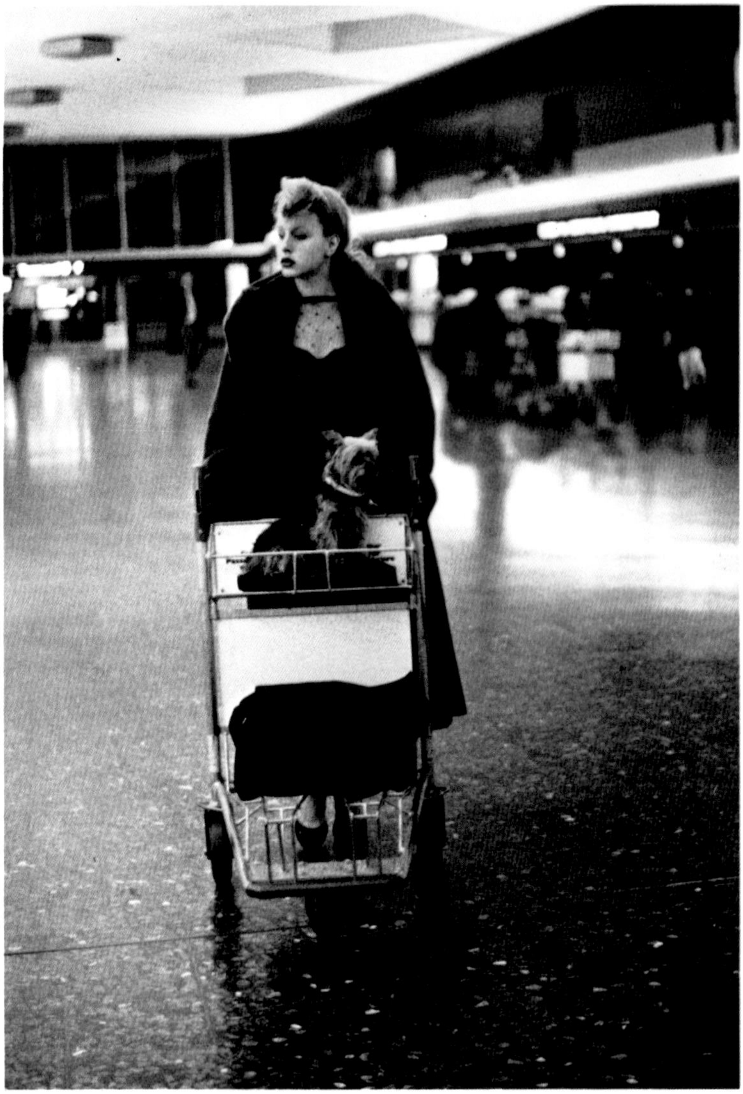

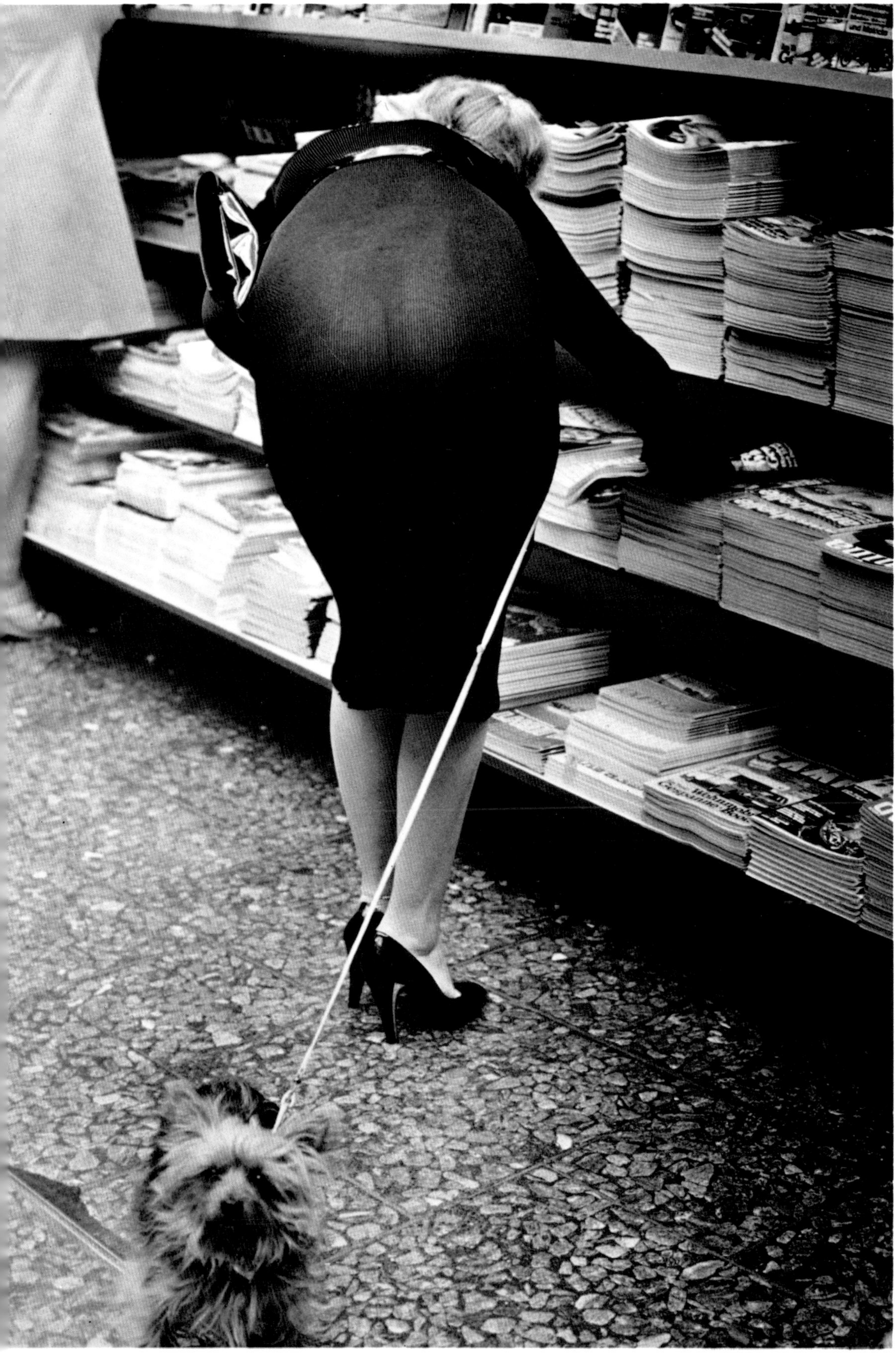

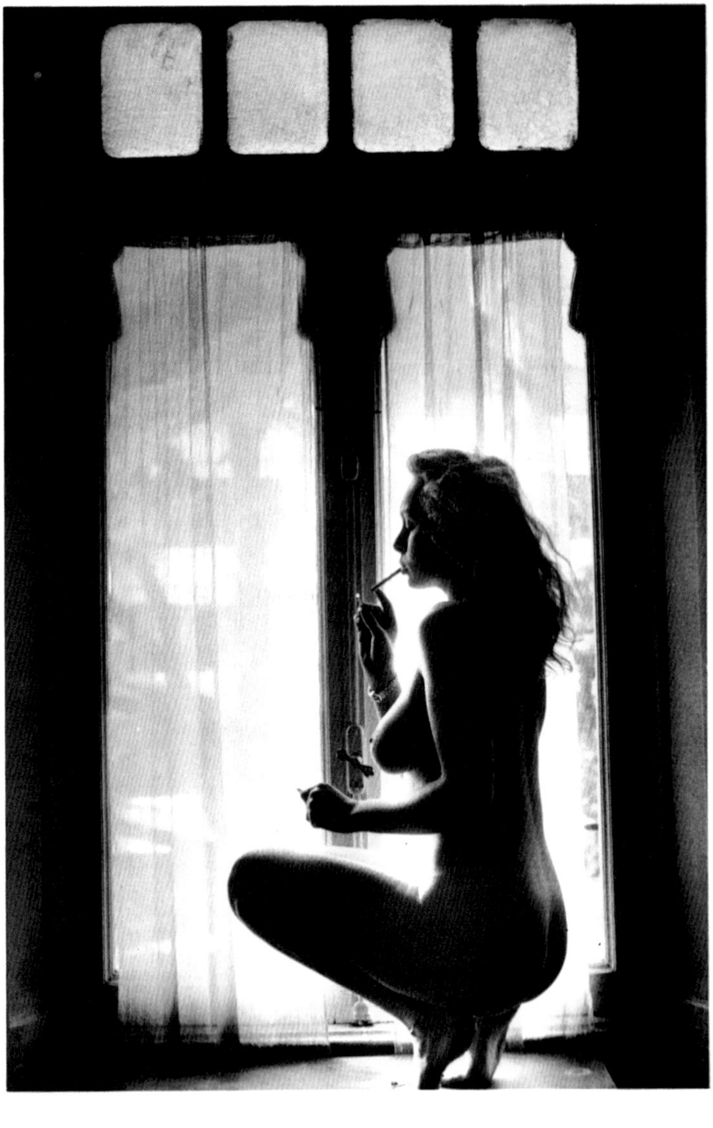

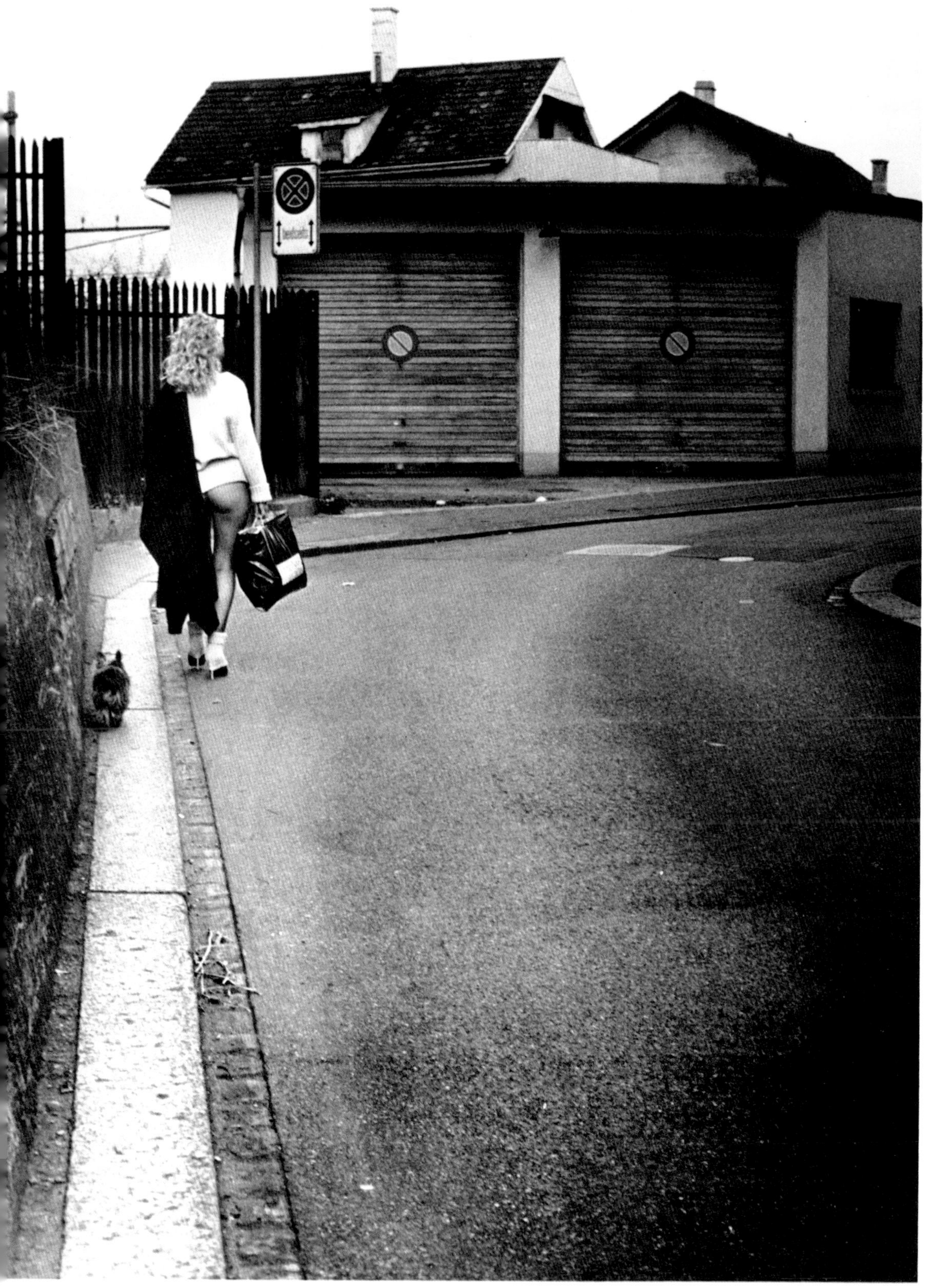

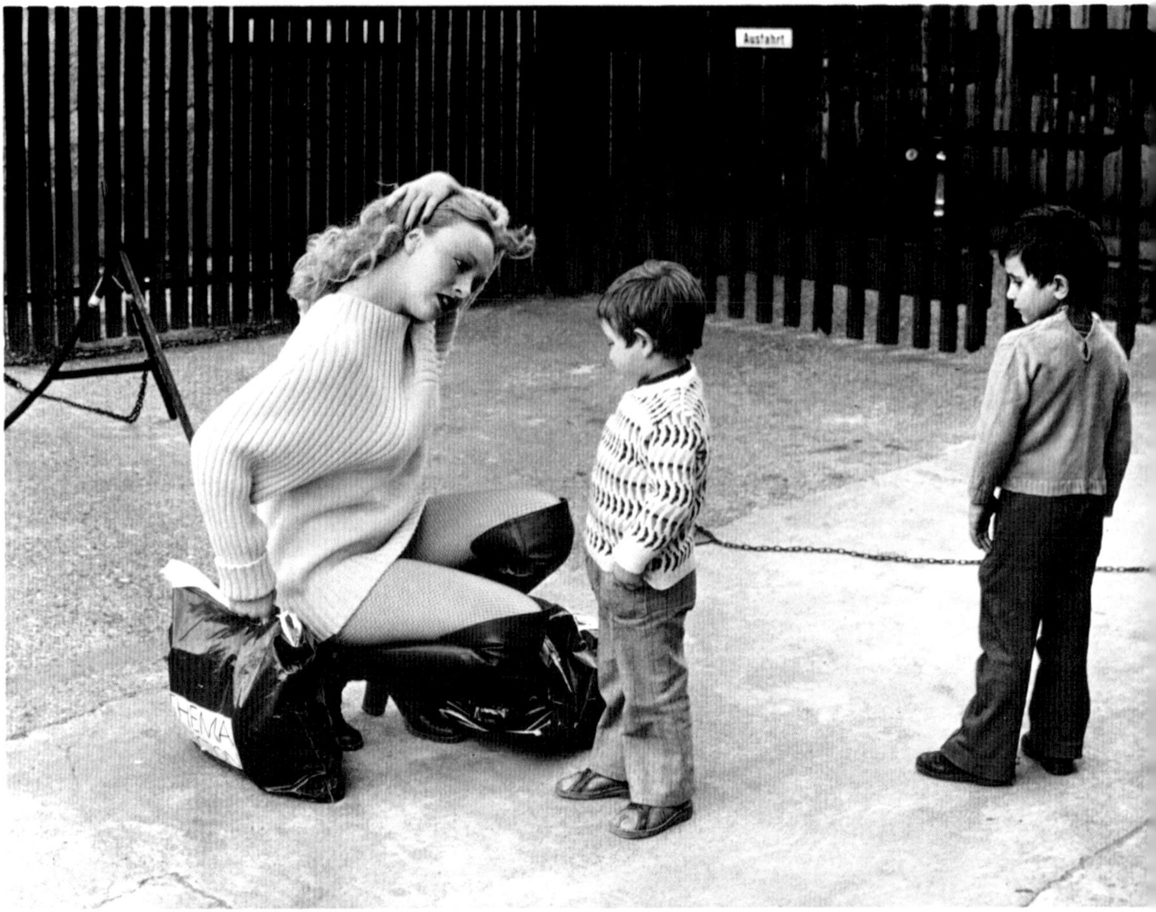
Ausfahrt

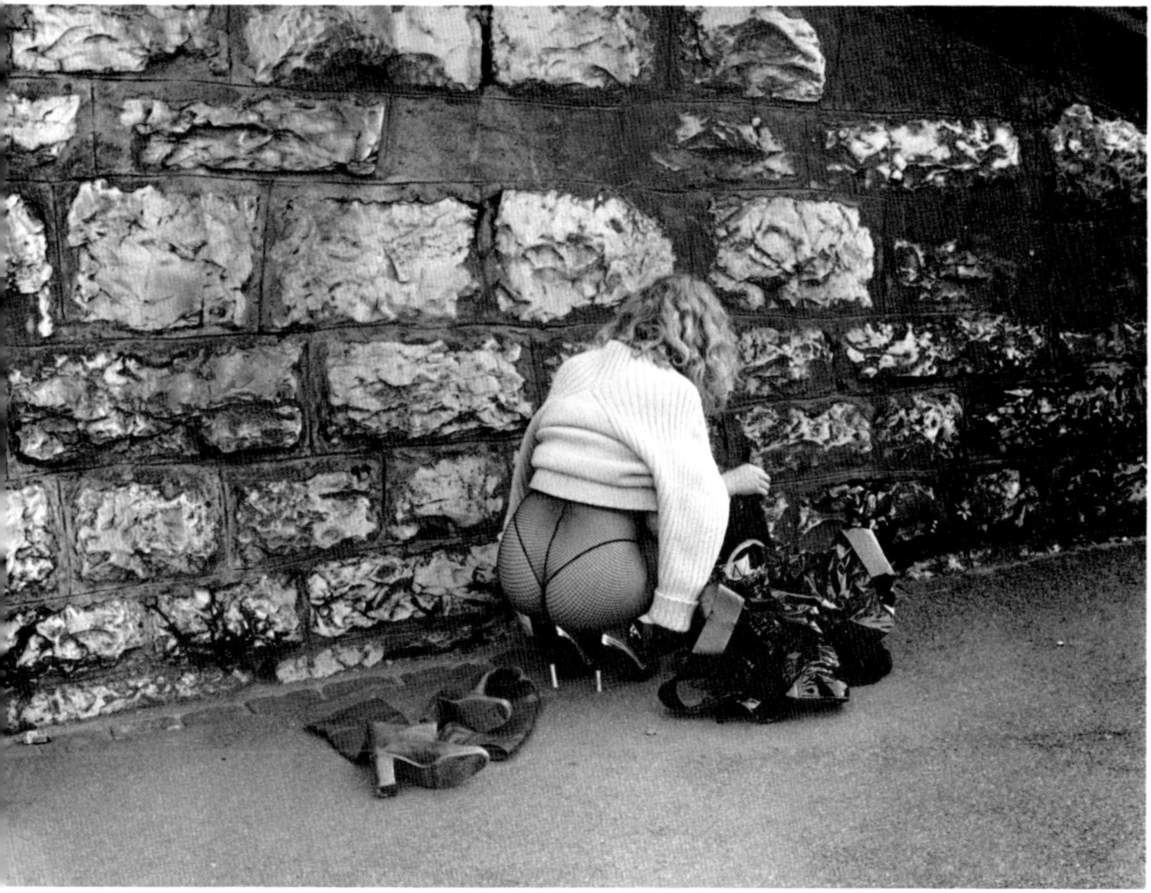

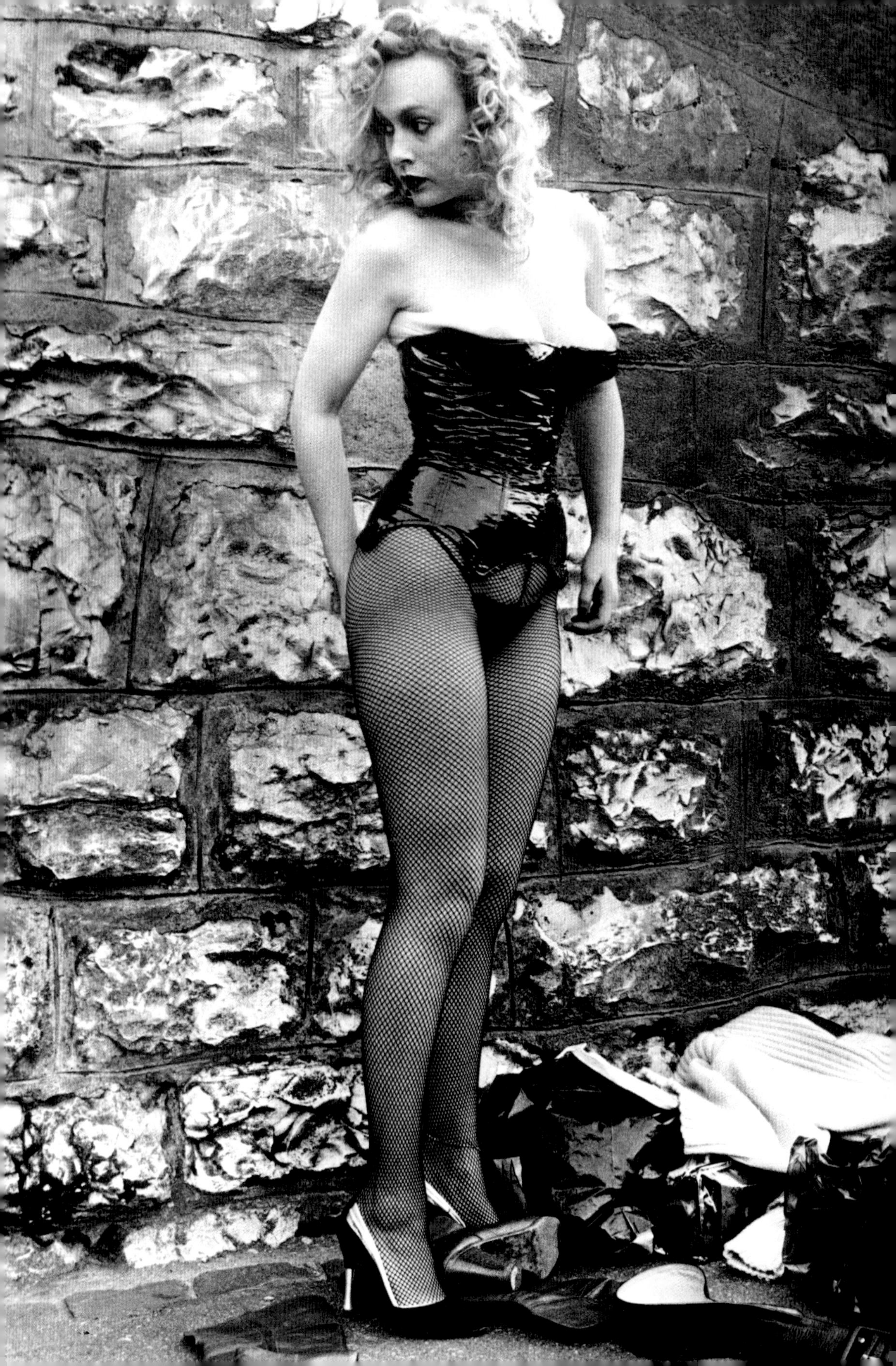

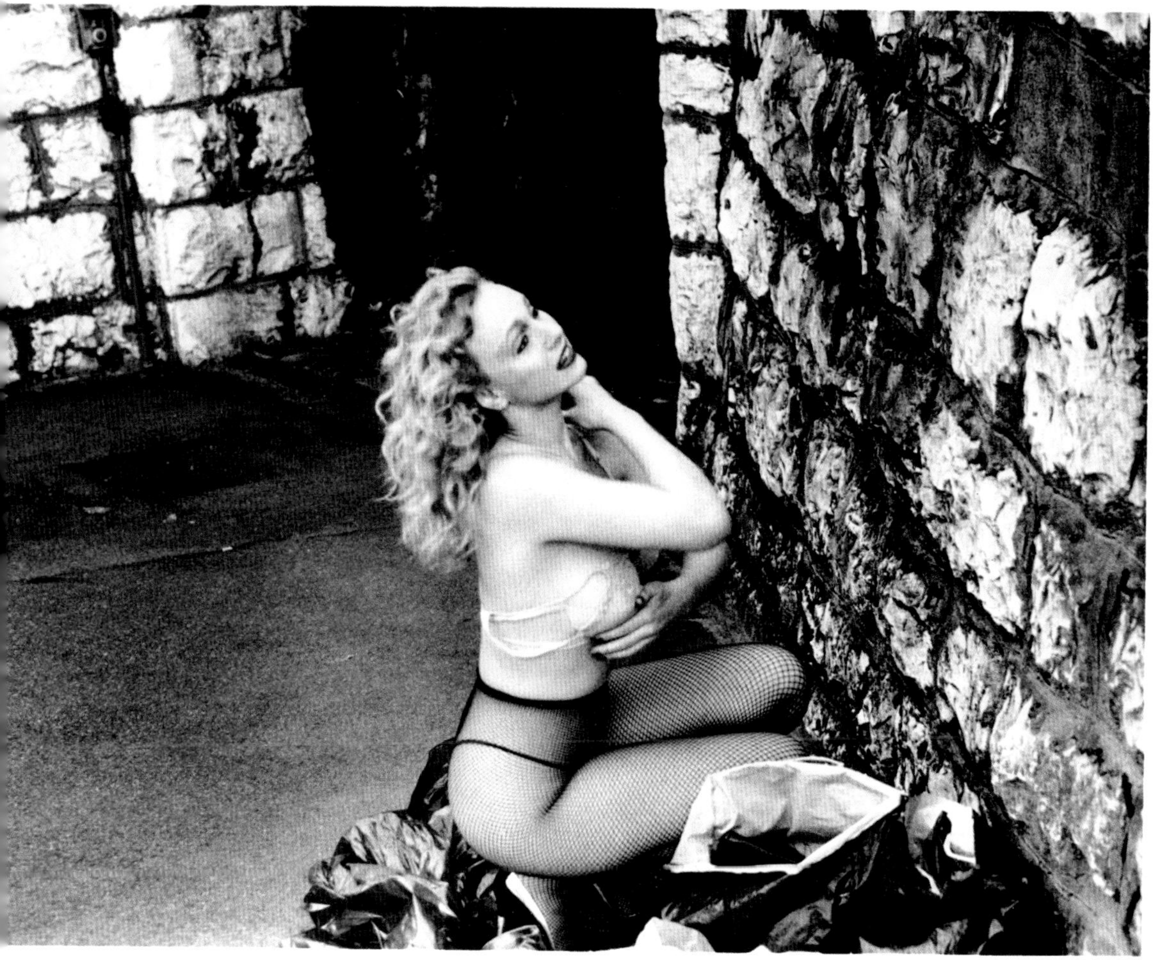

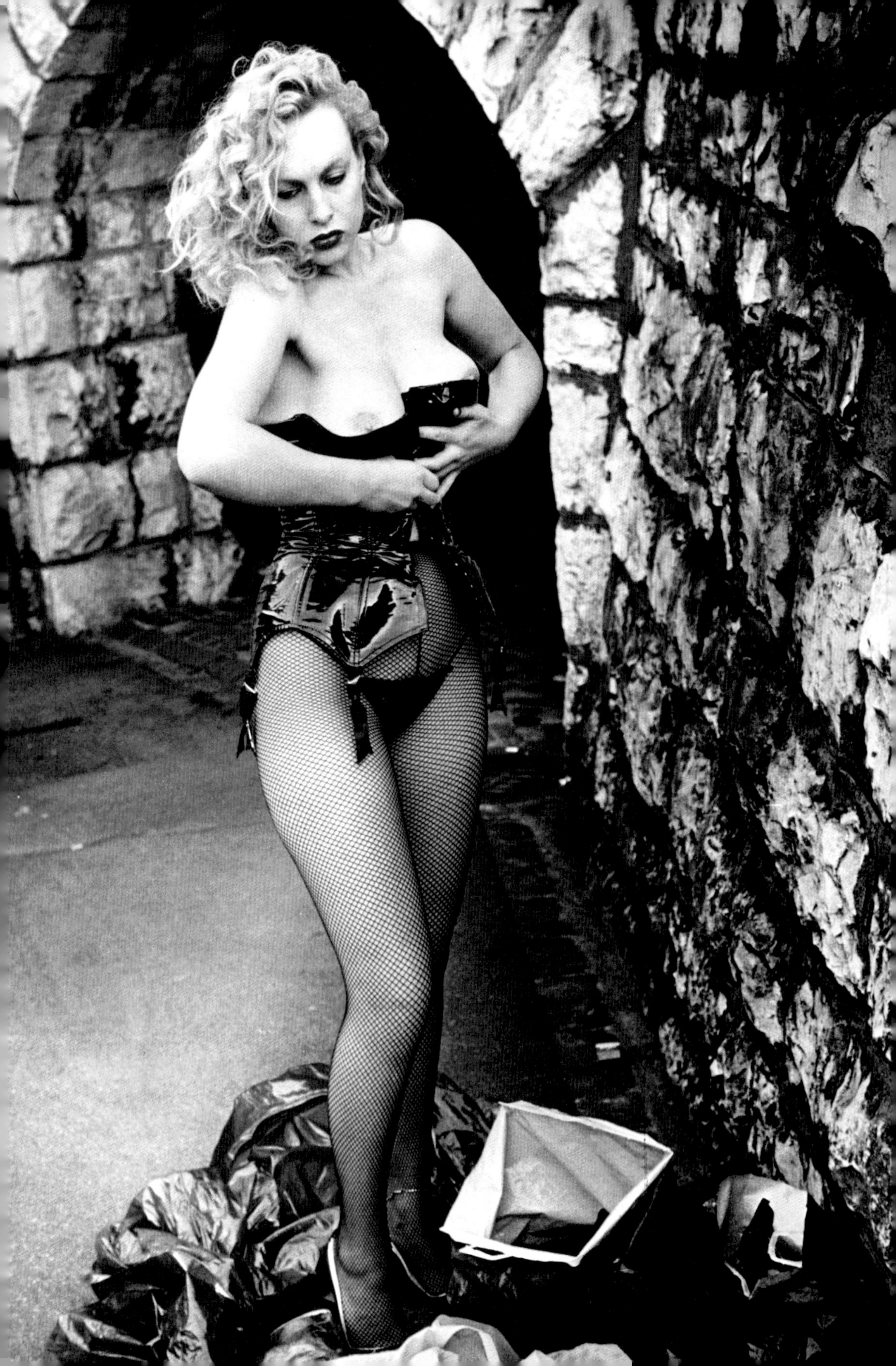

My female ideal is Jane Russell. A real woman. And not weak.
    Irene

What is love? The need to emerge from oneself.
    Baudelaire

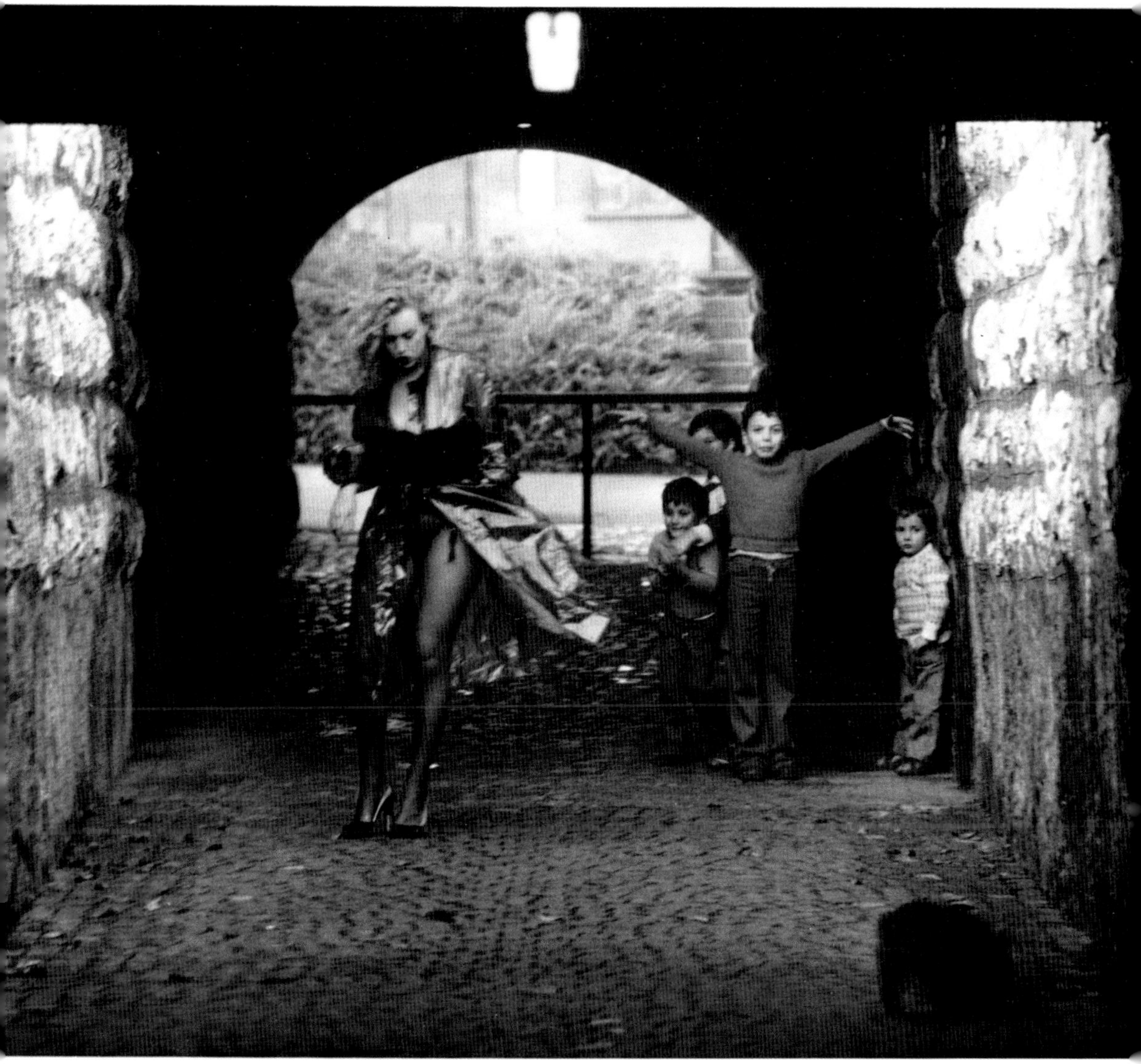

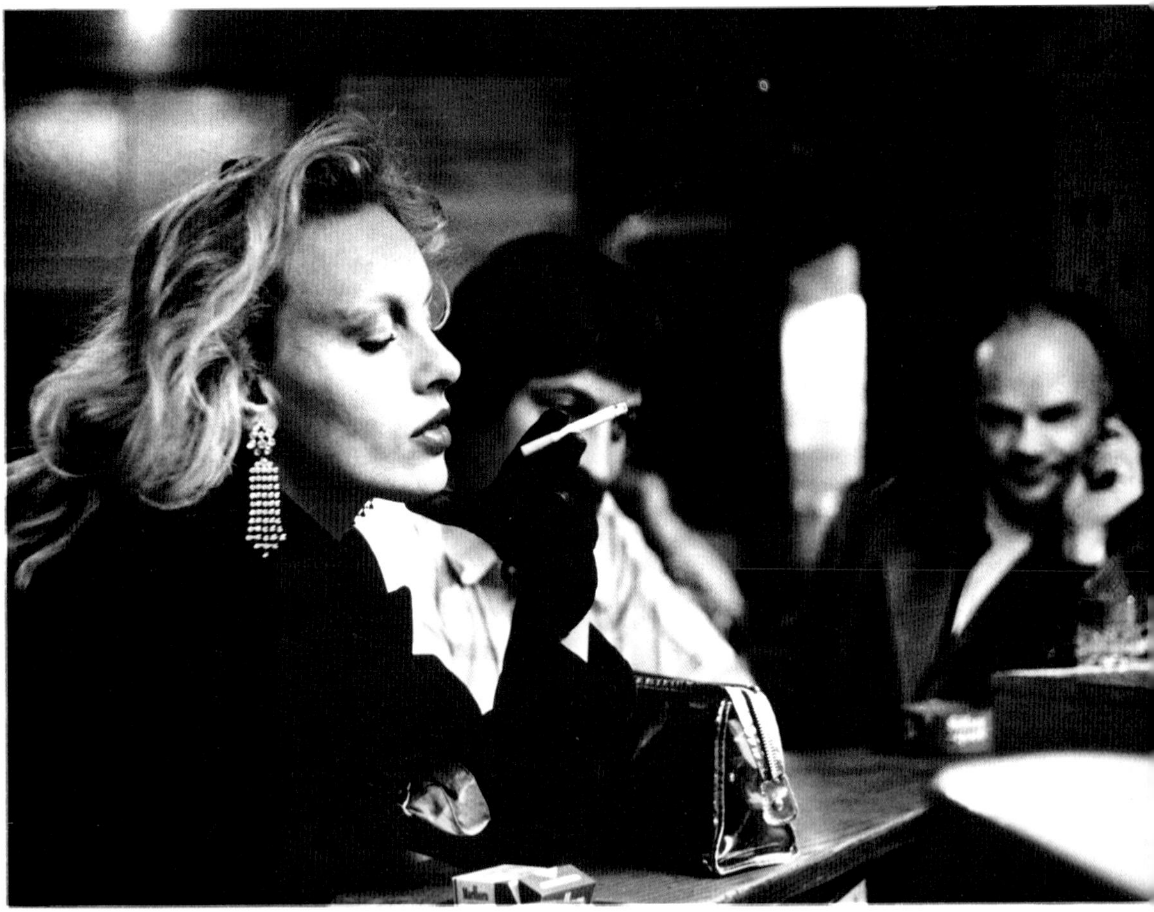

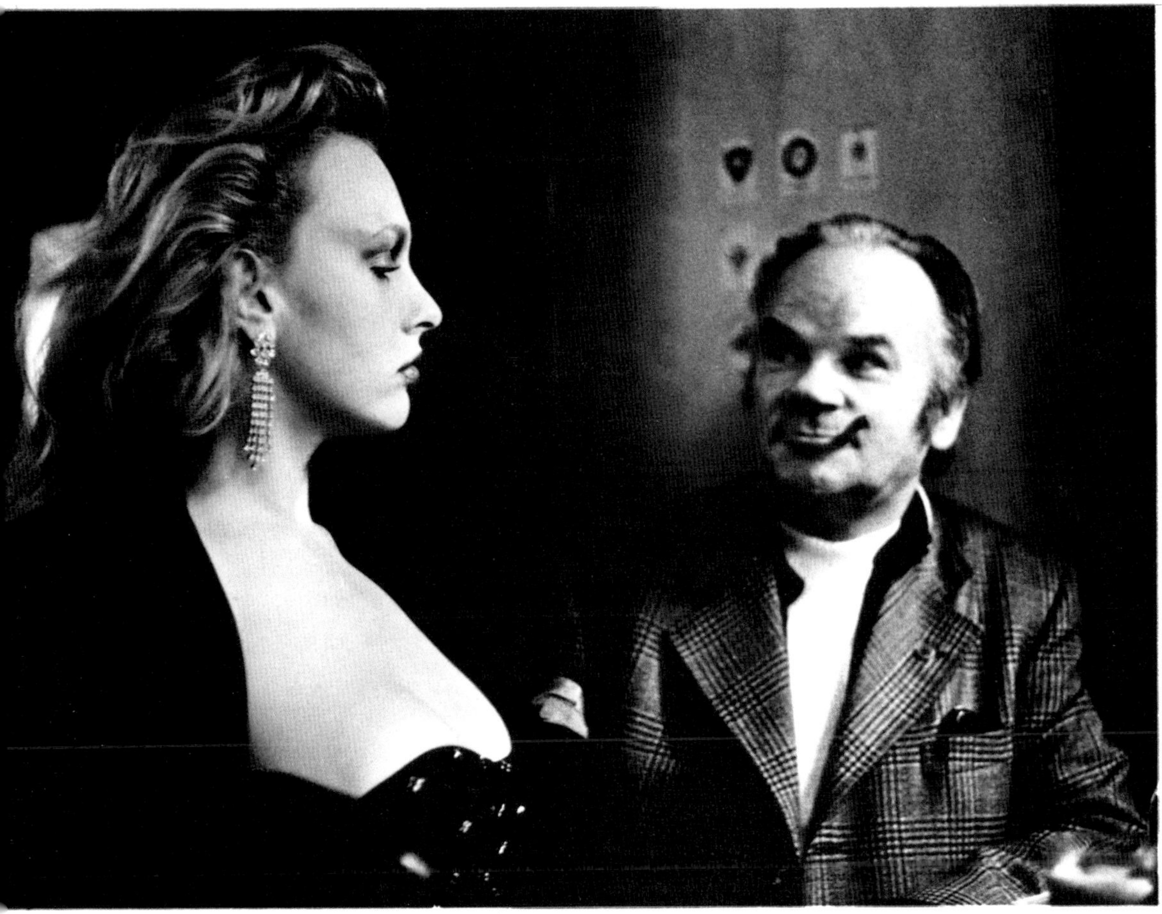

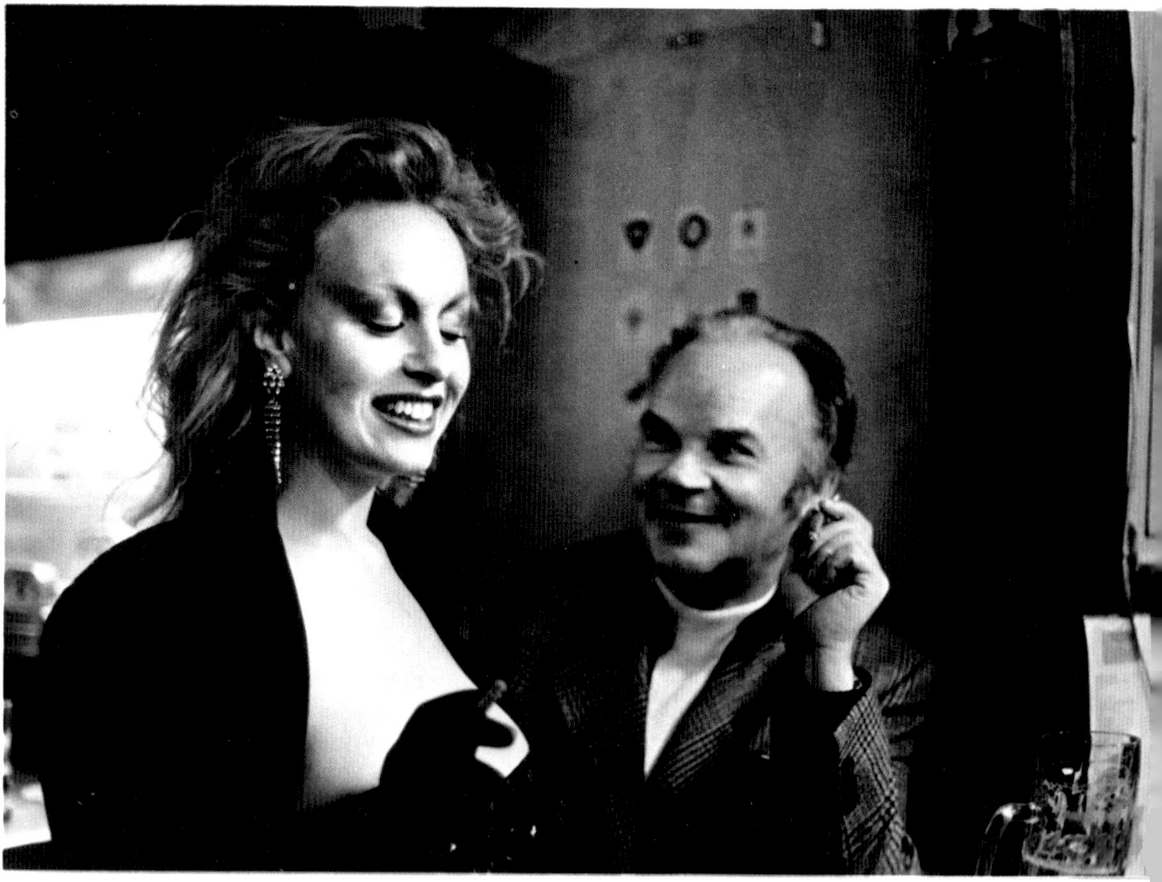

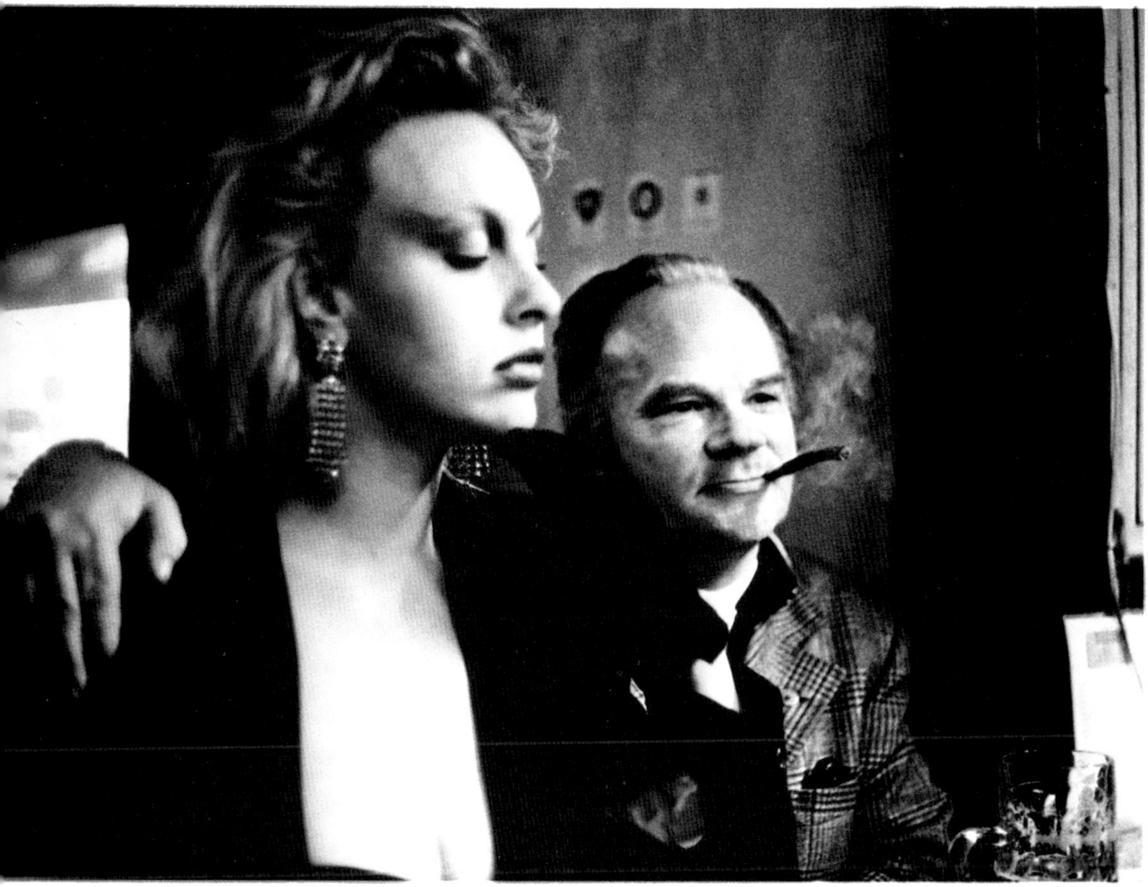

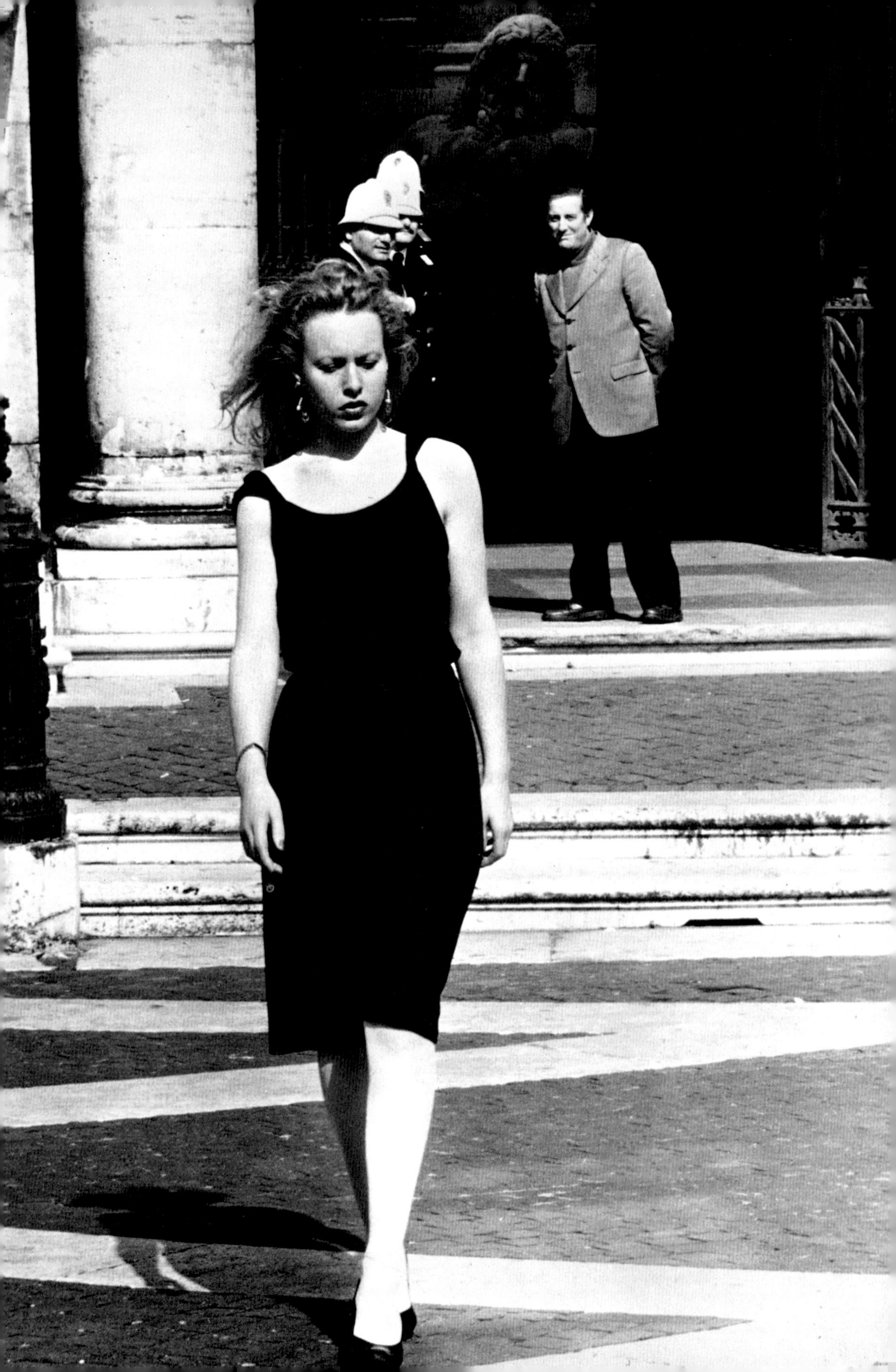

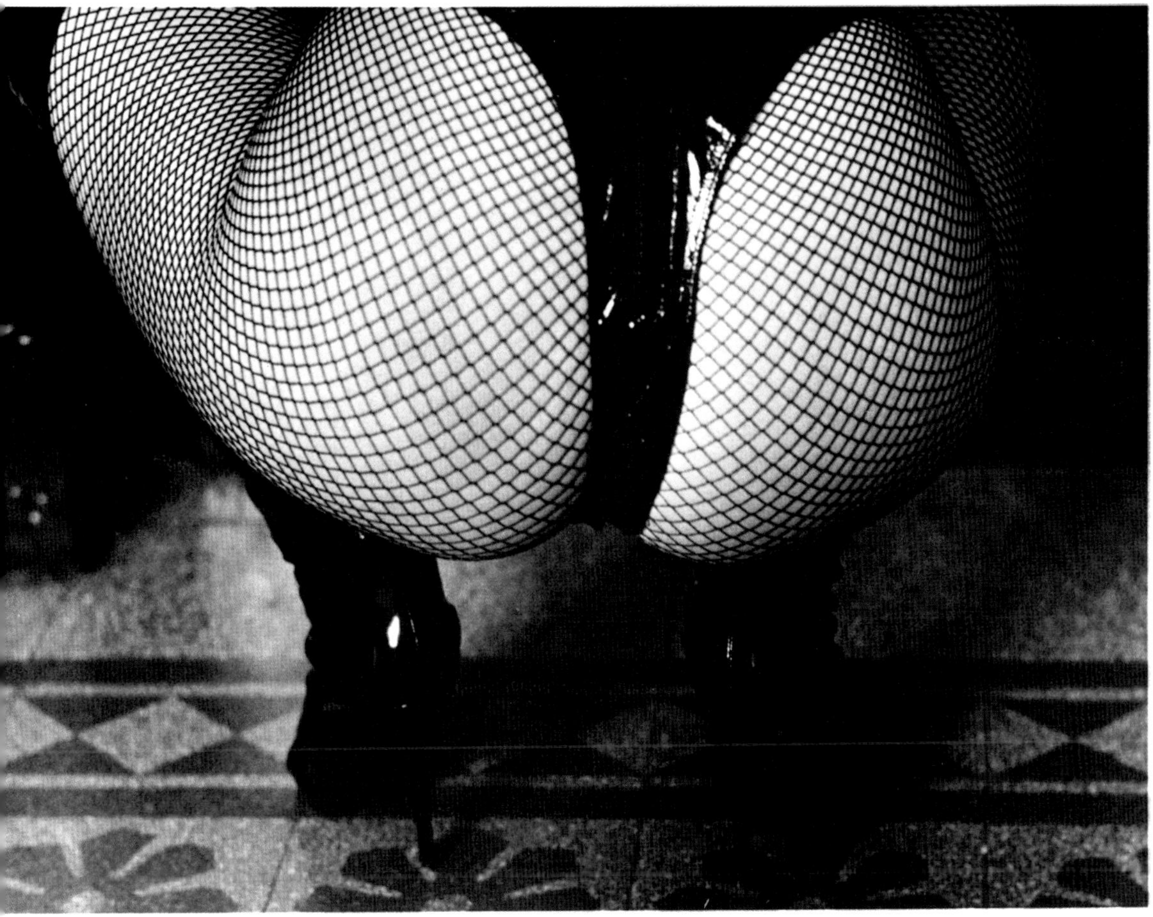

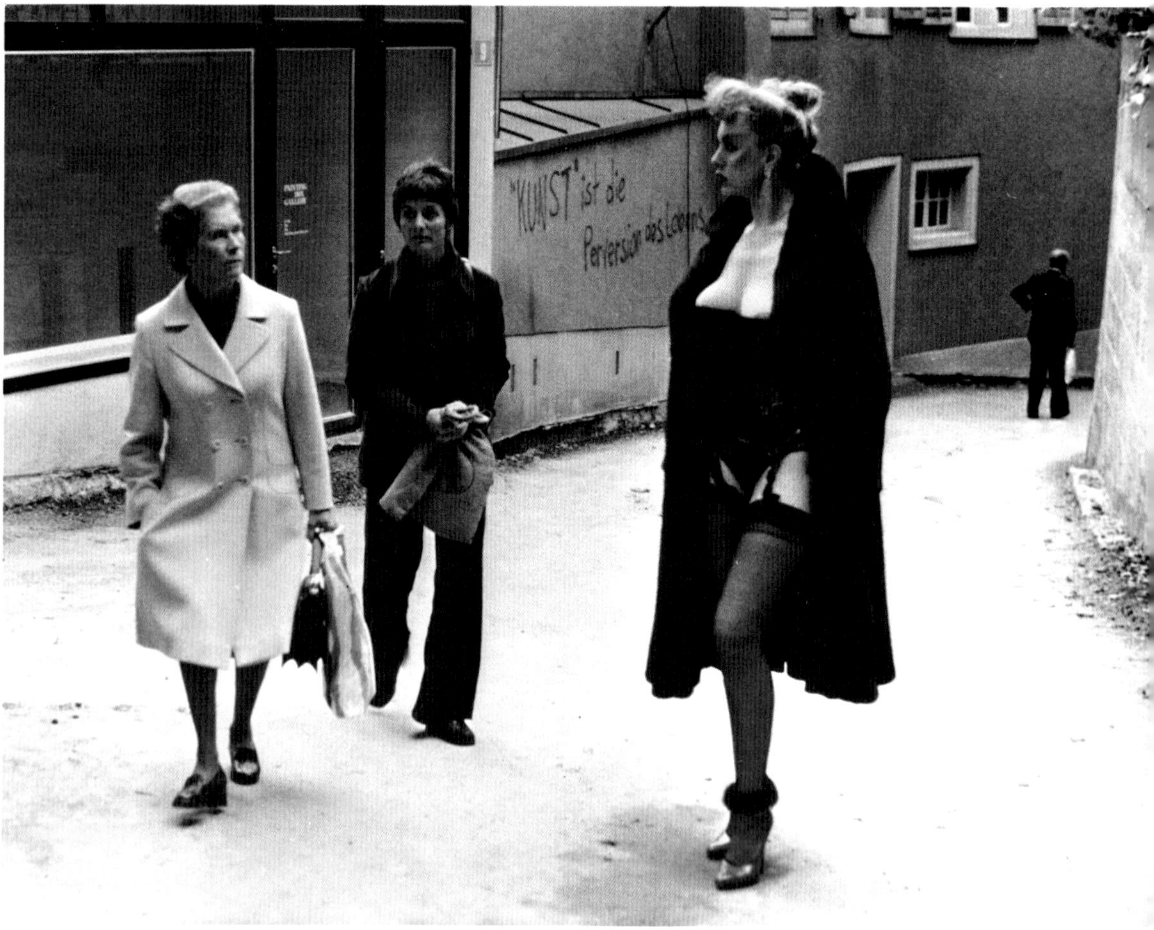
"KUNST" ist die
Perversion des Lebens

I love artists because they're perverse.
   Irene

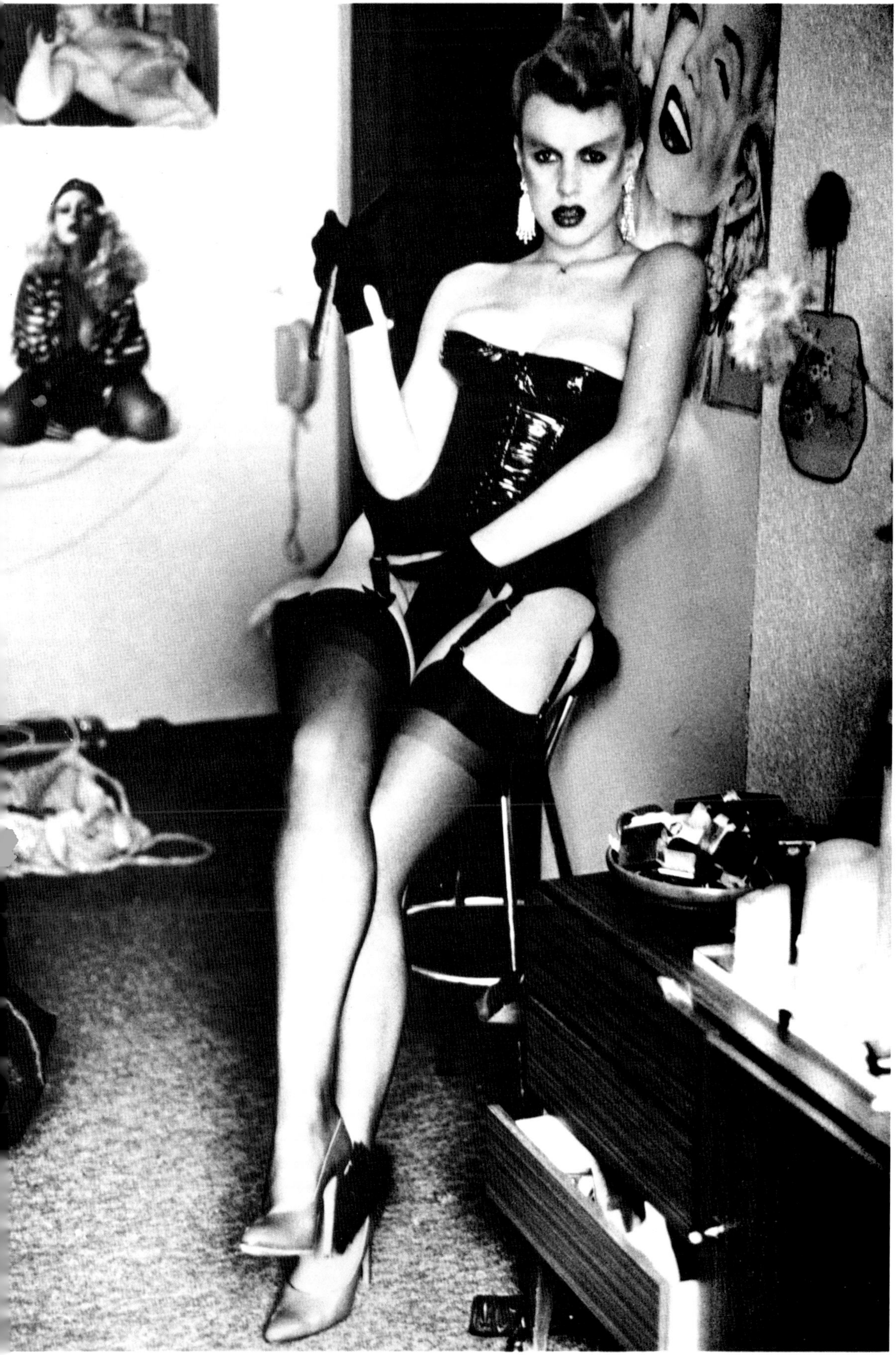

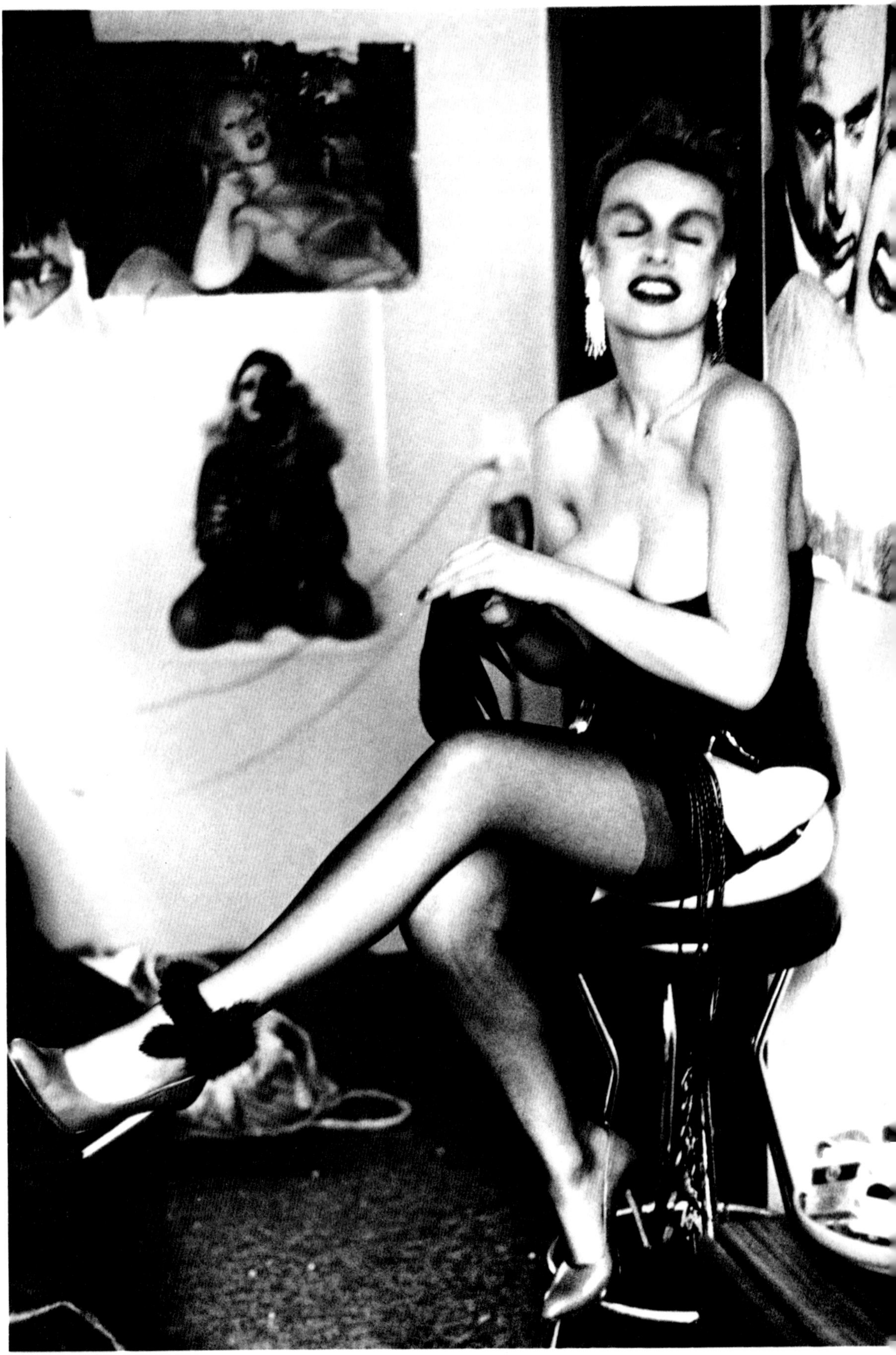

Love wants to emerge from itself, to become one with its victim, like the conquerer and the vanquished, yet still retain the privileges of the conquerer.

    Baudelaire

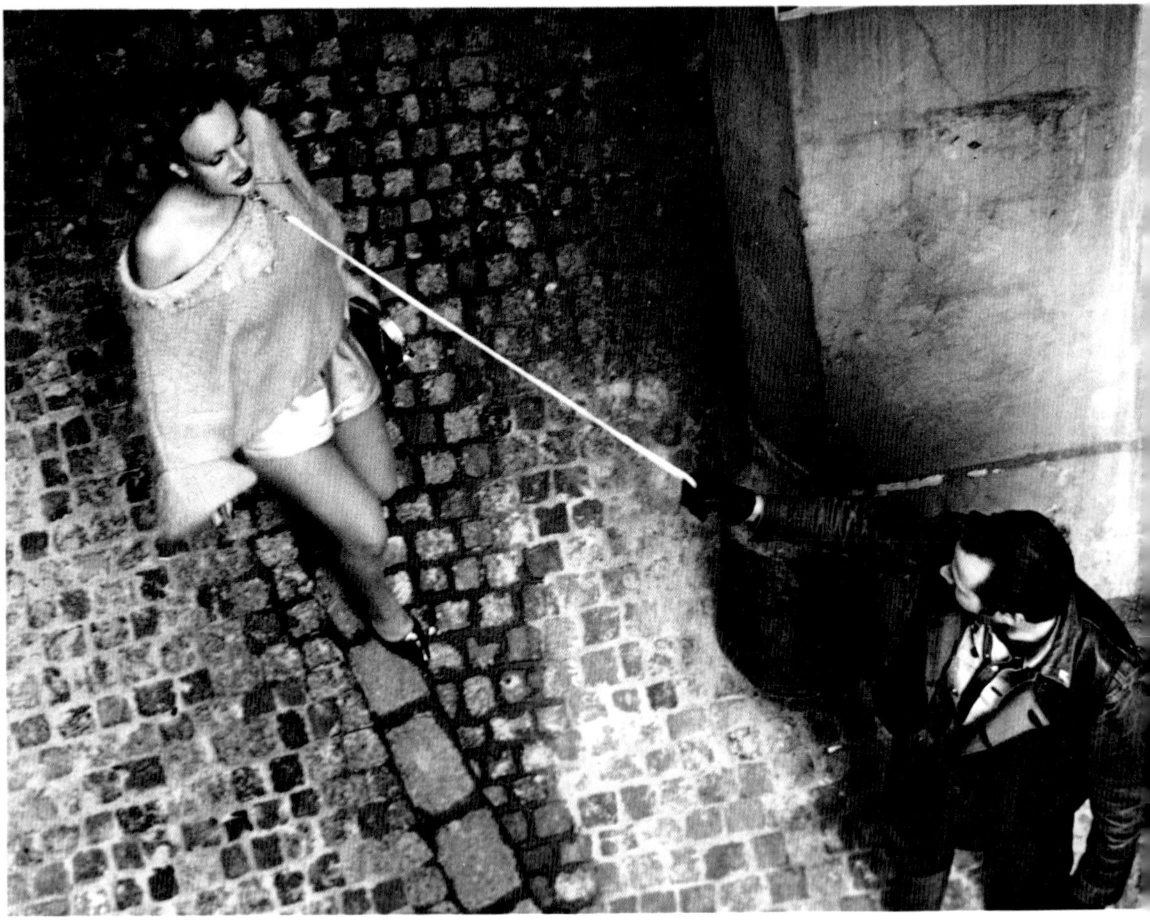

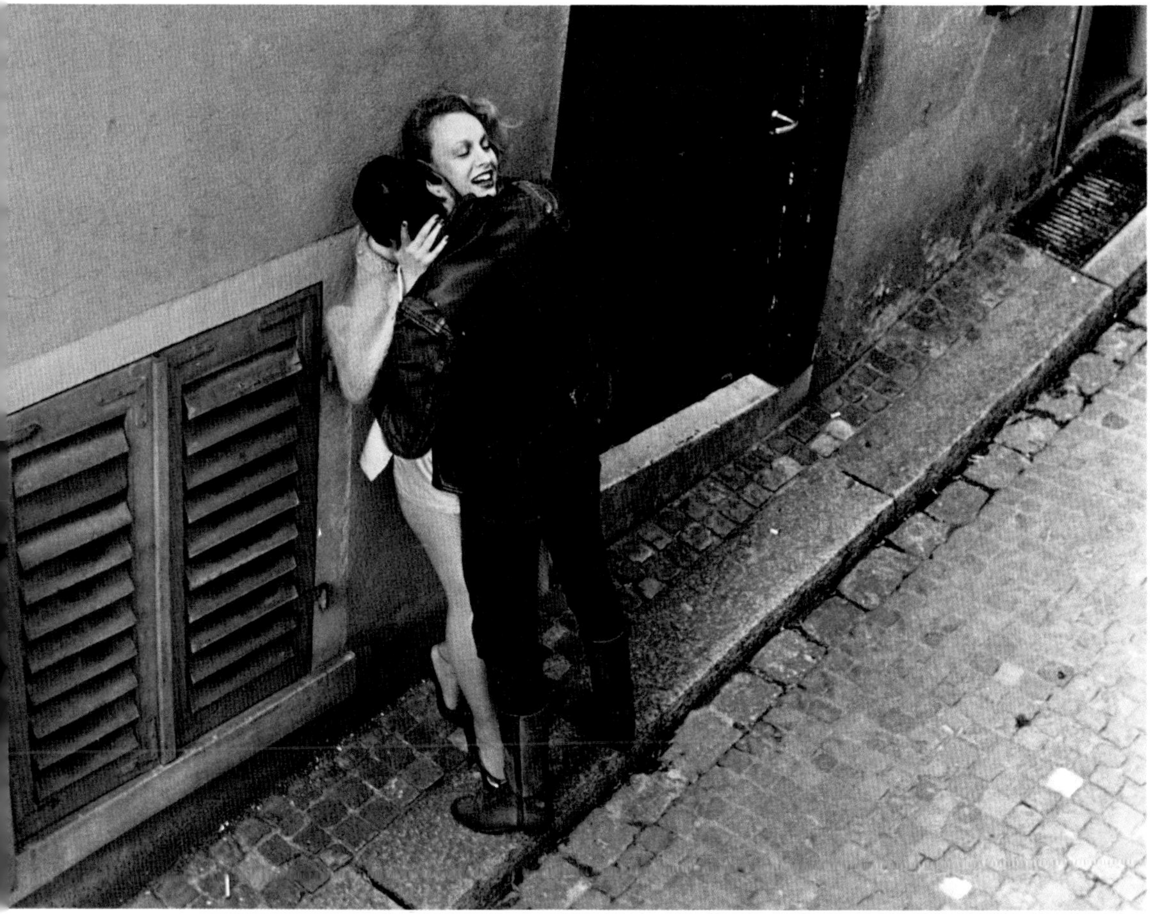

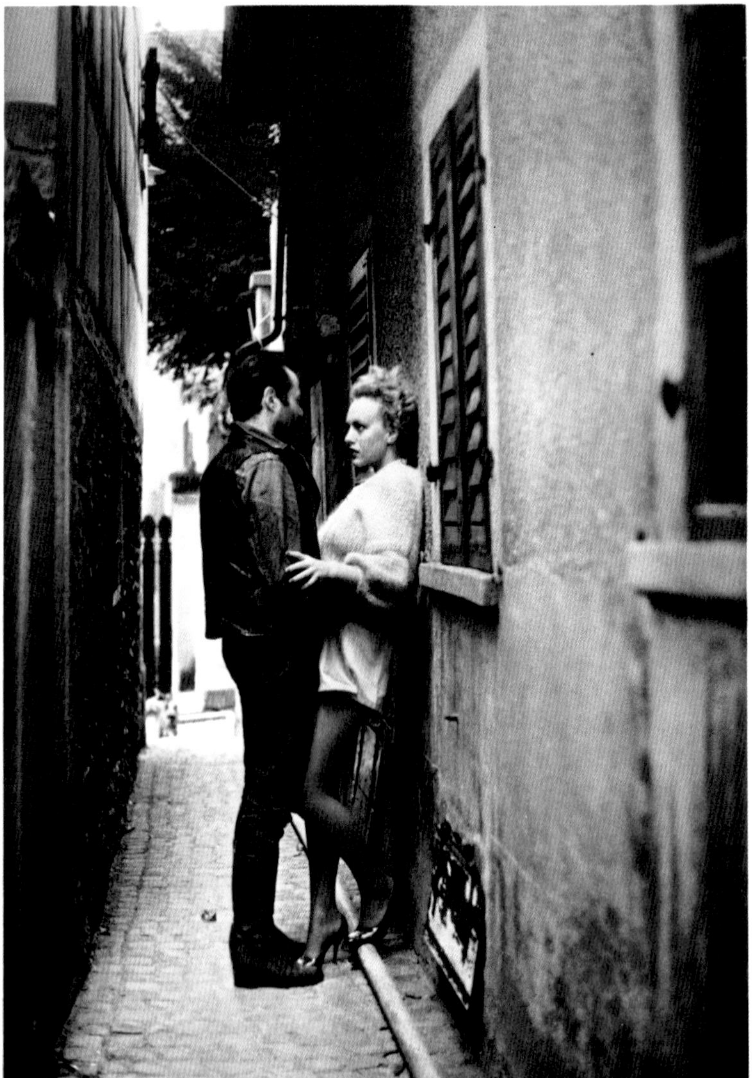

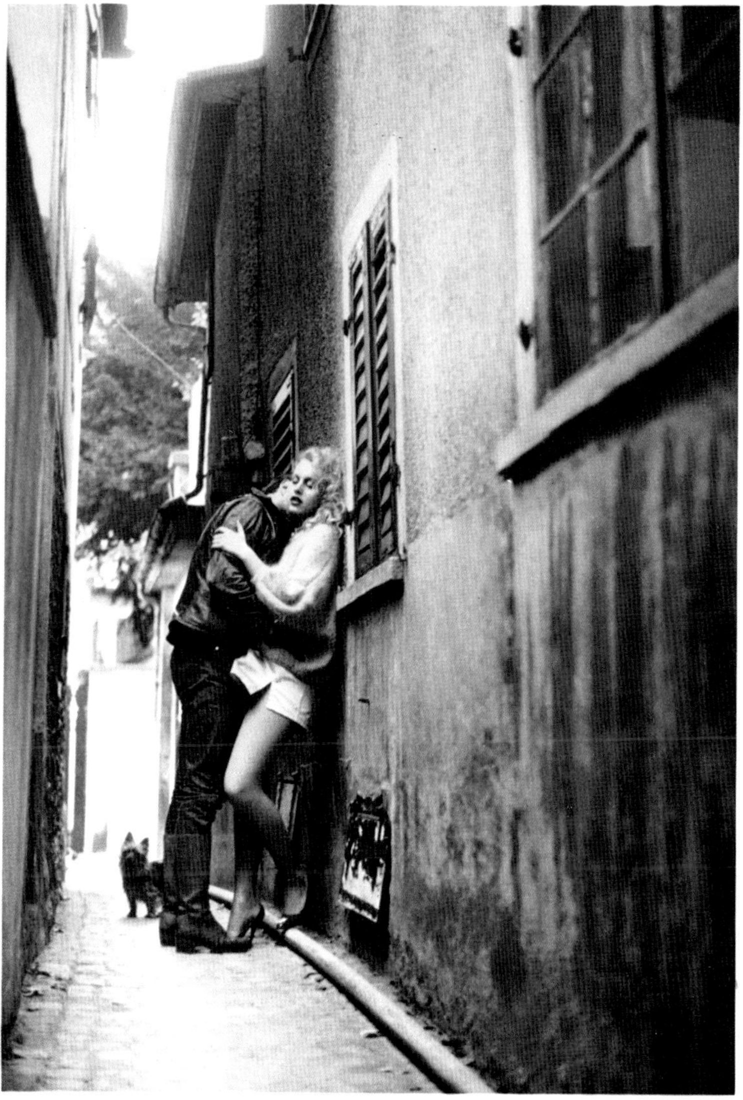

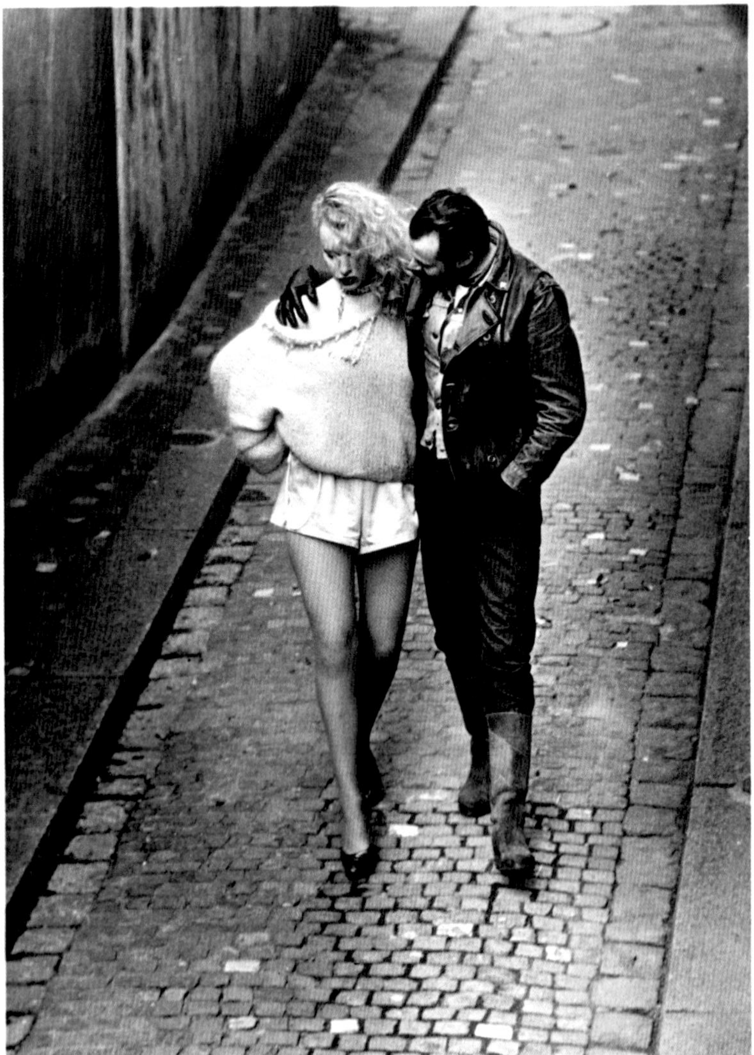

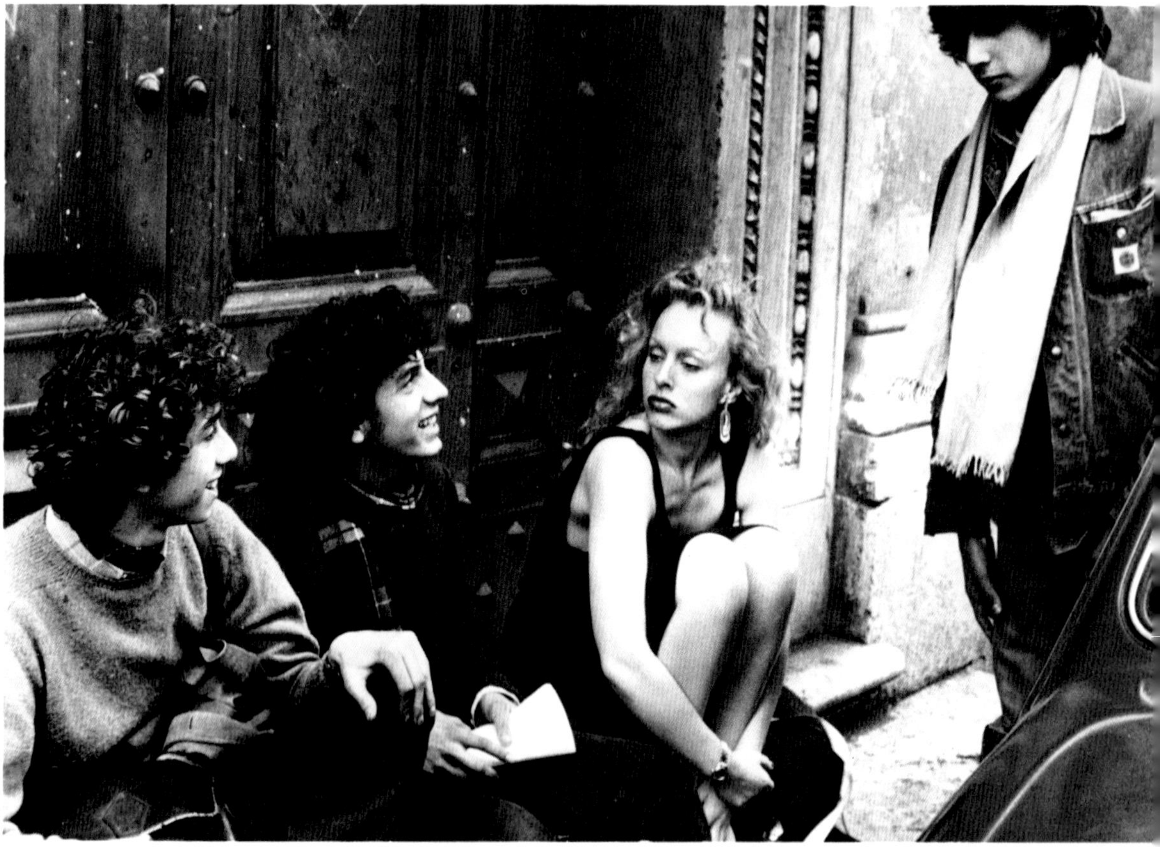

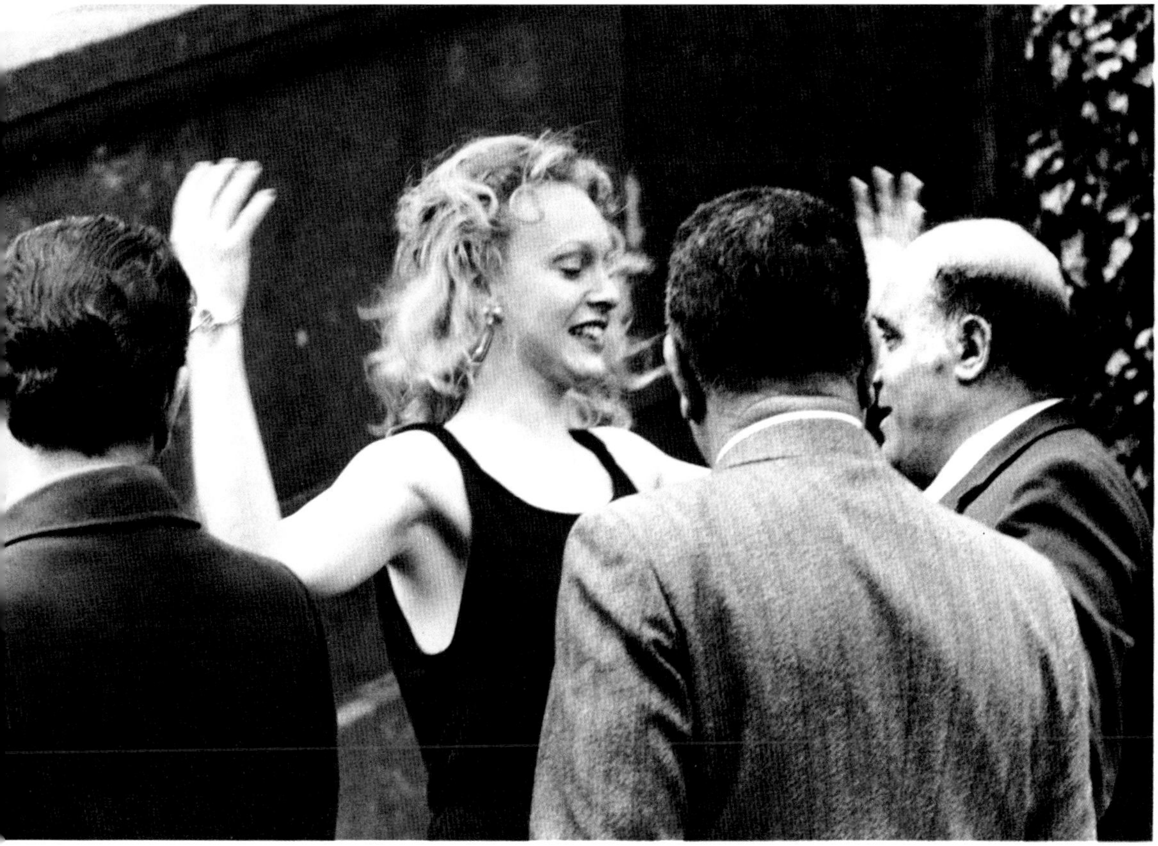

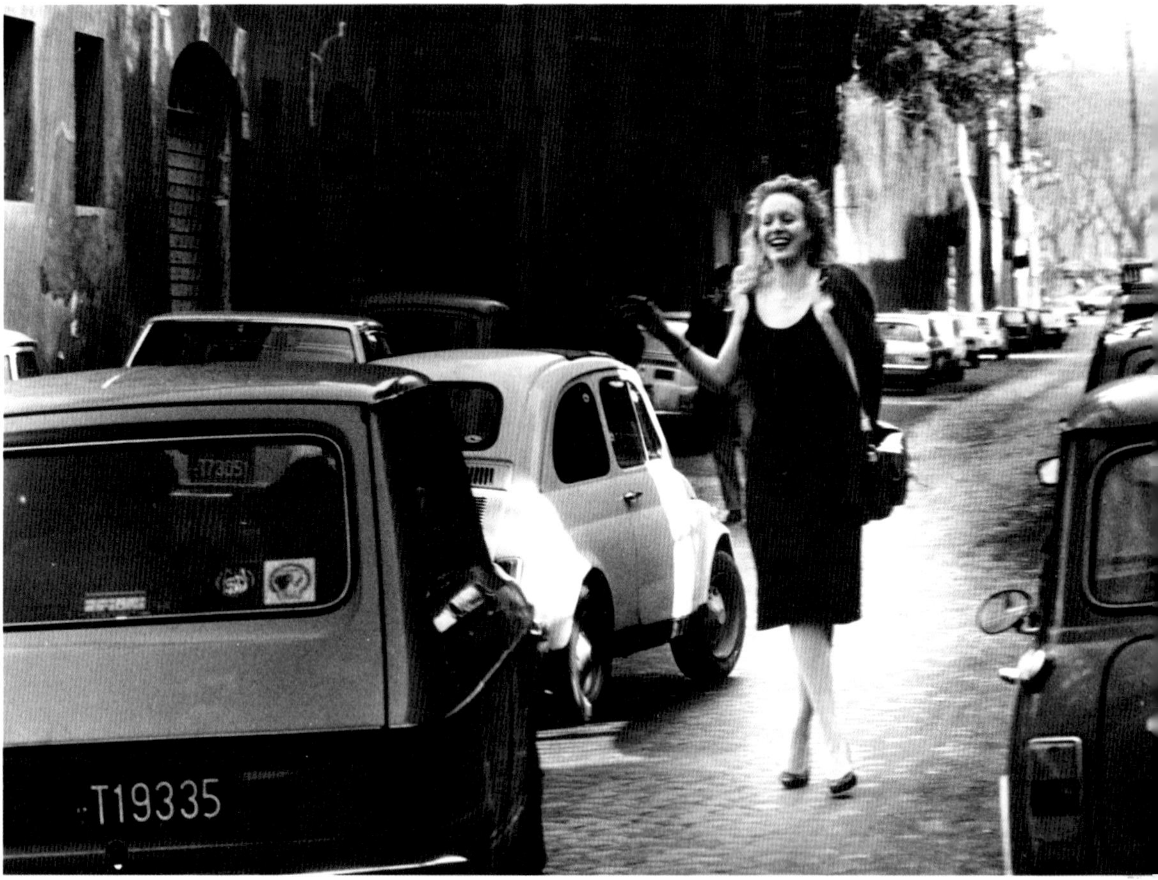
T19335

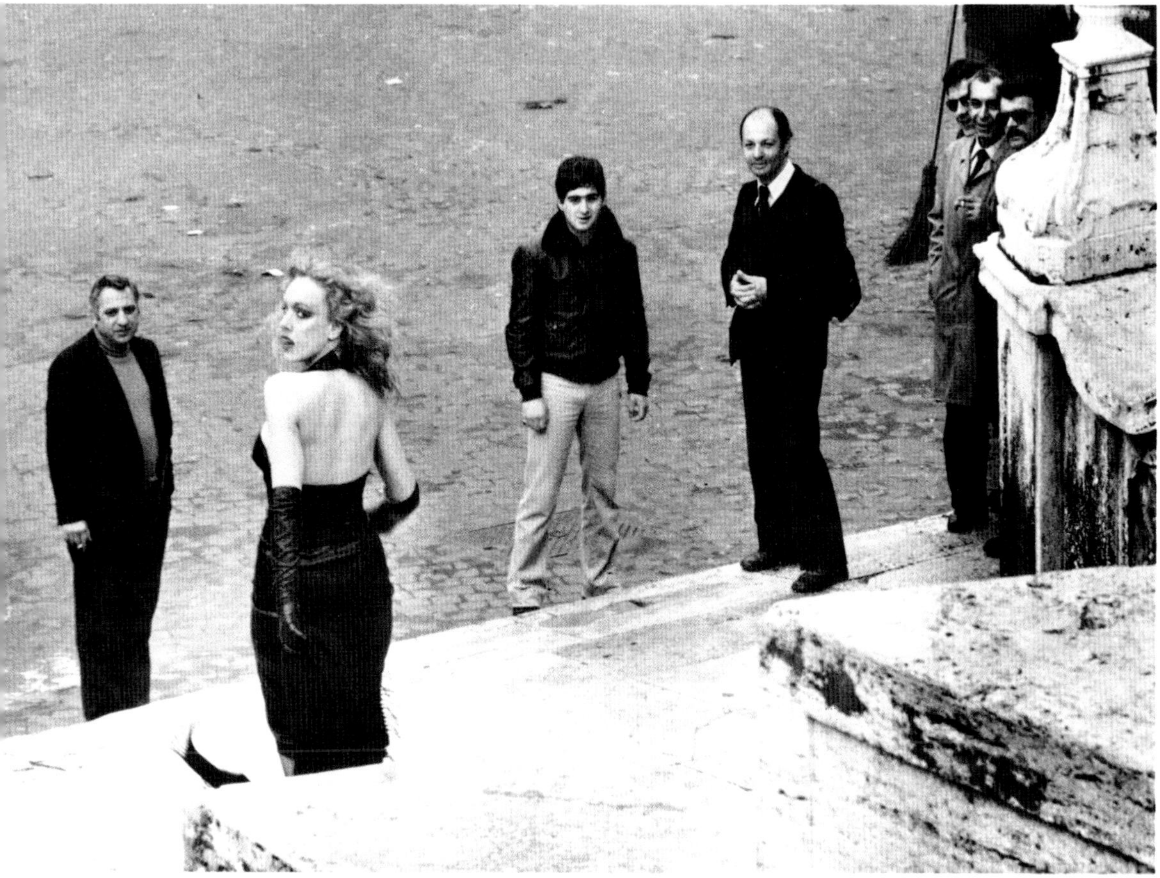

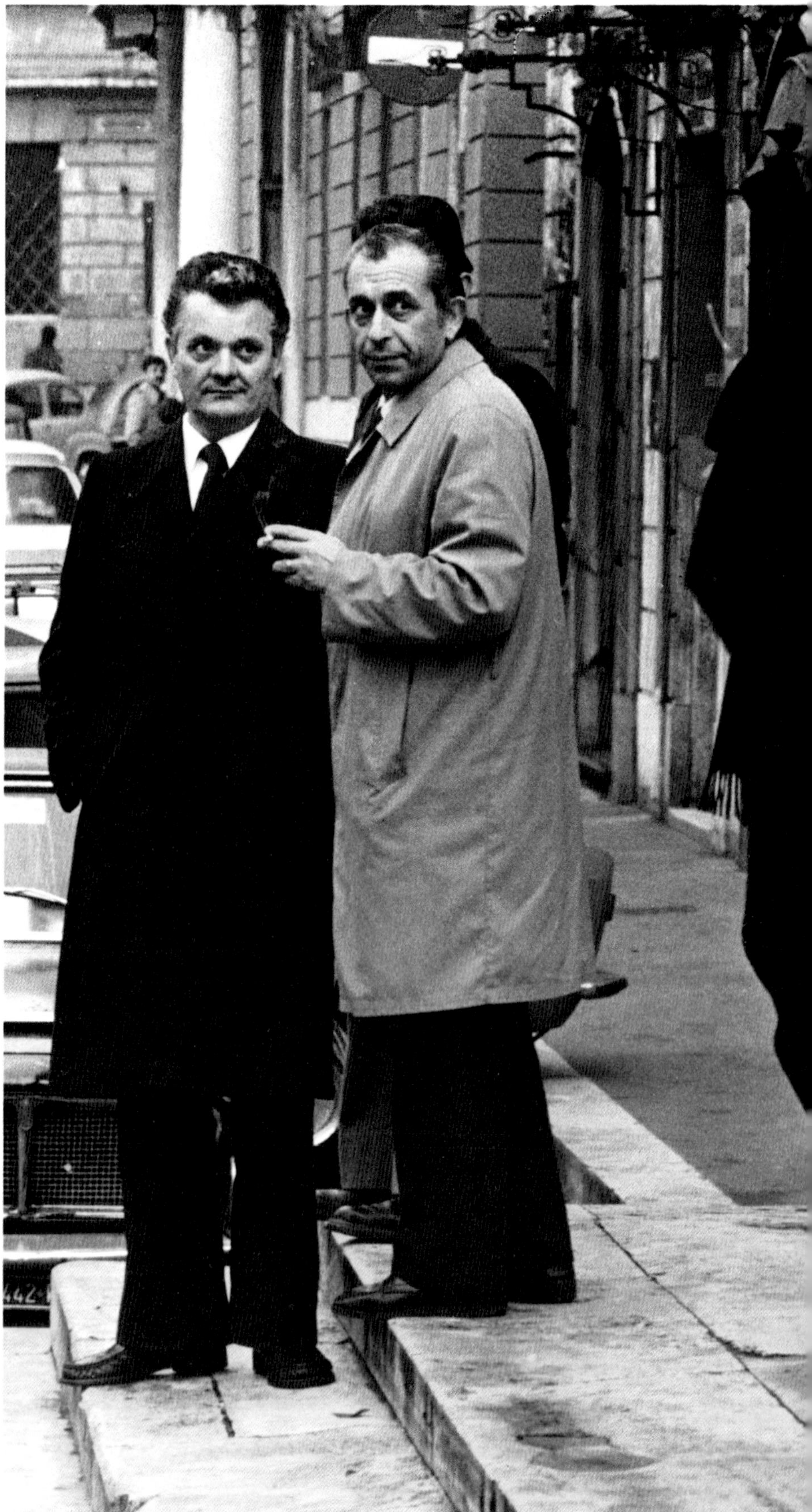

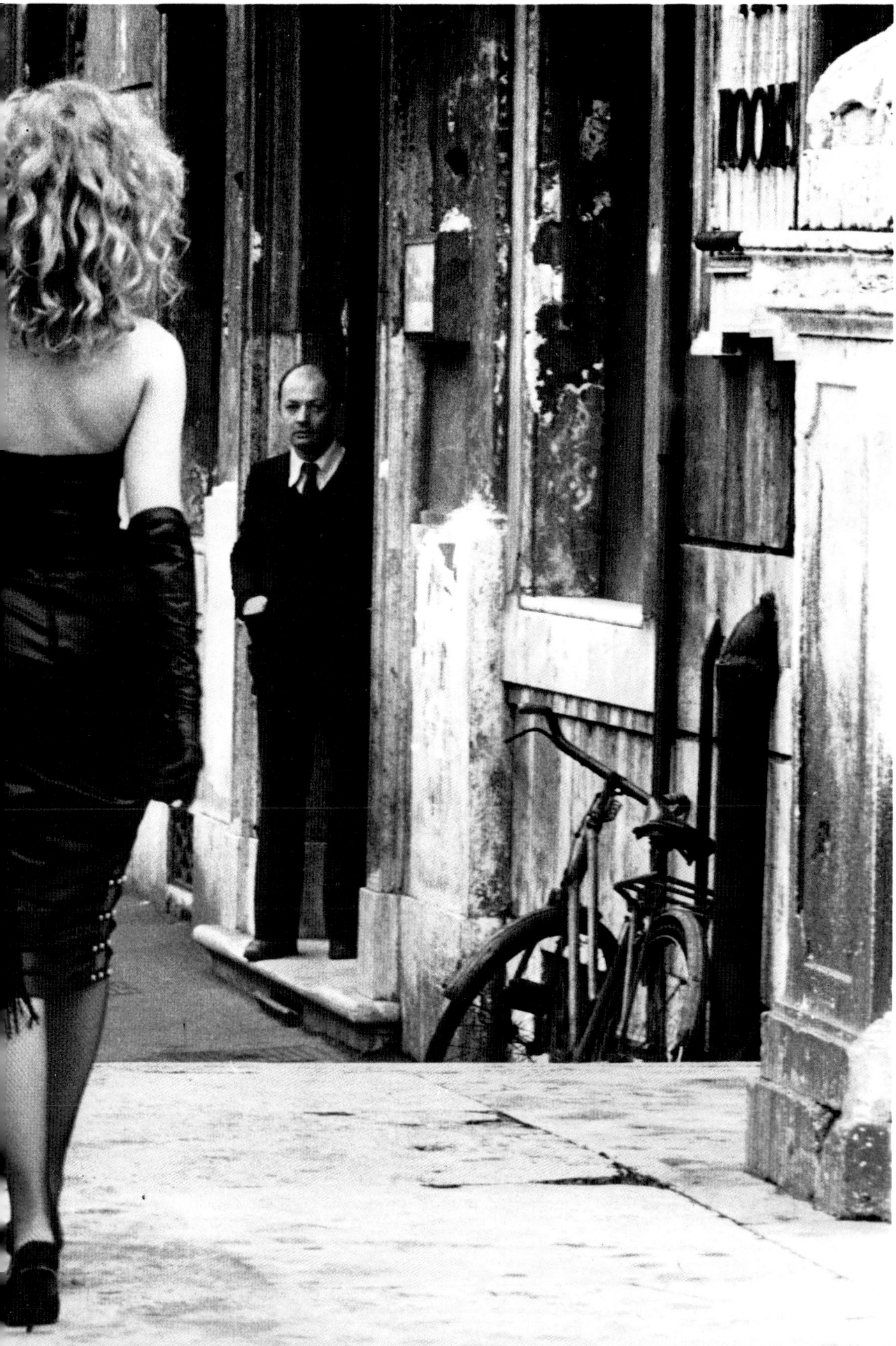

It's really too bad most men want to marry ladies and go to bed with whores. No wonder they don't enjoy sex with their own wives.

    Irene

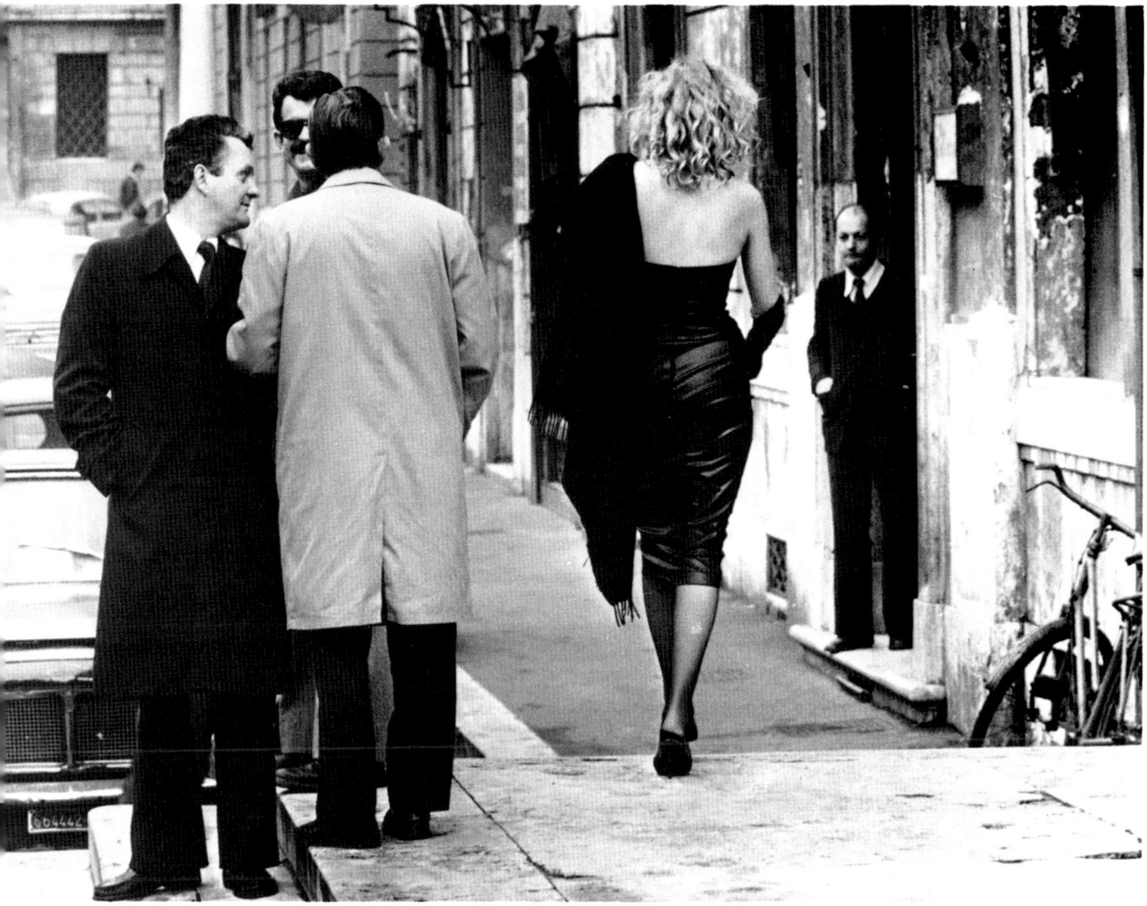

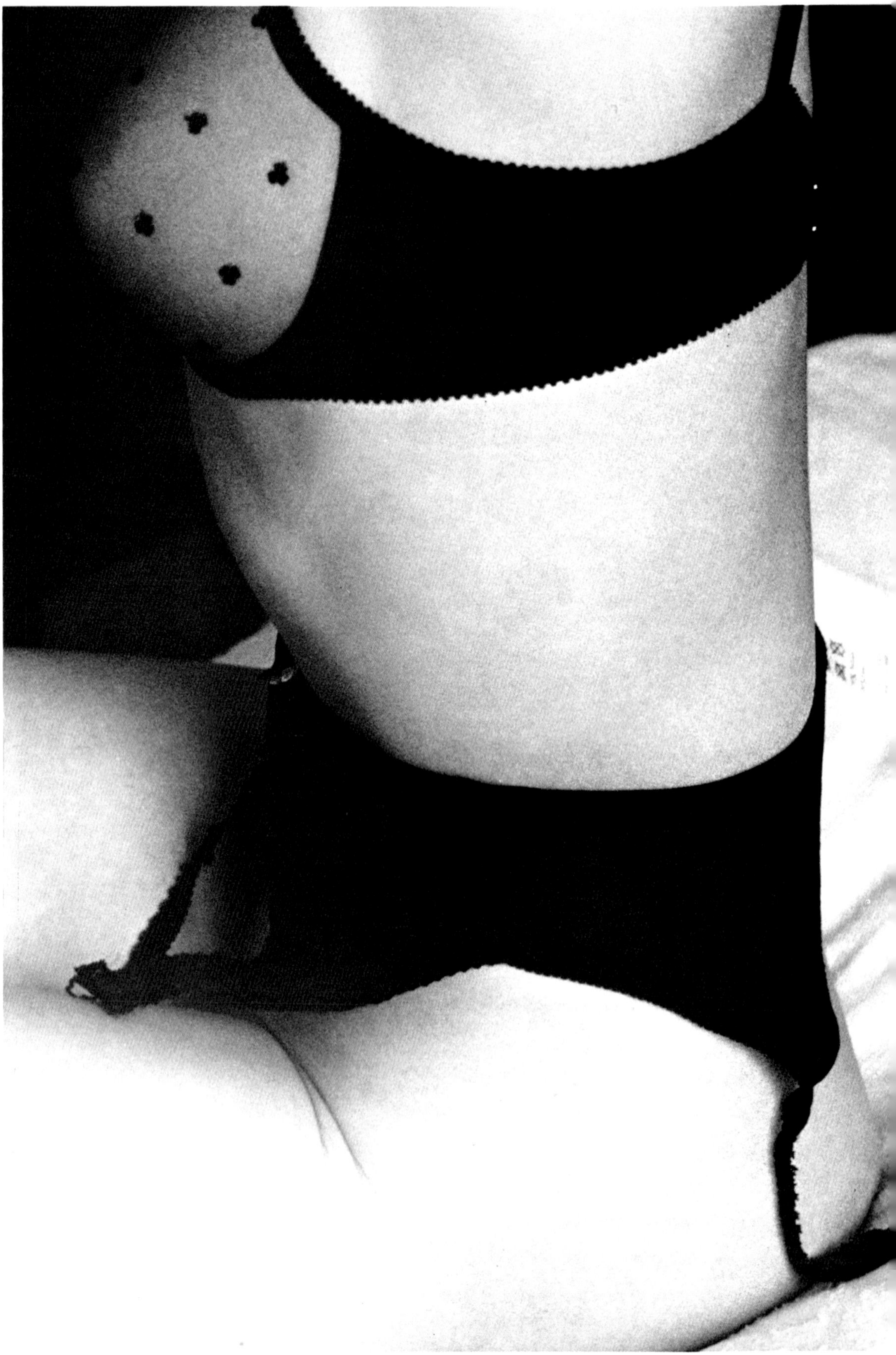

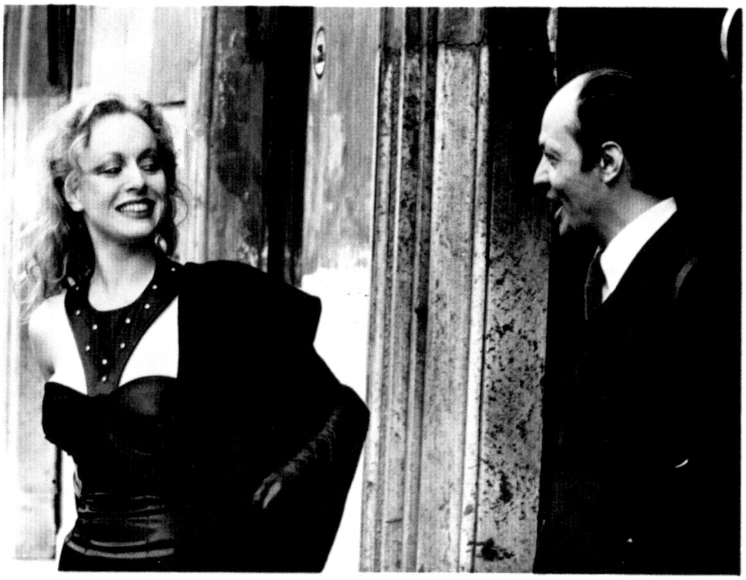

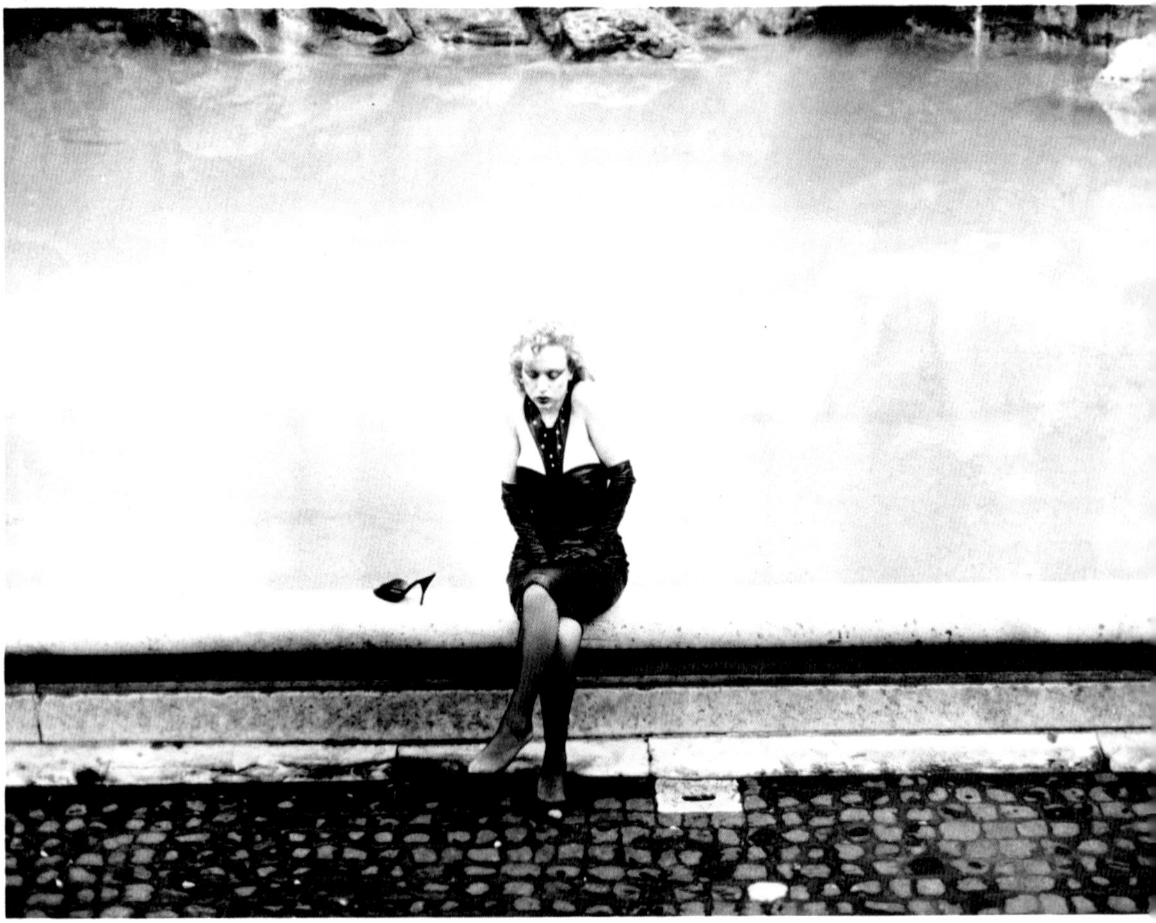

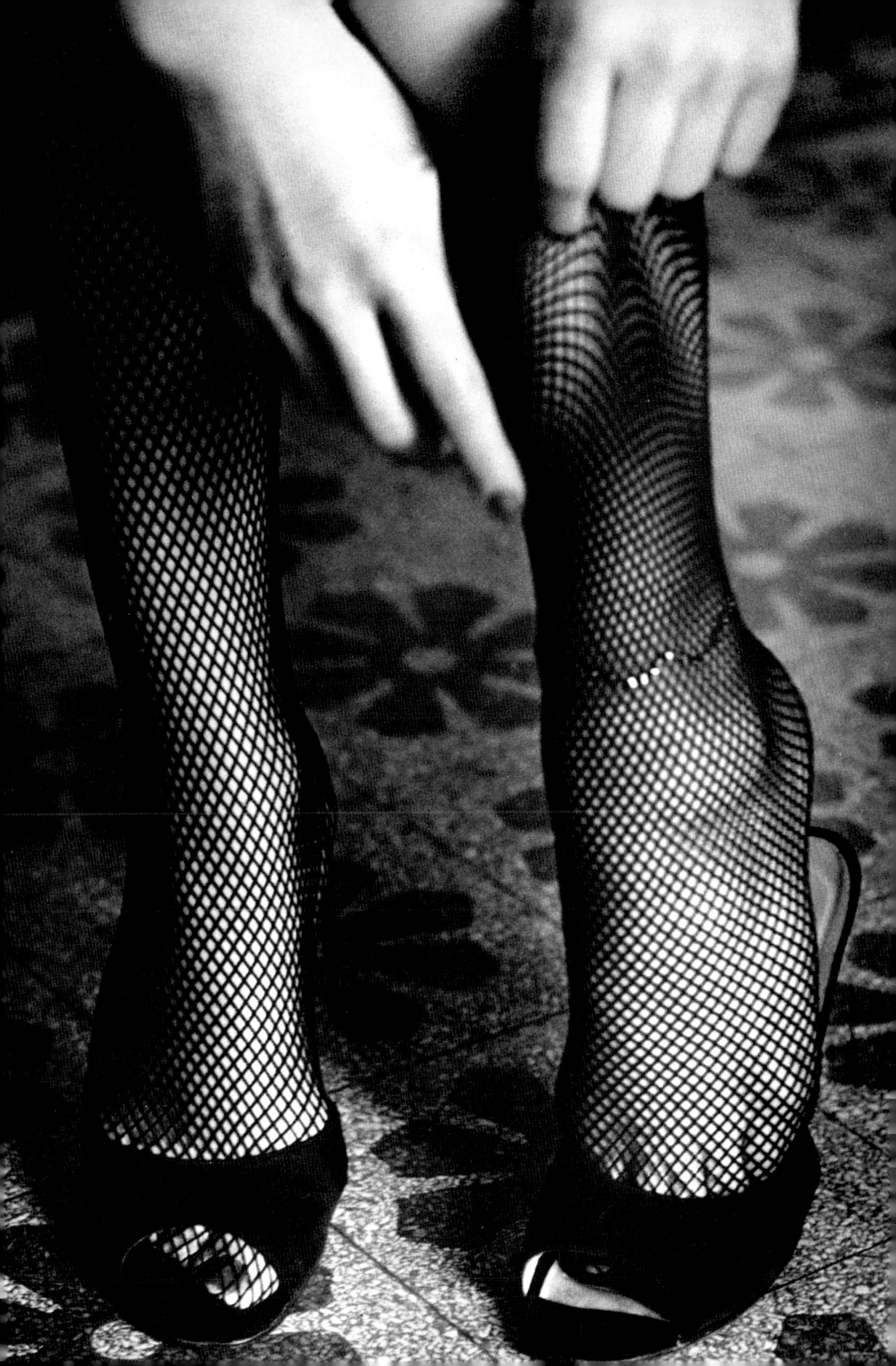

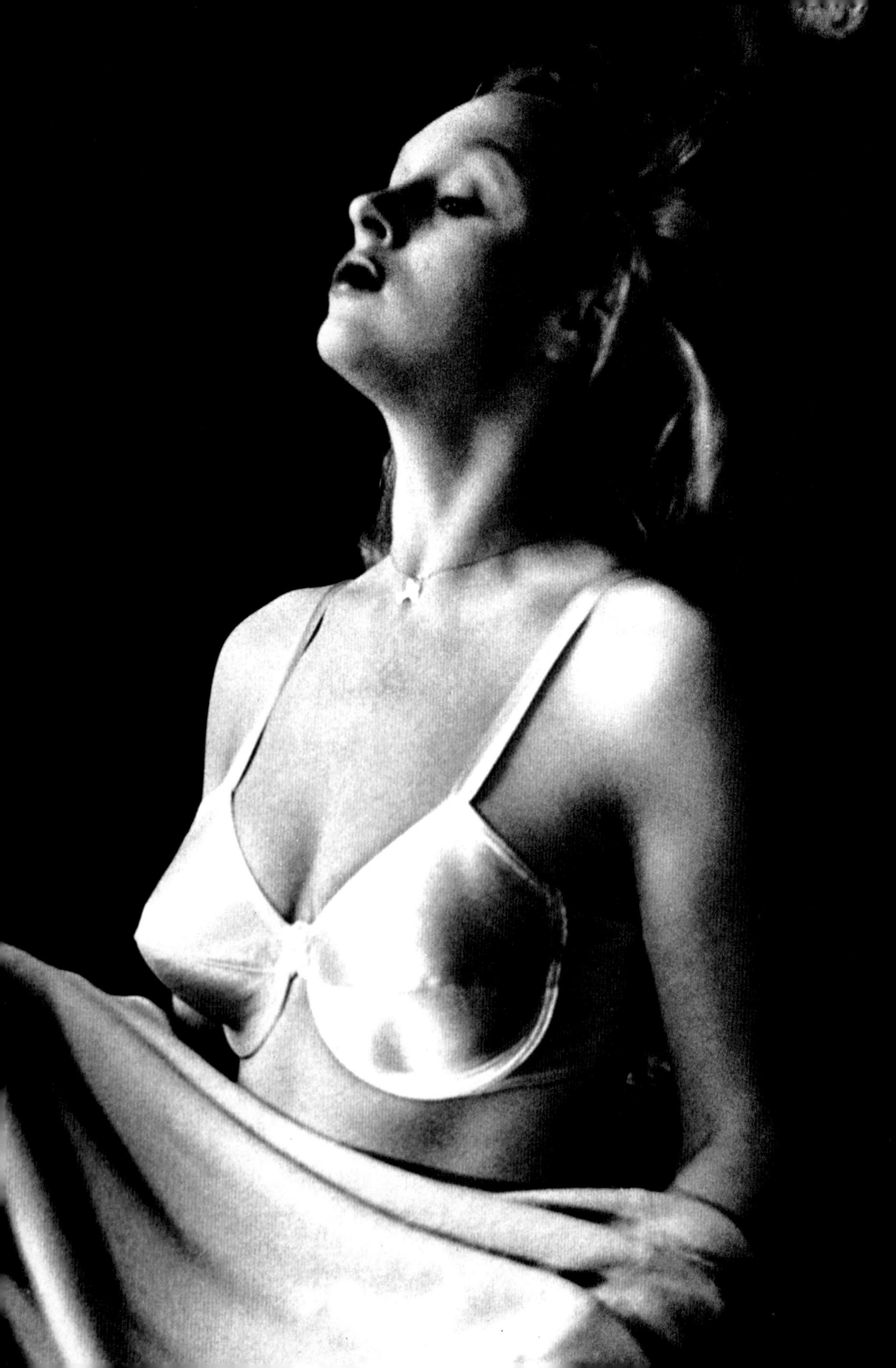

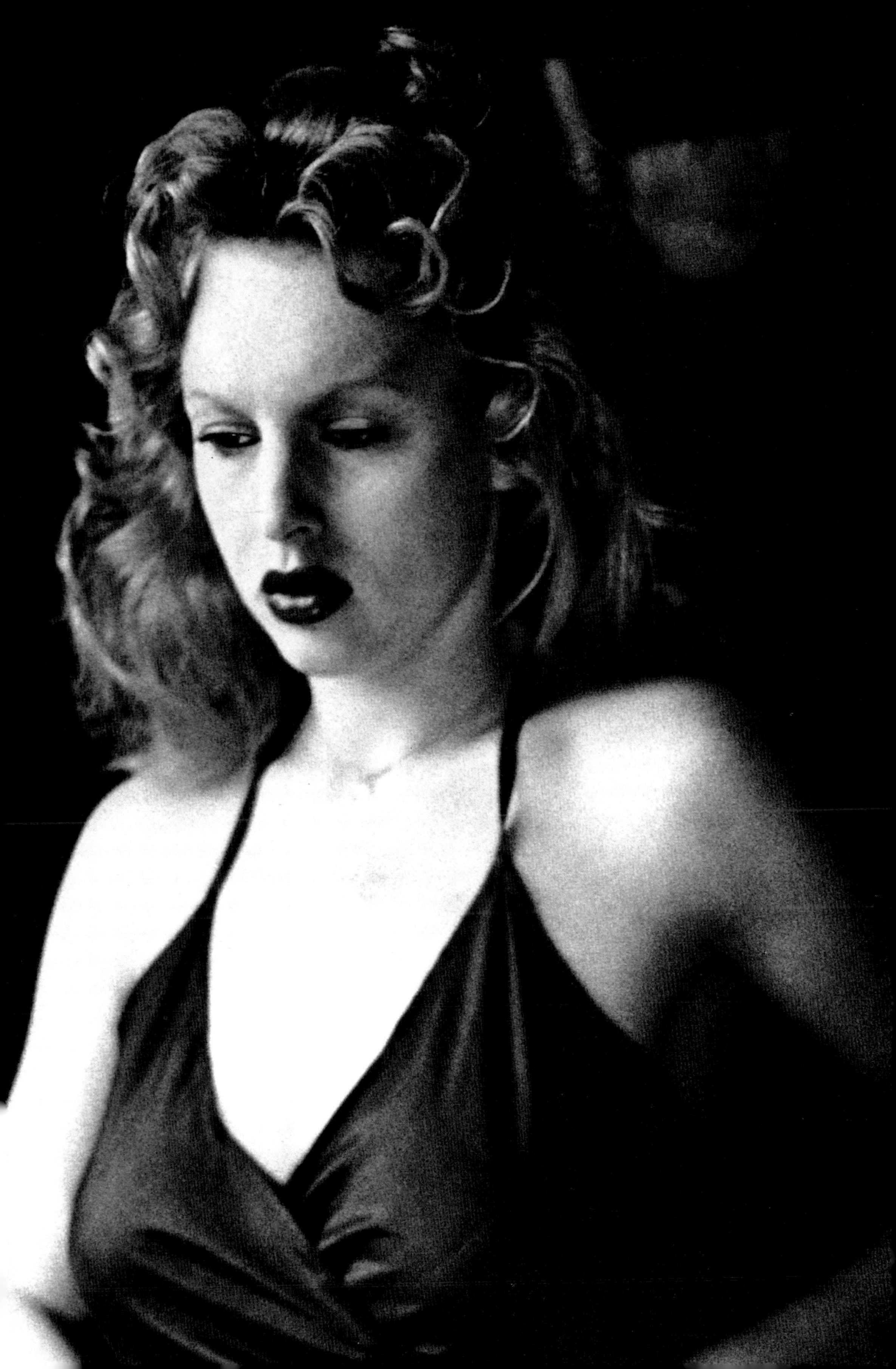

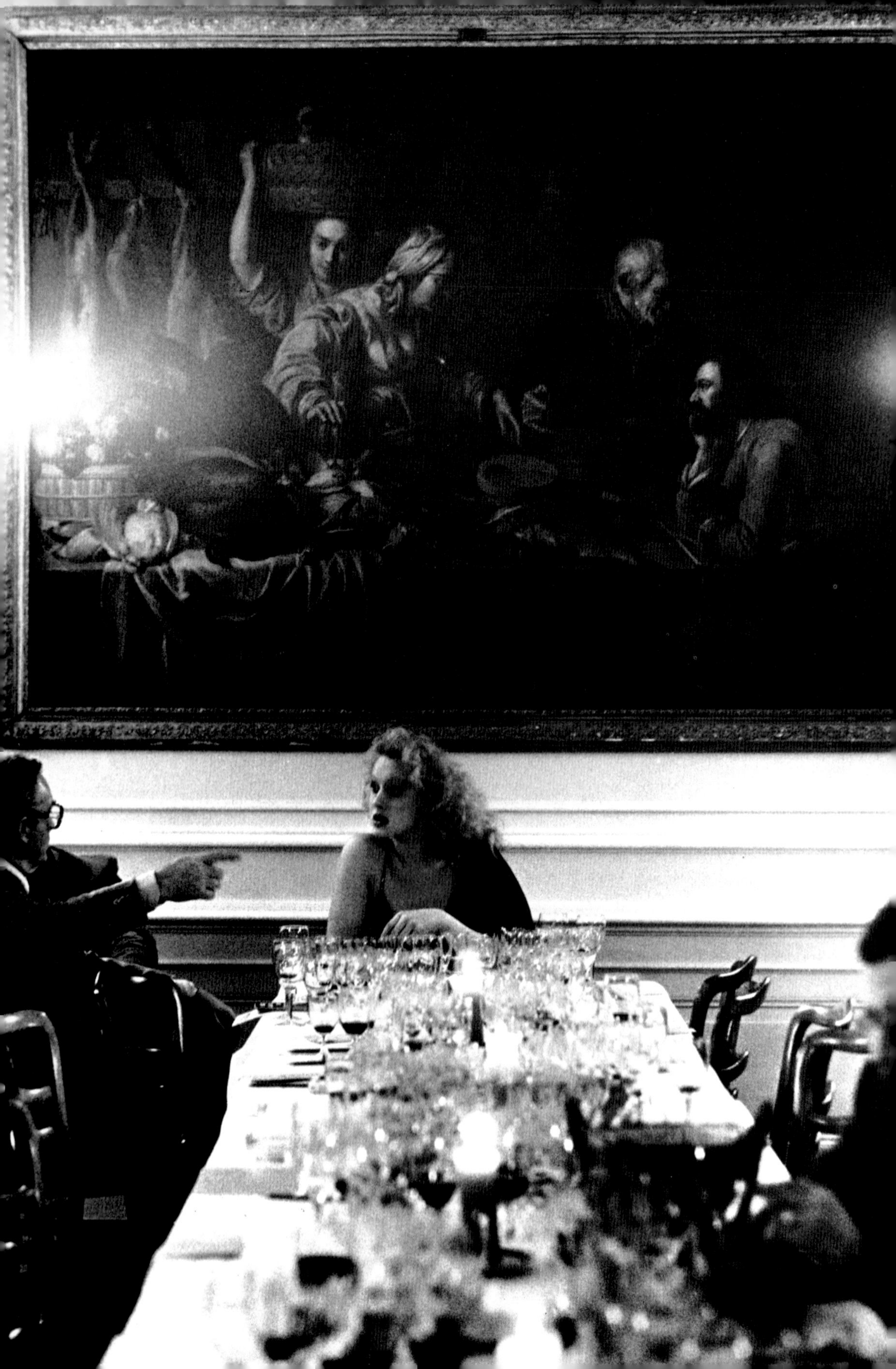

Man is an adoring animal. To adore is to sacrifice and prostitute oneself. Thus, all love is prostitution.
    Baudelaire

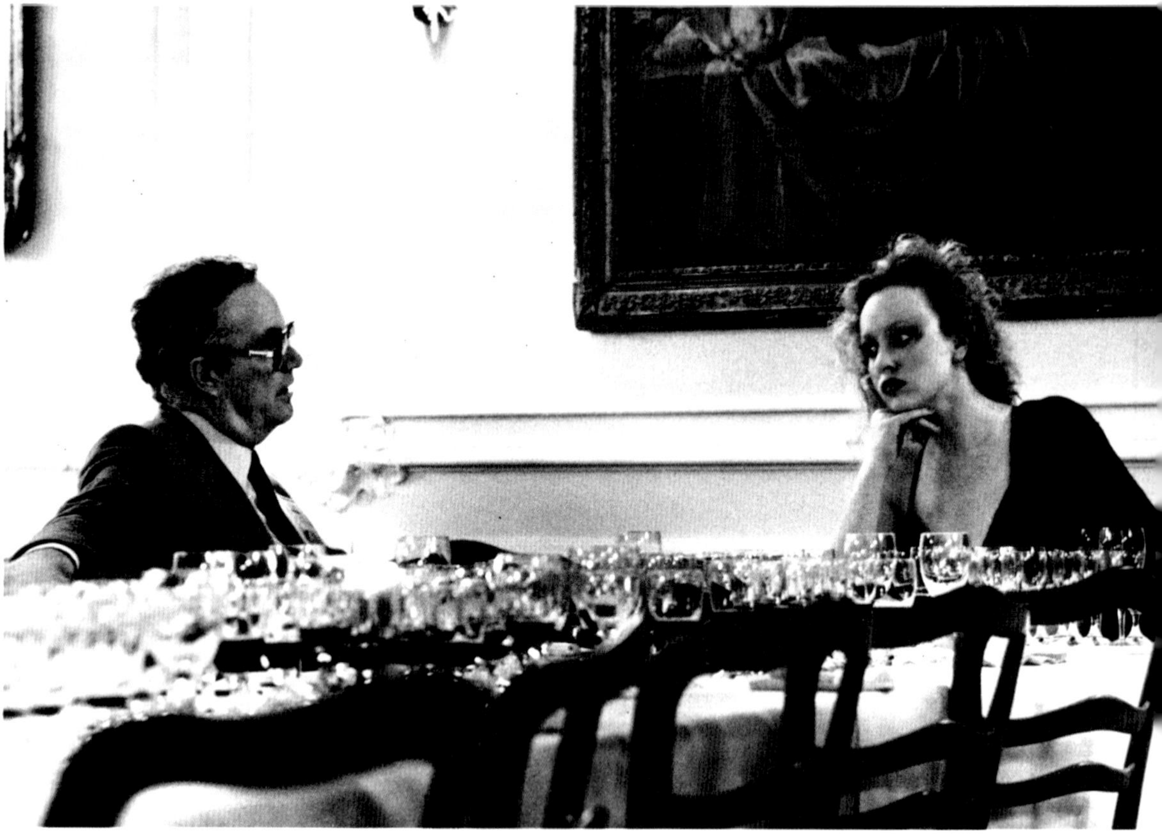

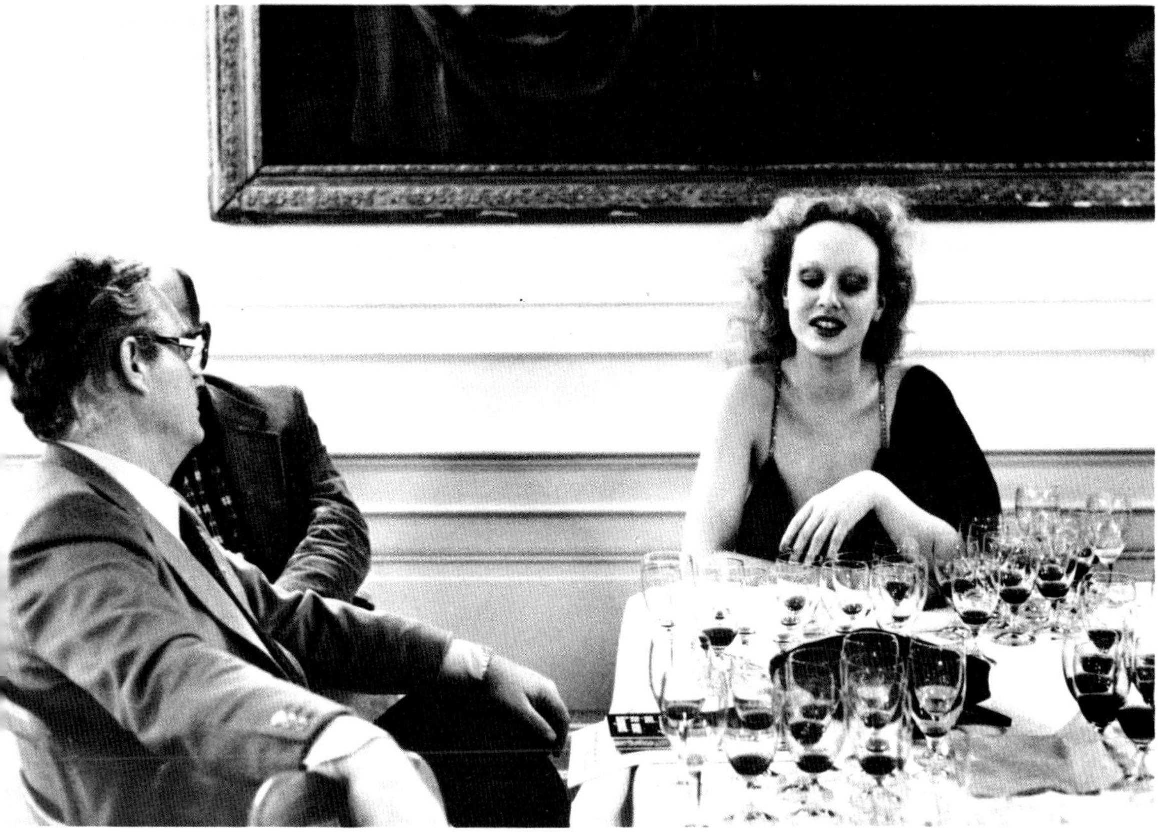

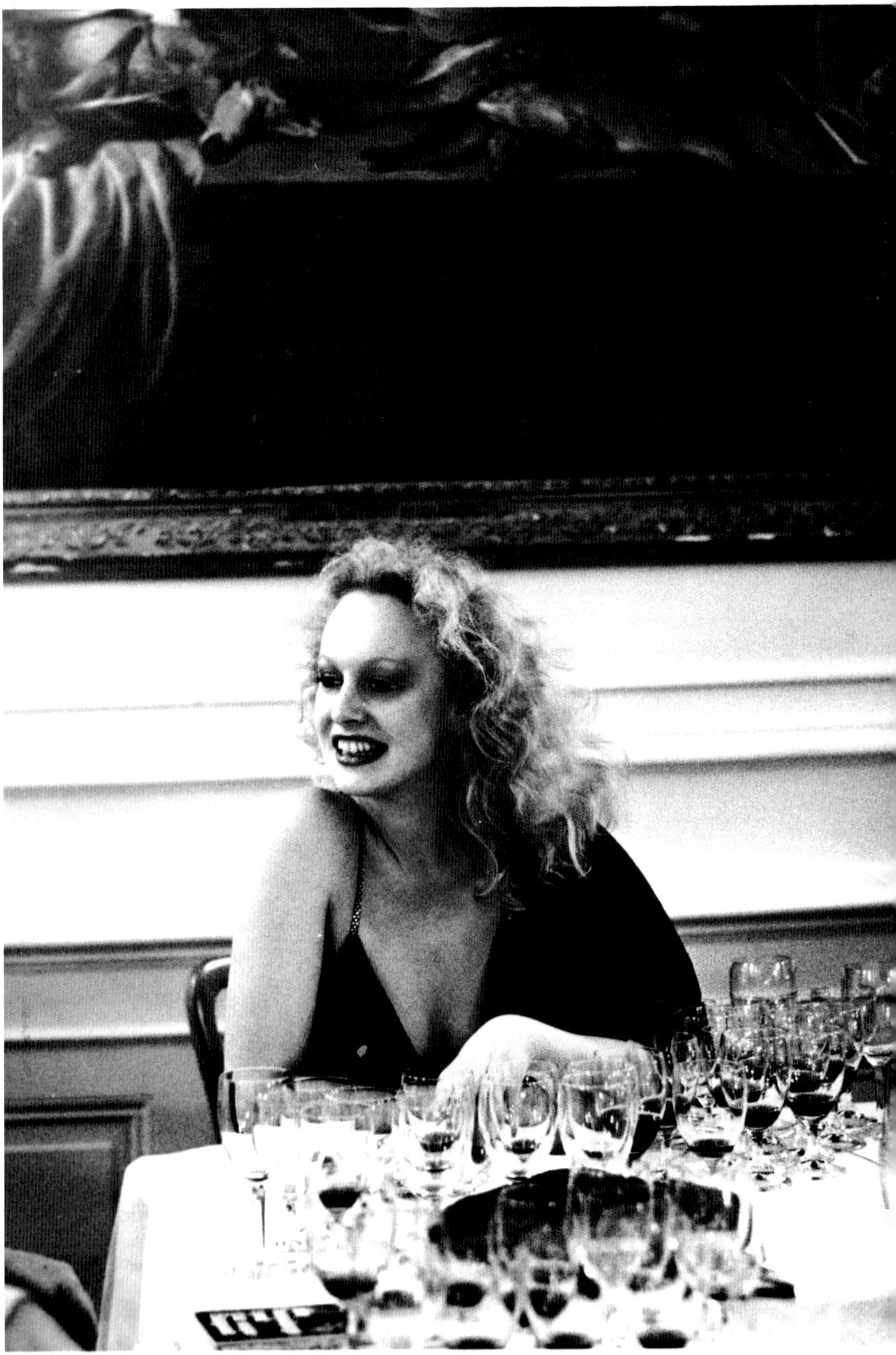

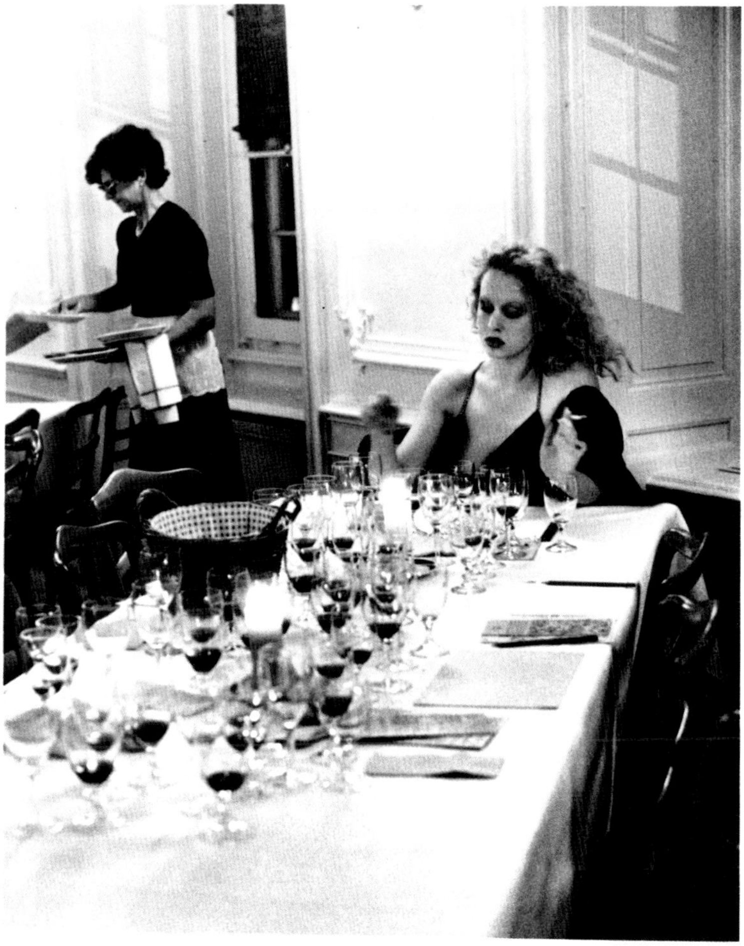

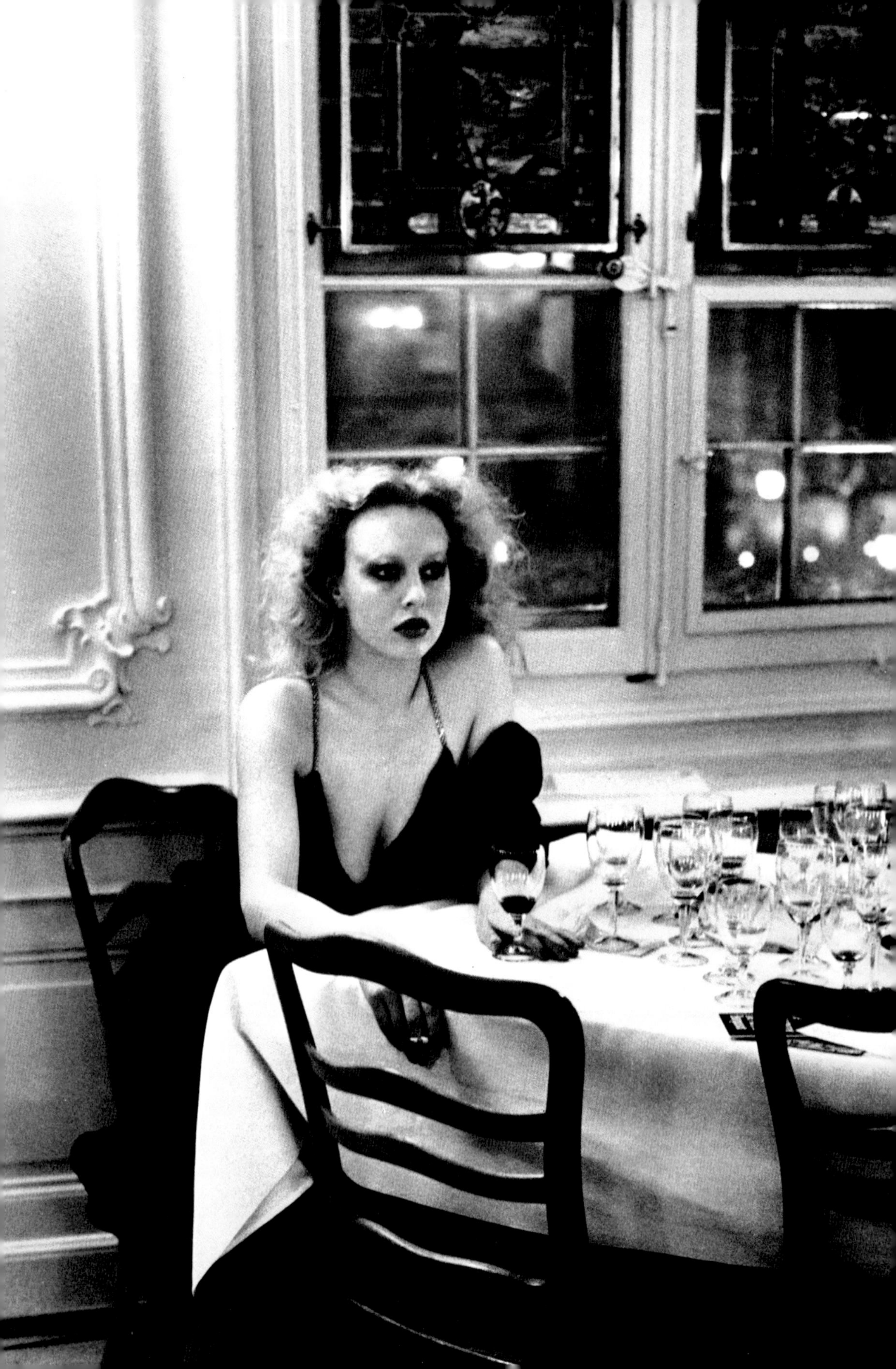

I'm a taker. It used to be the other way round. I don't want to be one of the victims anymore.
    Irene

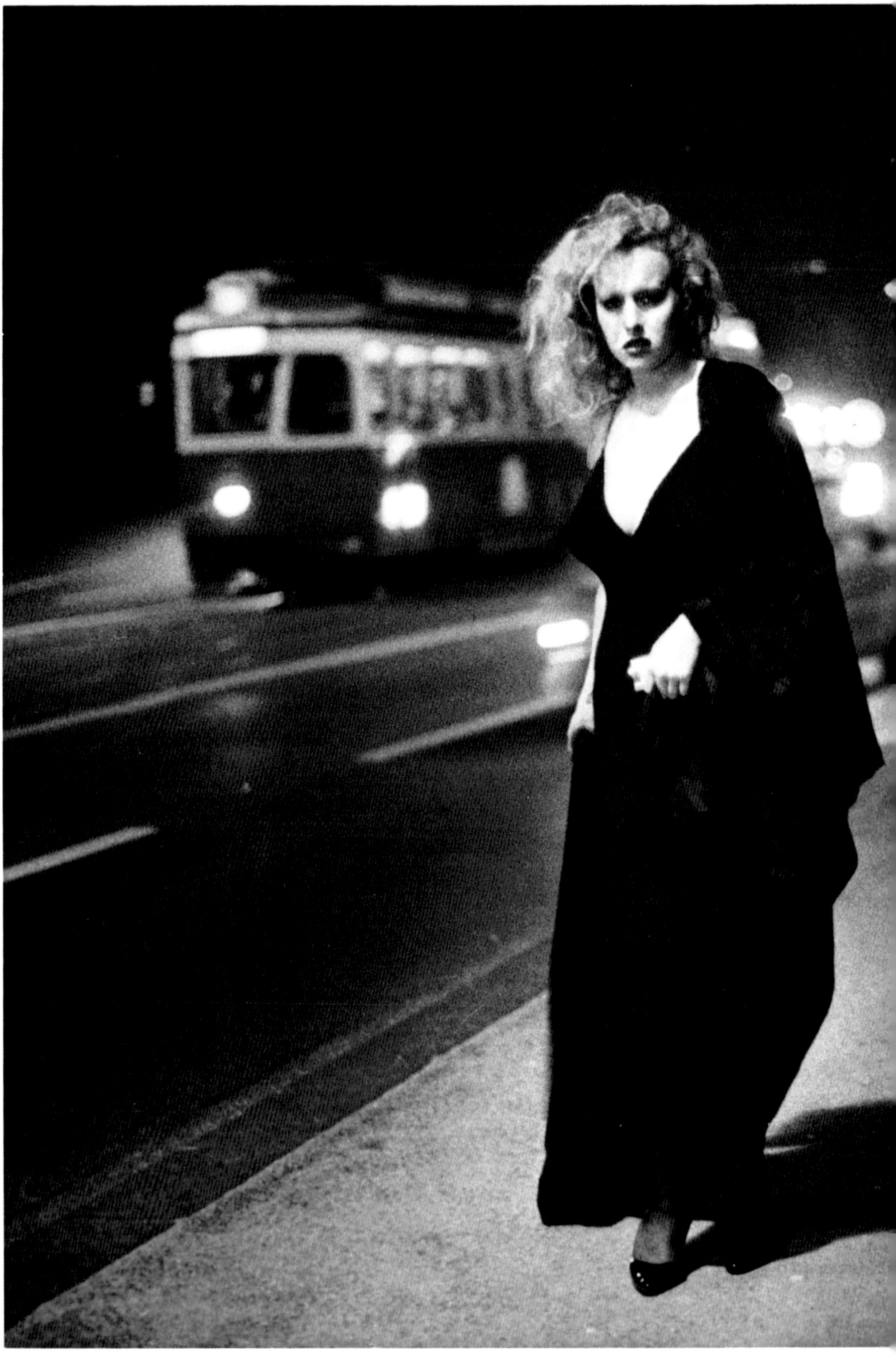

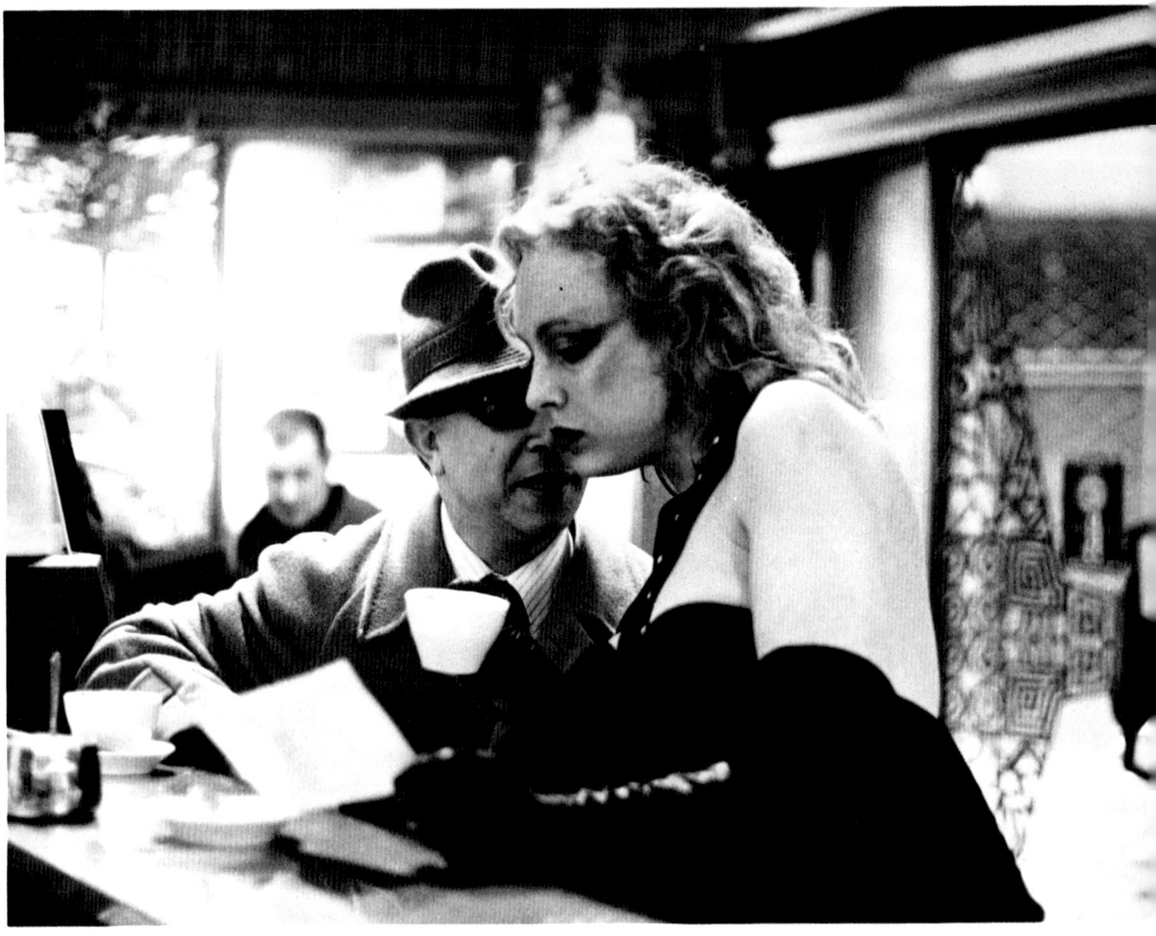

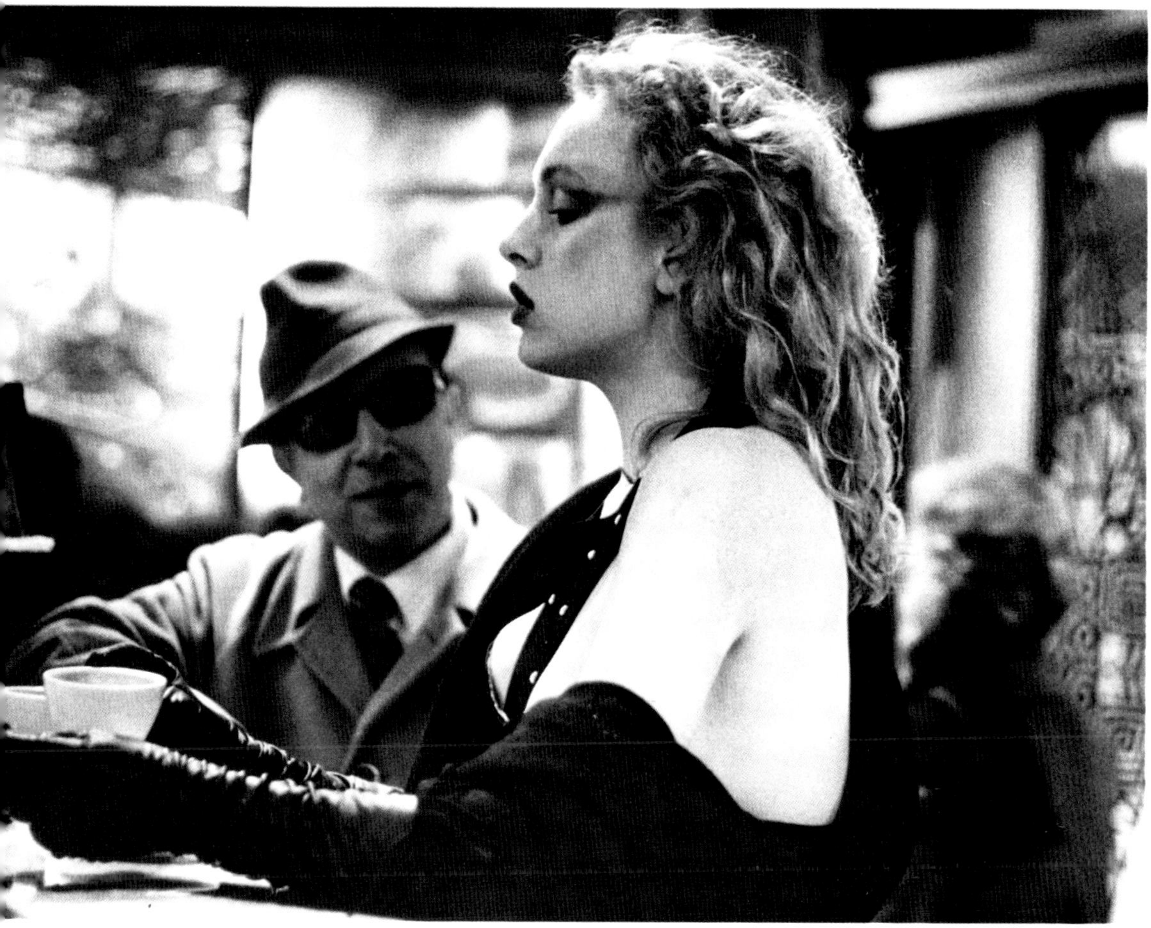

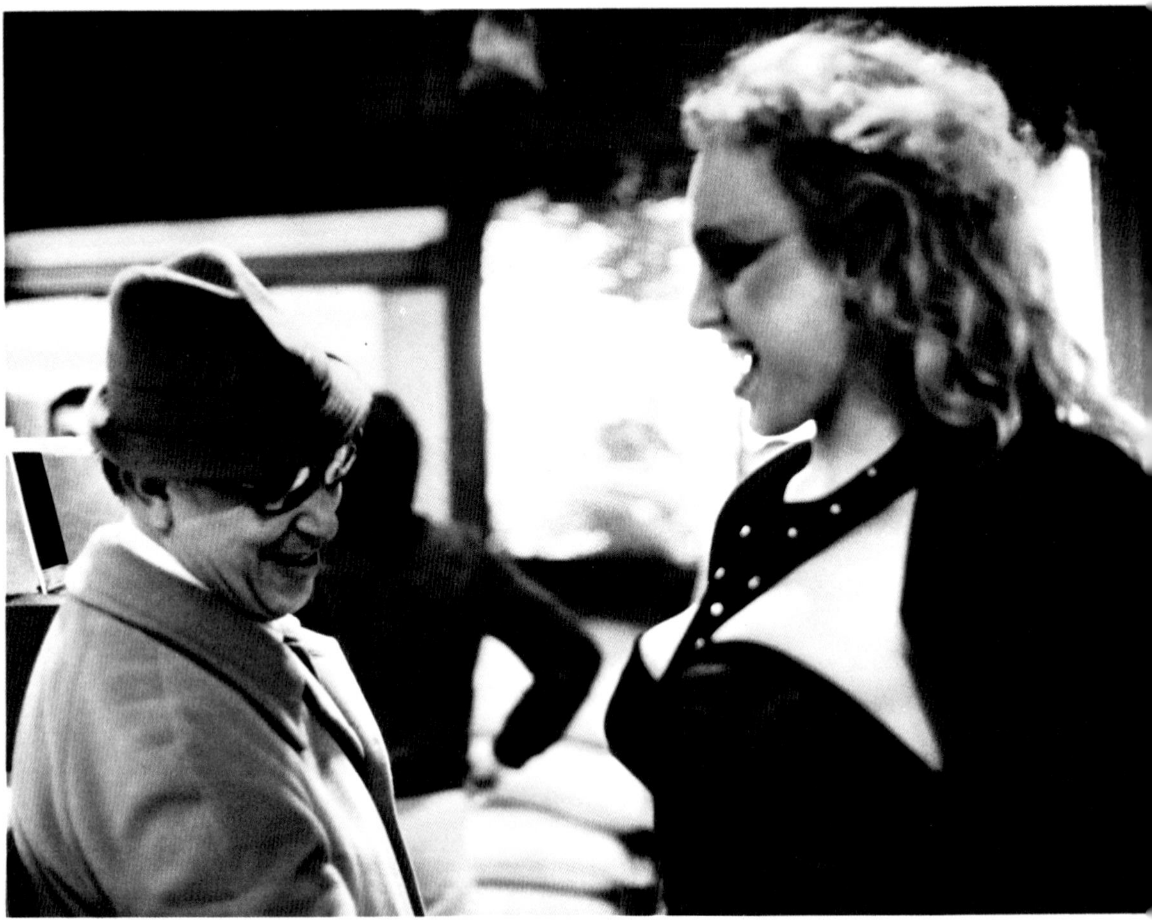

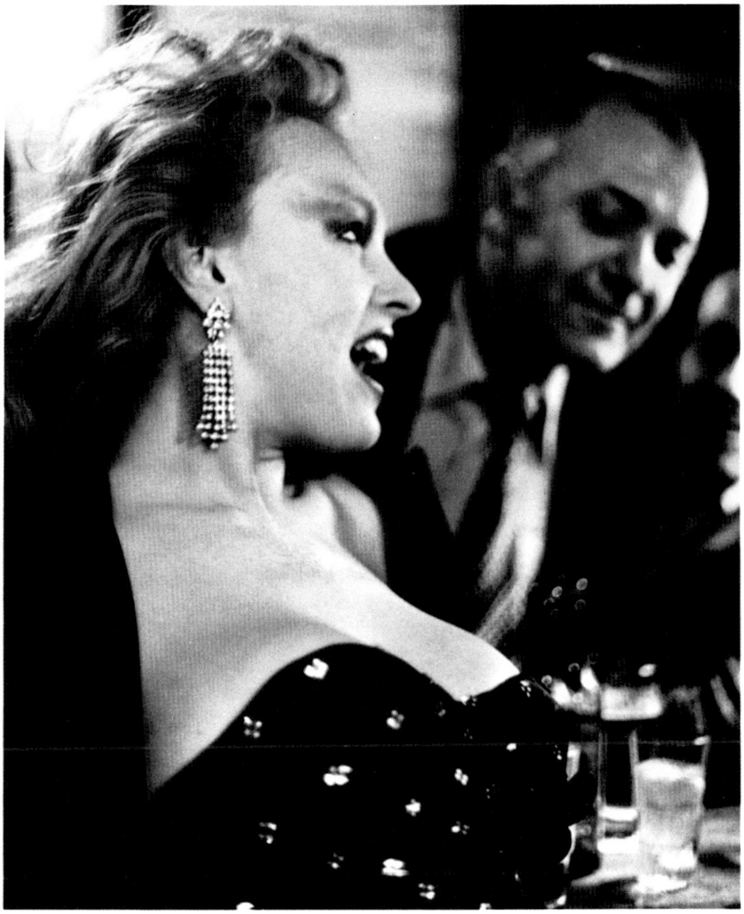

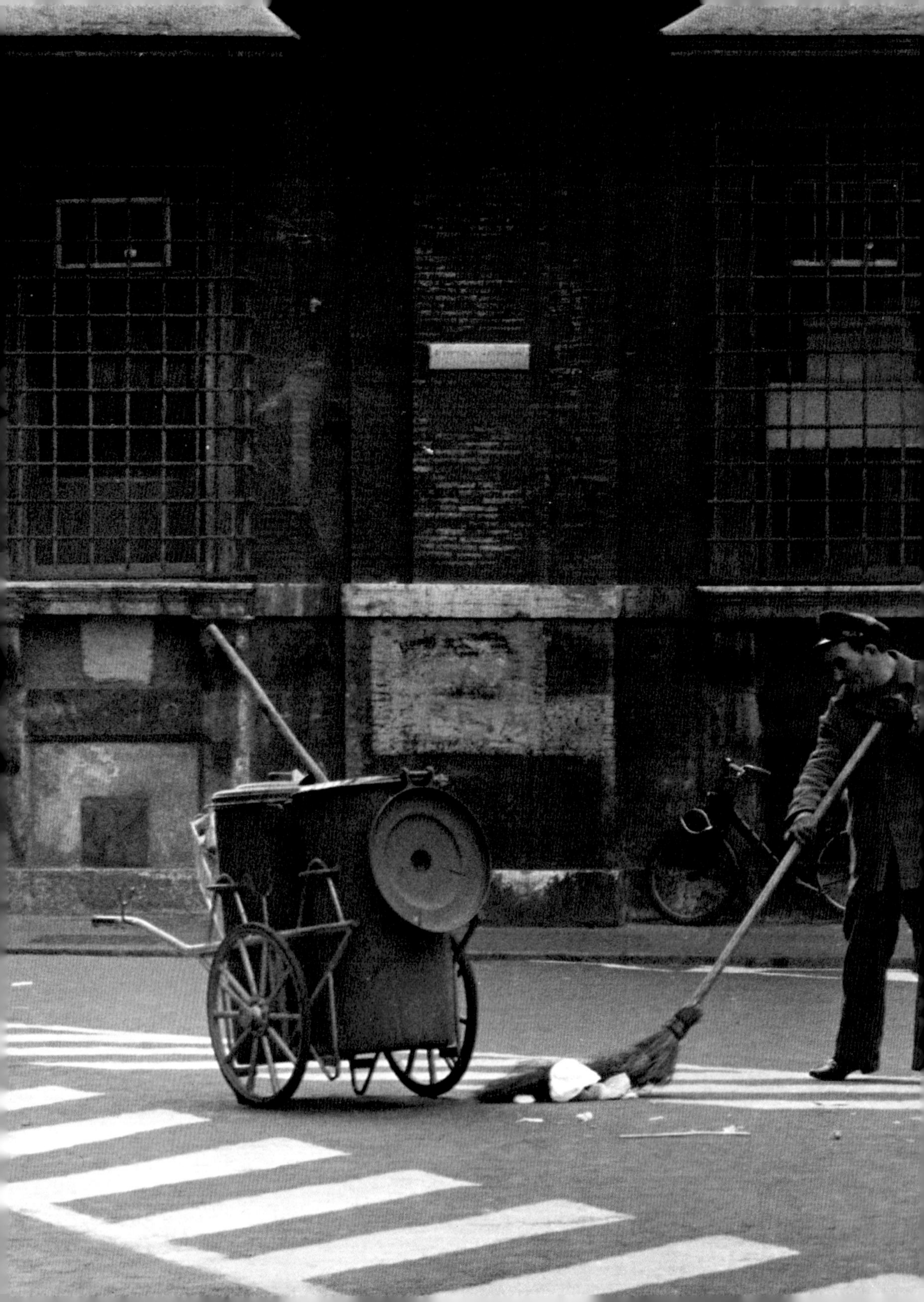

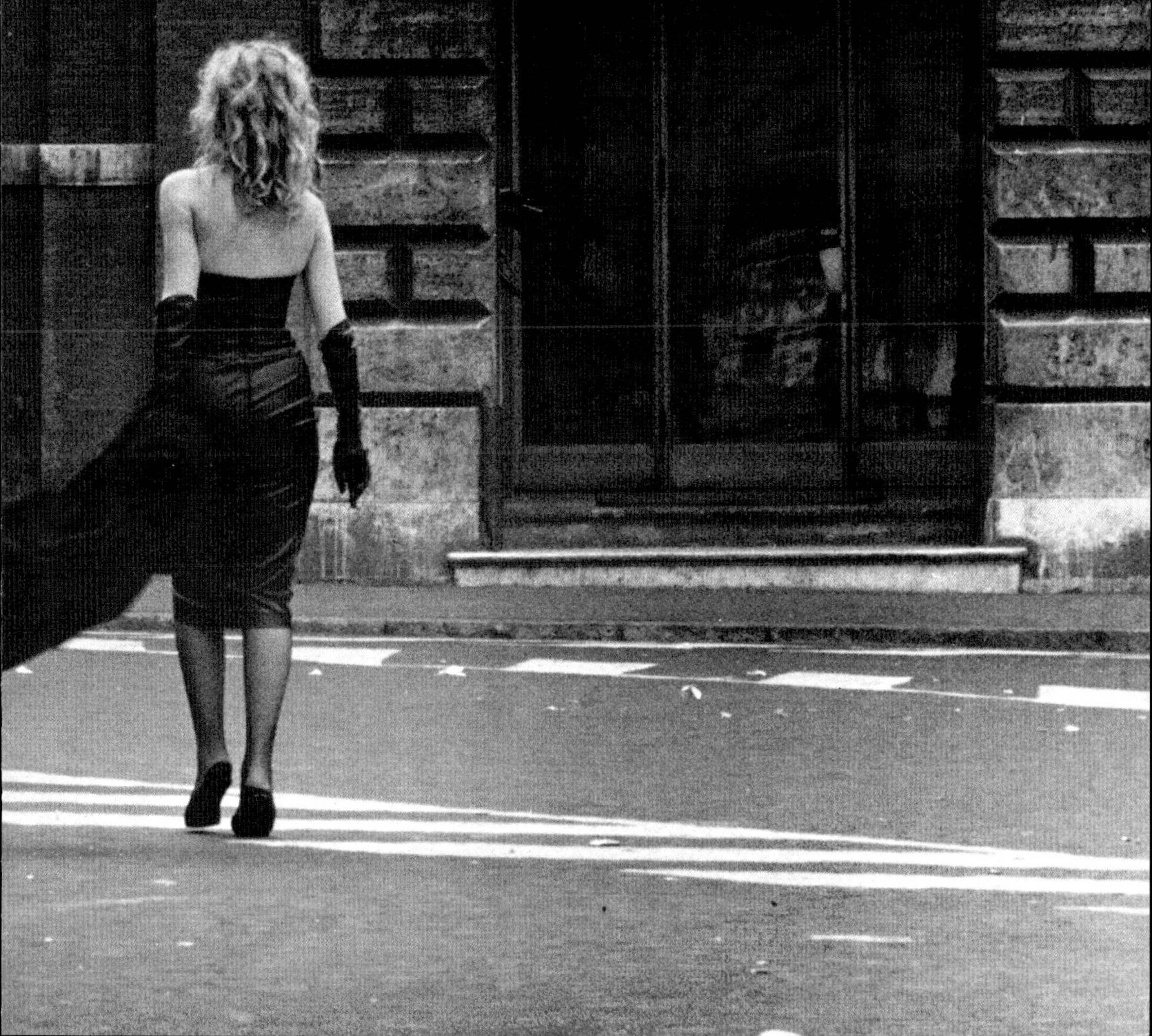

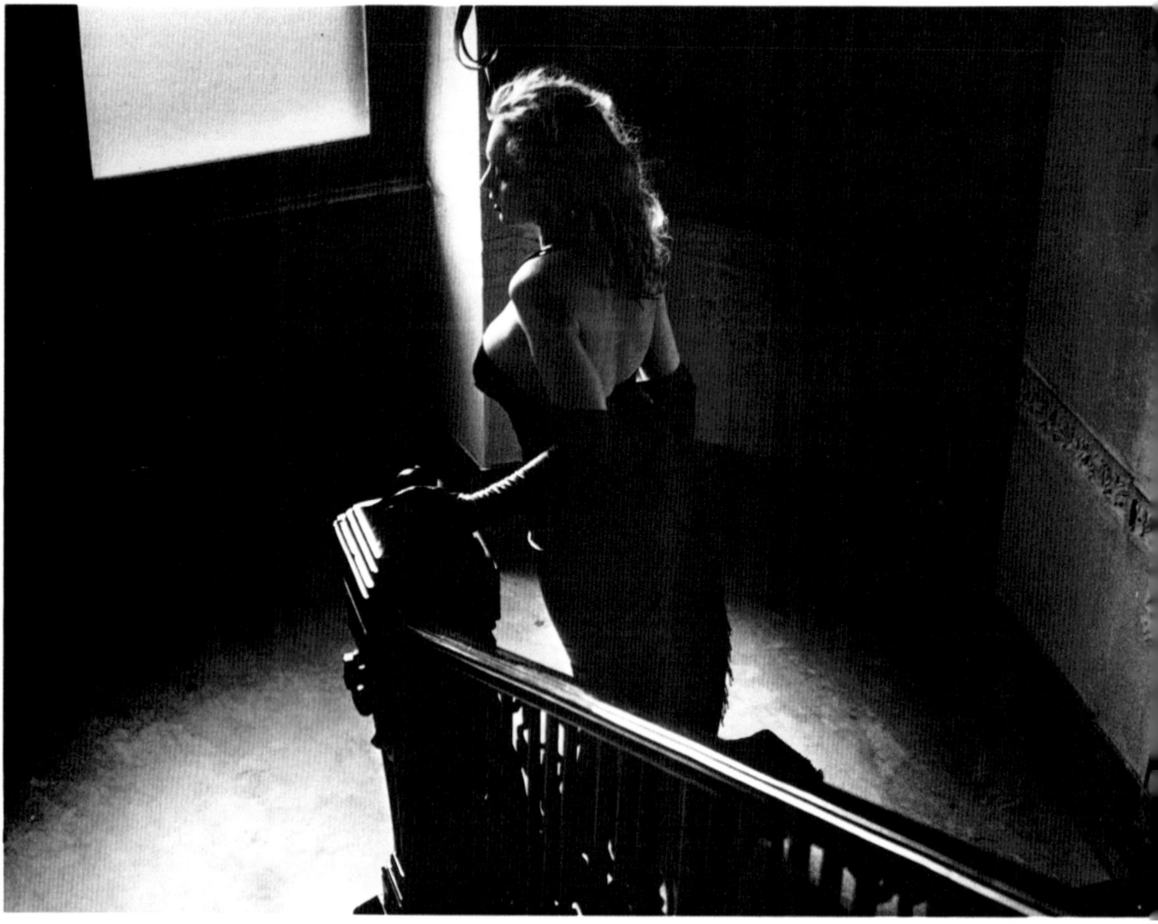

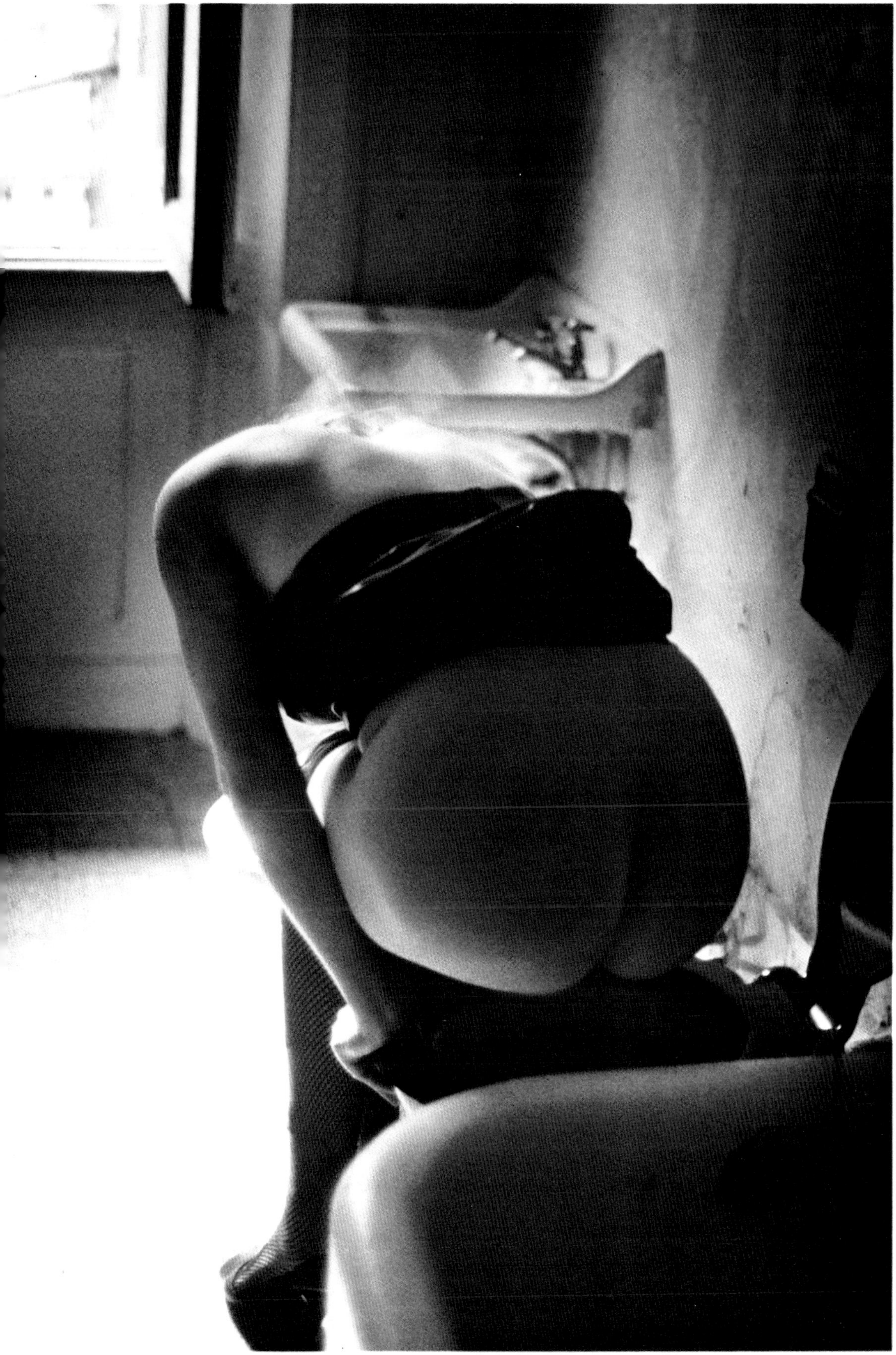

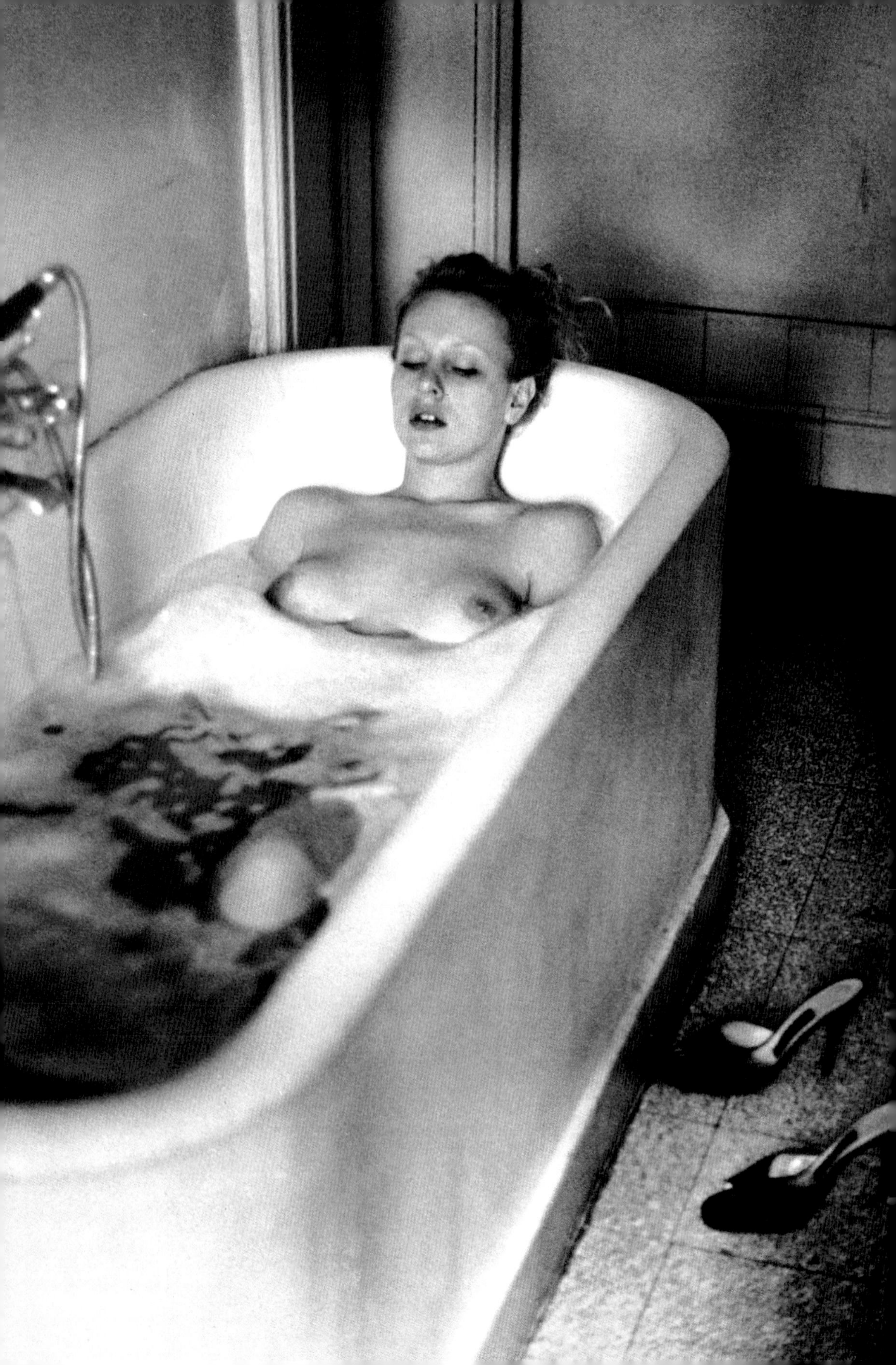

Sometimes I'm afraid of becoming fucked up, but then I'm saved by a hope in the uncertain which gives me strength and energy again.

    Irene

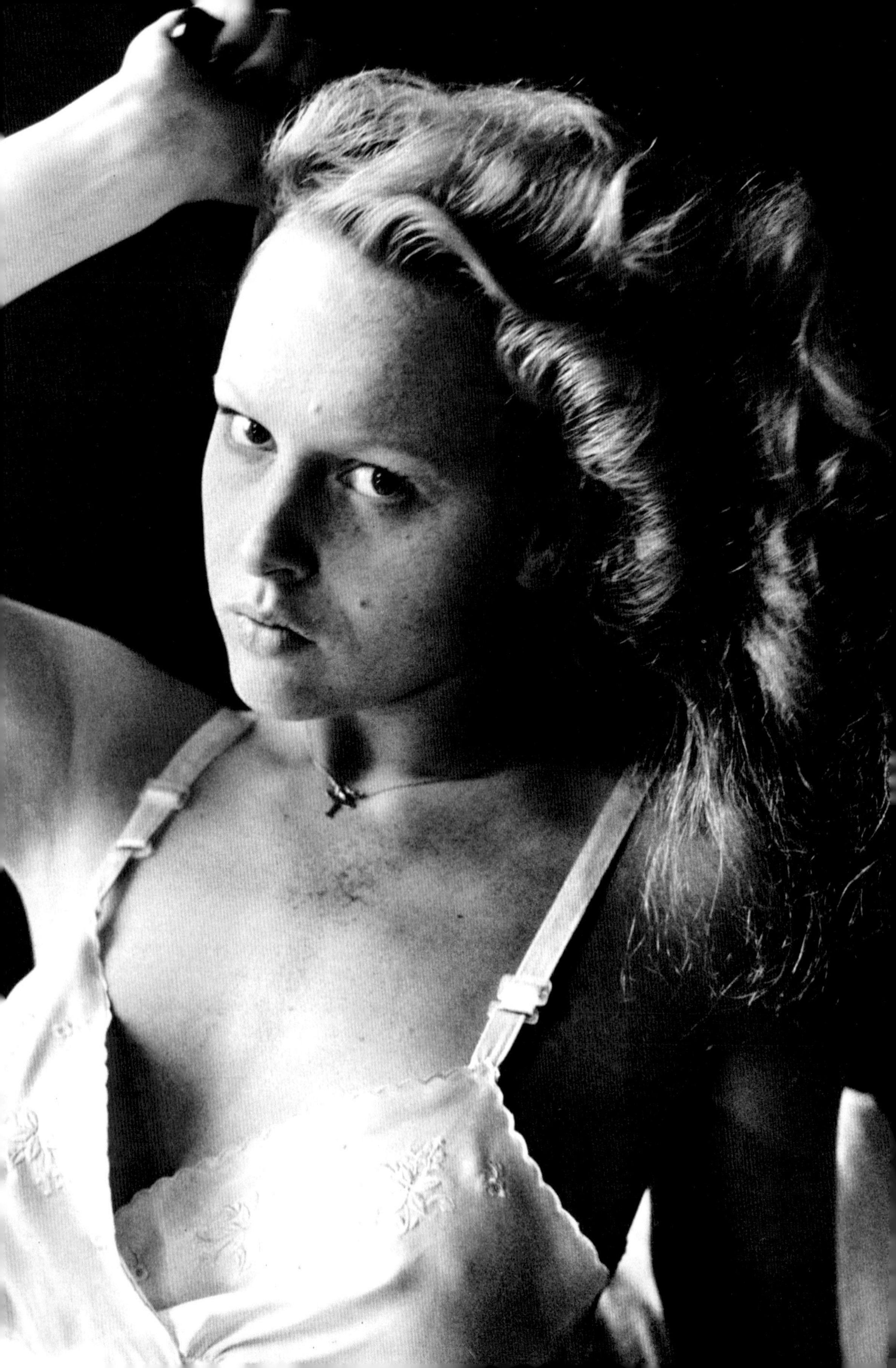

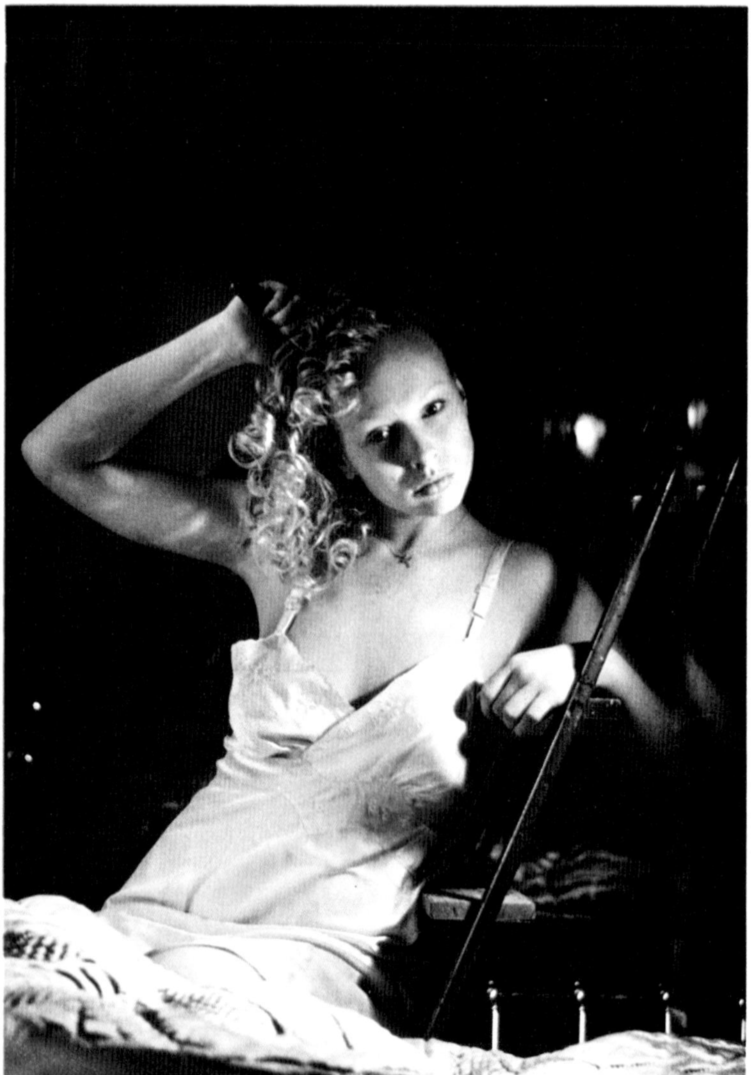

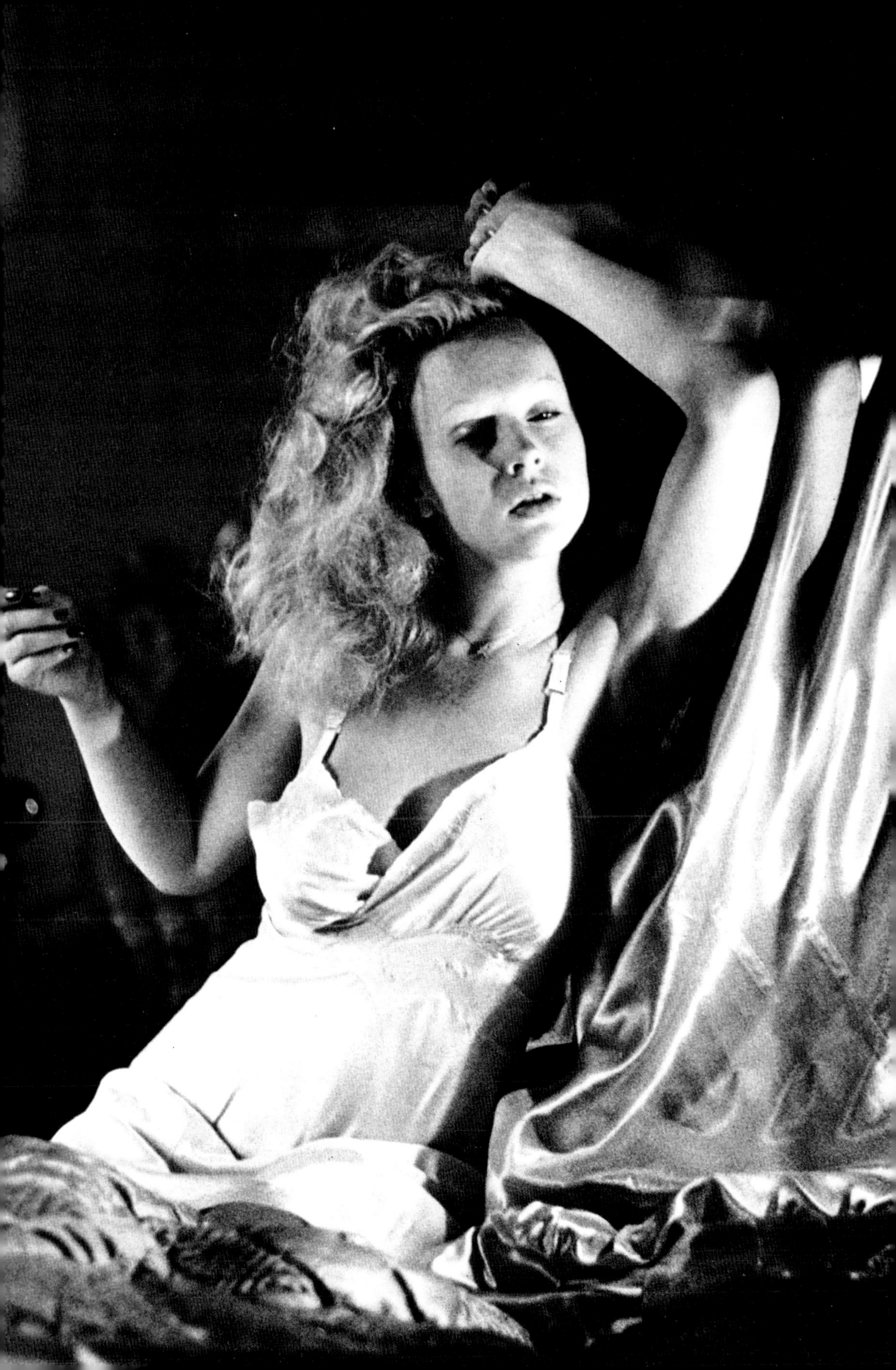

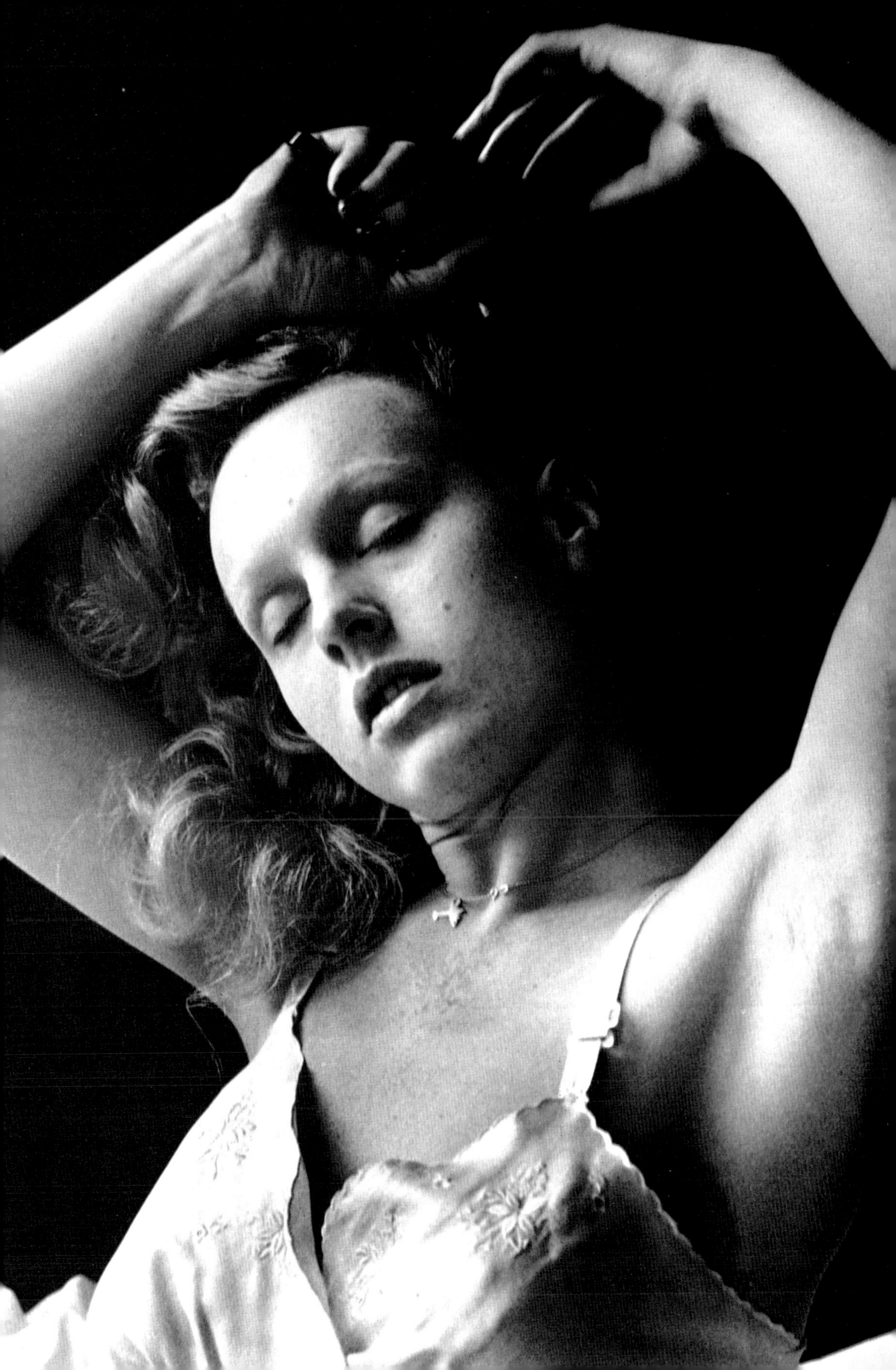

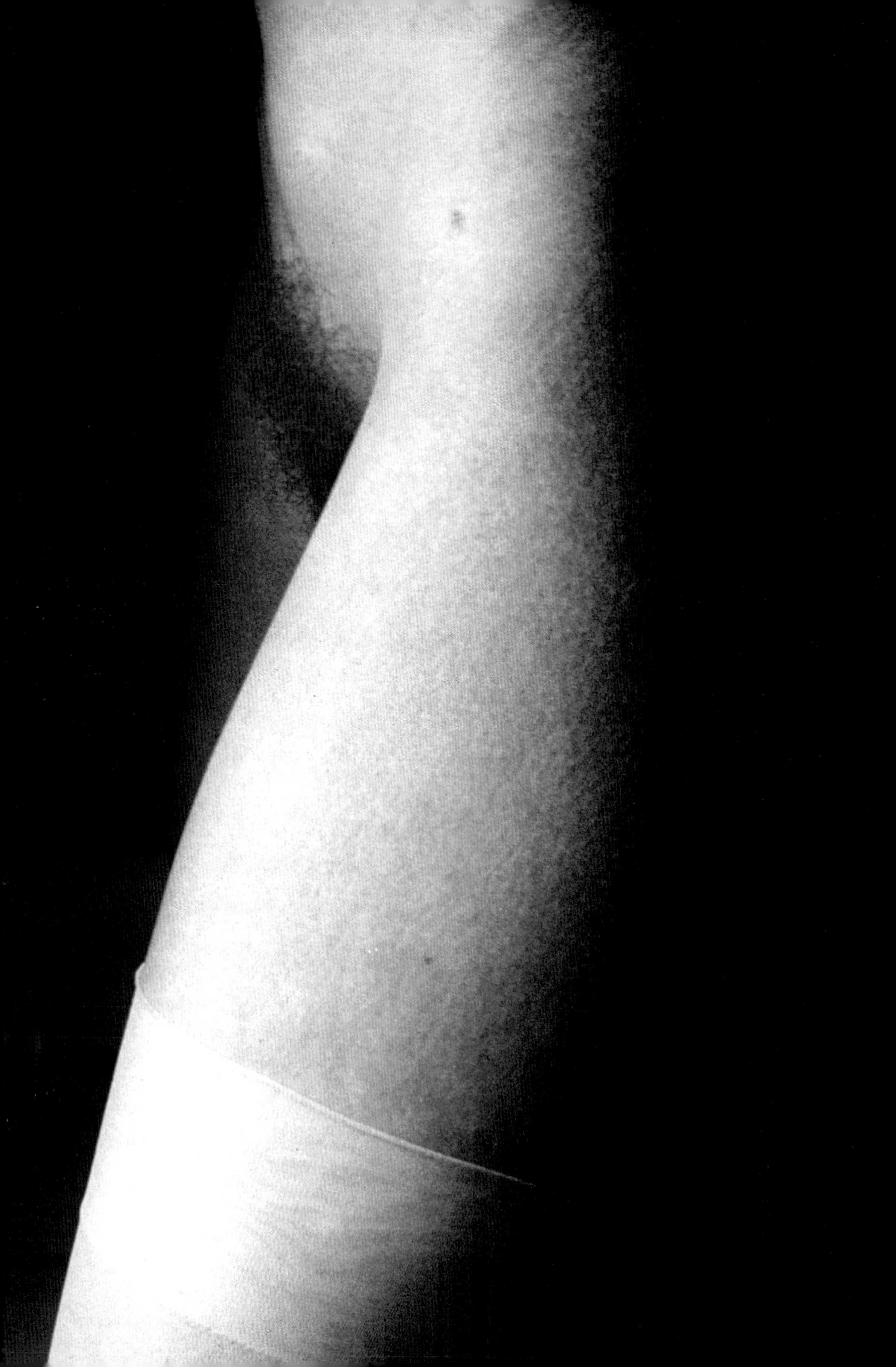

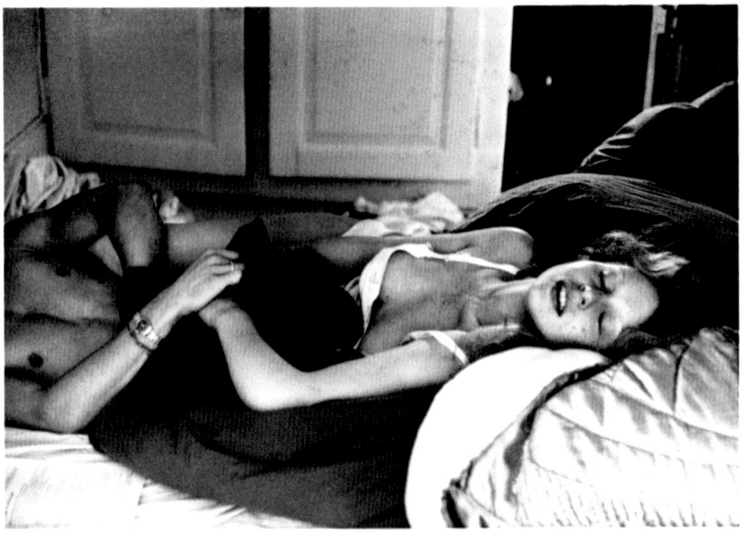

The unique and supreme pleasure of love lies in the certainty of doing <u>evil.</u> And man and woman know from birth that all pleasures are to be found in evil.

    Baudelaire

I have always been astounded that women are allowed to enter churches. What possible conversations can they have with God?

    Baudelaire

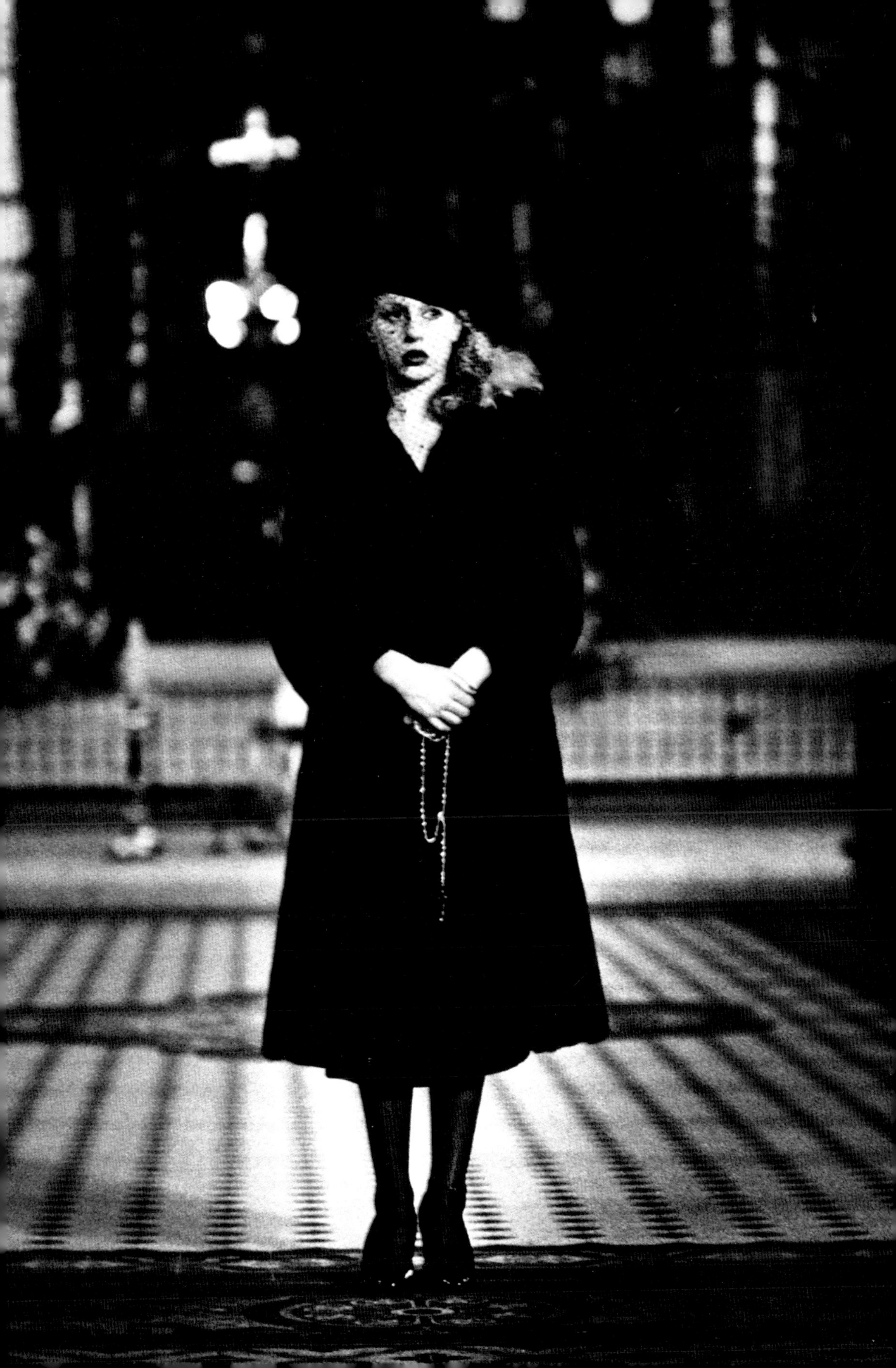

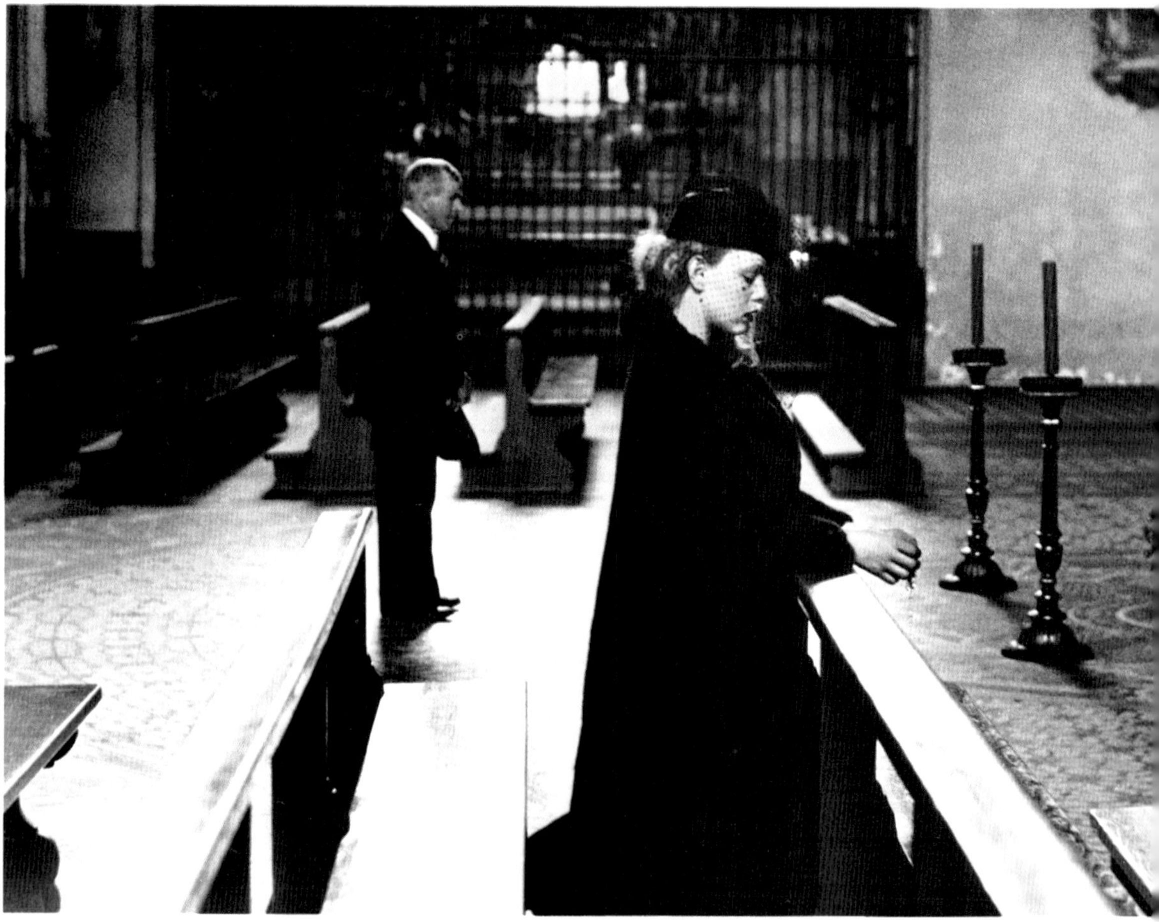

Man has two constant, simultaneous aspirations: one to God, the other to Satan.

    Baudelaire

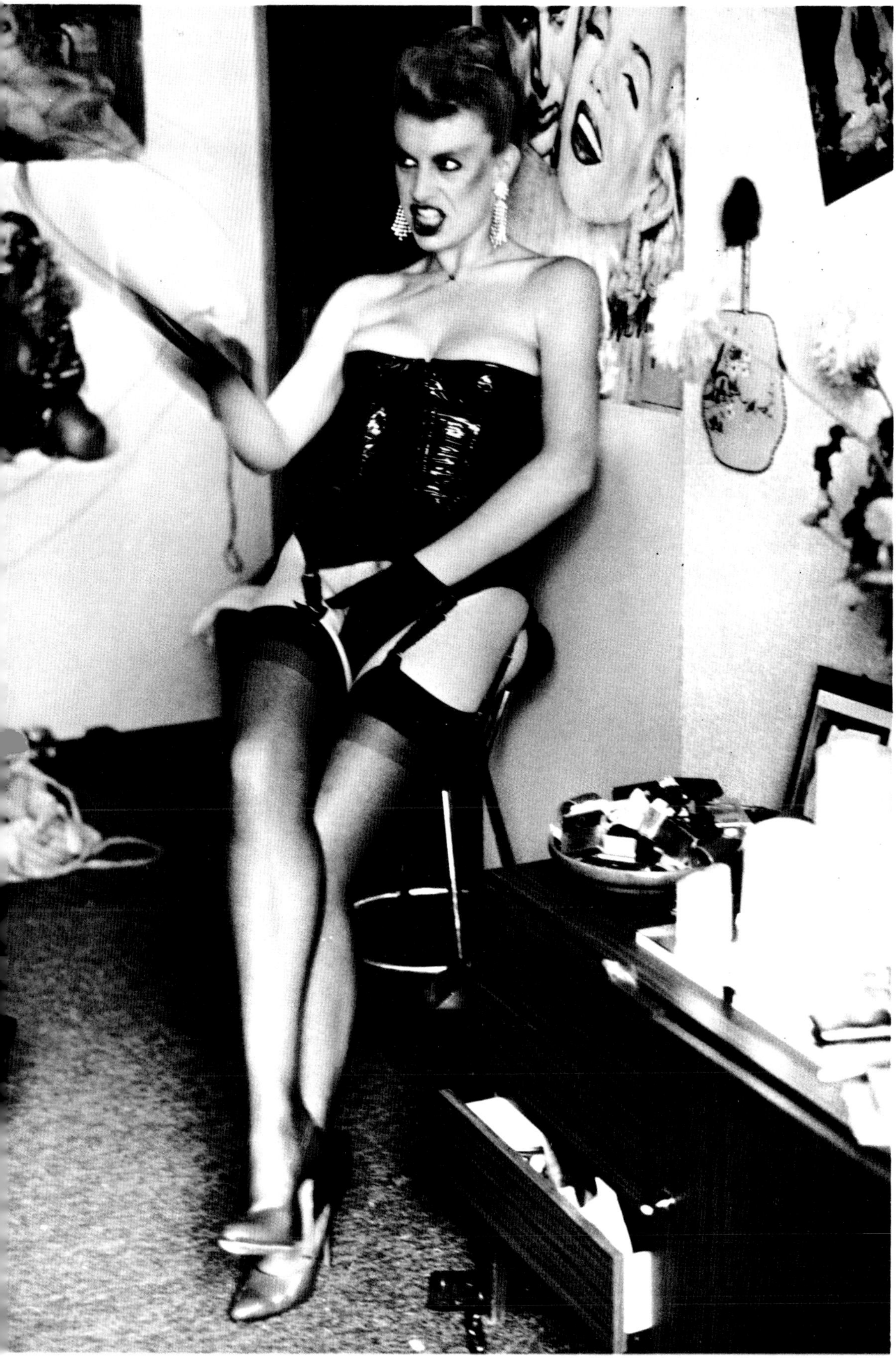

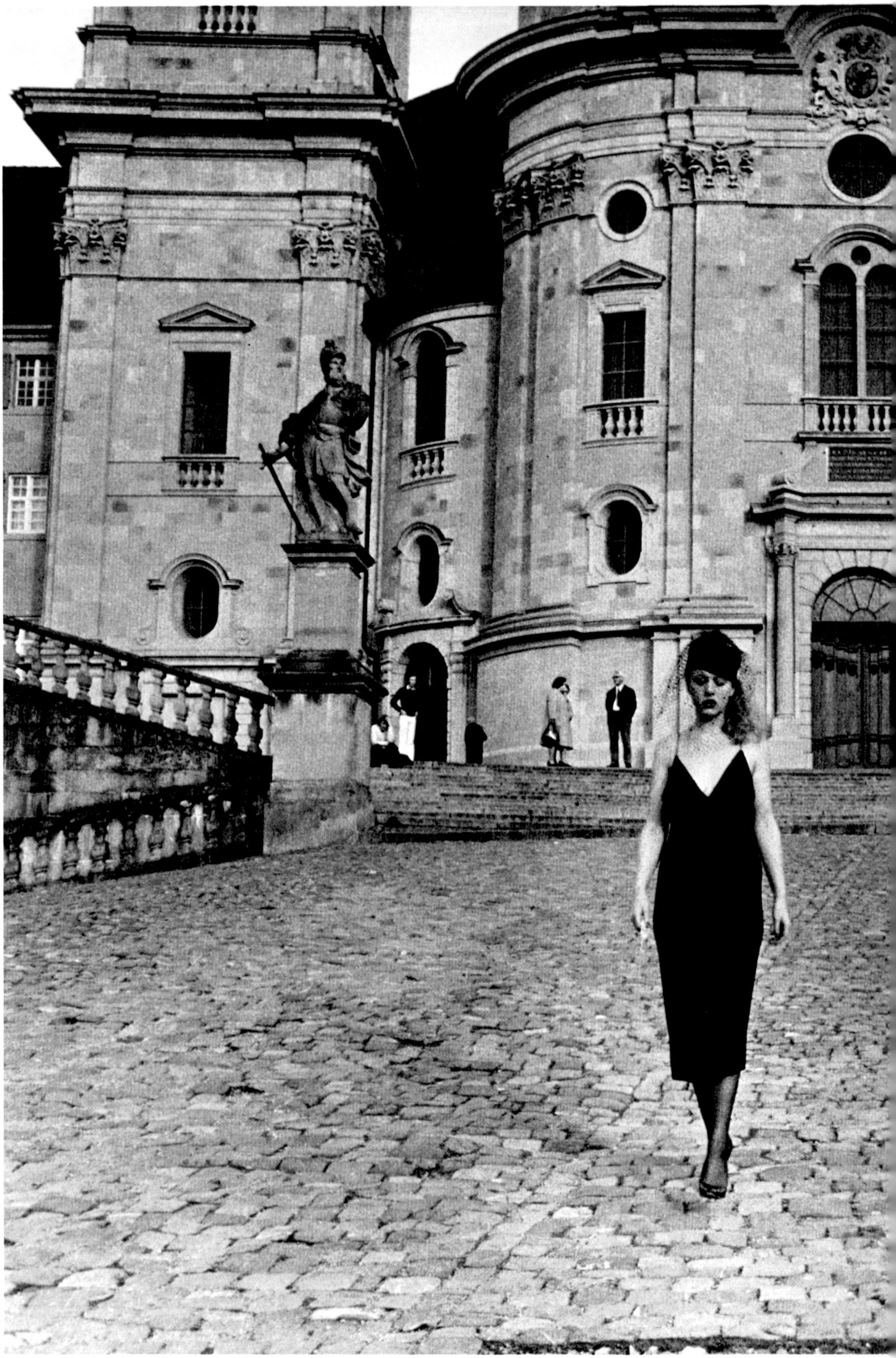

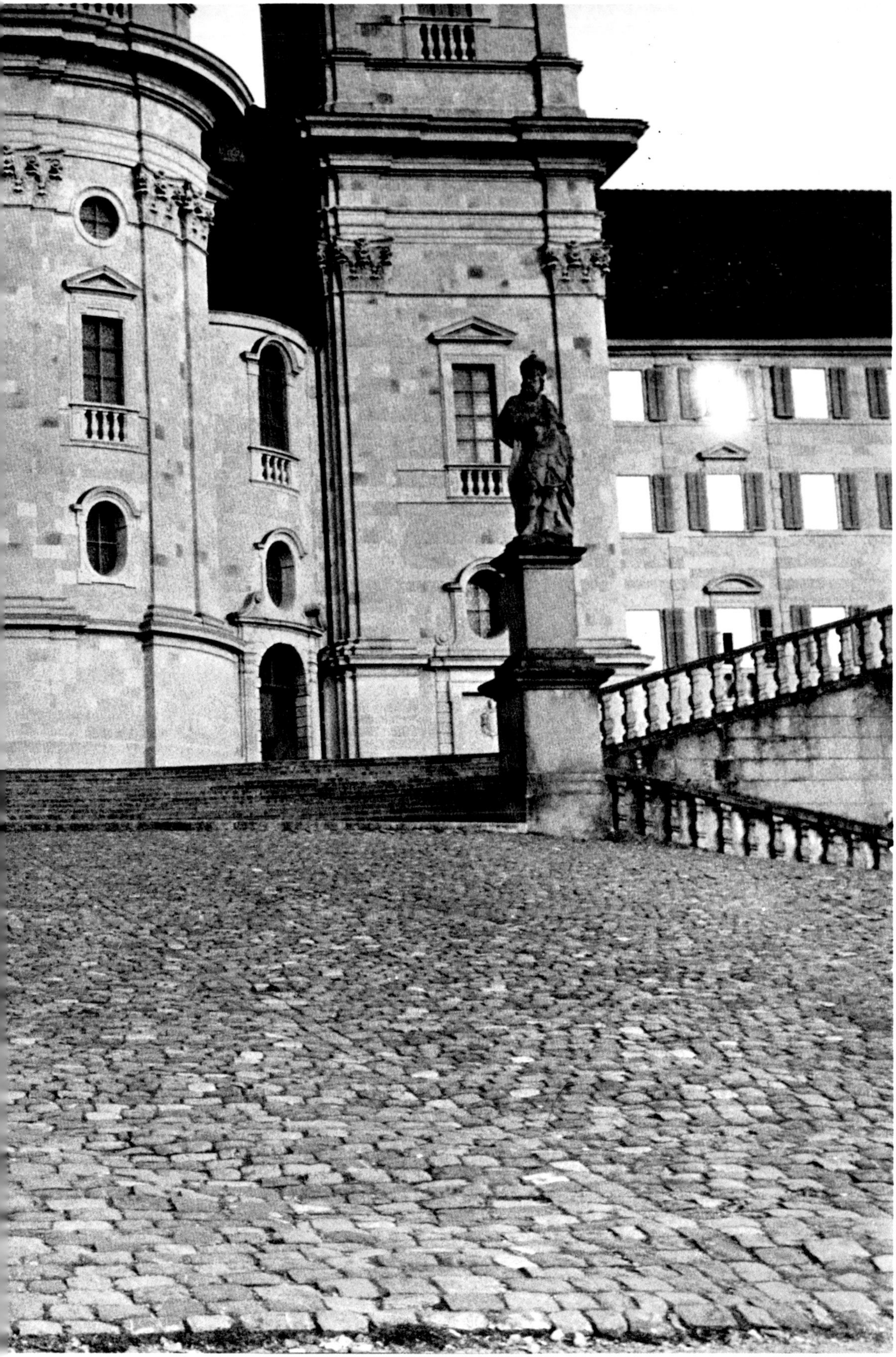

Actually, the only reason I want to marry is to experience the celebration in the church. It is the day one is most beautiful. It is something unique.
   Irene

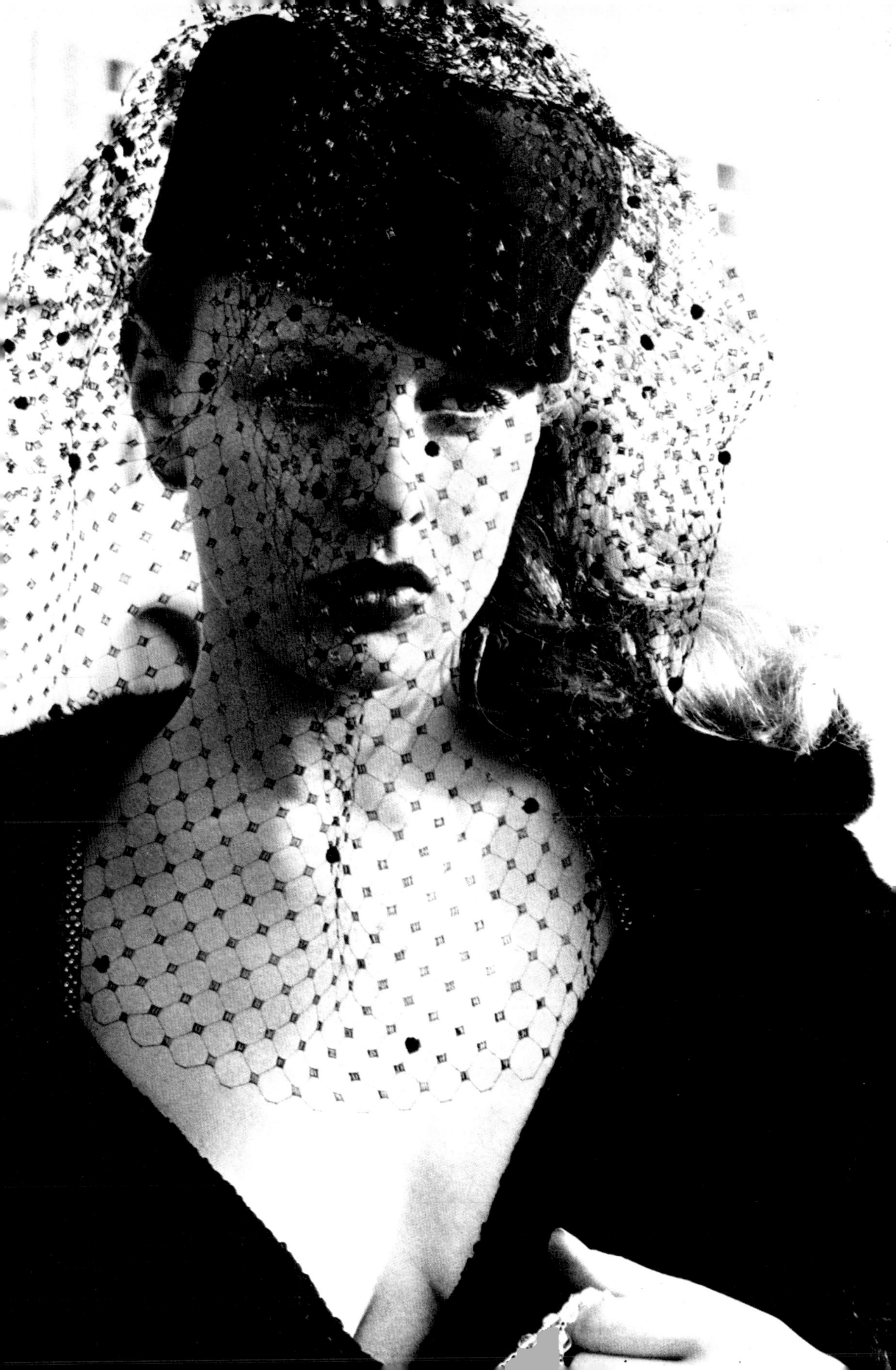

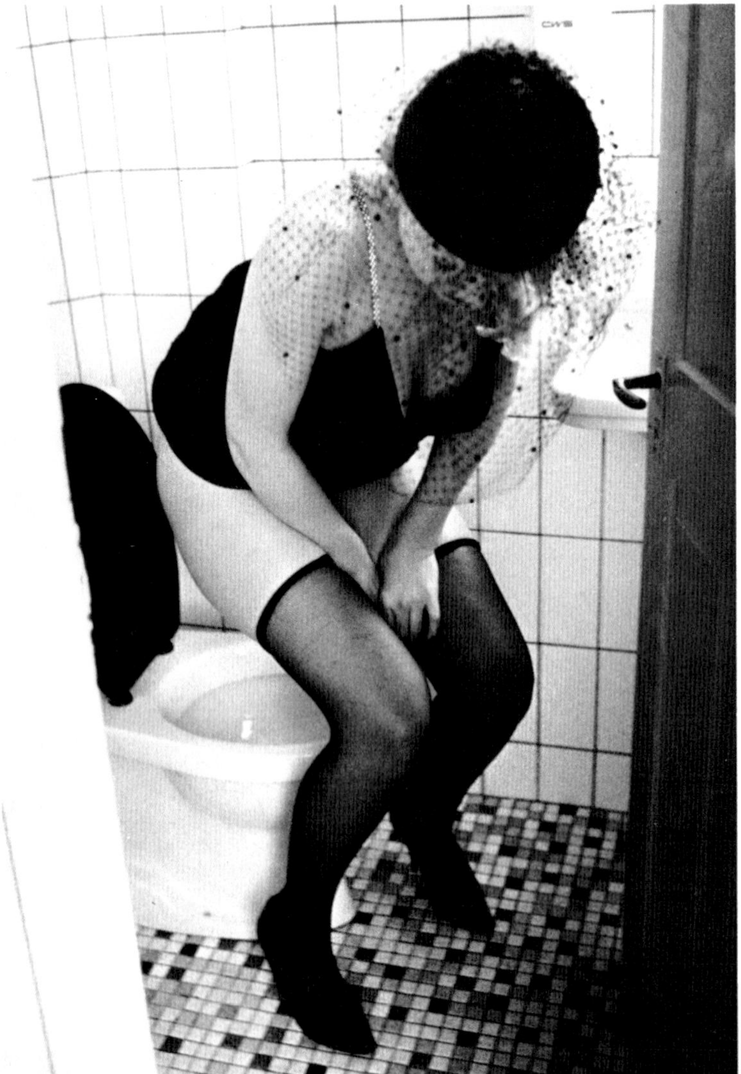

There are only two places where one pays for the right to spend: public latrines and women.
    Baudelaire

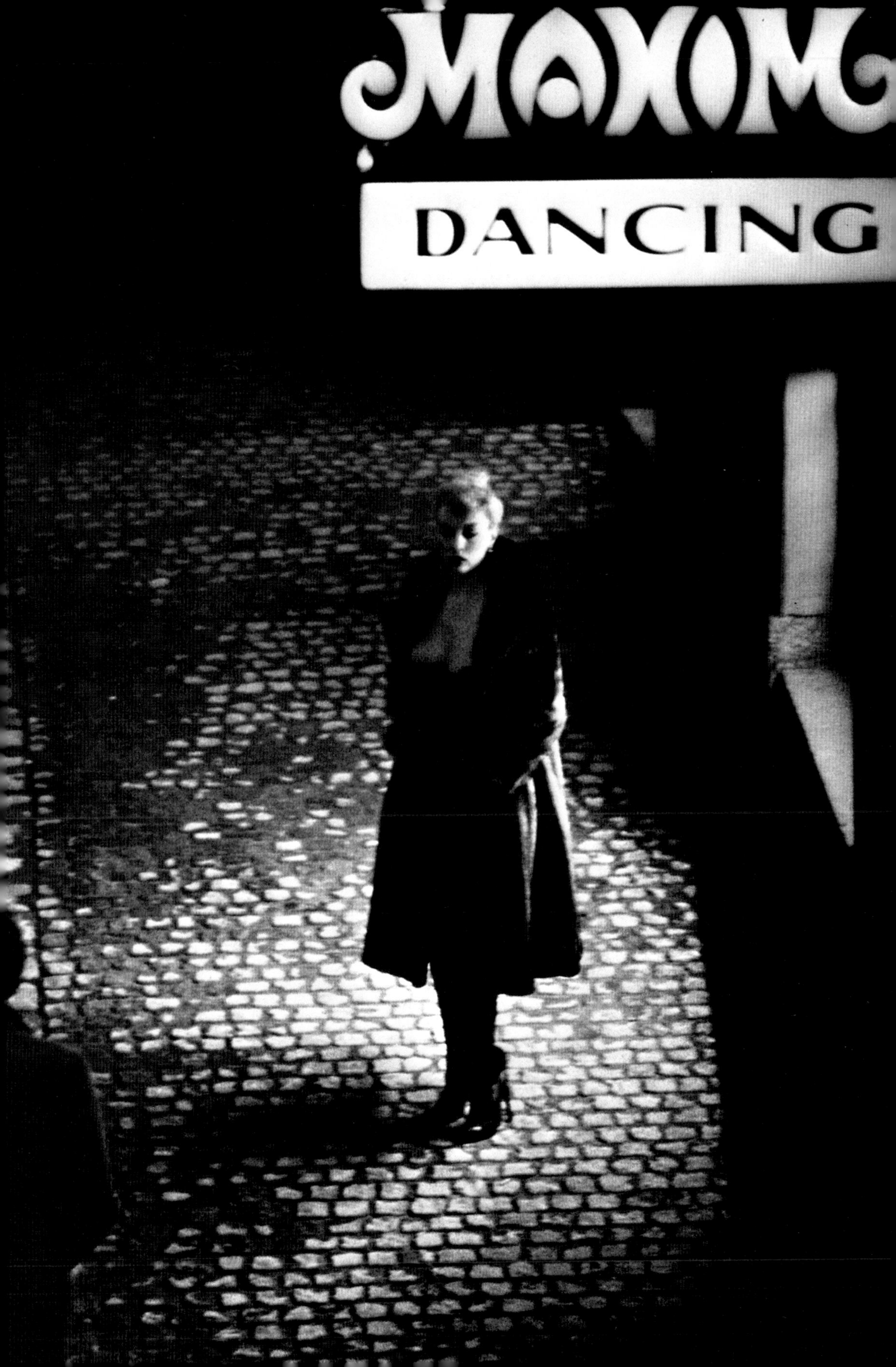
MAXIM
DANCING

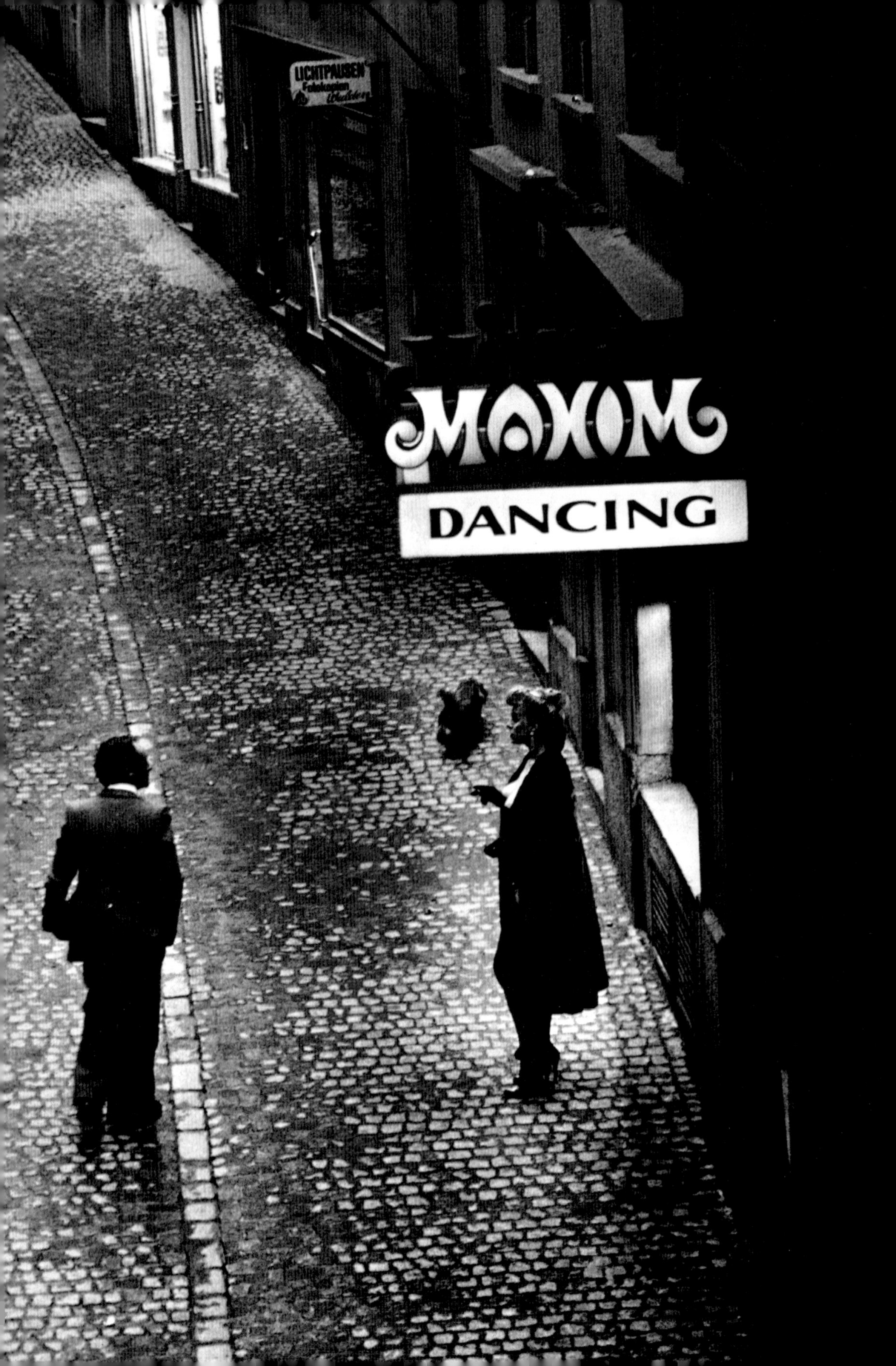
LICHTPAUSEN
MAXIM
DANCING

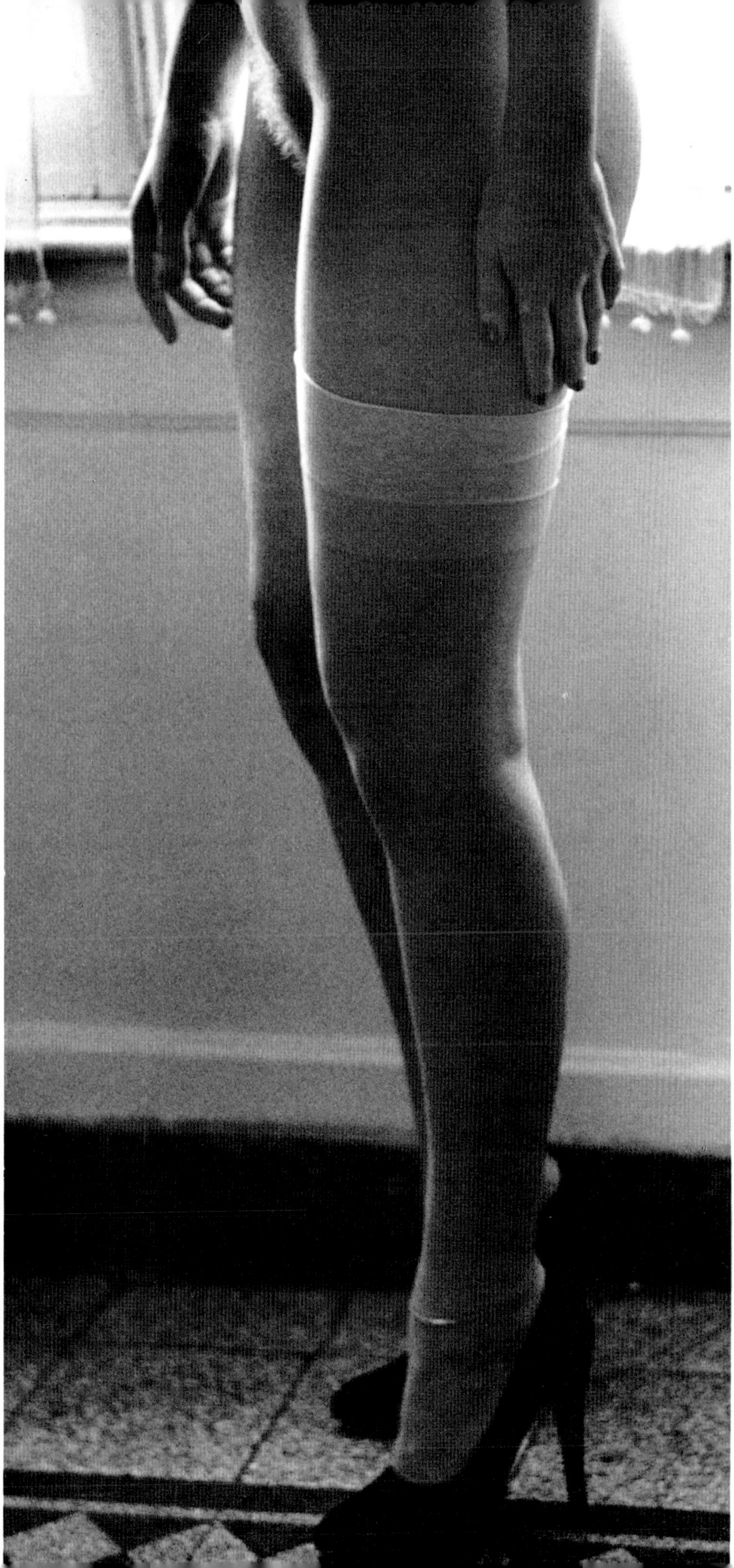

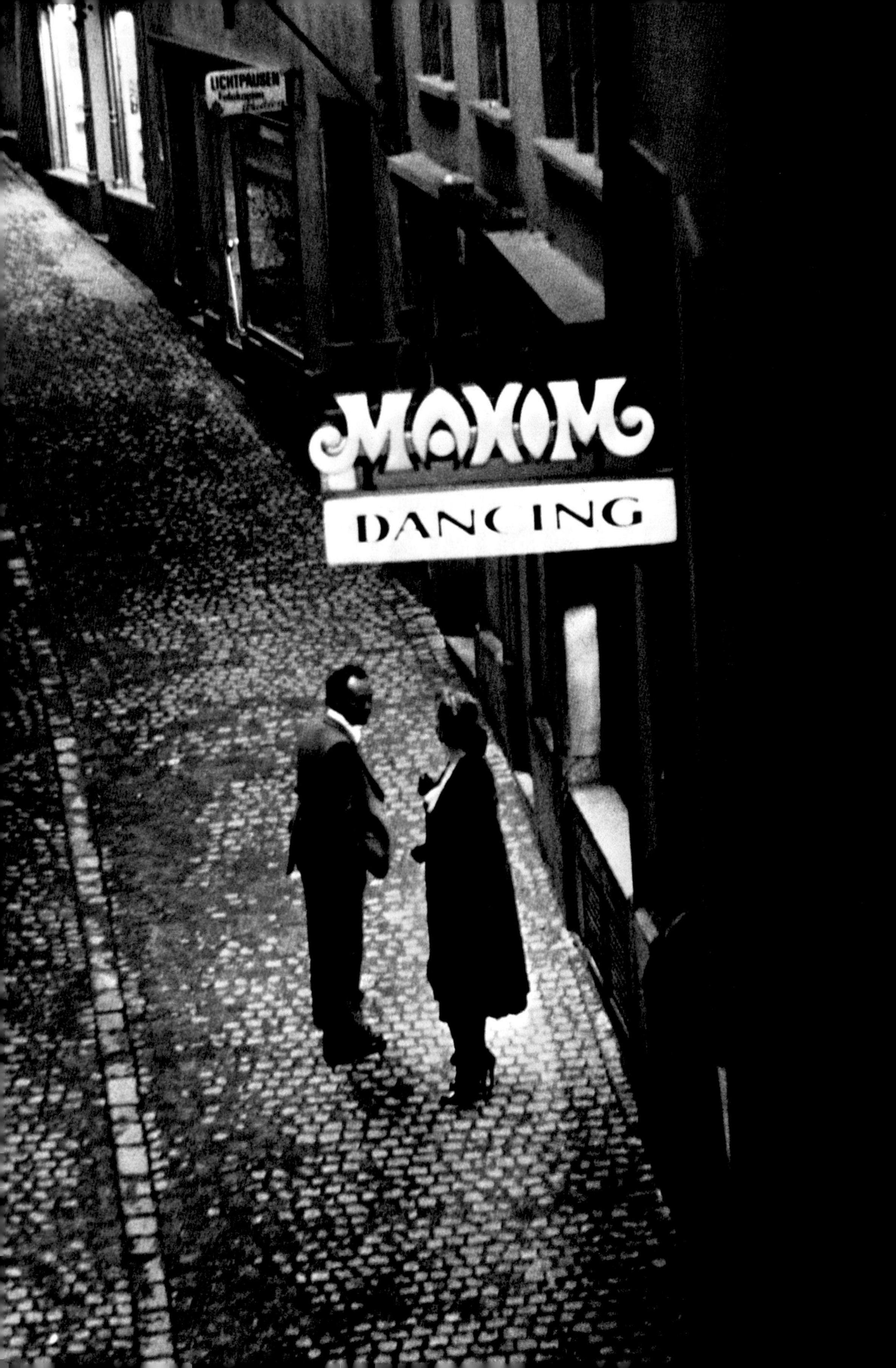
LICHTPAUSEN
MAXIM
DANCING

There is only one kind of man who may do with me as he pleases – a hustler.
    Irene

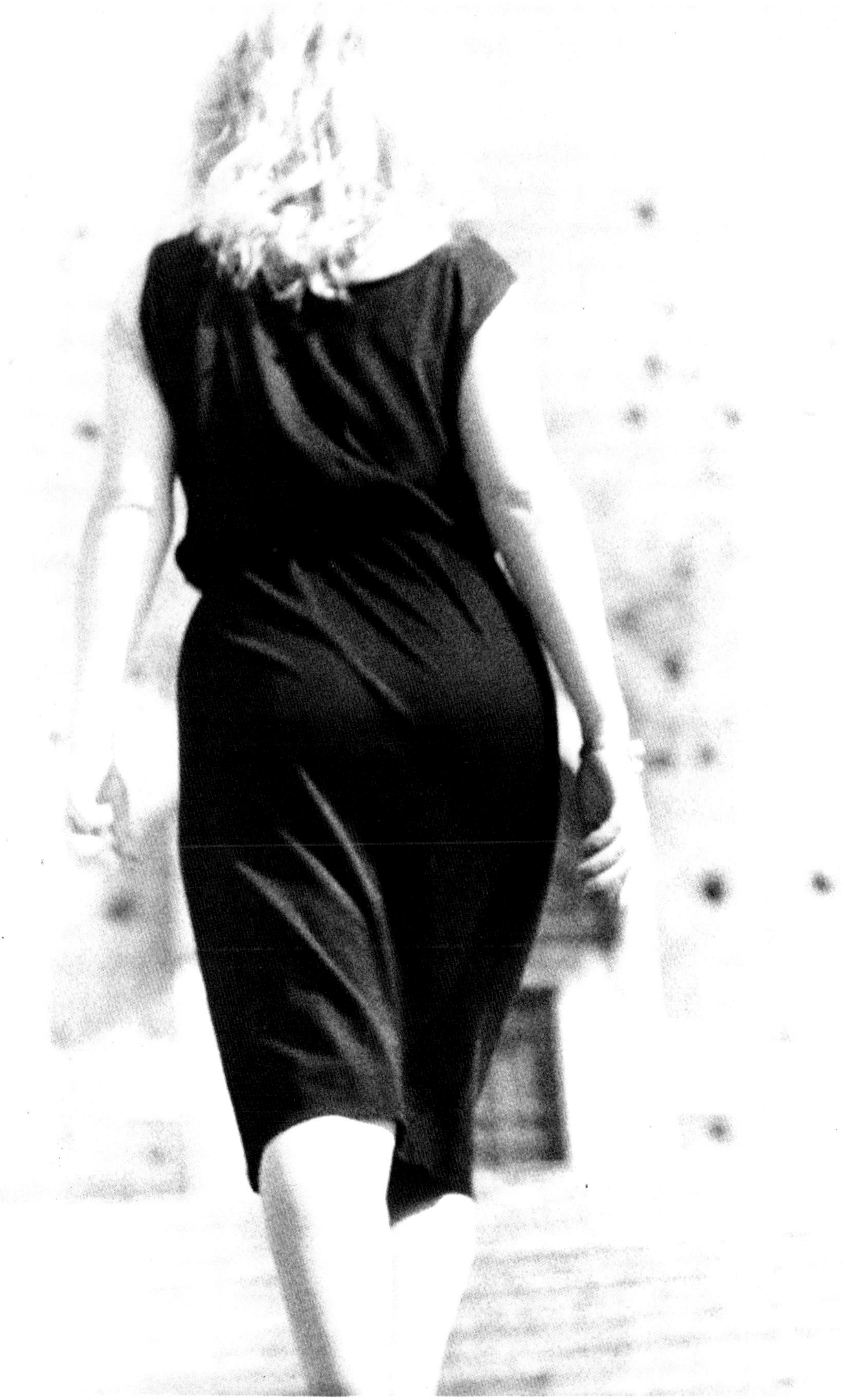

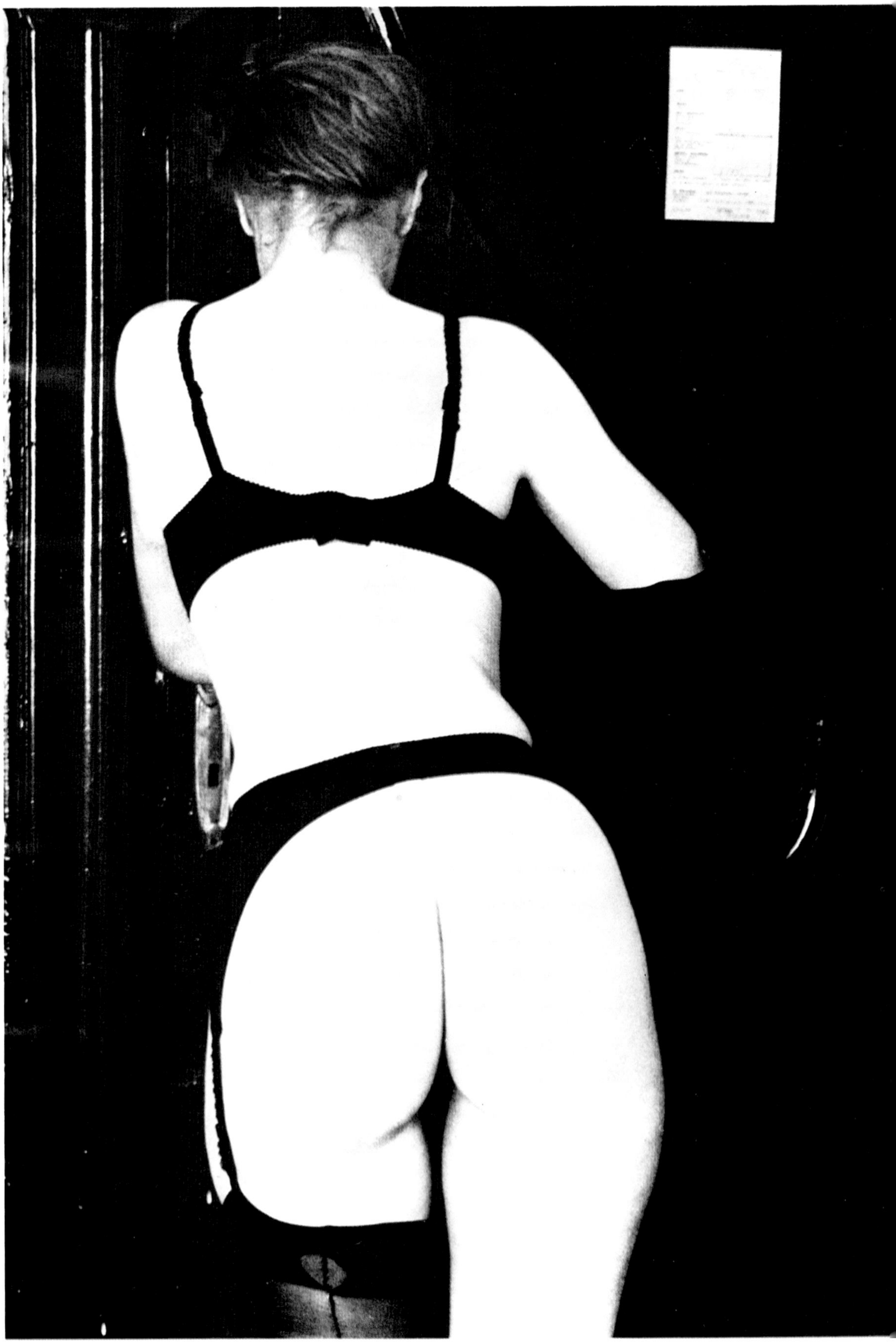

What is a young girl really? A stupid little fool, a little slut with all the depravity of a street urchin.

    Baudelaire

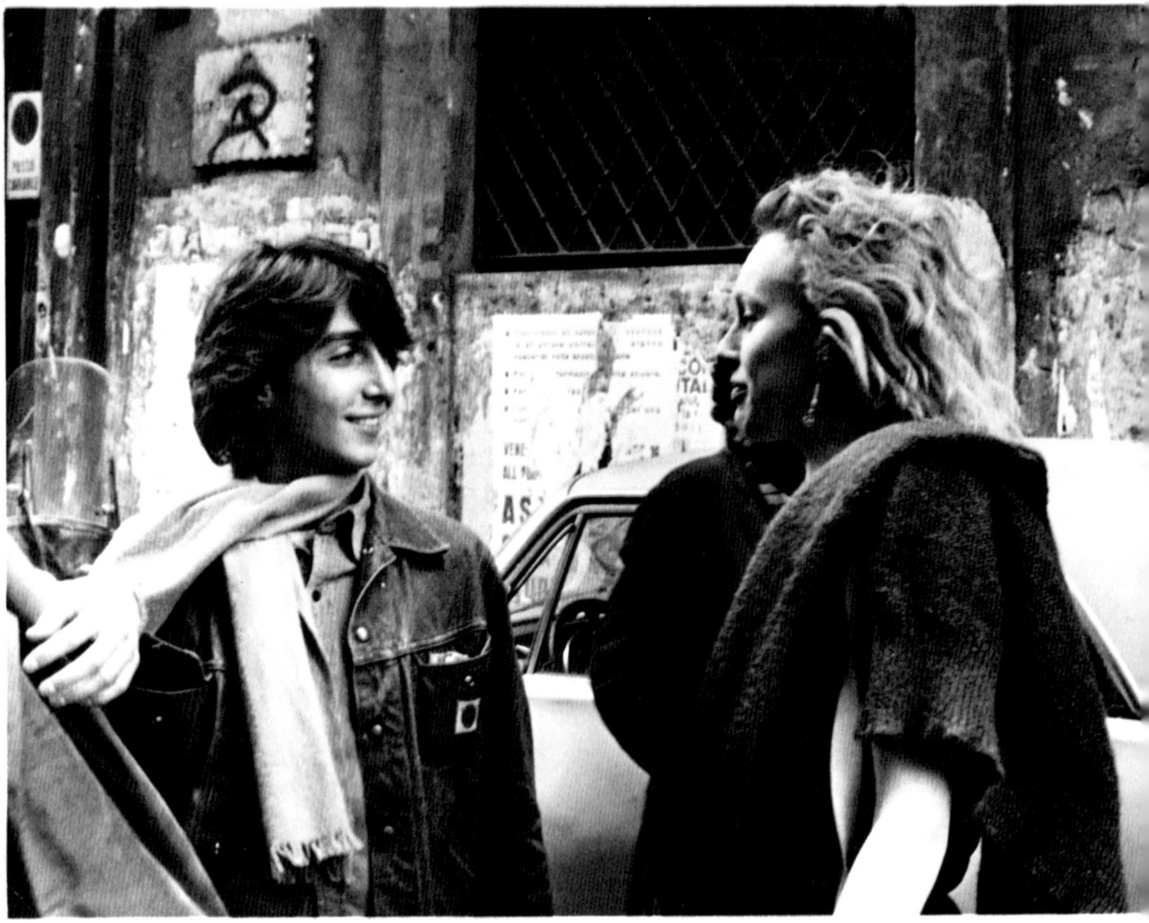

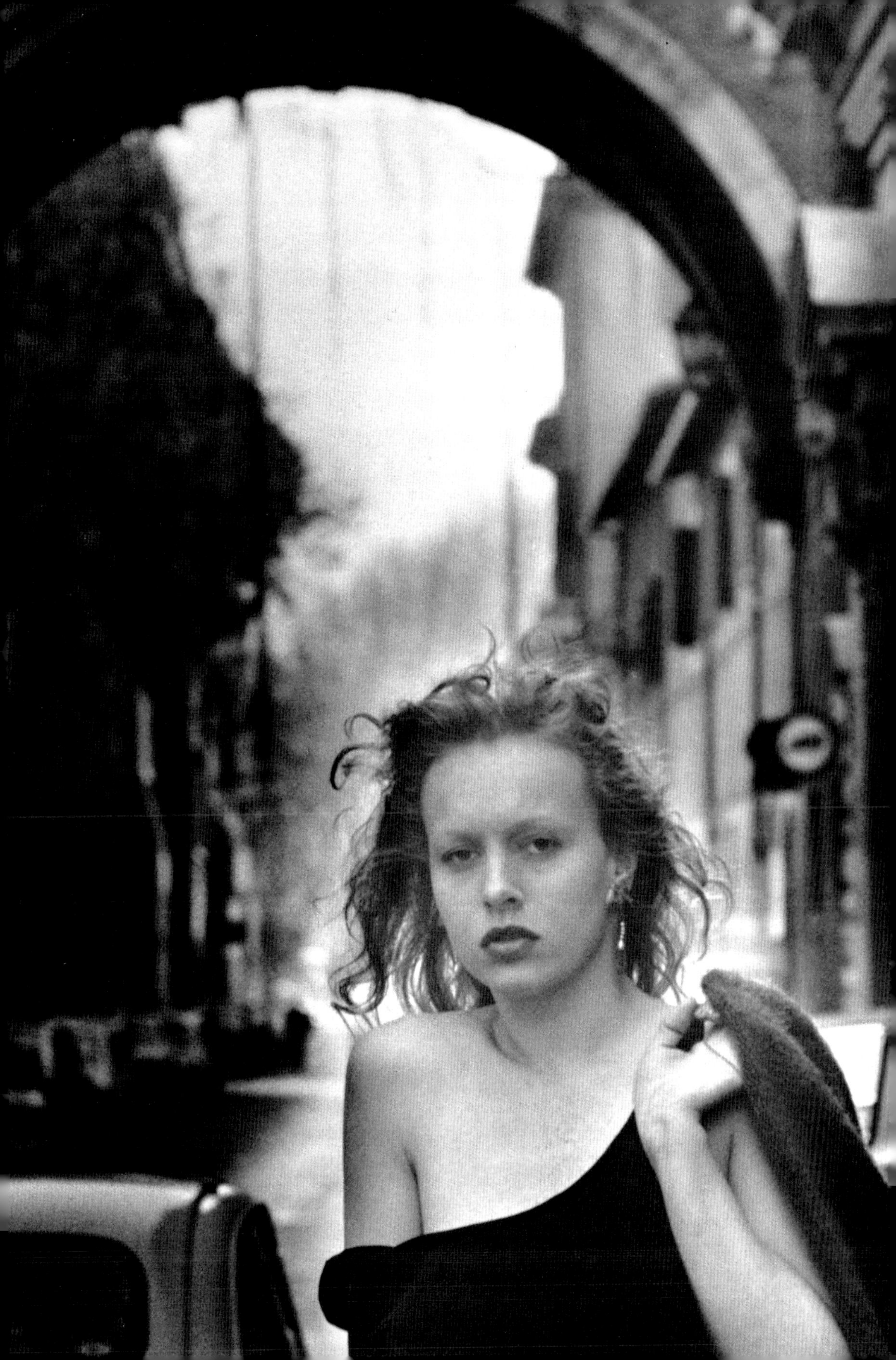

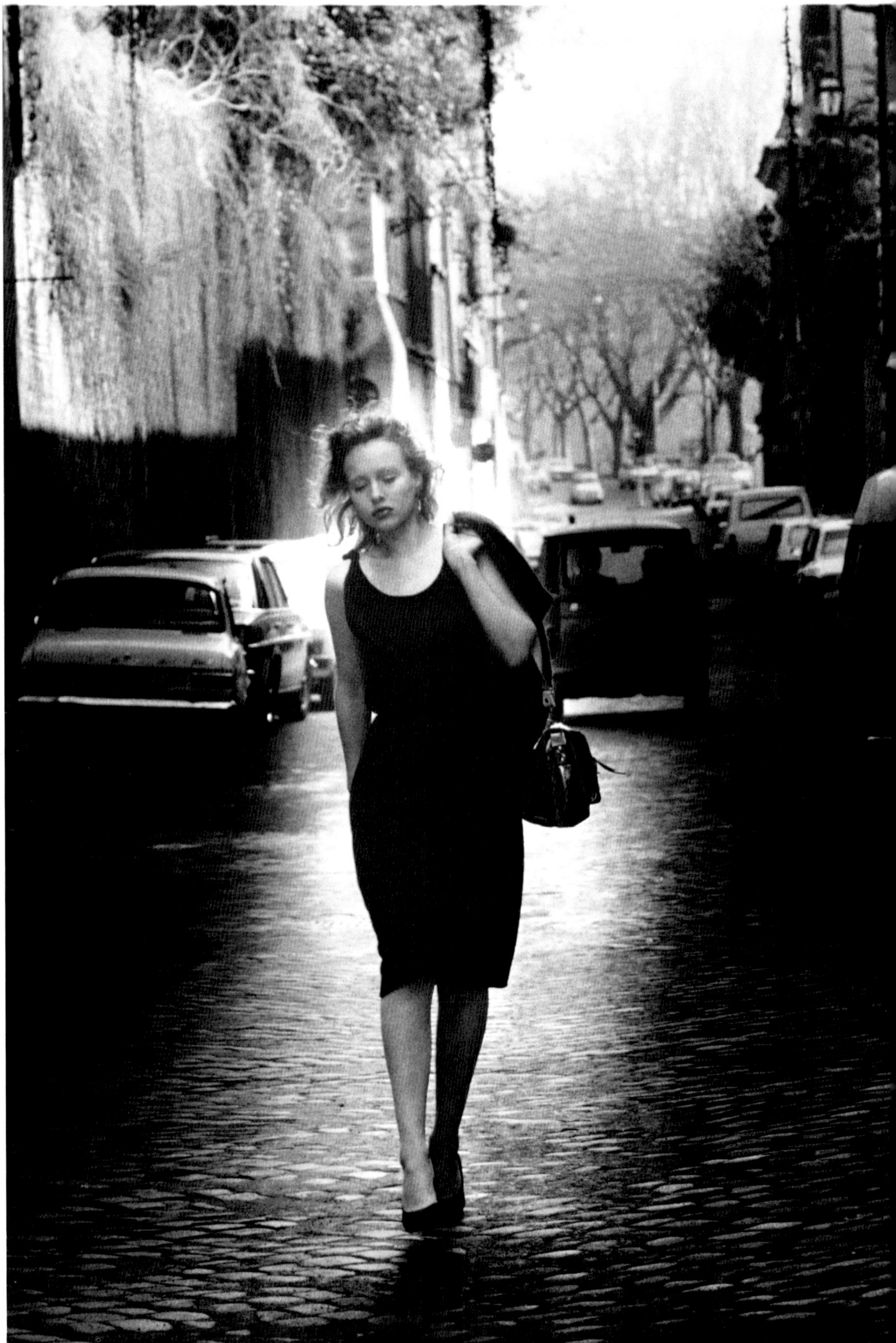

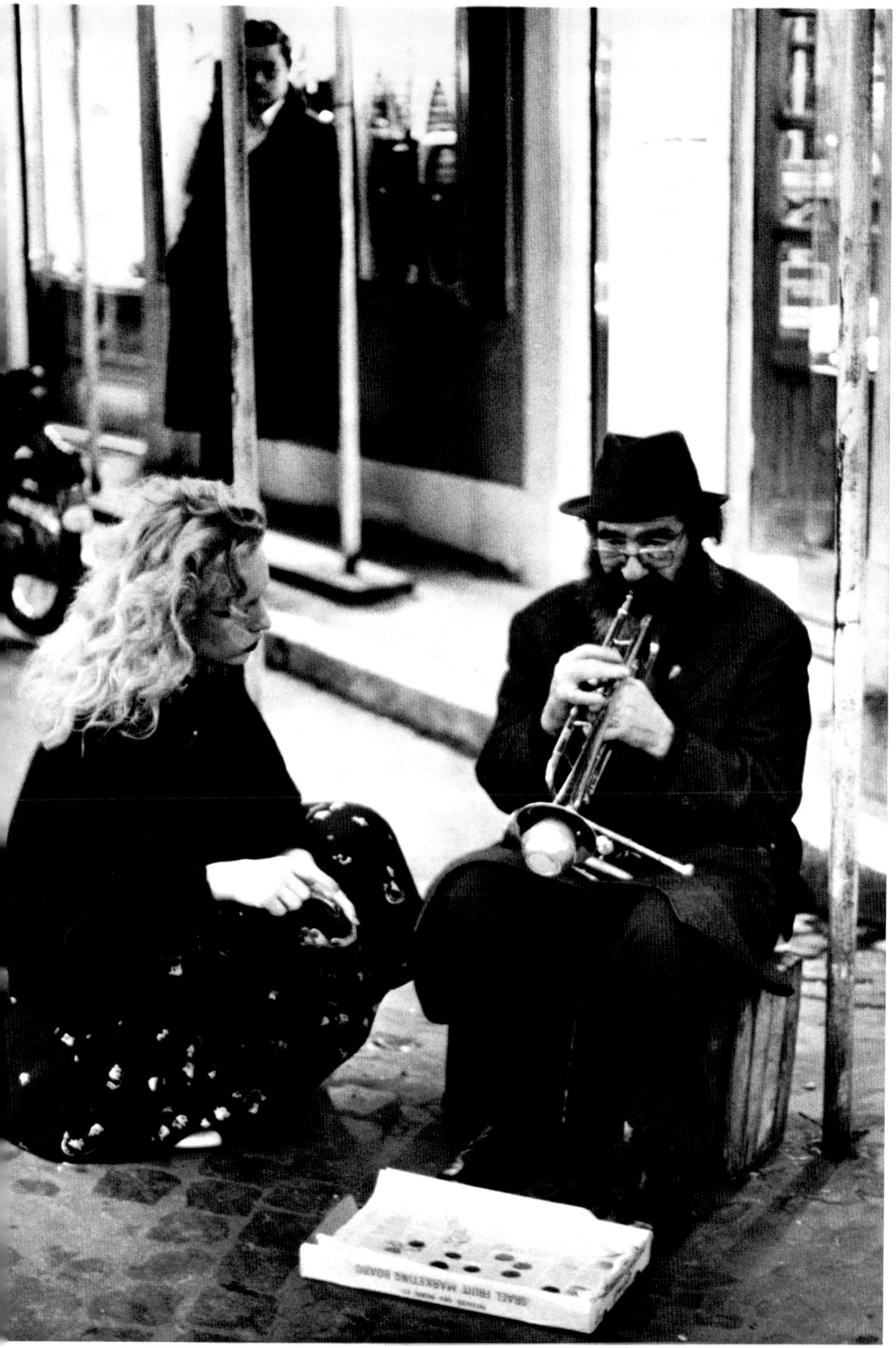
FRUIT MARKETING BOARD

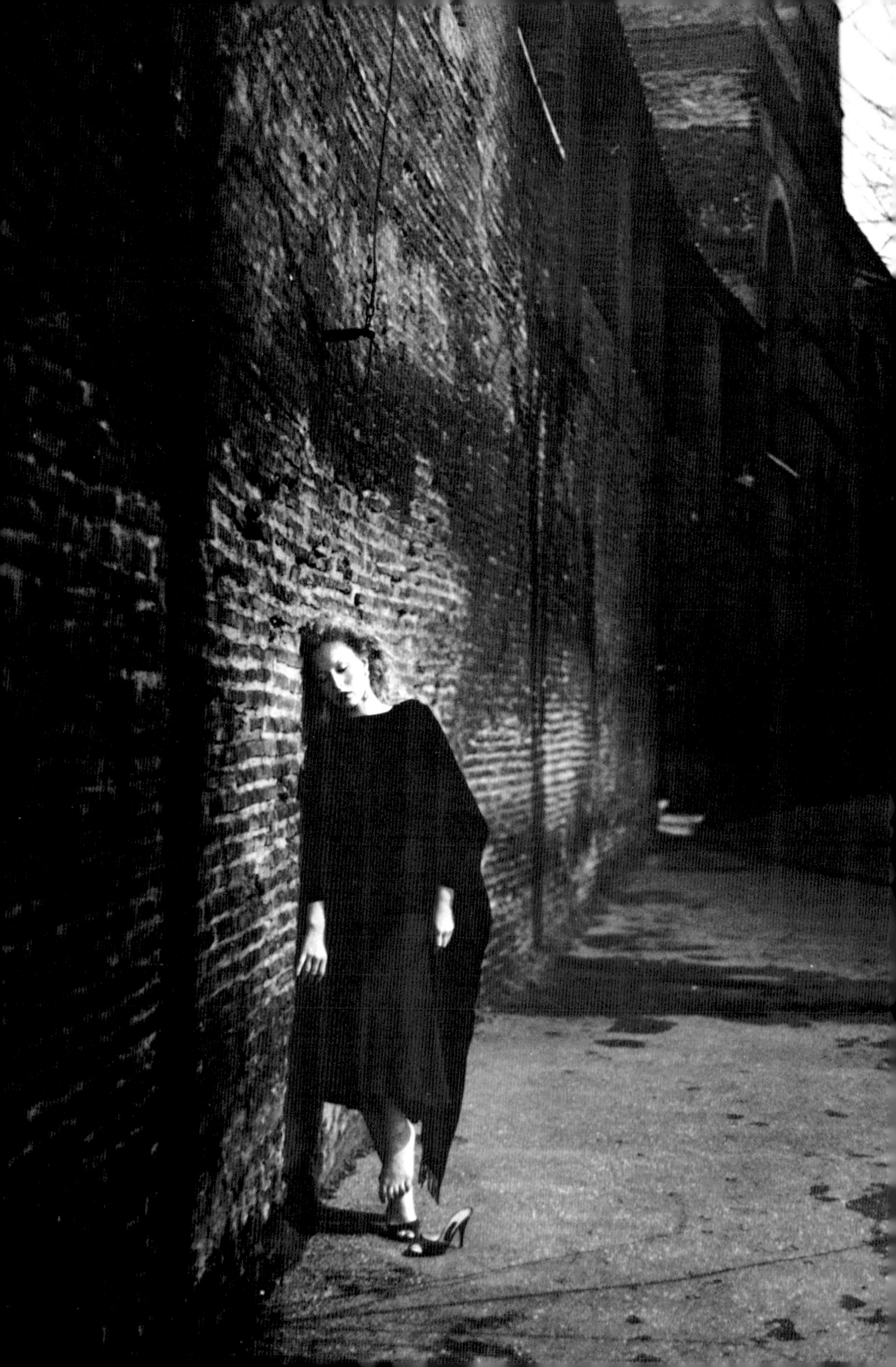

After each excess, one always feels even more alone, even more abandoned.
    Baudelaire

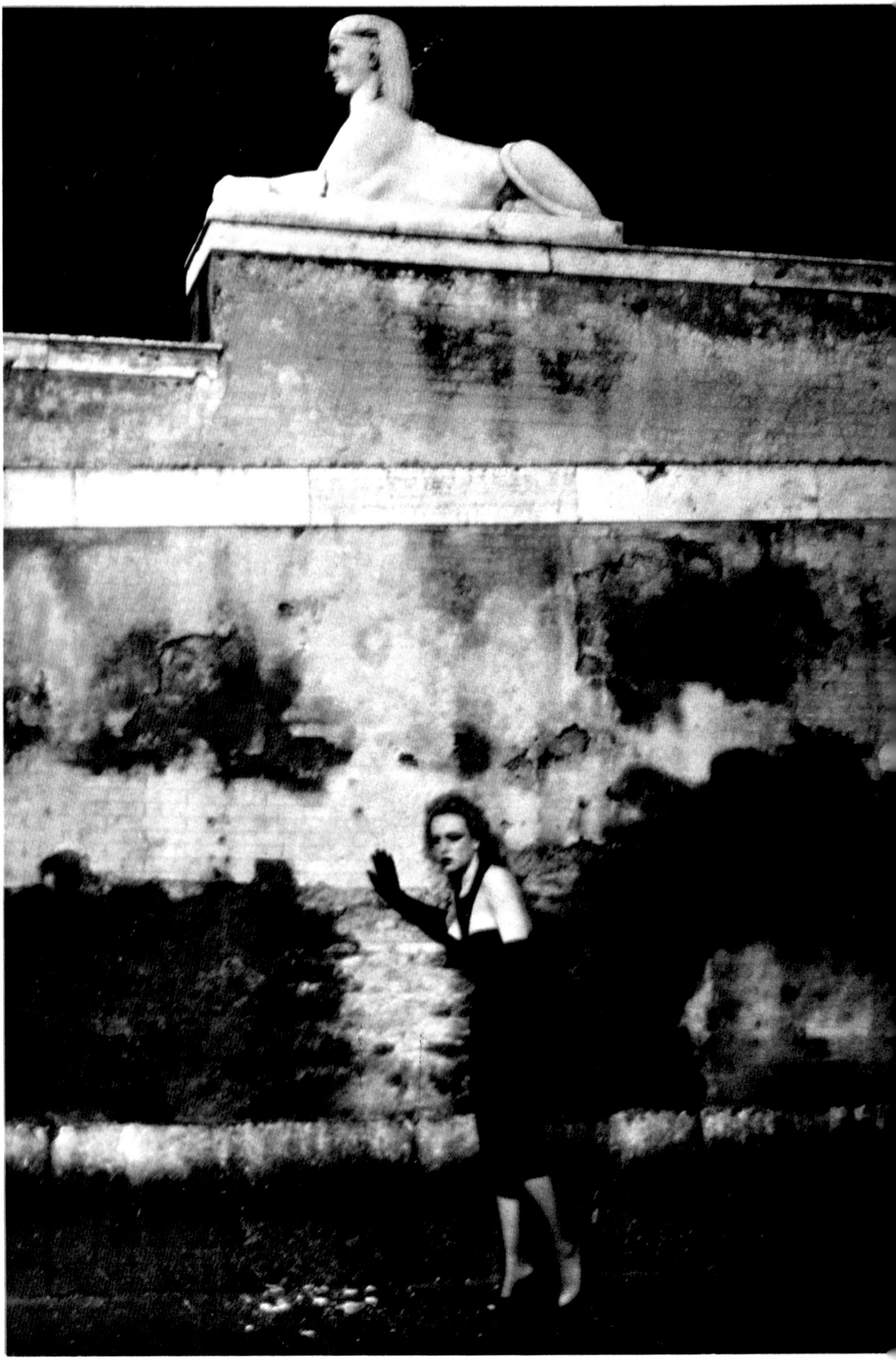

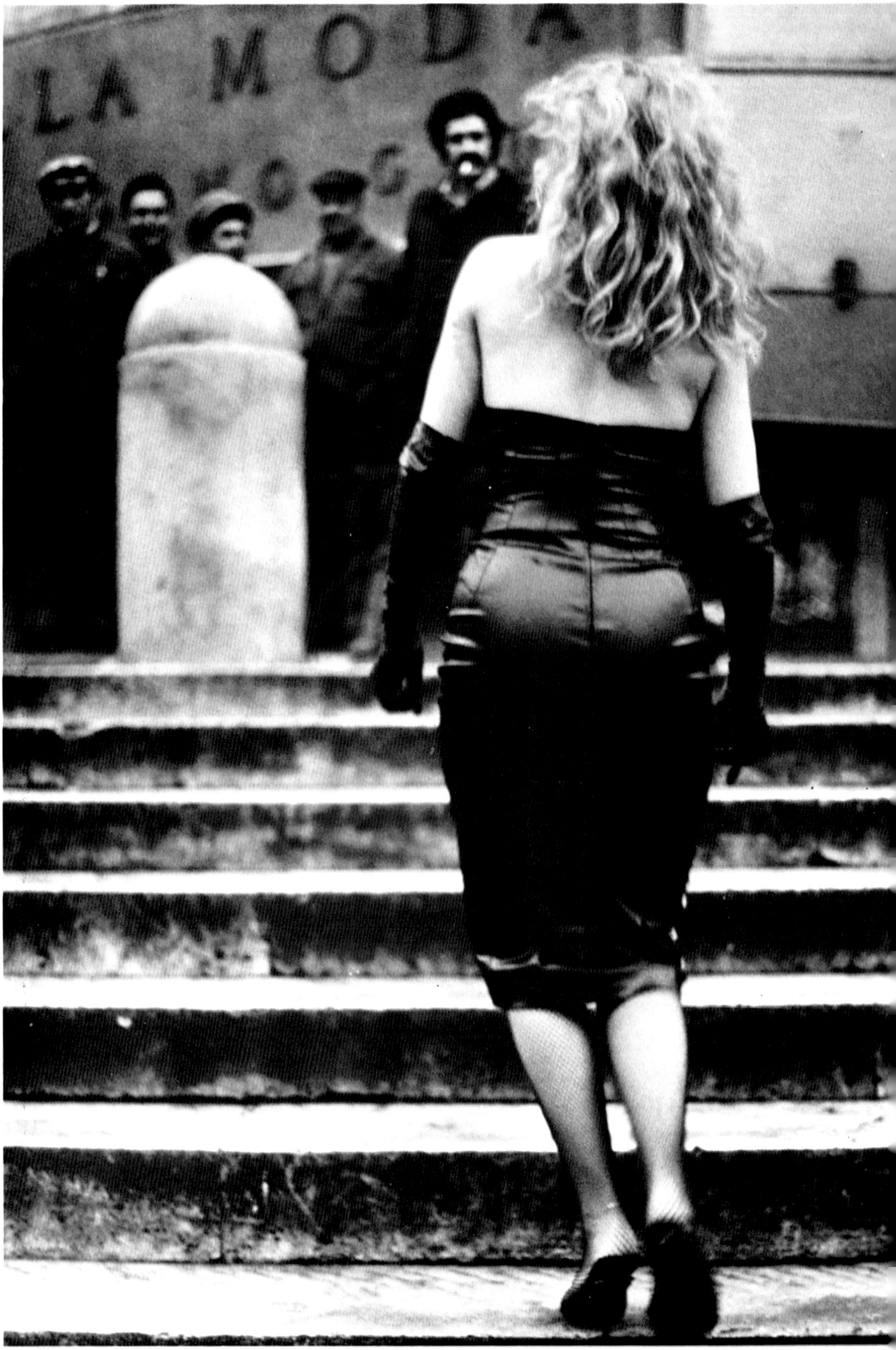
LA MODA

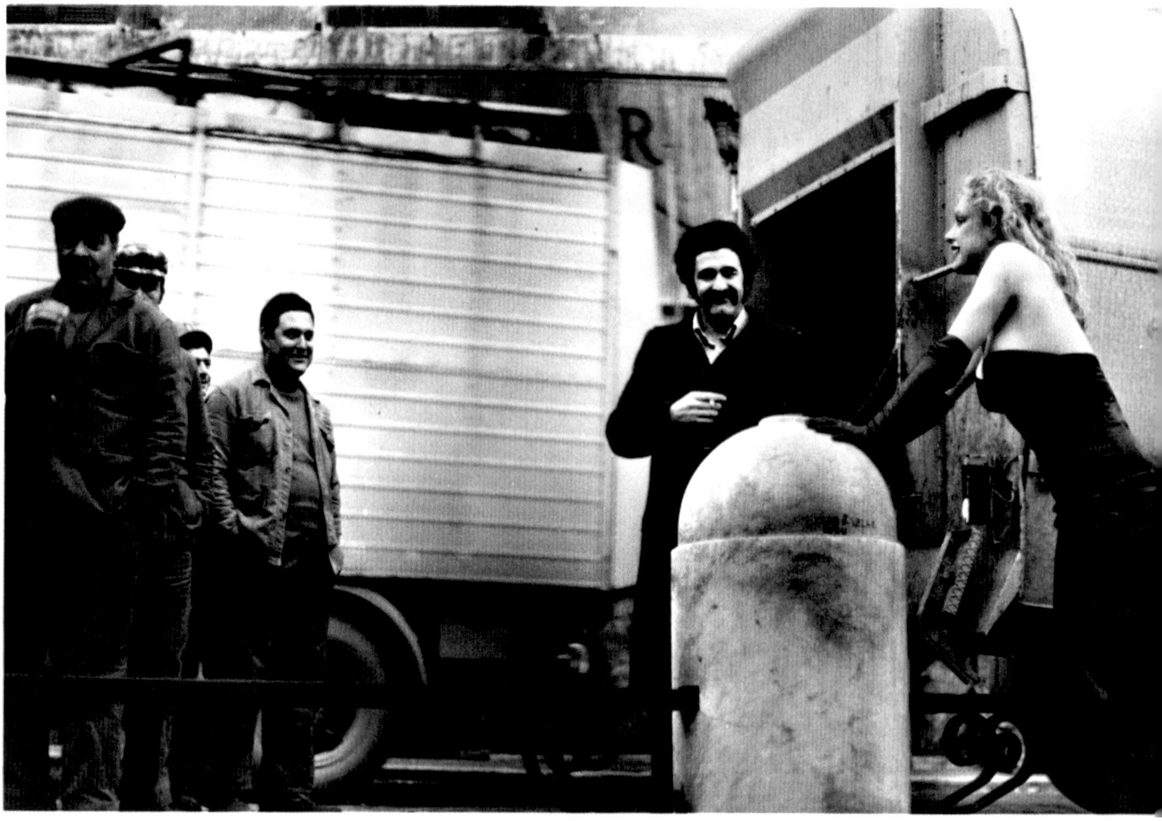

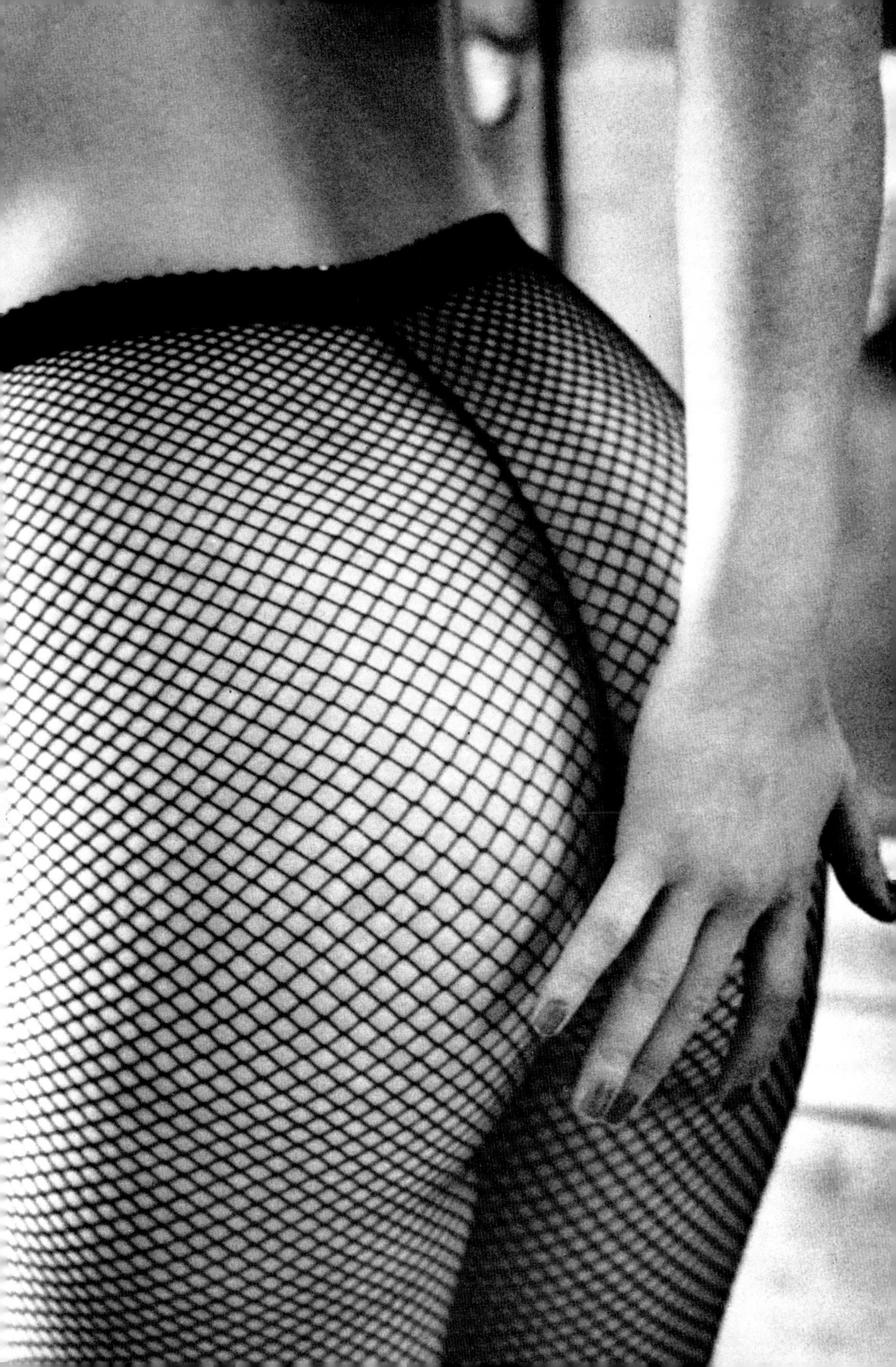

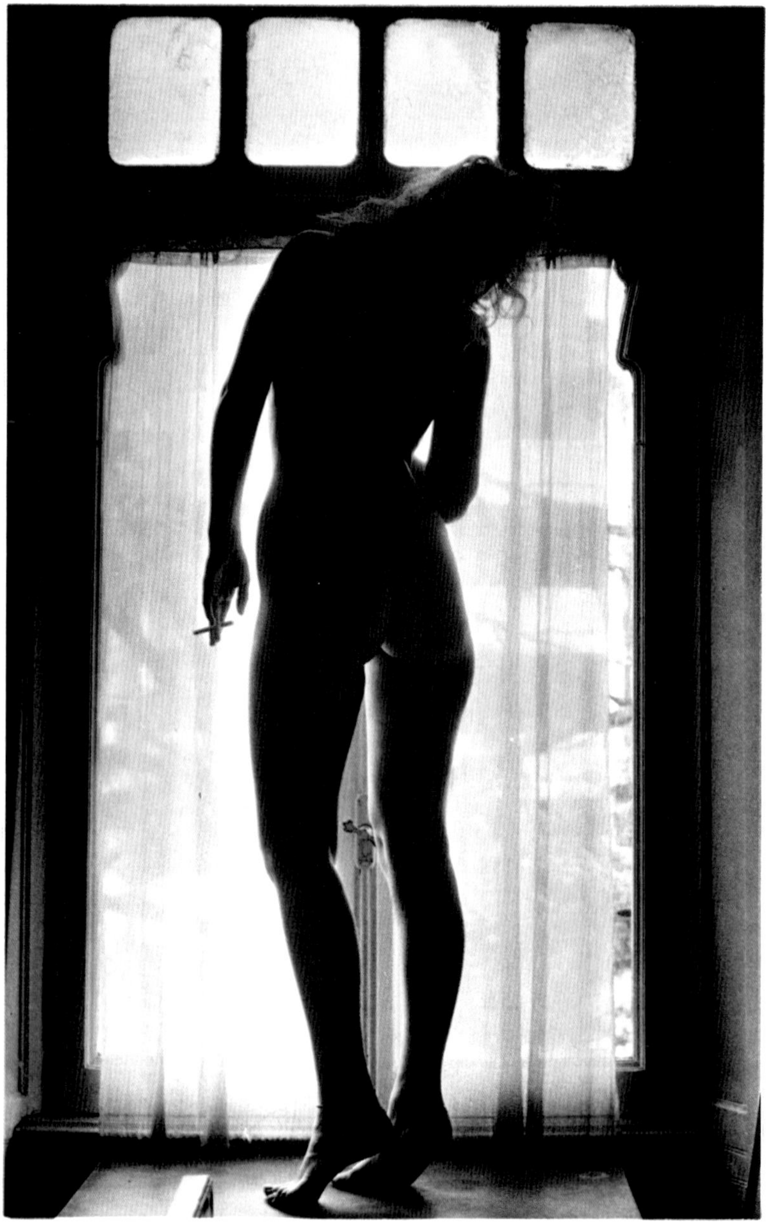

The fifties were really crazy. The men were the men and the women were ladies.
    Irene

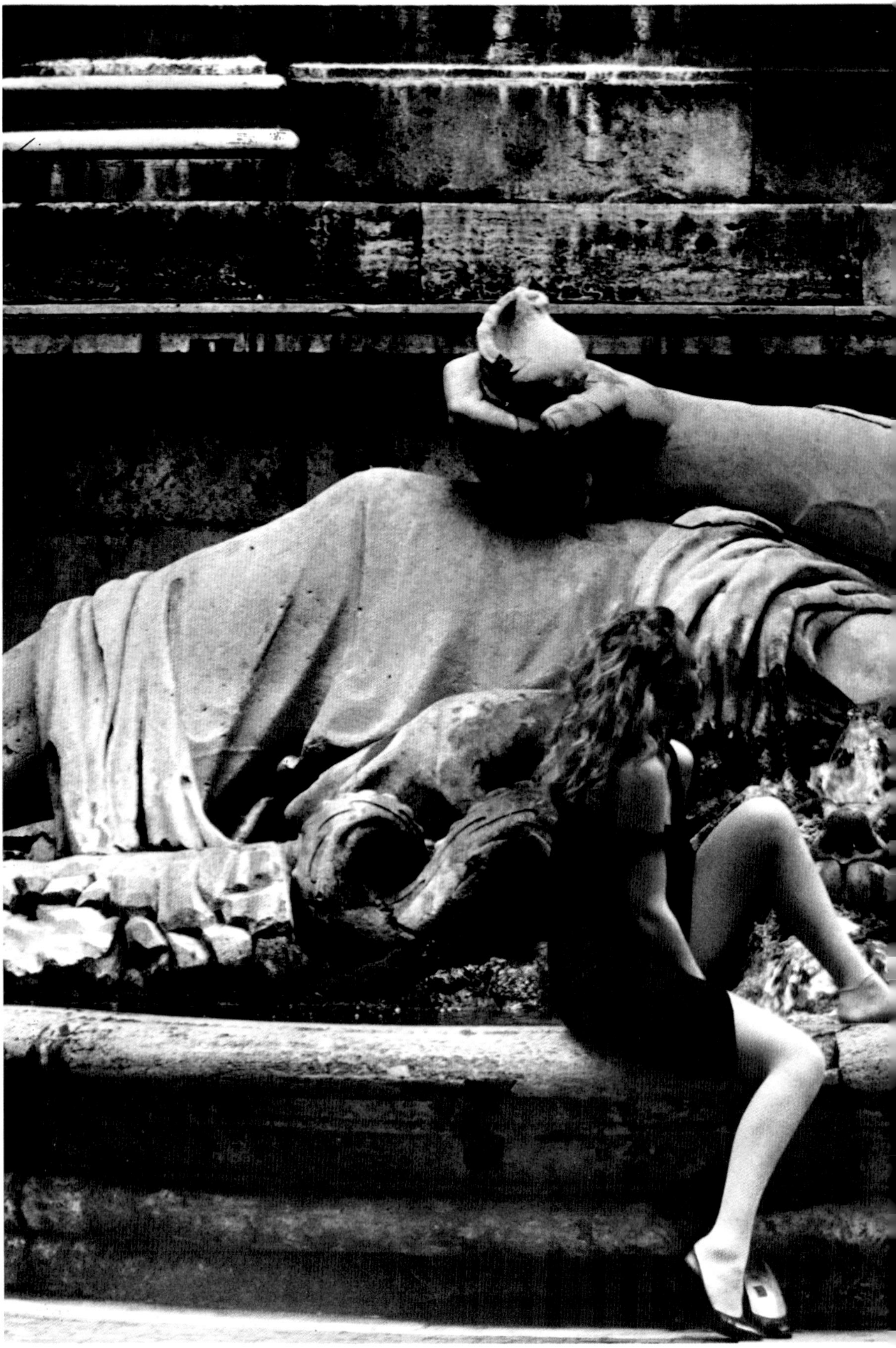

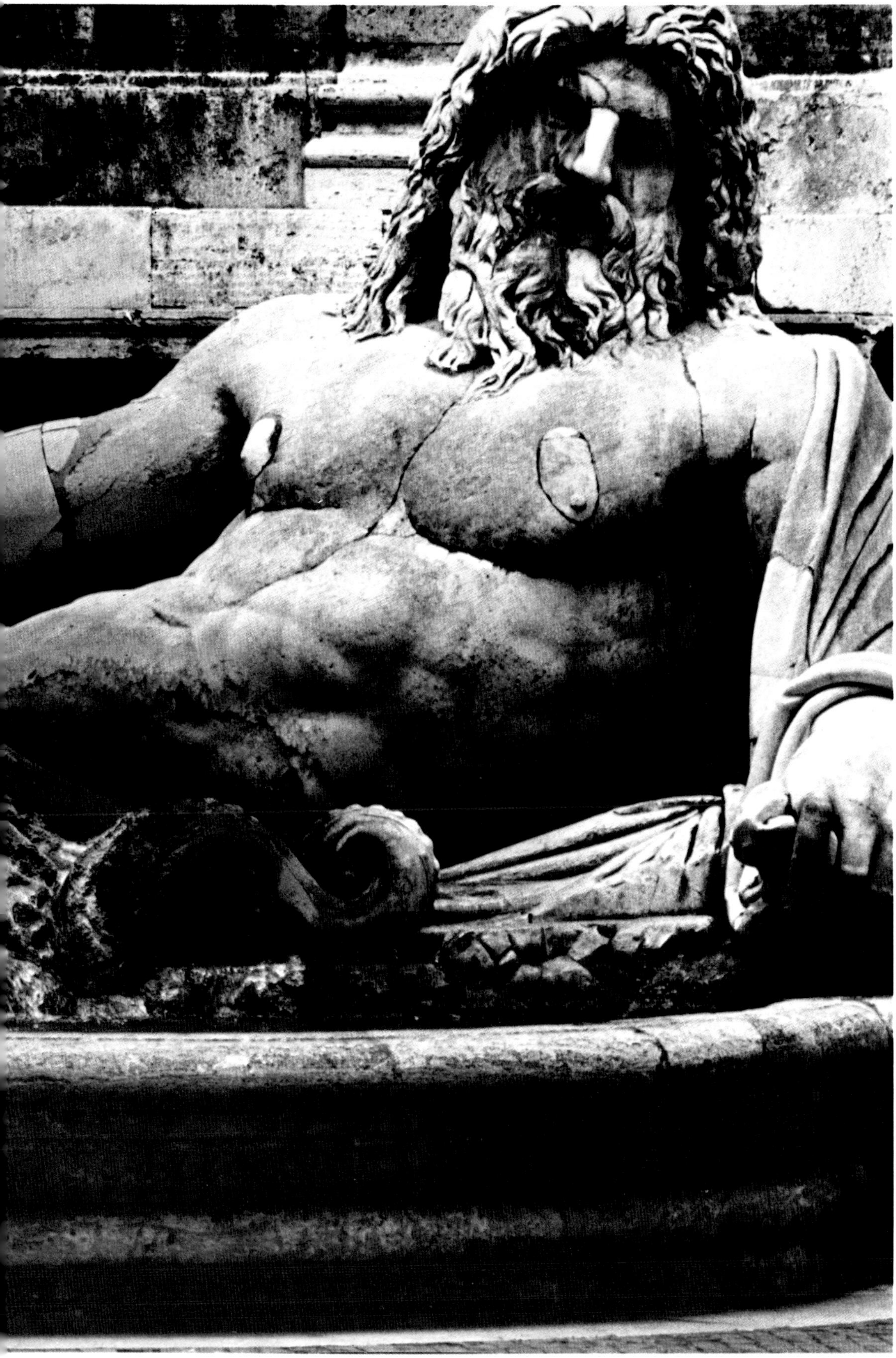

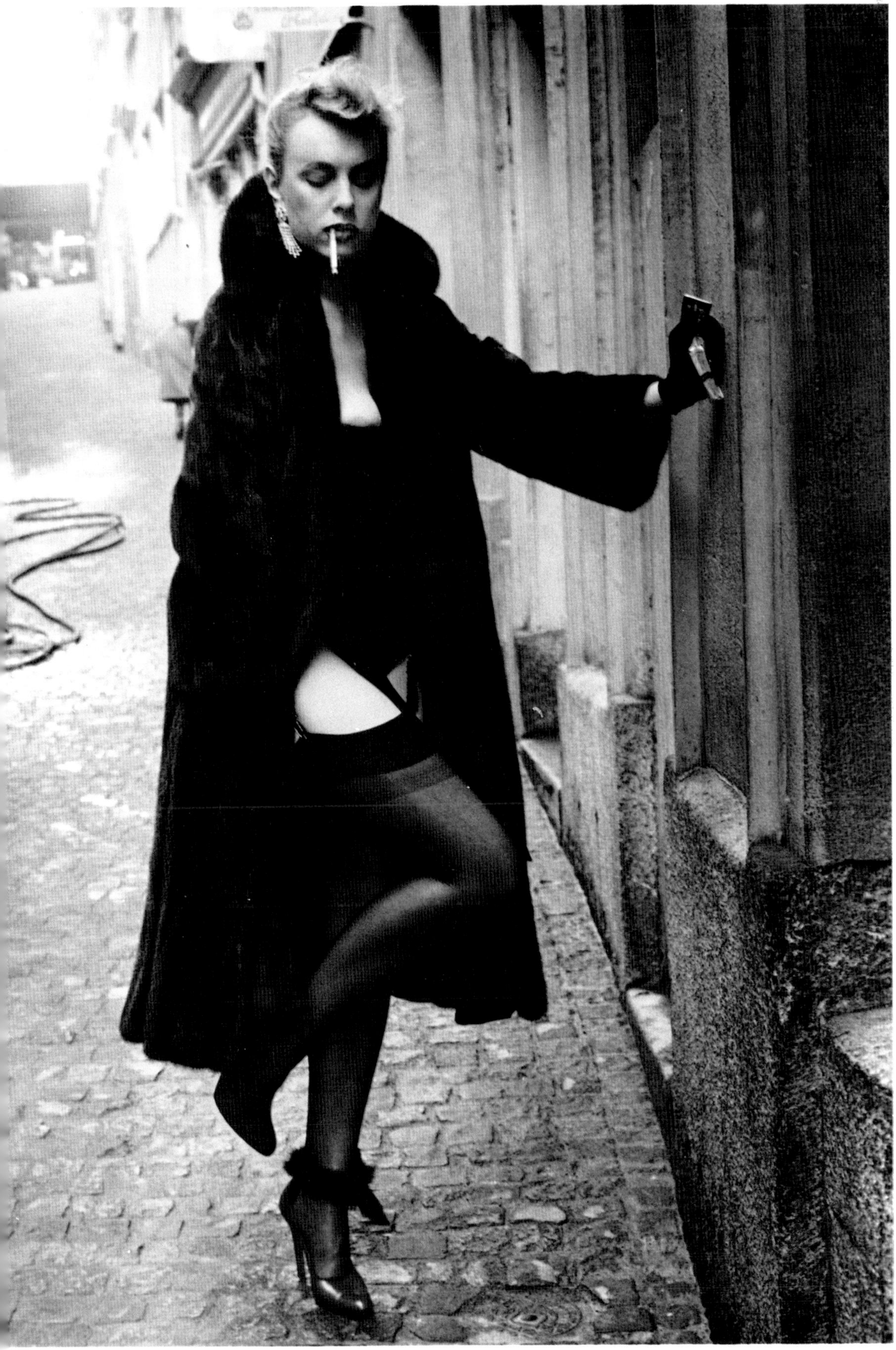

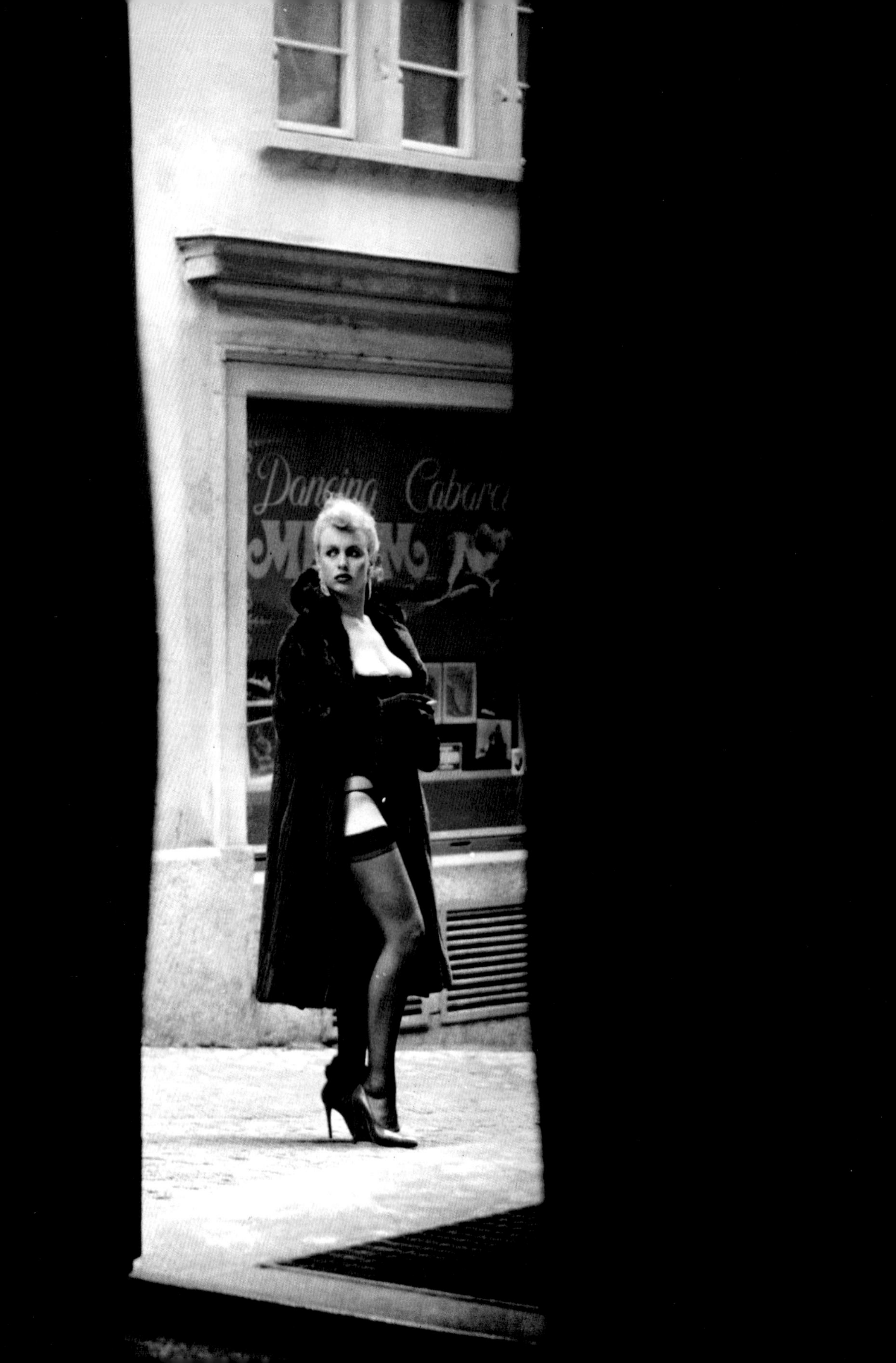
Dancing

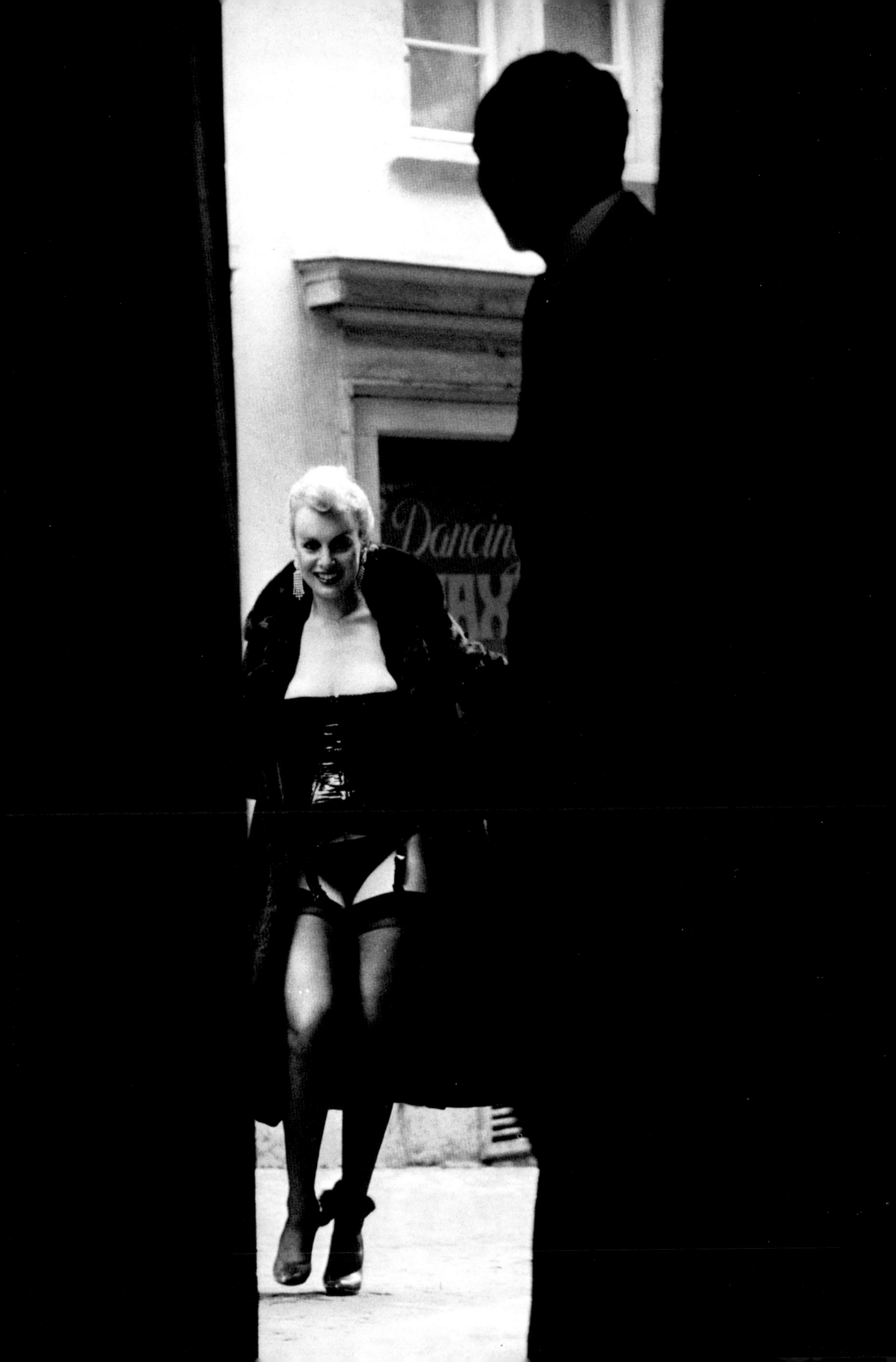

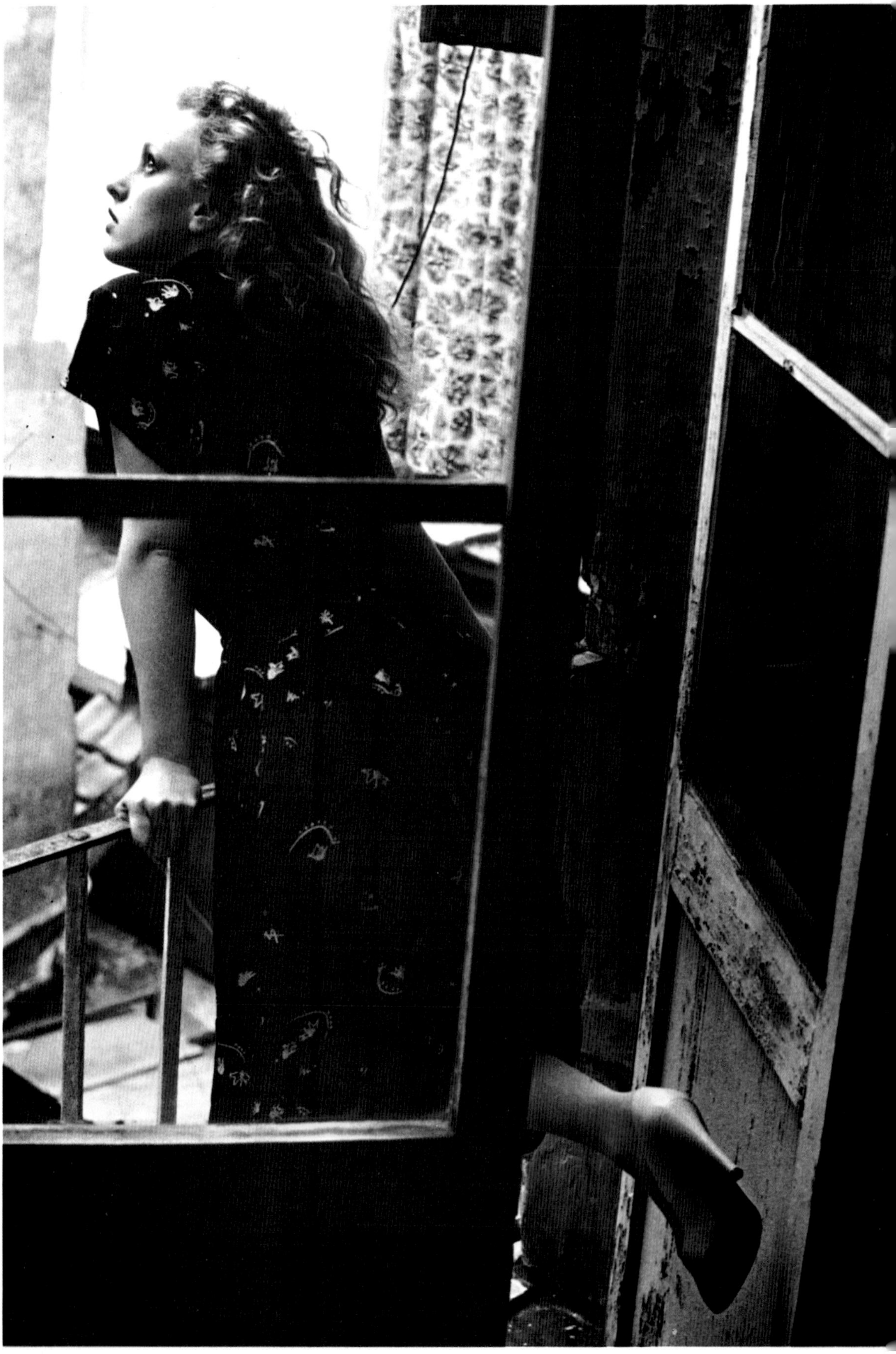

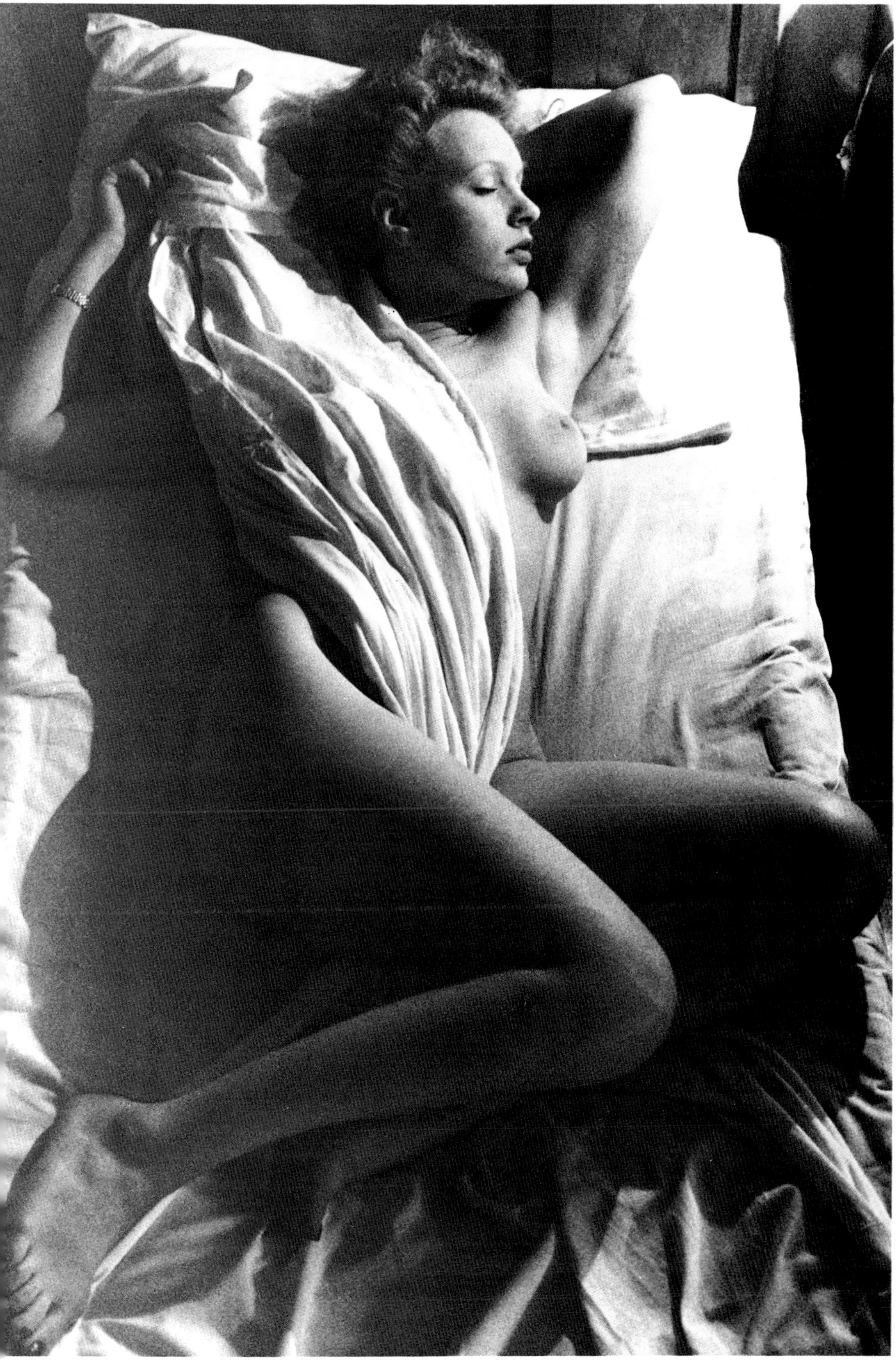

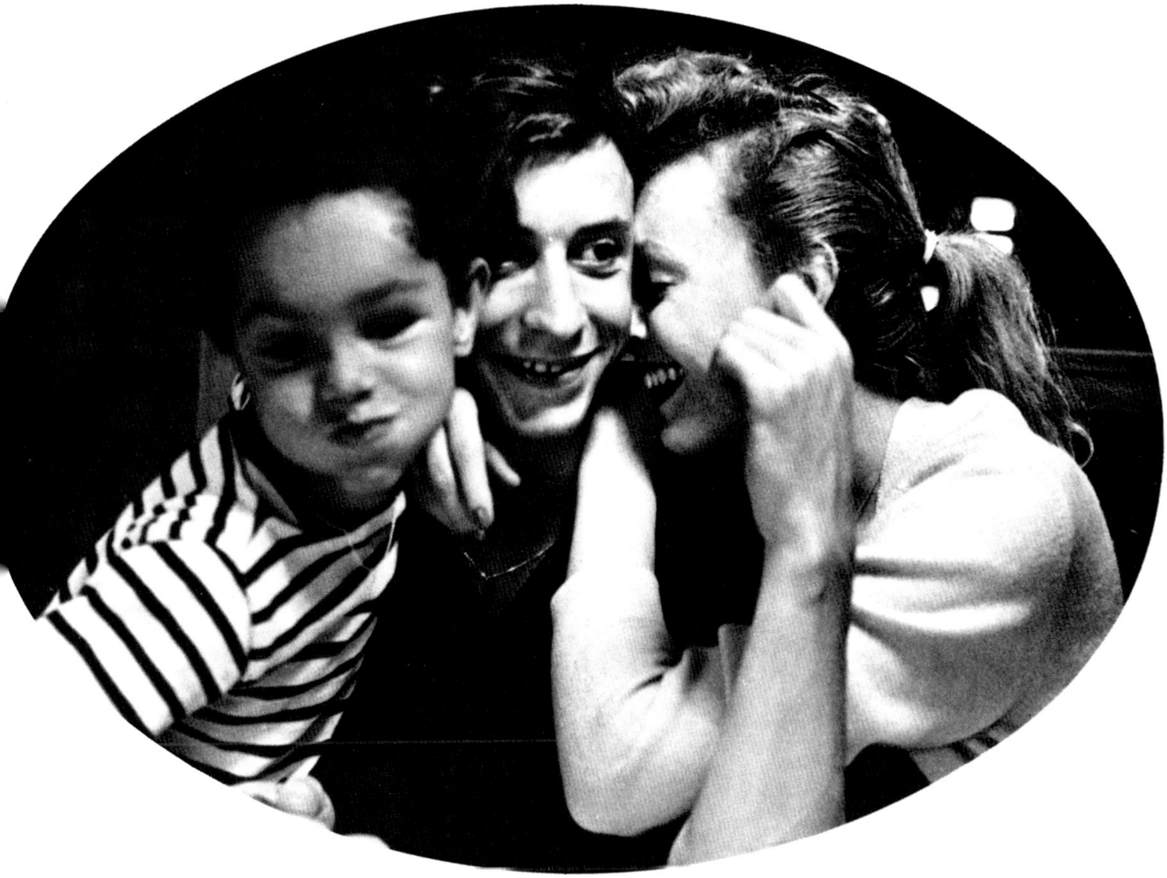

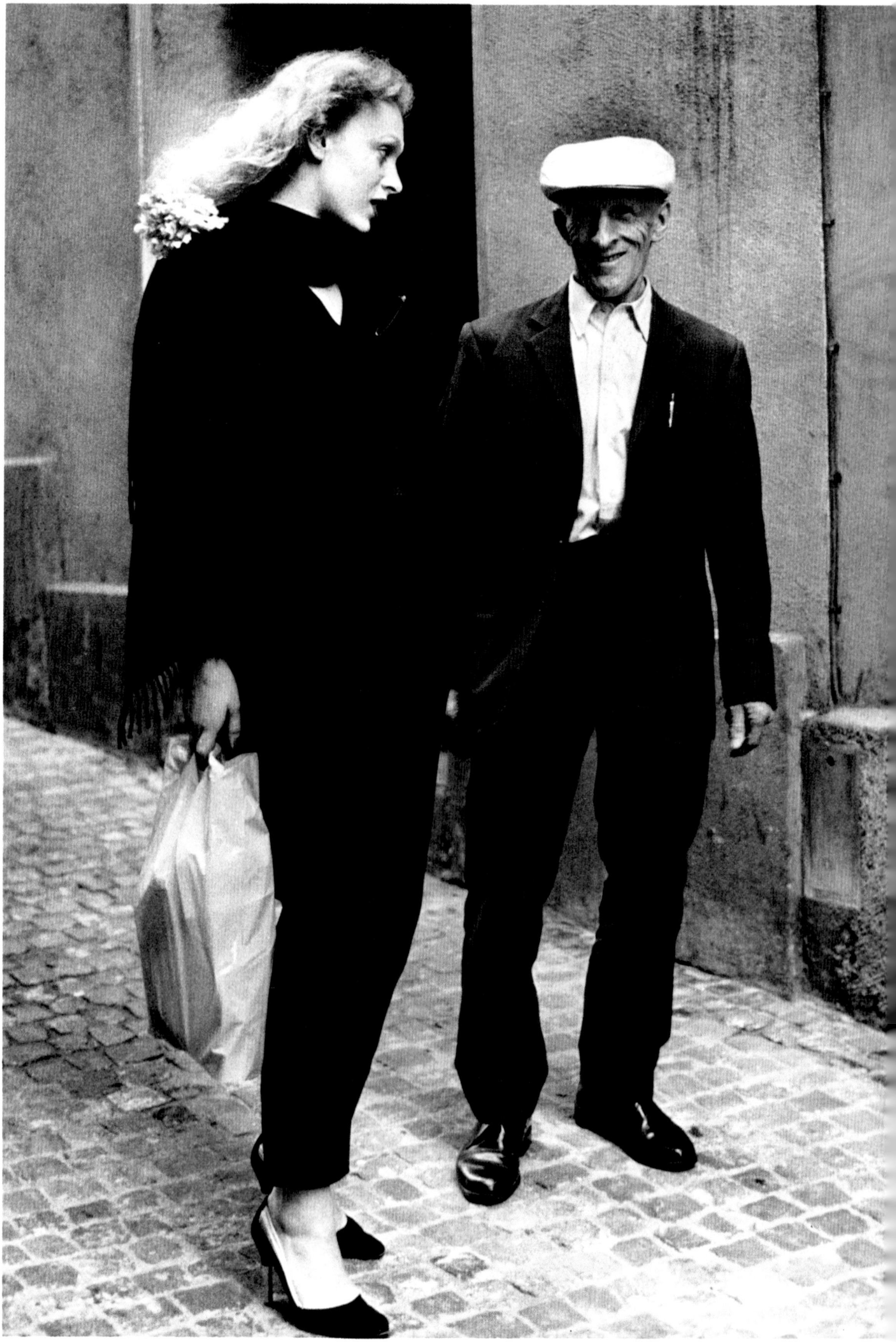

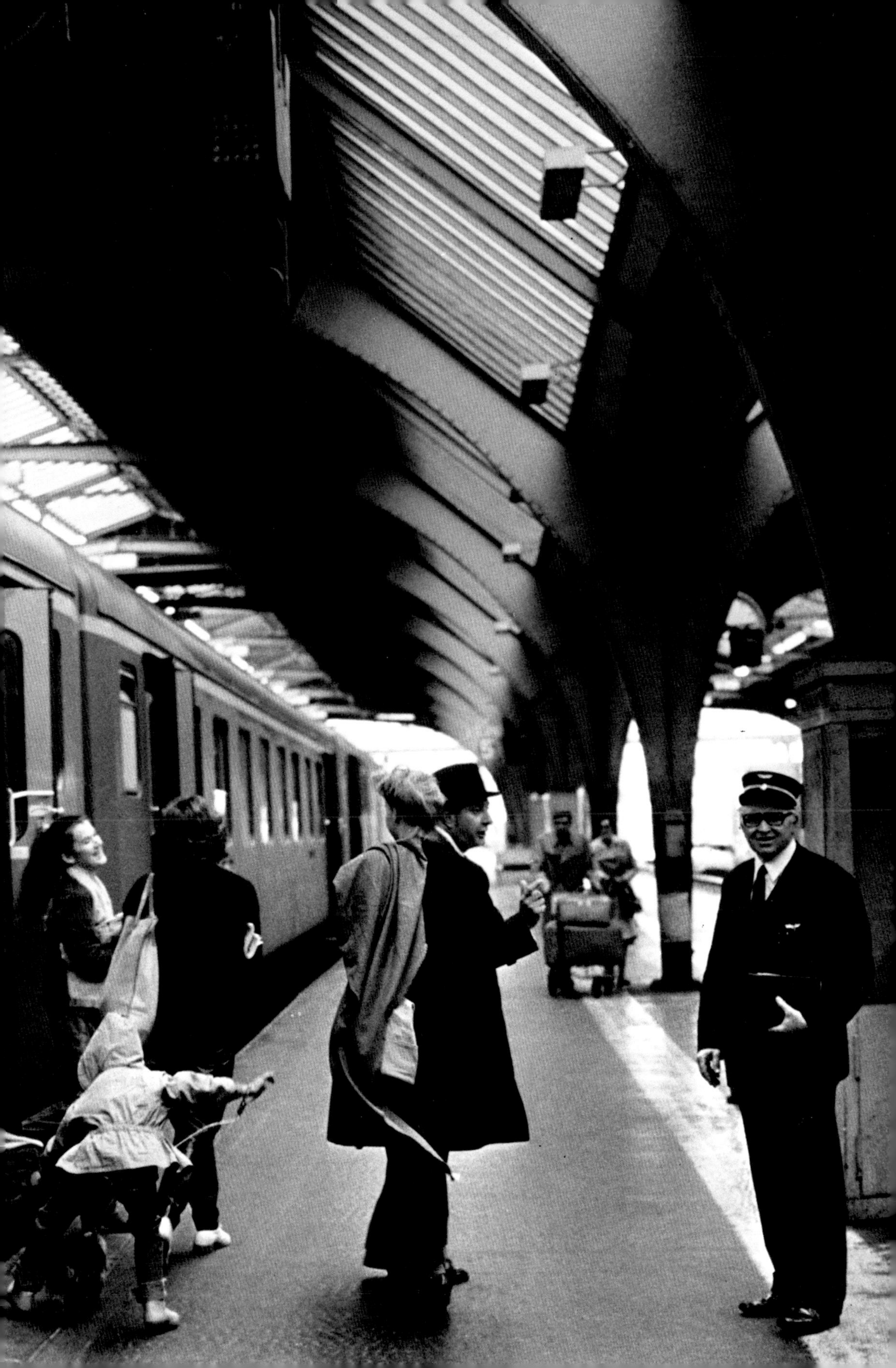

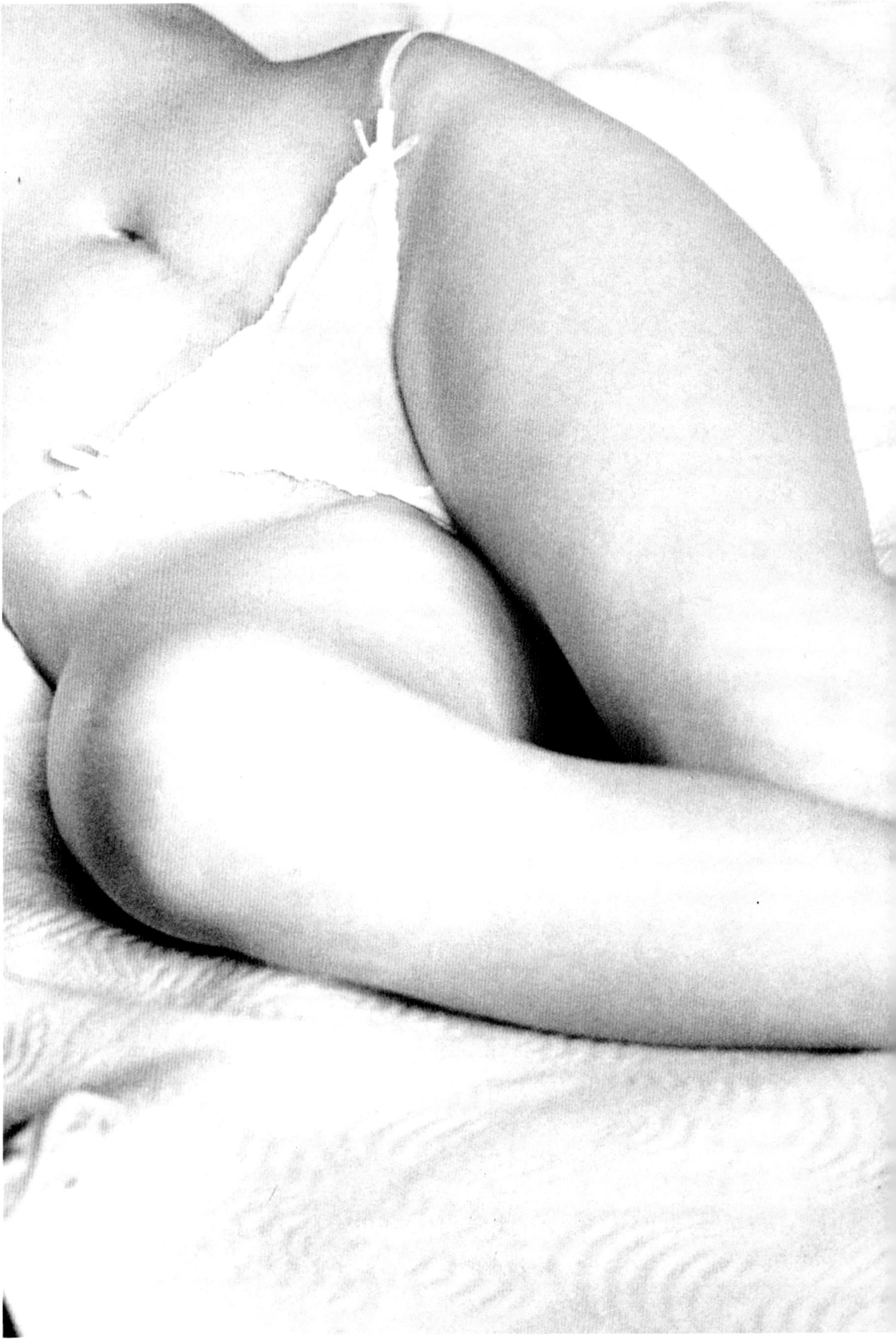

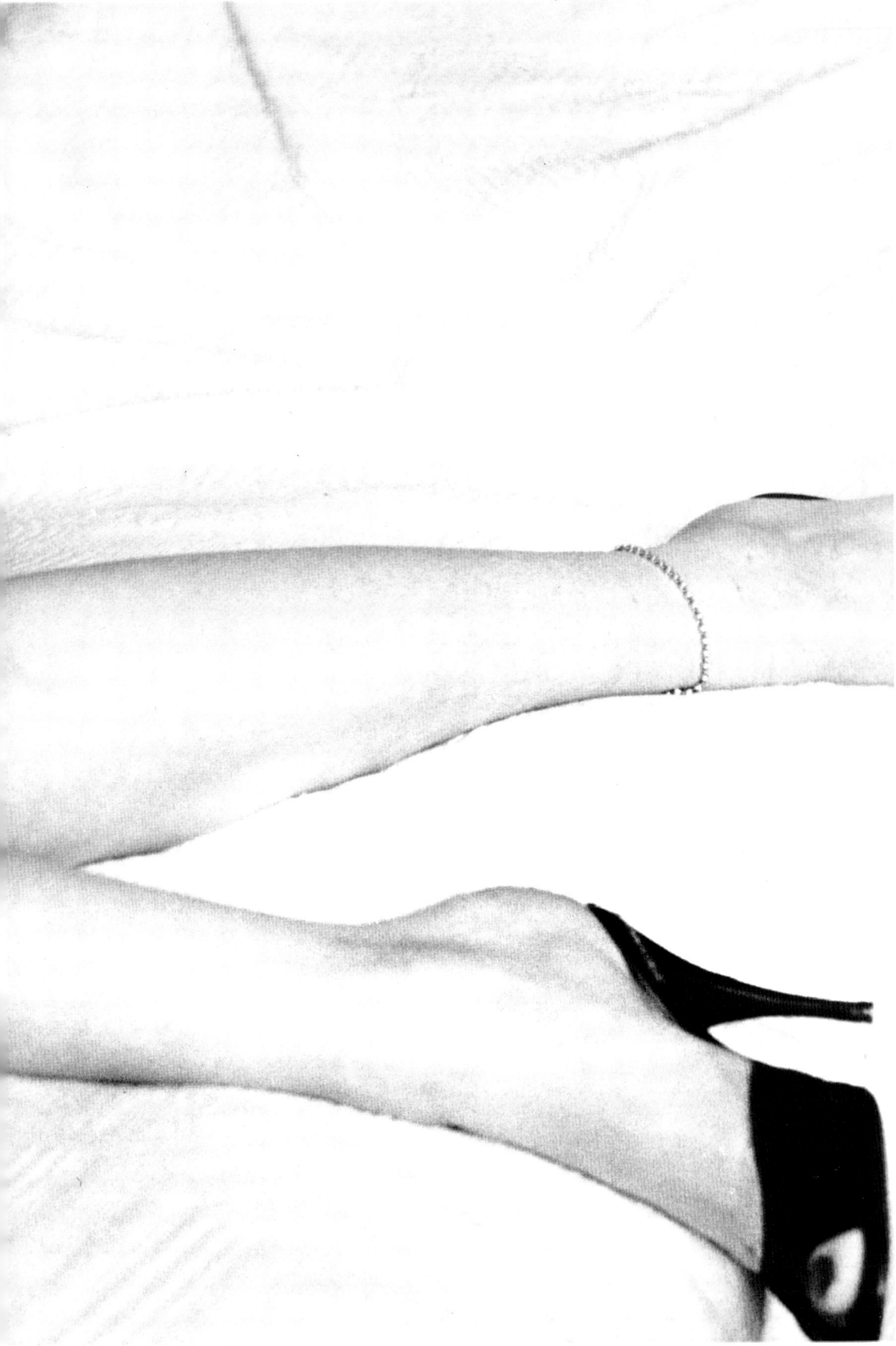

What is so annoying about love is that it is a crime which cannot be committed without an accomplice.

    Baudelaire

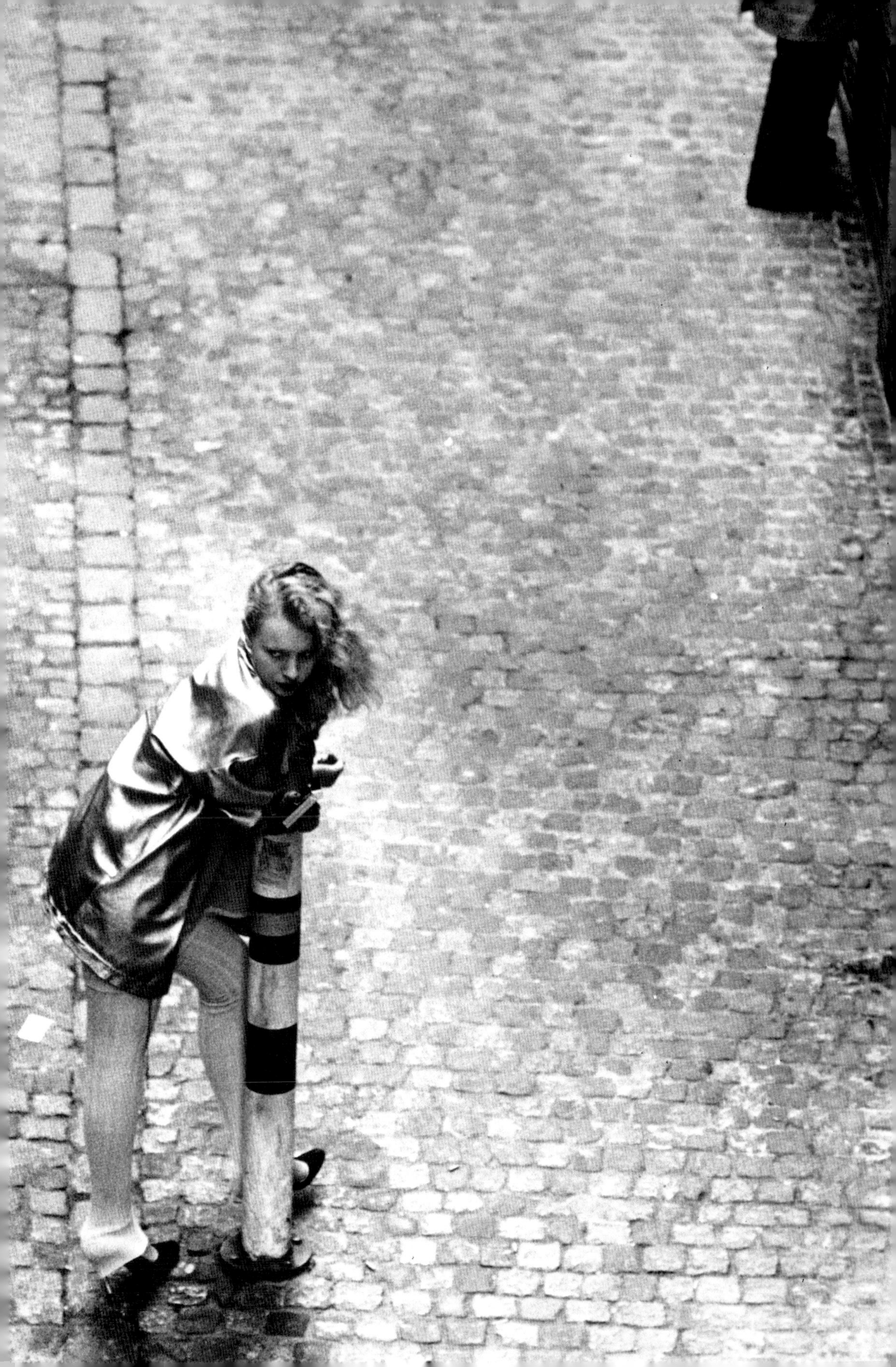

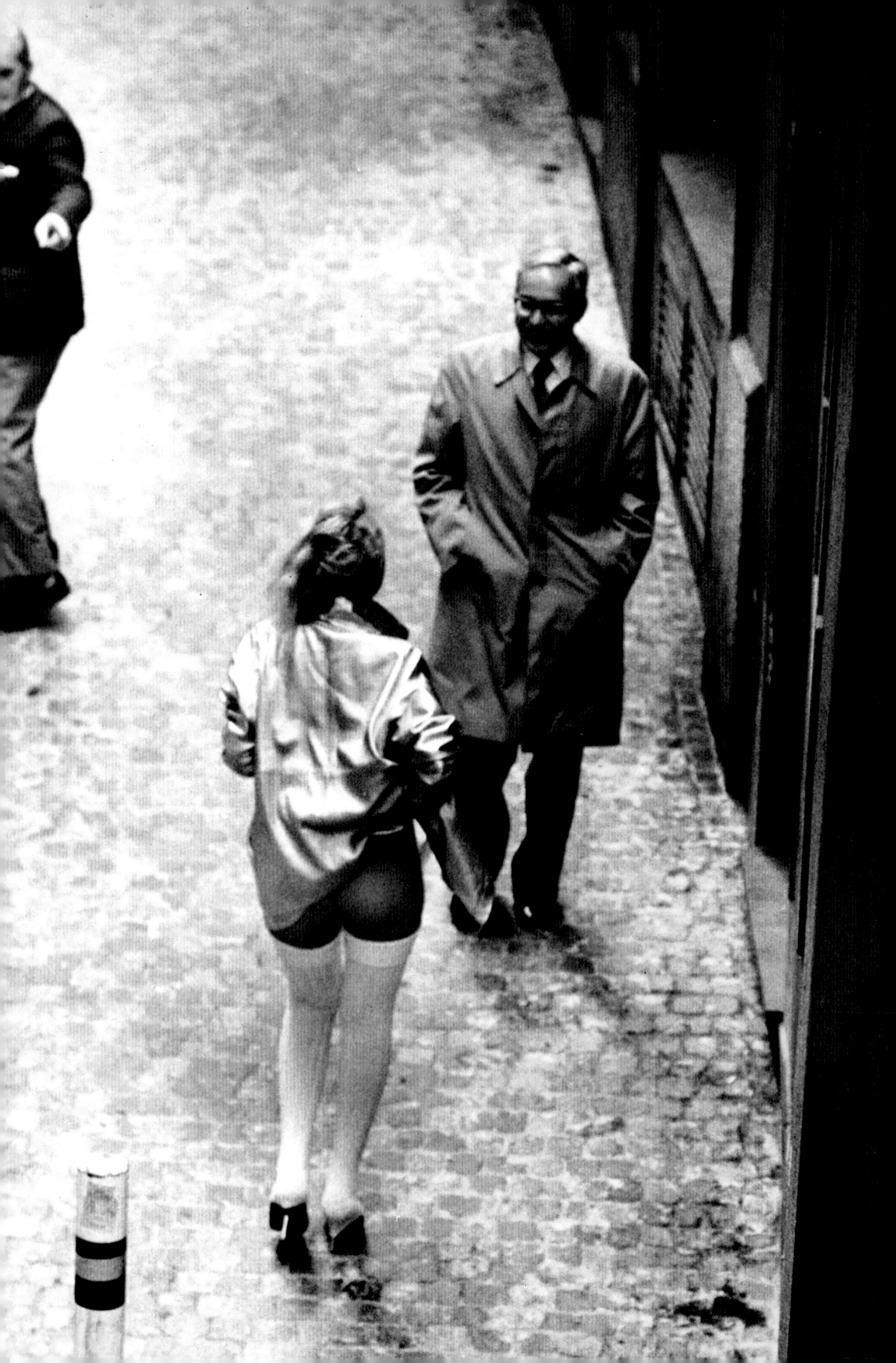

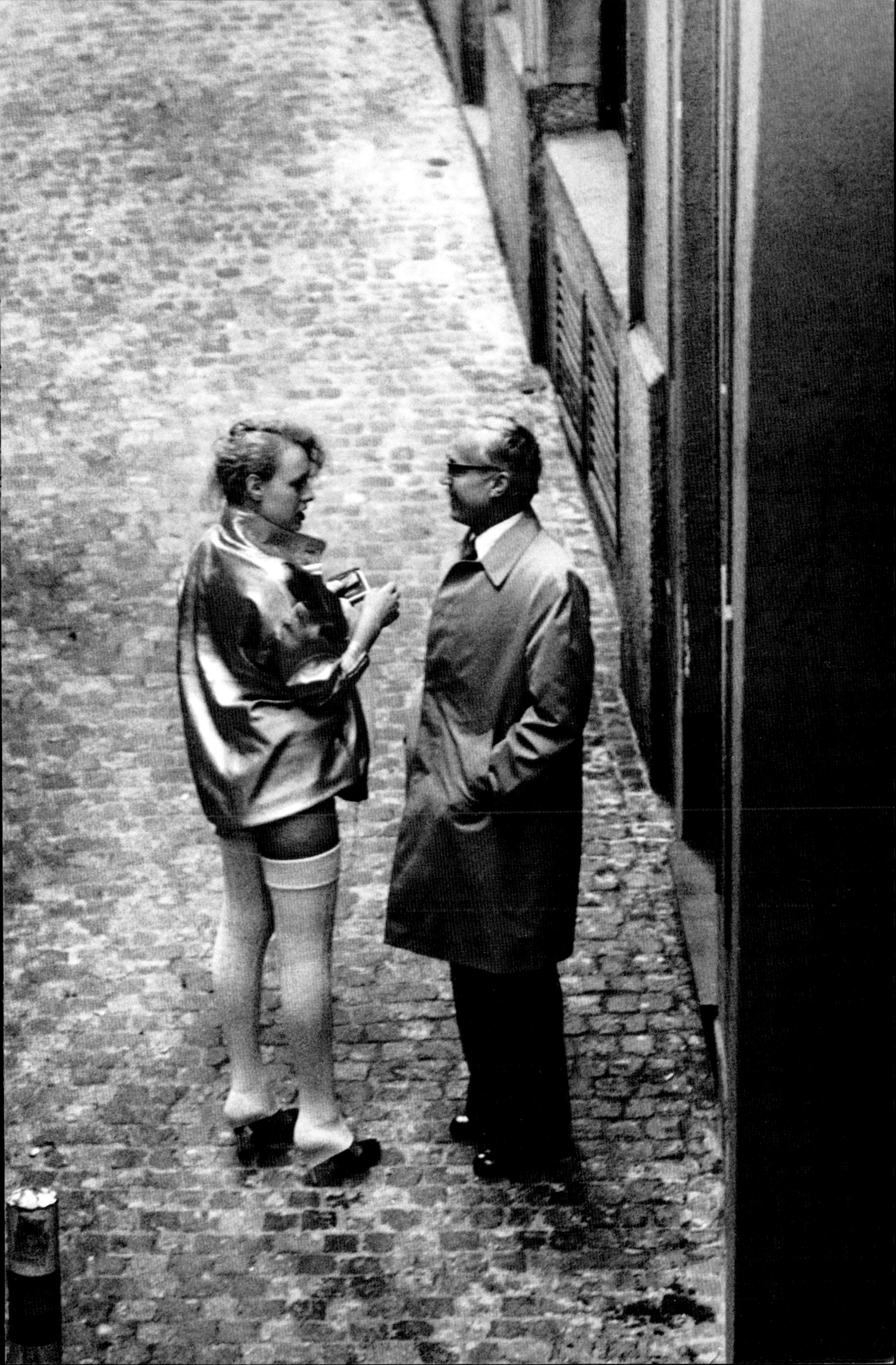

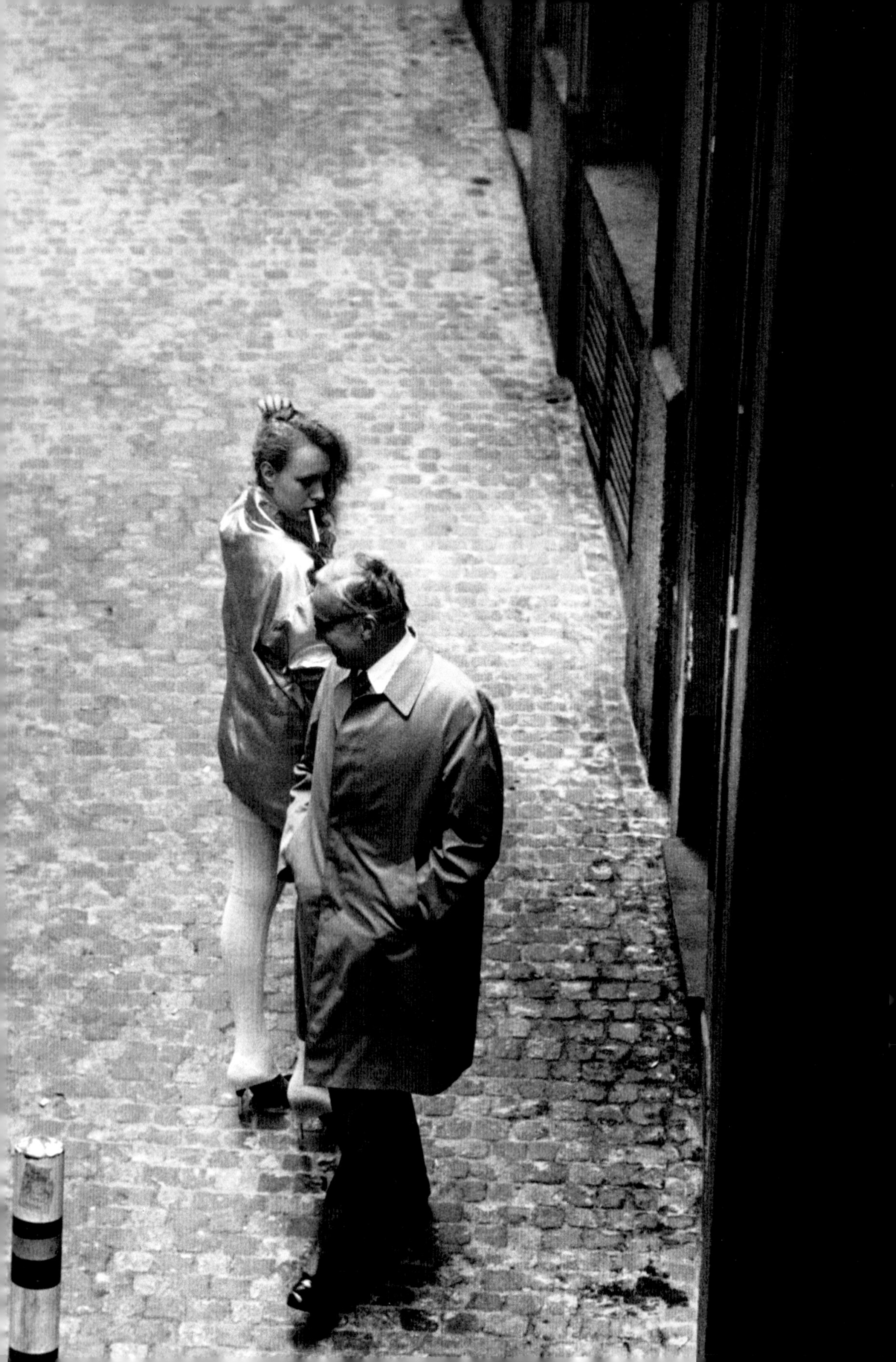

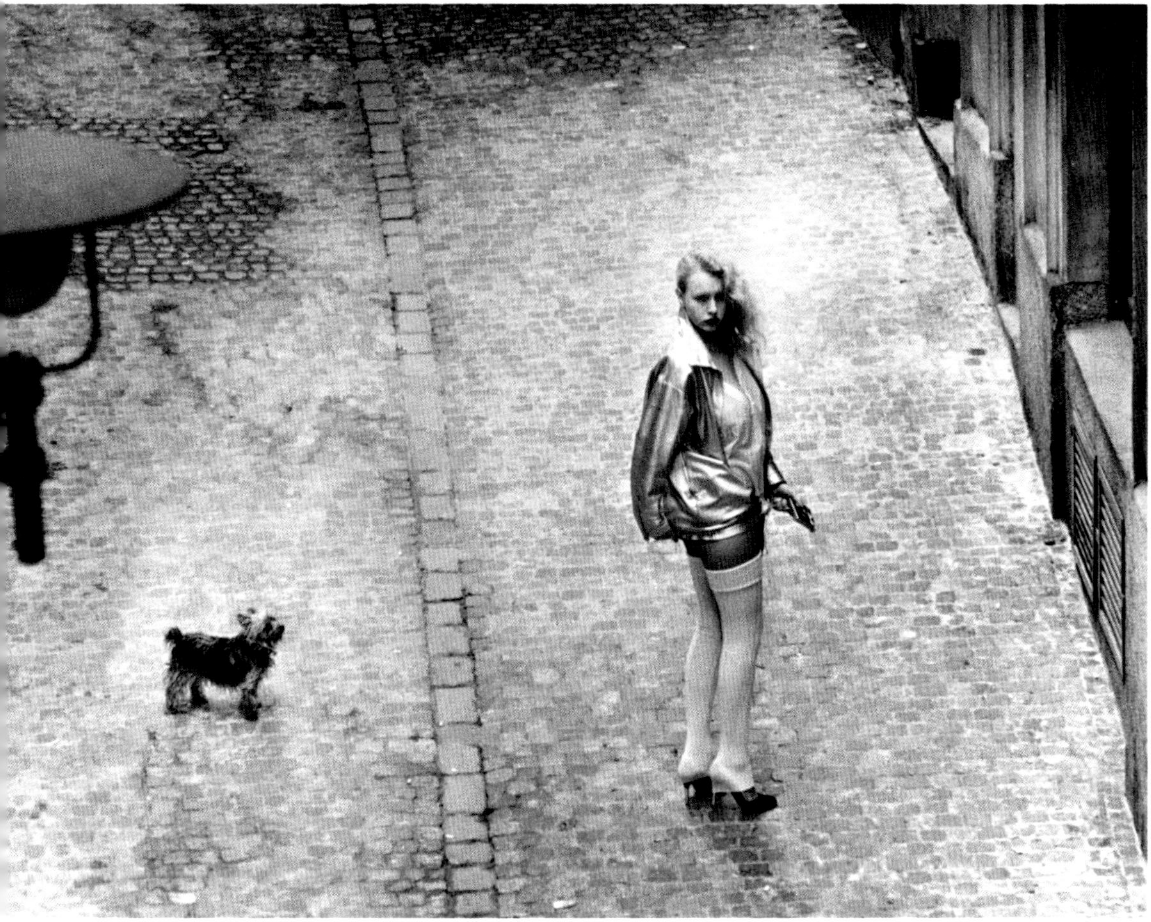

The stranger women seem to us, the more we love them.
Baudelaire

Translations by Christopher Doherty

This Is an R&B Book
Published in 1982 by Rogner & Bernhard, New York

Distributed by Grove Press, Inc.,
196 West Houston Street, New York, N.Y. 10014

Copyright ©1978 by Rogner & Bernhard GmbH & Co. Verlags KG, München

All rights reserved under International and
Pan-American Copyright Conventions.

No part of this book may be reproduced, stored in a
retrieval system, or transmitted in any form, by any
means, including electronic, mechanical, photocopying,
recording, or otherwise, without the prior written
permission of the publisher.

First Edition
First Printing
ISBN: 0-394-52894-8
Library of Congress Catalog Card Number: 82-48041

First Evergreen Edition 1982
First Printing 1982
ISBN: 0-394-62425-4
Library of Congress Catalog Card Number: 82-48041

Printed and bound in West Germany

GW01372966

READING CLIMBING CENTRE

Climbing & Bouldering

readingclimbingcentre.com

01189 756 298
Unit 33 Robert Cort Ind Est, Britten Rd, Reading. RG2 0AU

CONTENTS

Introduction ... 5

Warning ... 5

Acknowledgements ... 6

How to use this guide ... 7

Grades and the Fontainebleau system ... 9

Where's best to start out ... 11

Respecting your playground ... 13

Conditions and seasons ... 15

A quick look around the crags ... 17

Map of the Southern sandstone ... 18

Stone Farm ... 19

Bassett's Farm ... 39

Harrisons ... 43

Bowles ... 79

Eridge Green ... 111

High Rocks ... 135

High Rocks Annexe ... 183

Happy Valley ... 191

Toad Rocks ... 203

Elimination walls ... 209

Top 5's ... 213

INTRODUCTION

Welcome to Southern Sandstone Bouldering - a comprehensive guide to all the amazing problems found on the South Eastern sandstone crags.

This guide strives to capture the unique vibe that surrounds the sandstone. The laid-back and friendly atmosphere mixed with the excellent problems at all of the crags make this a must go destination for all boulderers.

The southern sandstone is the only rock in the South East and with its relatively close proximity to both London and Brighton, plays host to a wide variety of climbers. This is one of the reasons why we thought that it was about time this area had its own bouldering guide book.

To us the sandstone feels like home. We have spent so much time at all of the crags in the preparation of this book we feel that we now know the crags inside out.

We have had a great time writing this guide and along with it had some great experiences and adventures. We have discovered areas and problems that we have dismissed many times before but by putting the time into trying all of these problems our eyes have been opened to how many top quality lines there really are.

For too long people have climbed in the same areas year in, year out. These are normally the more well known areas as they are all that people have heard of or known how to access. We hope that by writing this guide we will push people into new areas that they may not have been aware of and in turn help to cut down on the erosion/damage that is being afflicted on these areas due to over use.

This guide has also been written to help inform sandstone climbers of the soft nature of the rock and what measures need to be taken to preserve this area for future generations. These rocks have been here for millions of years and will not be here forever at the rate things are going. Please make sure you take the time to read all of the notes on ethics in the respecting your playground section.

WARNINGS

Bouldering and other forms of climbing are dangerous sports and come with large amounts of risk and possible personal injury or death. All those taking part should be aware of these risks and make their own judgment if they perceive these activities to be safe for them to partake in. All material mentioned in this guide is just that 'A Guide!' It should not be taken as fact or used as an instructional manual. We have done our best to check all the grades but the information is not verified by any official party and the guidebook writers and publishers can not accept any responsibility, nor are they liable, for any injuries or damages to anyone that may arise from use of this guide.

We hope that you enjoy this guide and can find it useful in your quest to discover all the great lines that these crags have to offer.

James O'Neil | Harrisons | Route 99 | 6B

ACKNOWLEDGEMENTS

We have so many people to thank for their help and contributions to this guidebook.

From our friends and family, to the many climbers who we have met at the rocks or enjoyed a session with down at the crag.

Special thanks must go to Barnaby Ventham for his enthusiasm and help in getting this guide ready as well as keeping us on our toes! Also to Peter Wycislik for his consistent addition of new hard lines and for climbing nearly everything on the Sandstone which has helped greatly with consistency throughout this guide.

We must also take this opportunity to thank all of the people who have helped develop this area as without them this guidebook would not be possible. There are too many people to mention and to save offending someone who we miss we have decided not to list them all. Other publications have good lists of first ascents to which they are credited, but thank you again for all the time people have put into uncovering new routes!

To all our family and friends of whom again there are too many to mention. Special thanks to Katie, Jude and Kat who have been very patient over the months of writing this guide as we can't say that we've have had a lot of free time to see them!

The walls at which we work and play, such as Craggy Island and Evolution, have also been a massive help in getting the guide ready by keeping us sane when it is too wet to venture outside.

Everyone has been so helpful and supportive of this project and hopefully we have made it all worthwhile for you with this guidebook. Thank you again and we shall see you down the rocks!

Ben Read | High Rocks | Vandal | 7A+

HOW TO USE THIS GUIDE

We have tried to make this guide as fun and easy to use as possible. All the problems have photo topos to go with them and come with a wide selection of maps to help you locate them on the crag. In our eyes bouldering should be simple, so why over complicate the guide!

All of the climbing photos aim to capture the fun that comes with bouldering in the South as well as showing you some quality shots of some of the best problems! We have worked hard to try and get new and exciting angles that will show off the problems in a new light.

All of the problems have a short description with some basic information on the climb. We have decided not to give away any spoilers as to us part of the fun of climbing is the journey that you go through with each climb and the battle that you face as you try to unlock the correct sequence. To us this is a fundamental part and providing you with just the raw information means that you will have the enjoyment of this process as well.

We have very simple keys throughout the book that highlight just a few pieces of information. We appreciate that problems will feel different to different people and so obviously do treat this all as a guide and not as fact.

ROUTE DESCRIPTION KEY

H This symbol highlights a problem that goes above what is considered a normal bouldering height. Extra care should be taken on these and we would advise you to consider using ample pads and spotters on such problems.

SS This indicates that the problem is started from a sitting position on the ground. The starting holds should be obvious but if not then we have tried to include a short explanation in the descriptions.

David Bone | High Rocks | Route 228 | 4

⌇ The white line marks out roughly the path that is climbed on each problem. Sometimes these do vary slightly as people will climb the problems differently. Where the line stops is also where the problem finishes.

69 The number at the bottom of each line matches the description of the problem. These should be on the same page but in some situations they are on the following or previous page. These are just reference numbers and only relevant to this guide book.

Route Name   For problems that have been established as classic boulder problems we have included the name that it has been given. This is the name that has been given to the climb on its first ascent by the climber and would normally have a meaning to them. On there own sometimes they can sound a bit weird!

6A   This indicates how hard the said problem is. For more details on grades please see the 'Grades and the Fontainebleau system' page.

Dan Moore | High Rocks | Final Destination | 7C

GRADES AND THE FONTAINEBLEAU SYSTEM

The Fontainebleau or 'Font' grading system is a great way to distinguish how hard problems are. We have decided that this system is best for the sandstone and hopefully we have managed to get our heads around it. Being quite close to Fontainebleau means that it is much easier for us to work out how hard each grade is and hopefully apply these to the sandstone appropriately.

The sandstone has always traditionally been graded using English tech grades which work well for the roped routes but when it comes to boulder problems, which are usually a lot more condensed and powerful, the font system works best. This system is being more commonly used around indoors walls and therefore it has become one of the more accepted grading systems for bouldering.

We have tried our best to get the grades as accurate as possible but be aware that there are hundreds, if not thousands, of problems on the sandstone and we are bound to have got a couple wrong. Grades will also feel different to different people due to a number of reasons. Height and body type will play a major factor in how hard a problem feels and although we have done our best to take this into consideration there are some places where it would be impossible to please everyone.

The more that you climb on the sandstone though the more you will understand the grading system and the reasons behind each grade.

As with most rock types, conditions will also affect the grade in considerable ways. A route on slopers may feel impossible in hot weather but when it is cold and crisp it may feel like a path! Please read the conditions and seasons page in this guide for a full indication of when is best to climb.

One thing we must mention is that grades should not rule your climbing session. Please use these as a rough guide in your selection of problems and a vague representative of what level you are climbing at. Remember that the most important thing when climbing is that you are having fun.

The grade is made up of a letter and number combination and basically the higher the letter and number then the harder the climb.

The system technically starts at 1A and goes up accordingly but due to the small difference in grades and how hard it is to compare these difficulties we have decided on using 1, 2, 3, 3+, 4, 4+, 5, 5+ before going on to 6A and working upwards in A, B and C intervals.

ENGLISH	V-GRADES	FONTAINEBLEAU
1A – 1B	VB	1
1B – 1C	VB	2
1C – 2B	VB	2+
2B – 3A	V0-	3
3A – 3C	V0-	3+
3C – 4B	V0	4
4B – 5A	V0	4+
5A – 5B	V0+	5
5A – 5C	V1	5+
5C – 6A	V2	6A
5C – 6B	V3	6A+
6A – 6B	V3	6B
6A – 6B	V4	6B+
6A – 6C	V5	6C
6A – 6C	V5	6C+
6B – 6C	V6	7A
6B – 6C	V7	7A+
6C – 7A	V8	7B
6C – 7A	V8+	7B+
6C – 7A	V9	7C
6C – 7B	V10	7C+
7A – 7B	V11	8A
7A – 7B	V12	8A+
7A – 7B	V13	8B
7A – 7B	V14	8B+

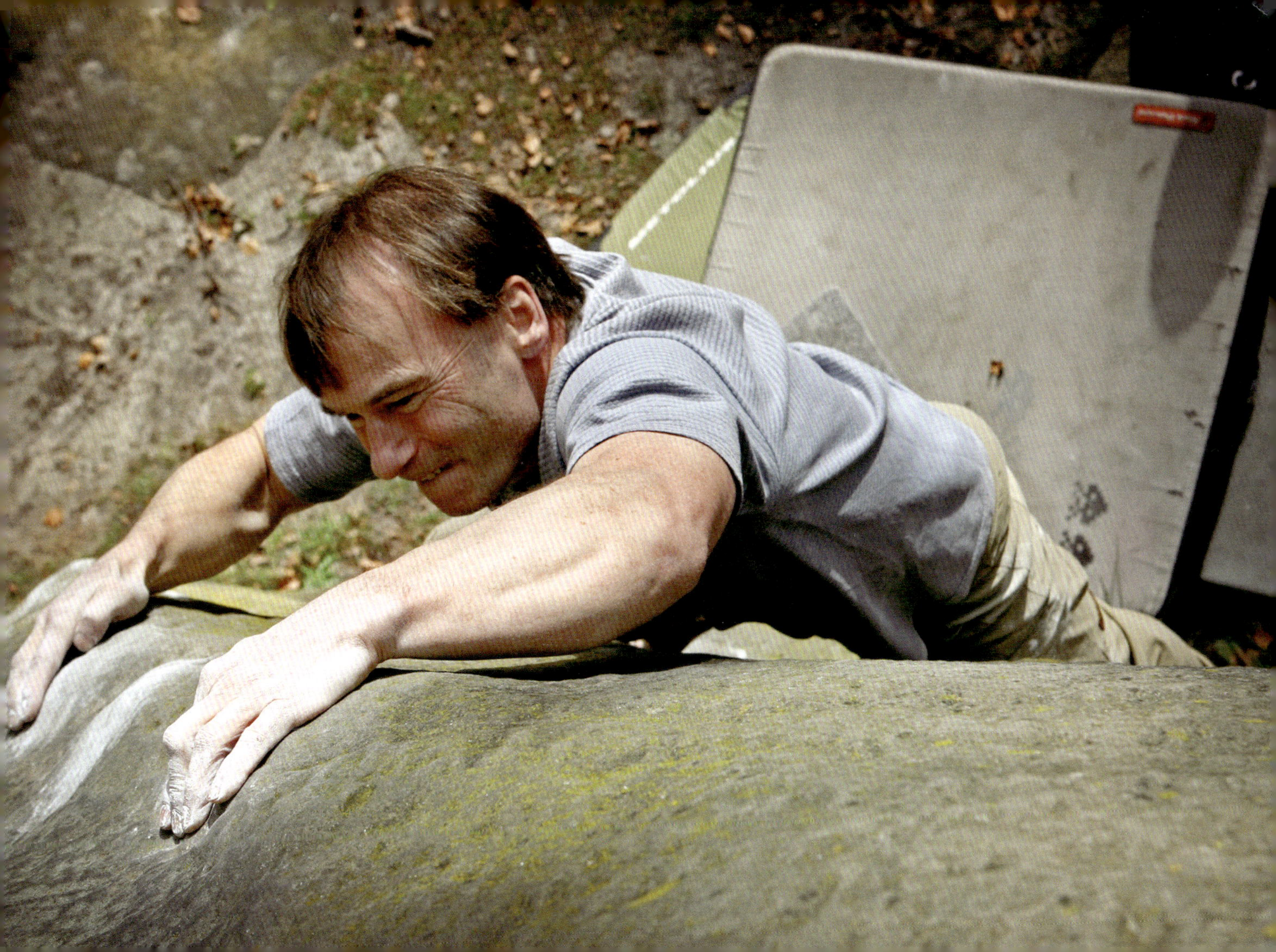

WHERE'S BEST TO START OUT

If you have never been to the sandstone before then here are some recommendations for your first visit to make sure you get the most out of your day.

The grade you are climbing at will help depict where you should start out. For those who are new to climbing you will prefer areas such as Bowles and Stone Farm which have a lot more in the lower grades to attempt. Crags such as Toad rocks and Happy Valley are great if you are looking for a chilled day. For those who are hunting out the sandstone's hardest then High Rocks and Eridge Green will suit you best as these hold some of the toughest problems.

All of the crags have a variety of grades so those with mixed abilities should be fine at most of the venues. On the introduction page of each crag we have broken down how many climbs of each grade are present which should help you in your quest for the right destination.

Each crag has its own feel and atmosphere as well. You will find that you may climb better at different crags and feel more in touch with the rock (as cheesy as that sounds) as the climbing really does vary massively between them.

Make sure that you check the 'respecting your playground' section if you are new to the area as the sandstone is not like other rock types and it is not just as simple as turning up and having a climb, there are a few more points to consider!

Brandon Crouch | Harrisons | Route 20 | 2+

ALL THAT YOU NEED

If you are new to climbing then all the equipment you should need is as follows:

ROCK SHOES Although not essential, there are a number of benefits to having these shoes. Firstly they will give you extra grip and will no doubt help in the development of your climbing. Secondly they will help to reduce the damage caused to the rock by heavy, muddy foot placements.

CHALK BAG AND CHALK Again this is not essential and some would argue that it should be banned but as you do progress on to smaller holds then chalk will definitely help to dry out your hands and improve grip. Please only use just what you need as over chalking ruins not only the climb and the rock but the look of the sandstone as well. If you can not climb it with a little bit of chalk then a lot of chalk is not going to help either!

TOWEL OR RAG This is to clean off excess chalk from the holds or any dirt that may have fallen upon it. It also helps to clean shoes before you start climbing.

BOULDER MAT For those who care about their ankles then a boulder mat is strongly recommended. A lot of the climbs go above the comfortable jumping off height and therefore the use of a boulder mat will help do reduce accidents and injury. It also helps to preserve the ground from erosion and from getting too muddy.

Where ever you go though please respect each crag individually. The sandstone varies between each area and with this comes different restrictions and ethics. We have tried to map out these as best we can but sometimes things change so be aware of signs and notices that may inform you of this.

Kat Assersohn | Harrisons | Route 101

RESPECTING YOUR PLAYGROUND

The southern sandstone is a special but very fragile rock type. It therefore carries with it a certain amount of rules that need to be adhered to in able to protect and preserve this rock for future generations. Here is a list of the simple rules and ethics that need to be considered when climbing on the sandstone. Please take time to read these as they will help you to understand the reasons behind these rules and why it is important for you to do your bit.

NO CHIPPING WHATSOEVER
The routes and problems on the sandstone have been around for hundreds of years. There are many routes that are considered all time classics not only in the area but also nationally. If you are finding that you can not climb a route or problem then move on and try something else. Chipping is a disgusting act and anyone caught doing so will be reported to the BMC and local climbing bodies.

NO BRUSHING
Brushing has unfortunately become common practice with bouldering but here on the sandstone the use of a brush, no matter what type or how soft you are brushing, can have very negative effects. The sandstone has a tough outer coating but the act of brushing can wear this away very quickly leaving soft exposed sand underneath. This will continue to wear with the lightest of touch not only ruining the rock but also the climb. We are therefore supporting a no brushing stance on the sandstone and will be recommending everyone to use a towel or rag to remove dirt and excess chalk build up from the holds.

USE MINIMAL CHALK
Chalk is a very visible substance that stands out on the rock. Please make sure that you are using the bare minimum that is required when climbing. Lots of the crags are not just climbing spots but many people also visit them for their natural beauty which can be spoiled by large heavily chalked sections. Excess chalk will have a negative affect on your climbing as well and will not help you succeed. Tick marks should also not be used to mark out holds and you should rely on memory and ability to locate holds.

CLEAN AWAY EXCESS CHALK
This is best to do using a towel or rag as referred to earlier. This will not only keep the presentation of the sandstone acceptable but will also not spoil route finding for the next set of climbers who attempt these problems.

NO USE OF RESIN (POF)
Although common practice in the not so distant Font, the use of resin (or POF as it is more commonly known) is strictly banned on the sandstone. Under no circumstance should it be considered or even thought about on this rock; if you want to use then I suggest you get on a ferry!

NO BLOW TORCHING
If you come across a wet hold dry it gently with a towel or come back on a windy day when it will have dried out naturally. Climbing on wet holds comes with a large risk of holds breaking off. When moisture is present in the sandstone it becomes very weak and fragile. For more information please see the 'conditions and seasons section.'

NO GARDENING
The sandstone has many types of indigenous vegetation and climbers must respect these when climbing here. Different crags have different rules on the removal of vegetation and no work should be carried out to remove these before consulting the relevant bodies.

DO NOT LEAVE CARPET PATCHES AT THE CRAG
Although they are very useful for cleaning shoes before climbing they soon become wet and are an eyesore for visitors to the crag. Please make sure you take all belongings home with you at the end of the day.

CLEAN YOUR SHOES
No one should step onto the rock, however easy the climb, without carefully ensuring that their shoes are completely clean. Please use a mat, carpet or a rag to make sure that your shoes are free from dirt before climbing commences! Dirt on your shoes not only makes the climbing harder but the small piece of sand and grit rubs heavily on the sandstone and wears through the hard outer coating.

USE A BOULDERING PAD
Not only does a boulder pad help to reduce injuries but it also protects the vegetation at the base of climbs. Continuous impact onto the ground at a particular point can have a very negative effect on the landing and damage the vegetation that may be living there.

DO NOT DROP LITTER AT THE CRAG
Make sure that you do your bit to help keep the rocks clean and tidy. Any litter that you have should be taken home with you and if you come across any please pick it up and take it to the nearest disposal point.

HOLD RESTORATION
Please do not try and fix any broken holds that you come across yourselves. There are many ways in which broken holds can be fixed, but if you get it wrong then it can have very negative and long lasting effects. If you come across any broken holds that you feel need urgent attention then please get in contact with us via the website and we can point you in the right direction.

Simon 'Karma' Fowler | Harrisons | Route 59 | 6B

CONDITIONS AND SEASONS

Conditions affect the climbing on the sandstone greatly and here we have tried to outline when and where is best to climb in the varying weather conditions.

Firstly we must highlight that you should not attempt to climb on wet or damp rock as this can have very negative effects. The sandstone works very much like a sponge and moisture is absorbed throughout the rock. When this water in present it makes the rock very fragile and can easily lead to holds breaking off causing problems to be changed and also could lead to possible injury.

Different crags need different amounts of drying time which we have estimated in the introduction page of each crag, but it is up to you to make your own judgment call to whether you think the rock is dry enough to climb. Try not to let your urge to get on the rock mask the fact that it may not be ready to climb as this leads to classic problems being ruined by impatience.

Ideally please allow for a couple of days of dry weather before hand to ensure that the rock has had a chance to dry out sufficiently but if it has rained recently then do still treat with caution. In addition climbing on wet rock will not help your climbing!

If you do come across slightly damp holds then please do not use any drastic measures to try and dry them. Please use a towel or rag to dry off any water present on the holds and then allow for natural conditions to dry it out fully. This is the only way that should be used to speed up the drying time as other acts can cause significant damage.

The use of blow torches will leave horrible scaring and can breakdown the strength of the rock drastically so these are an absolute no go. Other areas around the world have been known to use this method but on the Southern Sandstone it is not to be done!

Packing the holds full of chalk will not work. Chalk will become damp and sticky very quickly and will act as a barrier on the sandstone meaning that it will take longer for the moisture to be able to dry out of the rock, by doing this you will just be slowing down the process and it will be quite an eye sore.

Ben Littlewood | Fridge Green | Route 65 | 6A

When the rock is dry there are still a number of factors that come into play that will affect your climbing. In extreme heat the friction will be limited due to the make up of the rock and the fact that you will naturally sweat more which in turn will not help with grip. When the weather is like this it is much better to find crags in the shade or you will find that you will have to drop your grade significantly in order to get up anything!

As well as hot weather, cold weather can affect the climbing but normally in a more positive way. Cold crisp days can lead to increased friction on slopers and you will be amazed at how much of a difference it can make. Unfortunately though this weather only normally comes in winter and with that tends to come more rain.

Summer evenings are normally the best times to climb on the sandstone as the rock has cooled down in temperature but also has had all day to dry out any moisture that may have been present in the rock. This can lead to some great climbing conditions and at this point most of the crags have dried sufficiently that you have a wide choice of destinations.

Over the winter months the sandstone can develop a green coating and in some cases a slimy one as well. Do not be alarmed if you see this spreading over your classic problems when visiting during these months, the green disappears quickly with good weather so do not attempt to do any emergency gardening to help protect the climbs. The greenness is normally a good indication that the rock underneath is going to be far too wet to climb on so give these climbs time to dry out.

To sum up the different conditions and seasons: we must reiterate that you must use your judgment when picking what crags to visit and what routes to climb. The above is only a rough guide to when is best to climb and with typical English weather changing all of the time although it may be quite frustrating to be stuck indoors. Be patient and you will be rewarded with good conditions and with that success!

WINTER

Crags such as Bowles and Stone farm have some areas that are possible to climb at during the winter months but as mentioned previously please be cautious as normally the holds are still damp. During winter the early morning frost and ice can freeze the water that is trapped inside the rock and this will cause the holds to be even more unstable so it is best to avoid trying to get some early morning ticks during this time. Once the sun hits the crag it should de-ice them nicely, so again patience is required.

SPRING

This is when the climbing seasons really starts to kick off. By about March time we start to get a few days and sometimes even a week of good weather. This can lead to some really good climbing conditions and crags such as Eridge Green and High Rocks have sections that become climbable (but be warned there are still large parts of these crags that require more time).

SUMMER

When the summer months hit us we can then start to look at other destinations and begin to explore further down the crags. As mentioned before summer evenings are often best. Crags such as Toad Rocks and Happy Valley are great places to go during the hot summer days as they have a lovely laid back relaxed feel and also a nice selection of easy graded problems when friction is minimal.

AUTUMN

This tends to mirror the spring conditions fairly well. The closer you approach the winter months the less climbing there is to be had but normally due to the hot drying period during the summer many of the crags are still very accessible. Be aware that time moves fast and these crags will soon start to get ready for their winter hibernation.

① STONE FARM

The most westerly crag that is quick drying and has some great low and mid level climbs. This crag has a great view and a relaxed atmosphere which makes it popular for families.

p.19

② BASSETT'S FARM

An old quarry line that has a couple of great traverses on it. The red rock dries quickly as it is very open making it a great spring and autumn venue.

p.39

③ HARRISONS

The longest outcrop and probably the most well known. There are some truly great boulder problems all the way along nestled among the historic routes that make up this impressive cliff.

p.43

④ BOWLES

A popular crag that stays dry most of the year round if good weather permits. Bowles has some great classic boulder problems of all grades.

p.79

⑤ ERIDGE GREEN

A peaceful little crag that has had a lot of development in the last few years. The rock can be fragile in places and has some areas that are restricted, so please treat with caution.

p.111

⑥ HIGH ROCKS

This crag has the hardest lines of the sandstone and the largest quantity of hard problems. This is a privately owned crag and the owners charge a small fee for entry, but it is definitely worth it!

p.135

⑦ HIGH ROCKS ANNEXE

A little hidden gem of slabs and walls that look green and wet but can often be surprisingly dry even though it is well covered from the sunlight.

p.183

⑧ HAPPY VALLEY

A great little venue that has some classic problems to put a smile on your face. I guess that's why its called Happy Valley!

p.191

⑨ TOAD ROCKS

A great family location that has hundreds of boulder problems of all grades in a fun, complex field of boulders. The sandy ground make it feel like a beach and has a pub right on its doorstep.

p.203

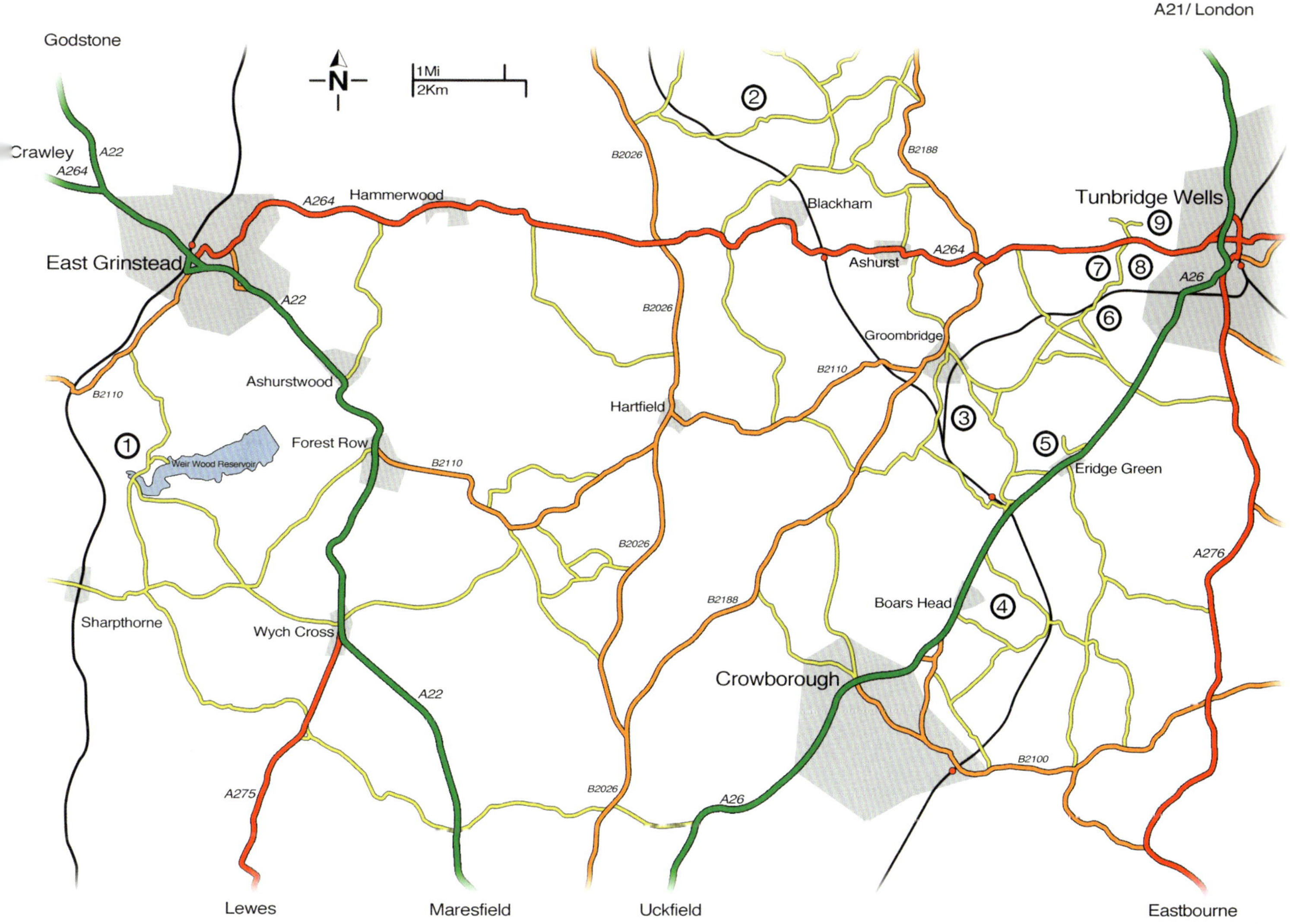
A21/ London
Godstone
N
1Mi
2Km
Crawley
A22
A264
East Grinstead
A264
Hammerwood
A22
Ashurstwood
B2110
Weir Wood Reservoir
Forest Row
B2110
Sharpthorne
Wych Cross
A22
A275
B2026
B2026
Hartfield
B2026
B2026
B2188
A26
Blackham
Ashurst
A264
Groombridge
B2110
B2188
Crowborough
Boars Head
Eridge Green
B2100
Tunbridge Wells
A26
A276
1
2
3
4
5
6
7
8
9
Lewes
Maresfield
Uckfield
Eastbourne

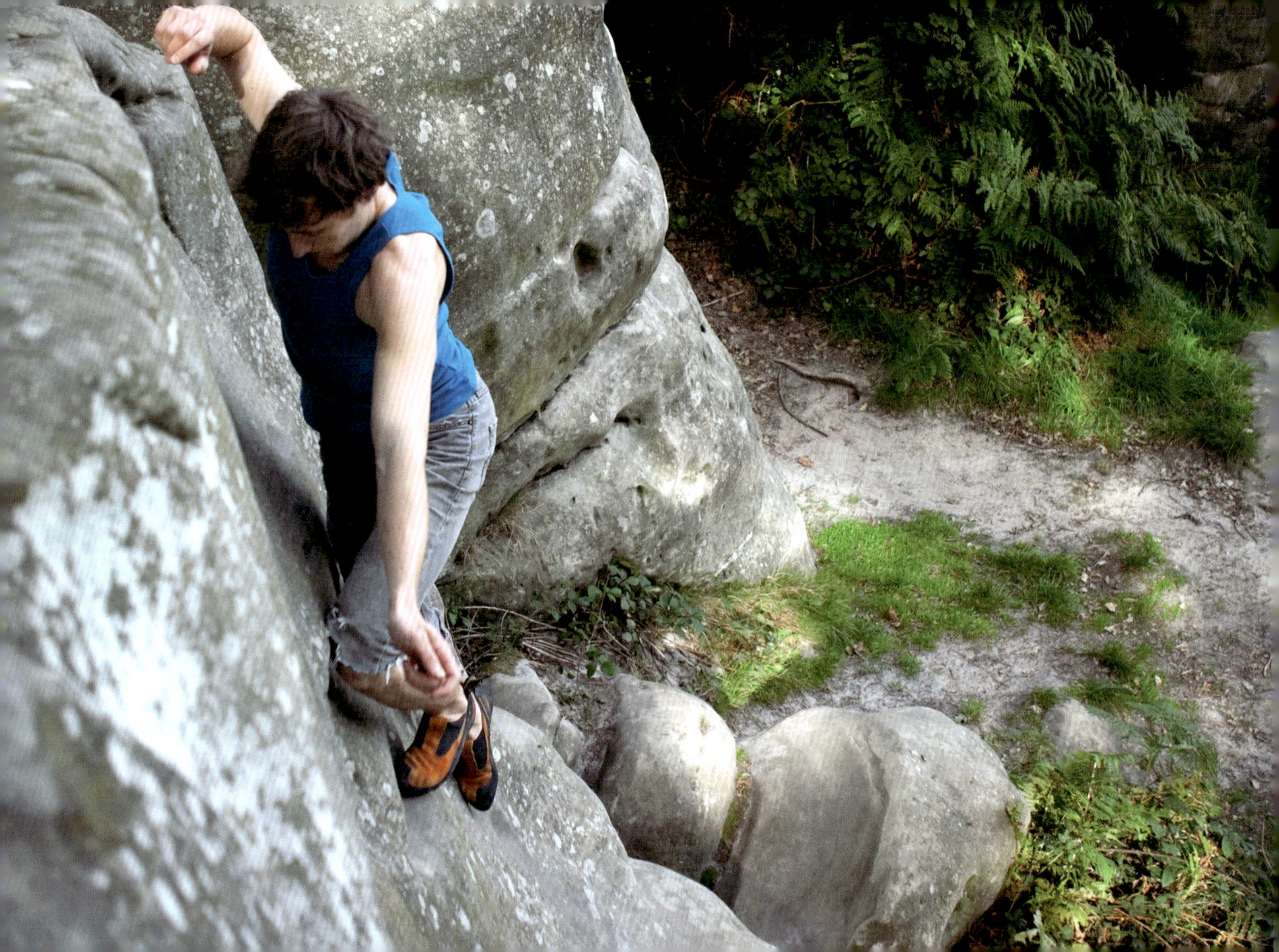

STONE FARM

INTRODUCTION

On the west side of Tunbridge Wells lays this little crag in a great setting with a brilliant view over the reservoir.

Stone Farm has some great problems, most of these lie in the lower grades but there are some great highball slabs that, although not too hard, will definitely get the heart fluttering. Classic lines such as 'Stinging Nettle' and 'Milestone Mantle' are great problems but unfortunately have been ruined a bit due to the overuse of brushes and some careless climbers, (this is a strong reminder that our rock is soft and needs to be treated with a lot more care than other rock types).

ACCESS AND APPROACH

Stone Farm is located very close to the Weirwood reservoir which is just south of East Grinstead. From East Grinstead take the B2110 heading south west towards Turners Hill. You will then be looking out for a signpost for Saint Hill Manor on the left-hand side. Take this turning and then follow this road to the end. At the T junction take a right hand turn and continue down this road. You will eventually come to a hill that leads down to the foot of the reservoir. About half way down this is a small road off to the left just before a sharp corner. Park in the lay-bys at the start of the road. The crag is then situated back up the hill on the left hand side down a footpath marked by a large overhang of rock (which is too soft to climb). This crag is now owned by the BMC but please take time to read the sign at the start of the crag which has all the important information regarding access and climbing here.

CONDITIONS

Alongside Bowles, sections of this crag, such as the Stinging Nettle area, are fast drying. As it is on a hill it gets the wind going straight through which helps with this drying process. As you move down the crag it does require more drying time the further you get due to the number of trees. Please make sure that chalk is kept to a minimum and you do not use tick marks as they look horrible and ruin the climb for the next person.

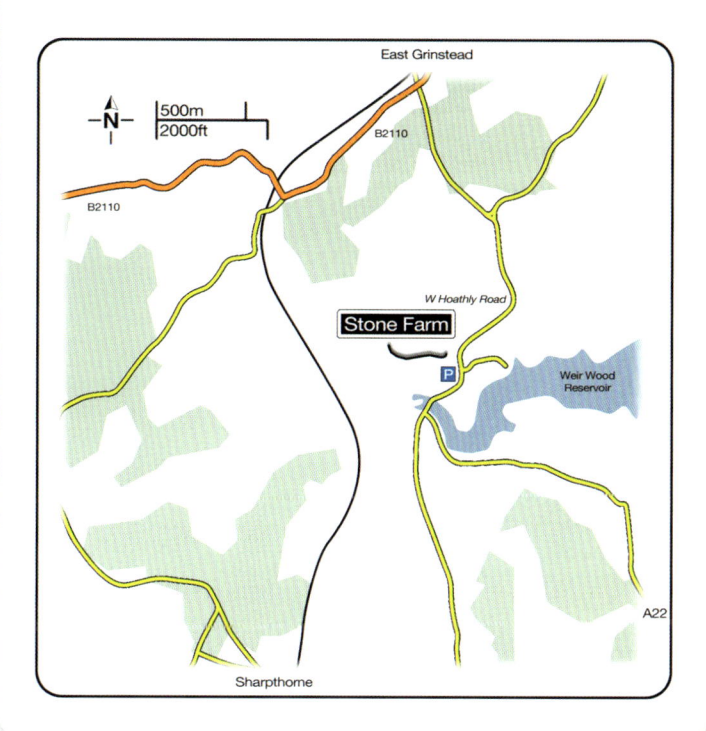

Matt Hutch | Route 87 | 2 (no hands)

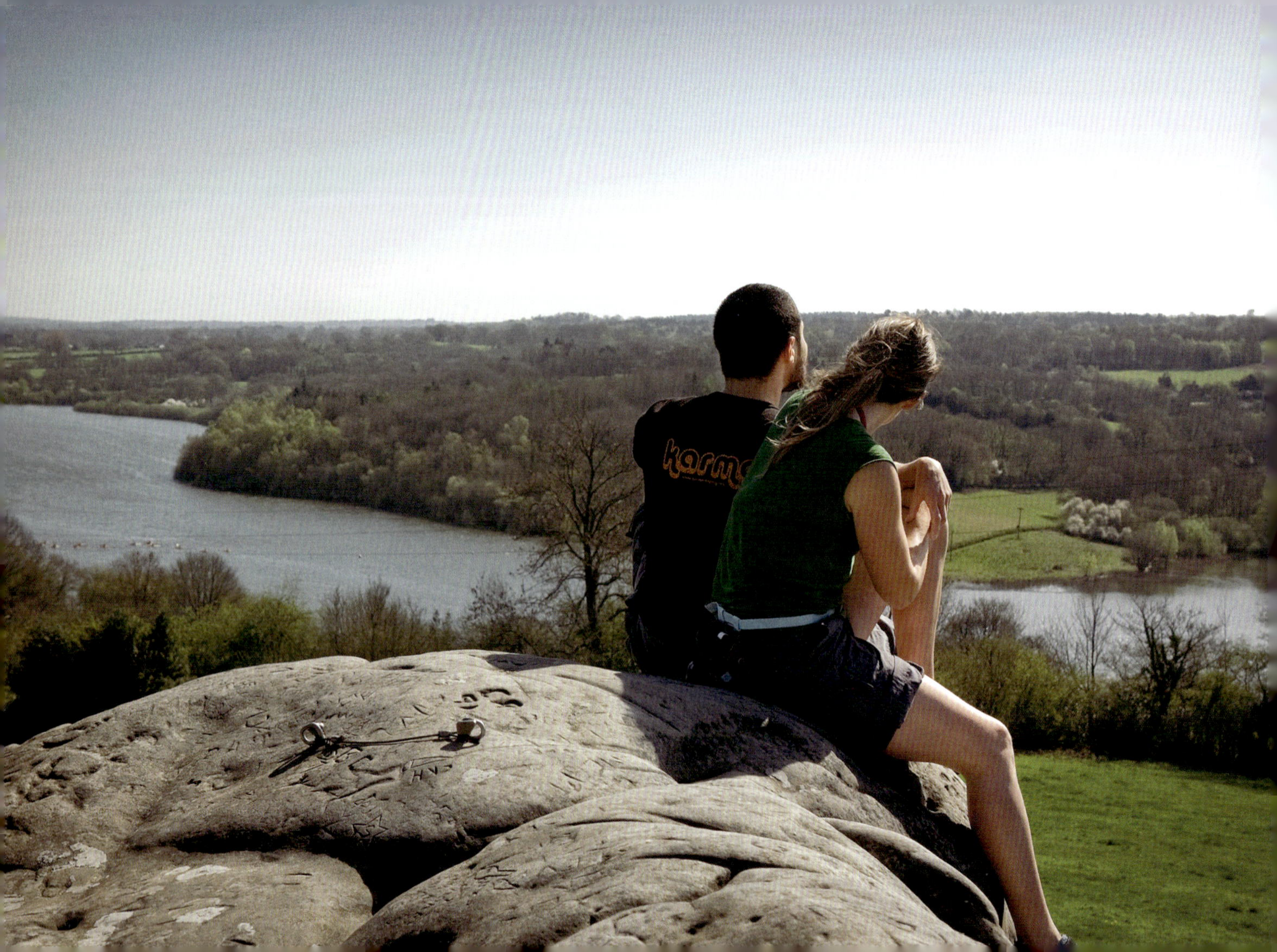

East Grinstead

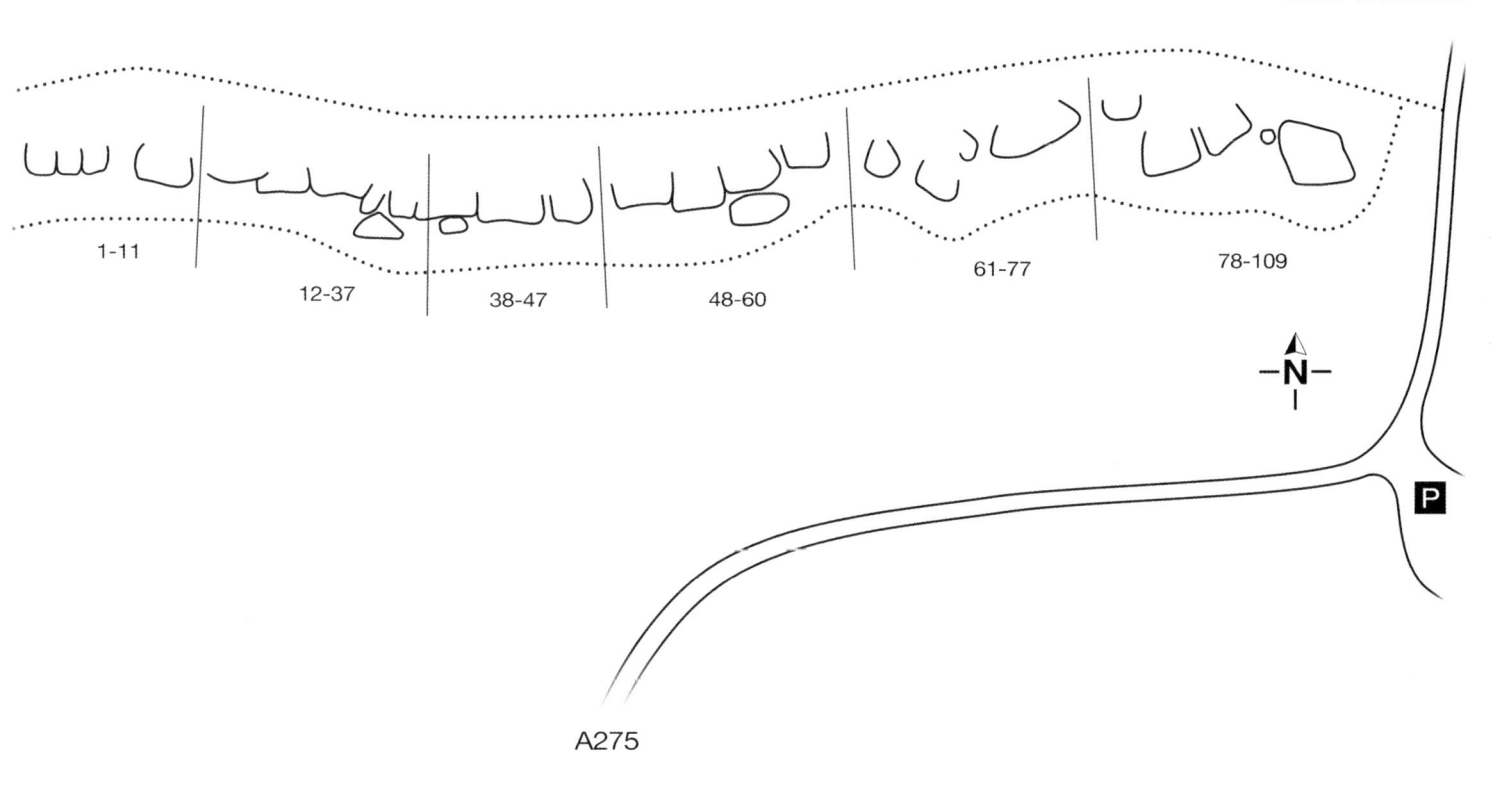

1-11   12-37   38-47   48-60   61-77   78-109

N

P

A275

Stone Farm 22

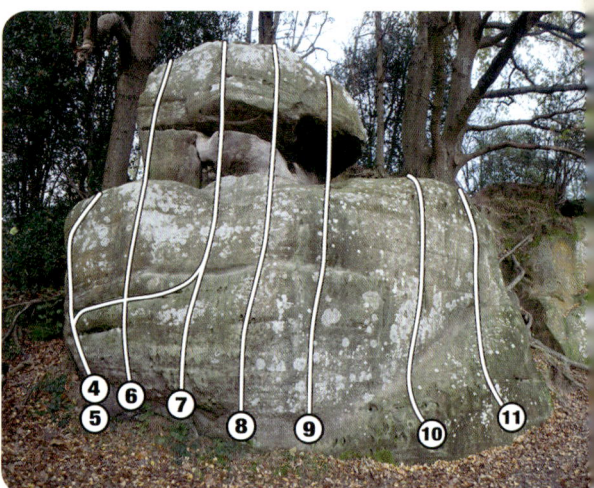

1. 2
Climb the easiest line up the middle of the boulder.

2. 1
Nice easy slab climb using holds on the boulder.

3. 4
Easy climb up the left hand side of the buttress.

4. 3+
Climb the arête to the large ledge and then exit around the top boulder.

5. 5+
Starting on the arête climb rightwards and up to the top of the of the boulder.

6. 4
Just to the right of the arête is this nice little climb, hard moves low down lead to an easier but scarier finish.

7. 6A
Straight up the middle of the slopey ledge, usually done as a mantle.

8. 5
Just to the right of the slopey ledge is this little climb finish at the top of the boulder.

9. 4
Straight up the blank wall and finish up the undercut side of the top boulder by some tricky moves.

10. 3
Easy line up the right hand side of the boulder from the start of the ramp.

11. 2
The far right of this boulder has a easy little climb up the slab and ramp.

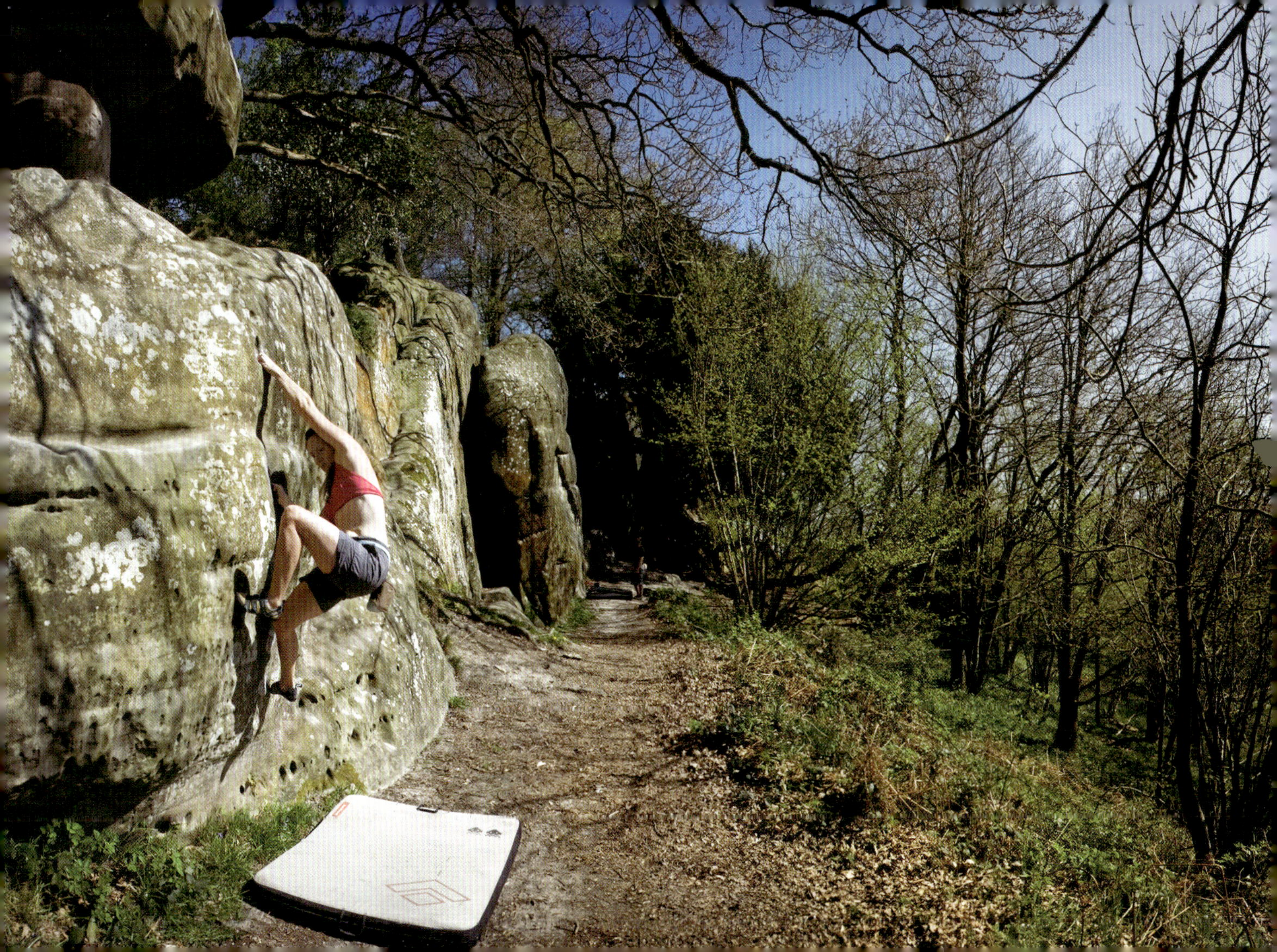

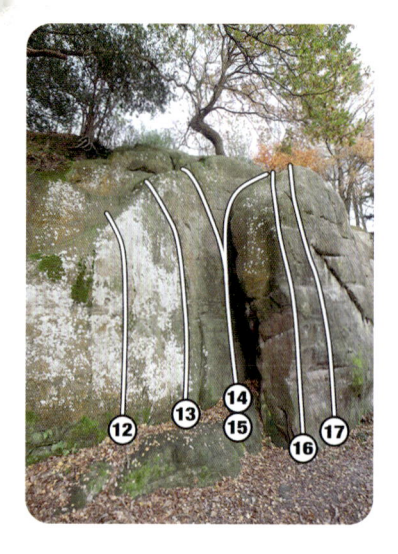

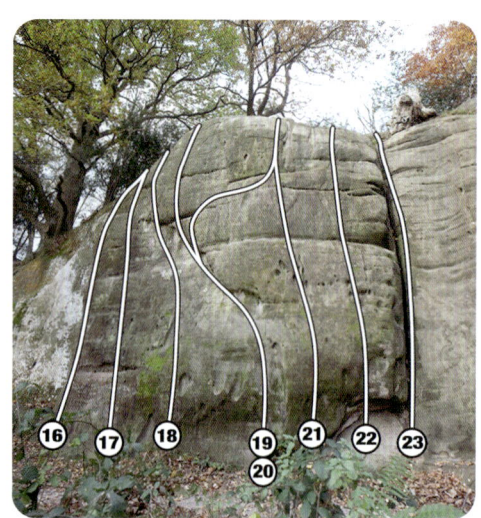

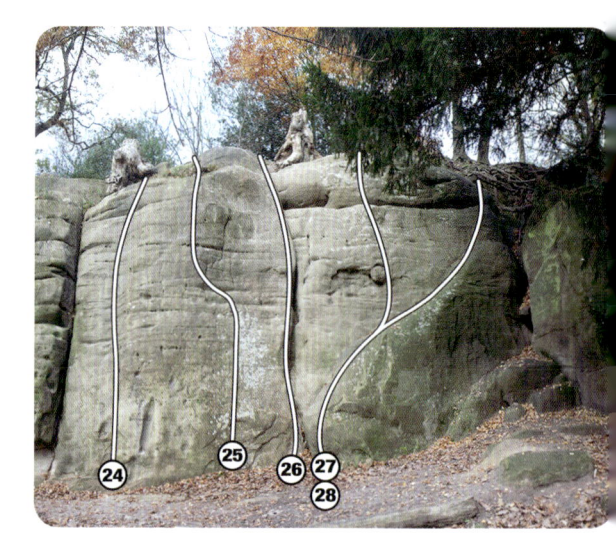

12. 6A+
Thin moves up the white wall above a bad landing. Finish on jugs at the back of the large ramp.

13. 6A
Nice layback moves up the flakes. Be careful of the landing.

14. 6B+ ⓗ
Start up the crack and the take the line of flakes up left near the top. Highball problem with a bad landing.

15. 2
Climb the crack/gully easily up to the top.

16. 6B *Chalk 'n' Cheese* ⓗ
Hard climbing up the arête, finish on the slab above without using any of the holds from the crack.

17. 6B+ *Kathmandu* ⓗ
Just right of the arête via some poor holds with a scary top out.

18. 6A+ ⓗ
Hard start leads to better holds and a highball finish.

19. 6A ⓗ
Follow the undercut flakes all the way to the top of the wall.

20. 6A+ *Cat Wall* ⓗ
Start the same as **19** up the flakes and then branch off right via some good holds in the breaks.

21. 6B ⓗ
Start just right of the flakes, climb straight up the wall via some hard climbing leading to a highball finish.

25　*Stone Farm*

22. 5+
Easy line just left of the crack using good but hidden holds.

23. 4 *Stone Farm Crack*
Nice crack line straight up the middle of the buttress.

24. 5+
Great technical slab line just right of the crack.

25. 6B+ *Biometric Slab*
Awesome slab line, holds from the crack on the right are out of bounds.

26. 4+
Crack line with a highball finish.

27. 5
Start up the ramp and then climb straight up via the smiley face hold.

28. 3
Follow the ramp all the way to the top of the wall using roots to finish.

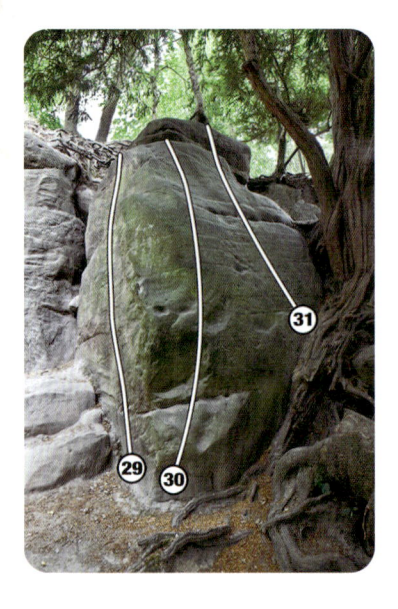

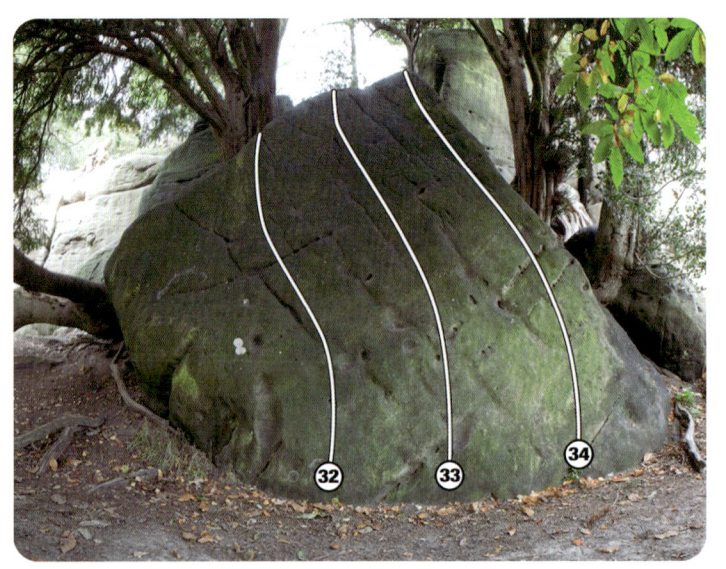

29. 5+
Climb just left of the arête.

30. 4+
Start up the arête then finish on the slab.

31. 3
Short wall above the roots of the tree.

32. 3
The left hand line of the diamond trio.

33. 3
Up the middle of the diamond boulder.

34. 2
Climb just to the left of the arête via some incut holds.

35. 6A+ *Yew Just Crimp*
Climb this short wall via some crimpy moves.

36. 6A *Yew Arête*
Climb the arête of the wall with a bad landing onto the roots.

Stone Farm

37. 6B+ *Yew Wall*
Climb up the centre of this wall via some hard moves. Highball with a bad landing.

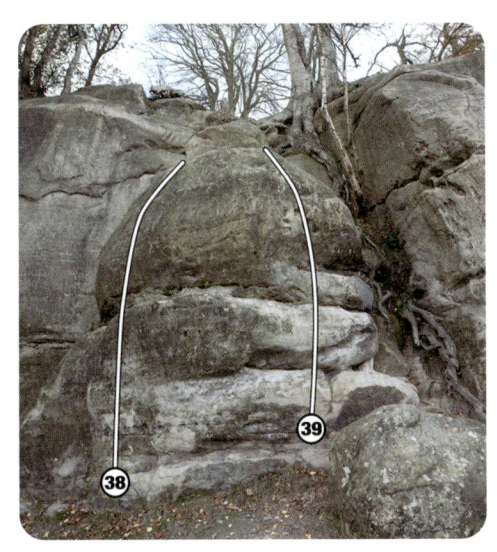

38. 6B
Hard slopey climb up the small boulder.

39. 6A+
Sandy climb up the right hand side of this boulder.

*There are a few climbs in between these boulders but these are too high to be considered boulder problems.

Christopher 'Orc' Searle | Yew Just Crimp | 6A

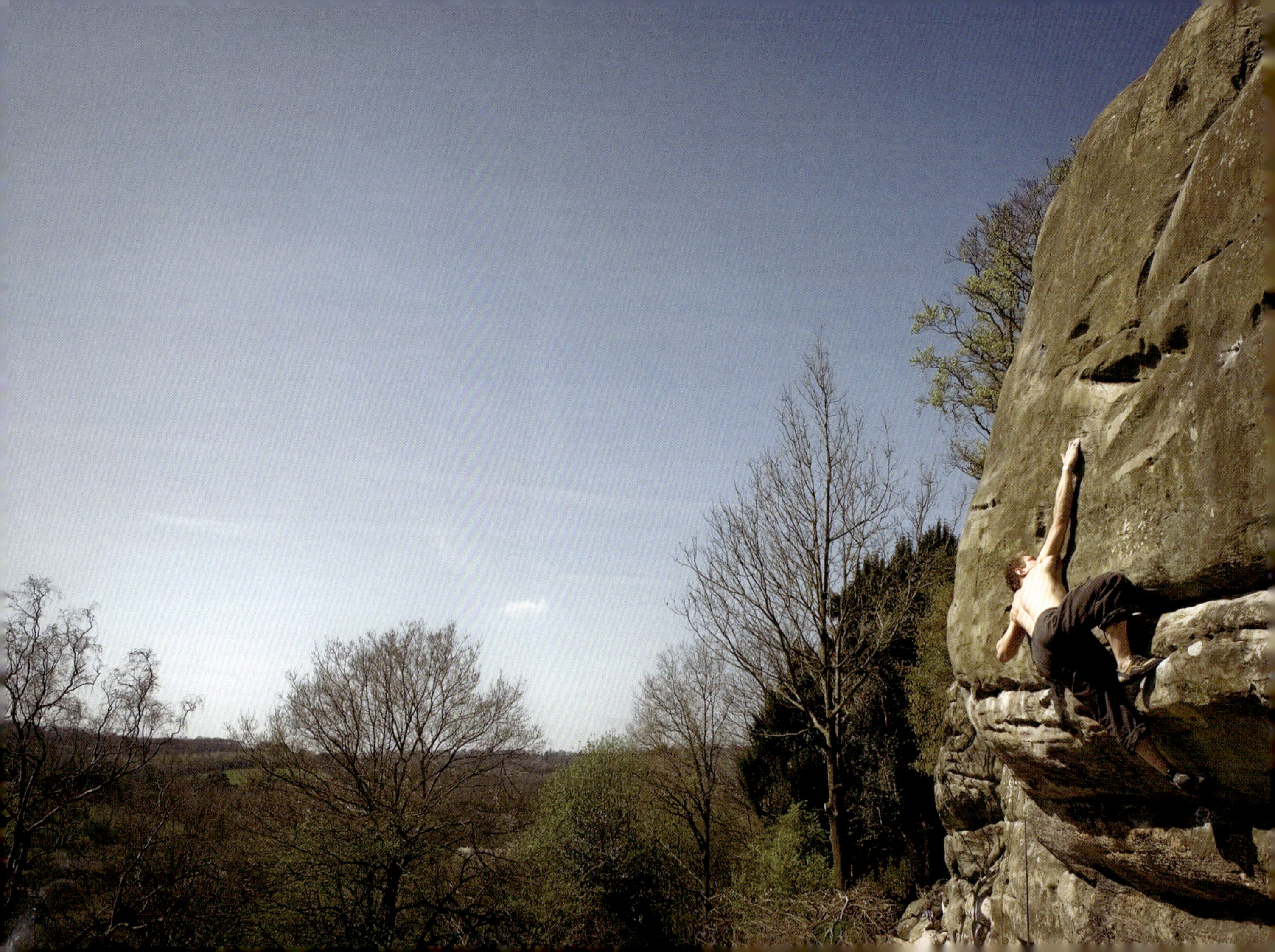

40. 5 *Thin*
Climb the arête via some nice lay-aways and positive holds.

41. 6B
Delicate climbing leads to an easy top out.

42. 6B+
Take the direct line off of route **41** to finish at the top of the wall. A hard last move and a bad landing mean that this is not one to be taken lightly.

43. 3 *Curling Crack*
A classic stone farm crack. Positive holds inside and beside the crack make this a very enjoyable little climb.

44. 6B
Not really a boulder problem but has been done as one before. Hard climbing up the middle of the wall without the arête. Lots of friends with lots of pads is advised before setting off.

45. 6A
The easiest line up the left hand of this buttress with a stiff top out.

46. 3+
Big holds all the way up make this a great introduction to the spicy world of highball bouldering.

47. 3
Easier than **46** but of poorer quality. Good holds direct you to the top.

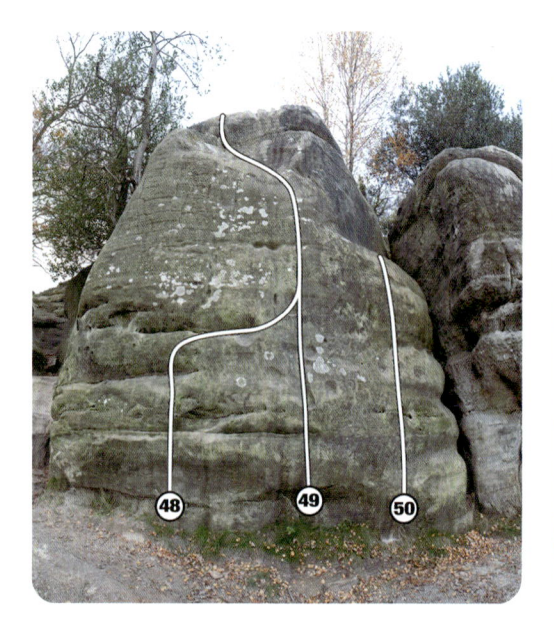

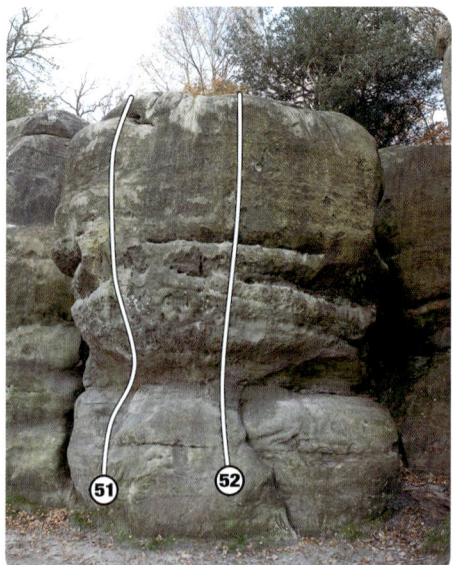

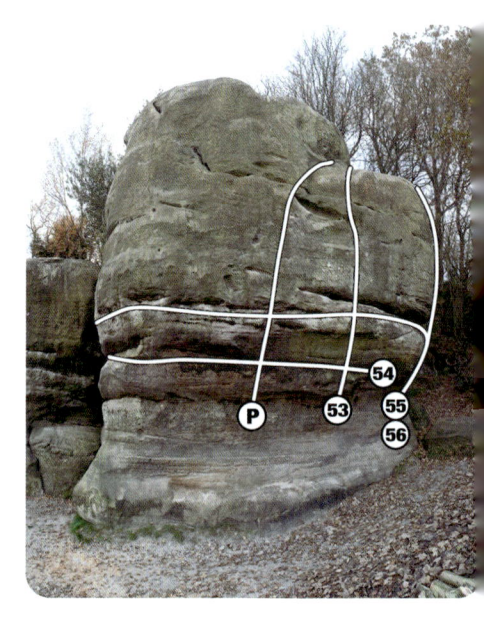

48. 5
Nice climbing low down leads to a balancy and airy finish.

49. 5+
The direct start to **48** makes this a technical route all the way.

50. 5
An easy start leads to a sting in the tail with a tricky mantle.

51. 6A *Bare Necessities*
Brilliant arête climbing with a good flat landing. A sand free sloper leads to an easier escape.

52. 6B
Hard climbing up the middle of this wall with a harsh top out.

Project.
The hardest line at stone farm via a massive reach off of poor holds. Can be finished direct or dart off right to finish up *Quoi Faire*.

53. 7B *Quoi Faire*
From the break fire upwards passing a good right hand hold. Finish either back left or direct over the bulge.

54. 7A *L'ottimista*
Staying on the left side of the arête. Make reachy moves to a sloping top out.

55. 5
Traverse R-L pleasant warm up for the harder climbs above.

56. 6A+
Traverse R-L more of a burly traverse as footholds can be hard to see.

Stone Farm

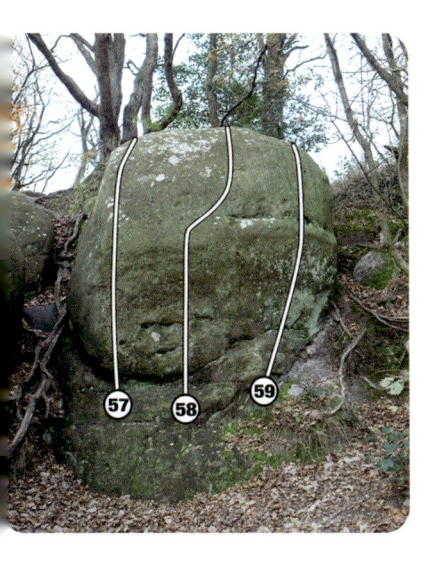

Full length Girdle
Form the start of **55** it is possible to traverse the majority of the way down the crag finishing by *Yew Wall* **37**. This makes a great adventure with some tricky moves crossing the highball slabs. It is possible to get further with some creative boulder jumping. Great fun for a bit of a warm up or warm down challenge.

57. 6B
The first of this trio of hard routes. Poor climbing up the left hand side of this stand alone boulder.

58. 6B+
The middle line straight up the boulder.

59. 6B
The right hand side provides this poor quality problem on bad rock.

60. 3+
The slab on the left of the Milestone boulder gives a nice delicate little number.

61. 3
Nice climbing on positive holds up the left hand side.

62. 3+
Traverse the break and finish up the front on in cut holds.

63. 6B+ *Milestone Mantle*
The undercut boulder provides a hard pull to get off the ground that defeats many climbers. Being taller definitely helps as the ground has worn away considerable amounts over the years.

64. 7B *The Painkiller* ss
The sit start to milestone mantle. From the right hands side get established on the sloper before flicking out to the left hand side and slap your way up to victory.

65. 6A+
Some tricky moves via the large hole finishing up the groove to the top.

Stone Farm

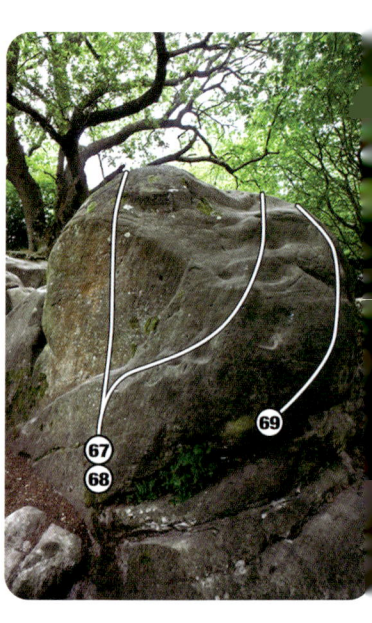

66. 3
Easy climb up the small boulder.

67. 2
Nice slab with goods holds most of the way up.

68. 2
Starting the same as **67** follow the ramp rightwards to the top.

69. 4+
Climb up the nose with some tricky moves to mount the beast.

Ben Read | The Painkiller | 7B

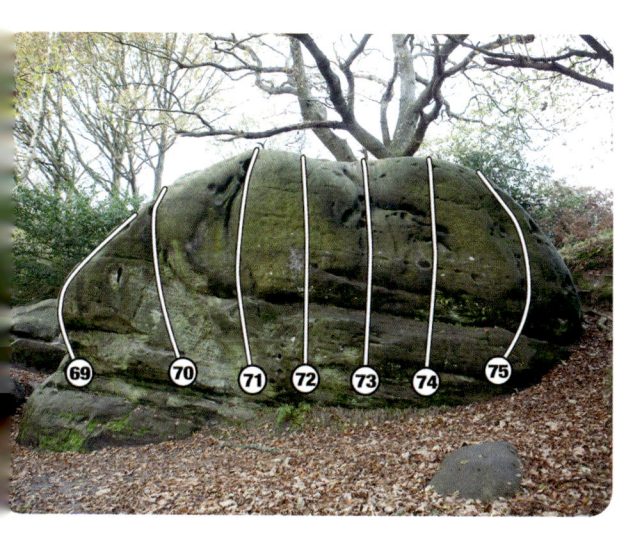

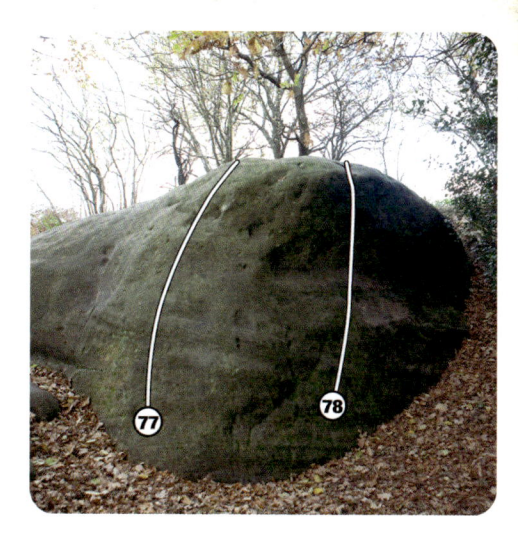

70. 4+
   The left hand side provides a nice climb.

71. 5
   Climb straight up to the large crack.

72. 7A
   An eliminate up the middle of the wall not using the large holds on both sides.

73. 5
   Easy climb up the middle on good holds.

74. 3+
   Just right of **73** gives another pleasant climb.

75. 4
   Climb straight up the right hand side.

76. 3+
   On the back side of the boulder has this little slab climb.

77. 1
   A short easy slab climb that is great for kids to play on.

78. 1
   Just to the right is another easy climb that is great for kids.

Stone Farm 34

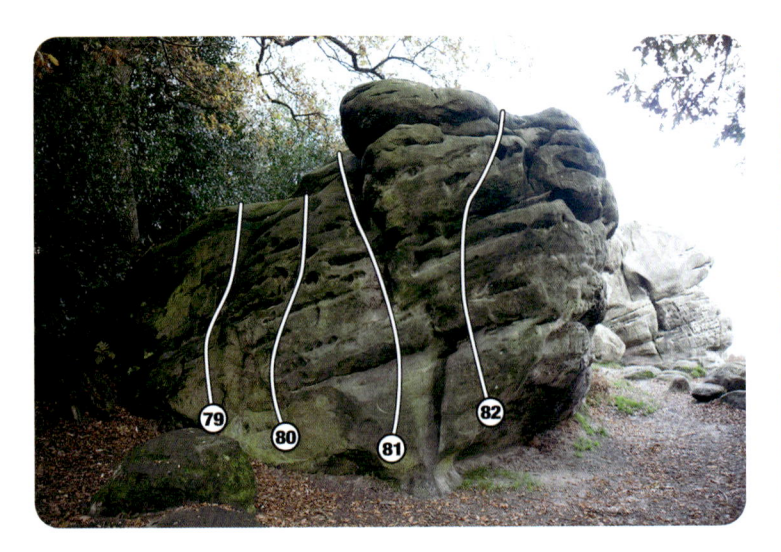

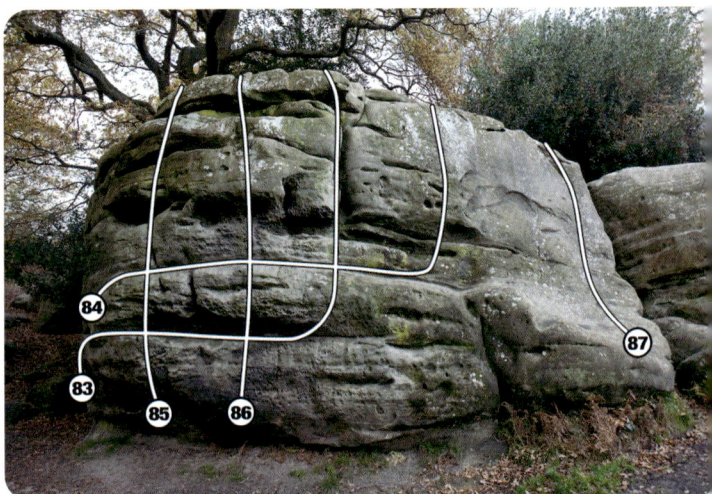

79. 3
Hidden in the shade is this easy little climb.

80. 3
Good holds lead all the way to the top.

81. 3
Climb up the groove with big holds everywhere you look.

82. 4+
Just right of the groove climb up trending rightwards to the top of the boulder.

83. 6A *ss*
Starting on the sloping holds at the bottom of the ramp, traverse rightwards at the same level to finish up the crack.

84. 6B
Starting on the right hand side, traverse the sloping break all the way along to the ramp at the end.

85. 6A *ss*
Climb up the good holds from the undercut start. There are many eliminates on this wall that you can spend hours playing on.

86. 5+
A direct line using a mixture of slopers and good edges.

87. 2
Easy slab. For added style points try this without any hands.

Stone Farm

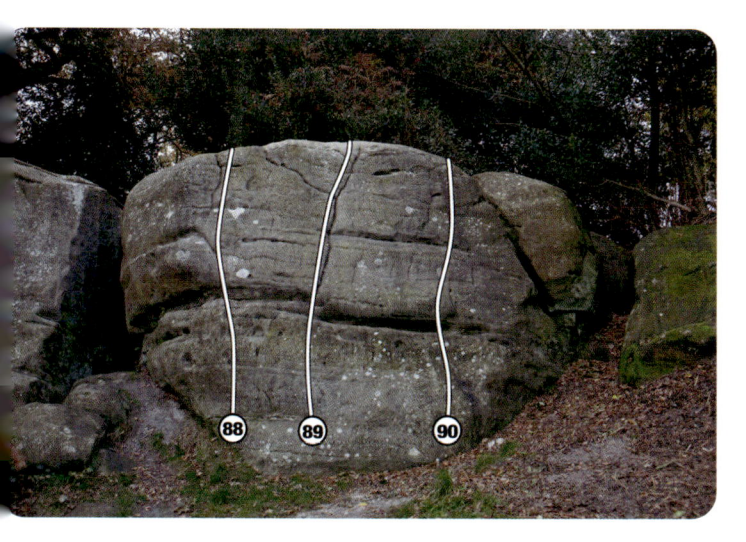

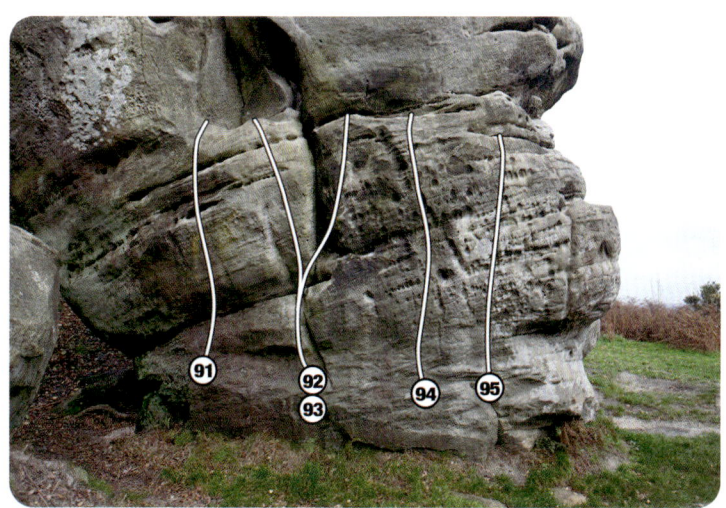

88. 2
The left side of the easy face.

89. 3
Direct up the centre.

90. 2
The right hand side! Woohoo!

91. 5
The mildly overhanging wall, making big moves on positive holds to finish in the groove.

92. 4+ ss
Straight up the crack to the groove.

93. 5 ss
The right hand side of the crack finishing on a good hold.

94. 5+
Direct up the pocket laden face using anything you can get your hands on.

95. 5+
Just to the right of **94** is another pocket covered climb.

Stone Farm 36

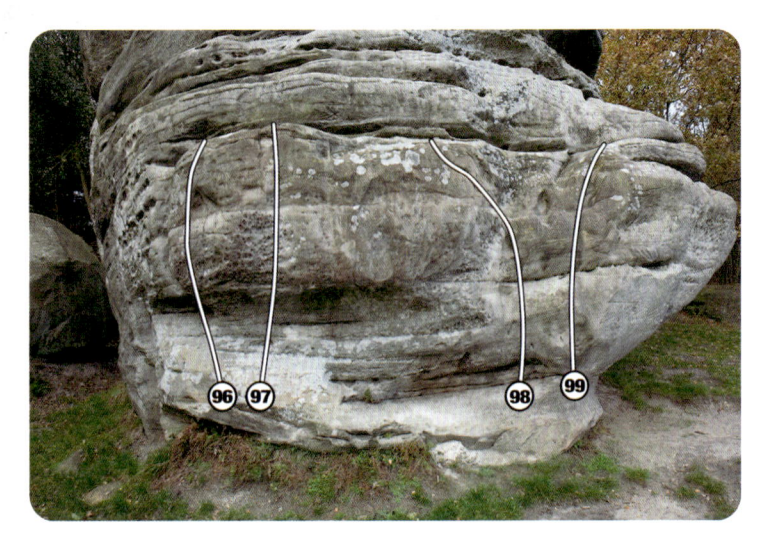

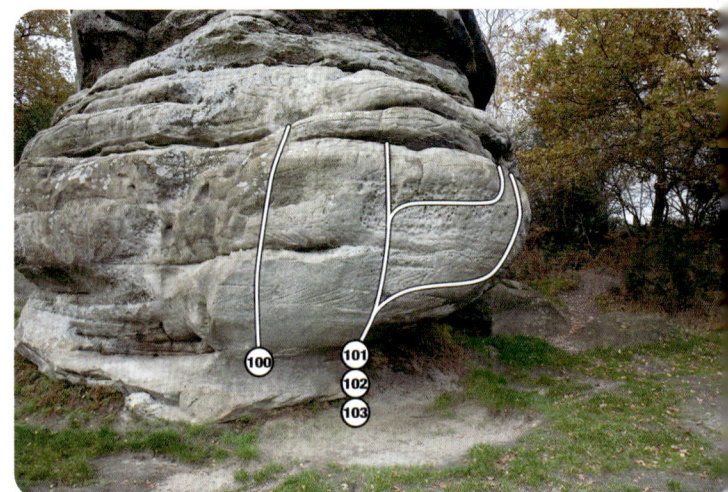

96. 6A
Climb the blunt arête on slopey side pulls to an interesting finish.

97. 6A
Another great little climb that can be very frustrating when you don't know the beta.

98. 5+
Starting in the break trend diagonally left.

99. 3+
The easy way up or down.

100. 5+
Starting in the break make a big move to the, tough to hang, slopey top out.

101. 6B ss
Starting in the large pocket, reach to the good edge and make a flick to the top.

102. 6B+ ss
Starting as **101**, from the good edges take the large side pull and move right wards to finish up Stinging Nettle.

103. 6C+ *Stinging Nettle Variation* ss
From a sit start, slap up with the left hand to a good edge. Then by some big slaps round to the right it is possible to surmount the nose!

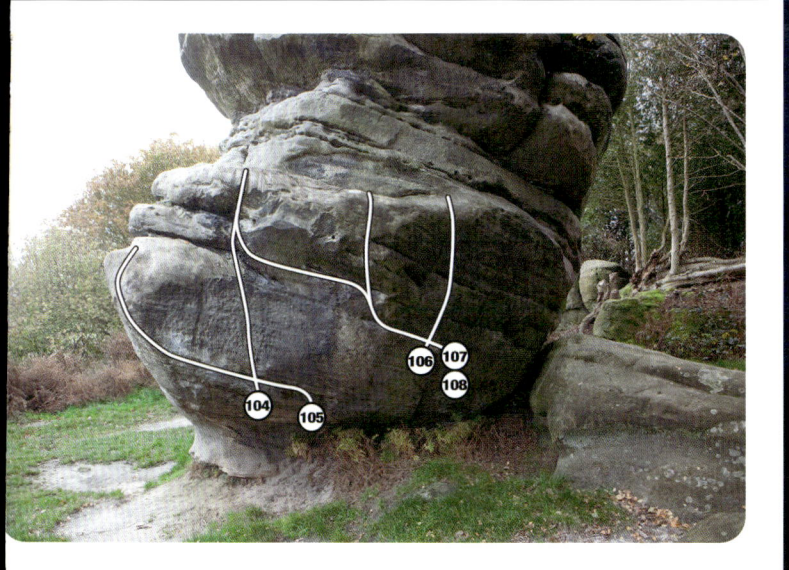

104. 4
The easiest way up the East face.

105. 7A *Stinging Nettle* ss
The original *Stinging Nettle* that is often forgotten.

106. 6A
A crouching start leads to a hard mantle.

107. 6B
Hard pulls to start then traverse left to finish easily up **104**.

108. 6B
Start as **106** but take an early exit to a tricky mantle.

James O'Nell | Stinging Nettle Variation | 6C+

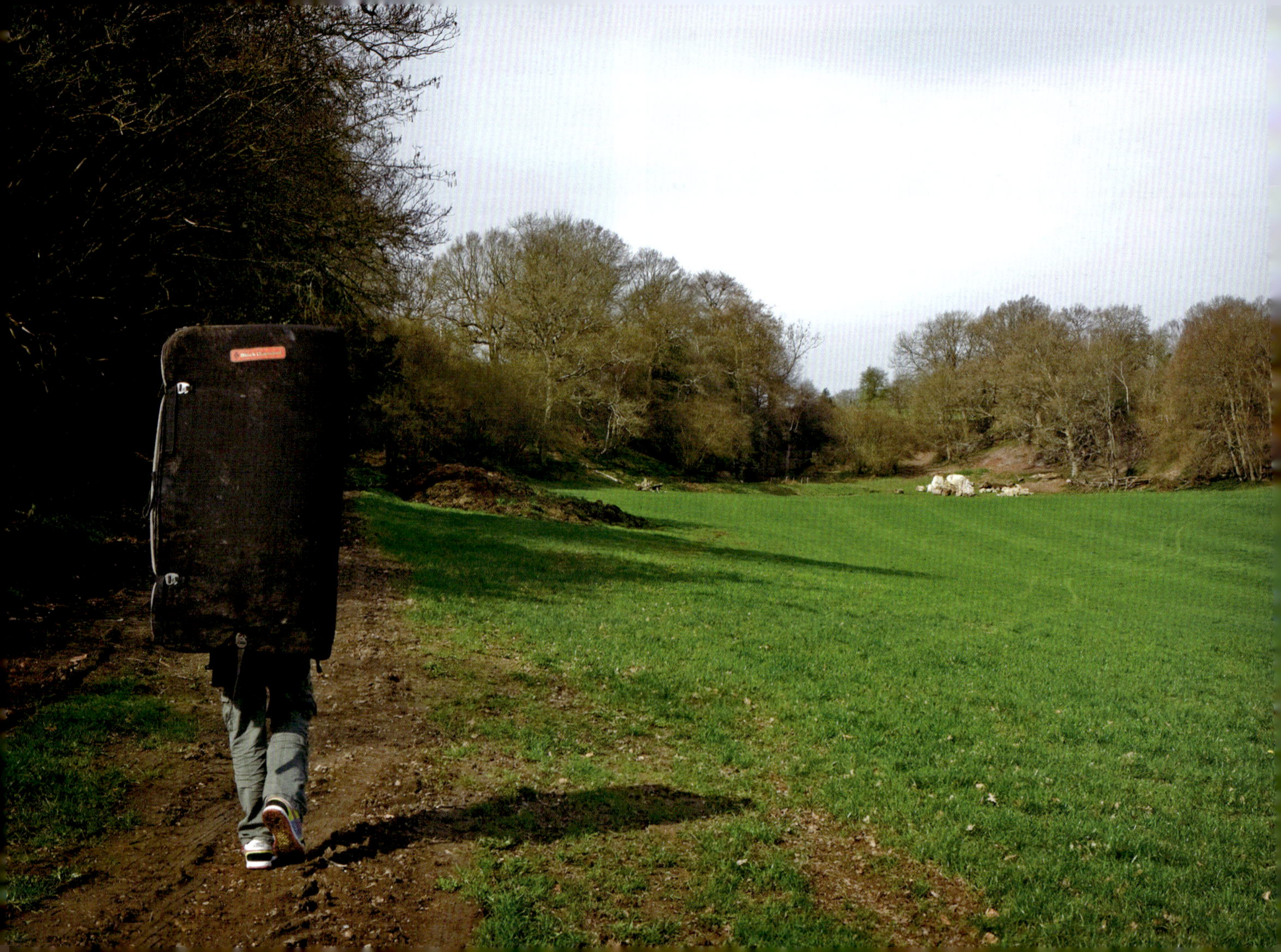

BASSETT'S FARM

INTRODUCTION

This small wall is of unique quality for a number of reasons. The red colour of the sandstone makes it stand out in the fields that surround it and catches your eye as you cross the footpath.

The bouldering here is very limited due to the small amount of rock present but the few traverse lines that we have listed make for great little adventures across the main wall.

ACCESS AND APPROACH

From Tunbridge Wells head west along the A264. You will then need to take the B2026 signposted for Edenbridge. Follow this road until you a greeted by a sign for Cowden Rail station, take this turning and continue along looking for a small road on your right hand side called Moat Lane. Take this turning and continue for about 1.5 miles along this small country road. Parking for this crag is very limited but there are a few bays by the entrance of the footpath at a sharp right hand bend. Further parking can be found if you continue down the road.

For the crag follow the marked footpath across the large field and the crag should come into view as you wander down towards the woods at the end.

CONDITIONS

Because of its open setting the rock tends to dry reasonably quickly but again as with all crags please be cautious if it has rained recently. The wall tends to be best climbed during the summer months and can be very peaceful in the evenings during sunset.

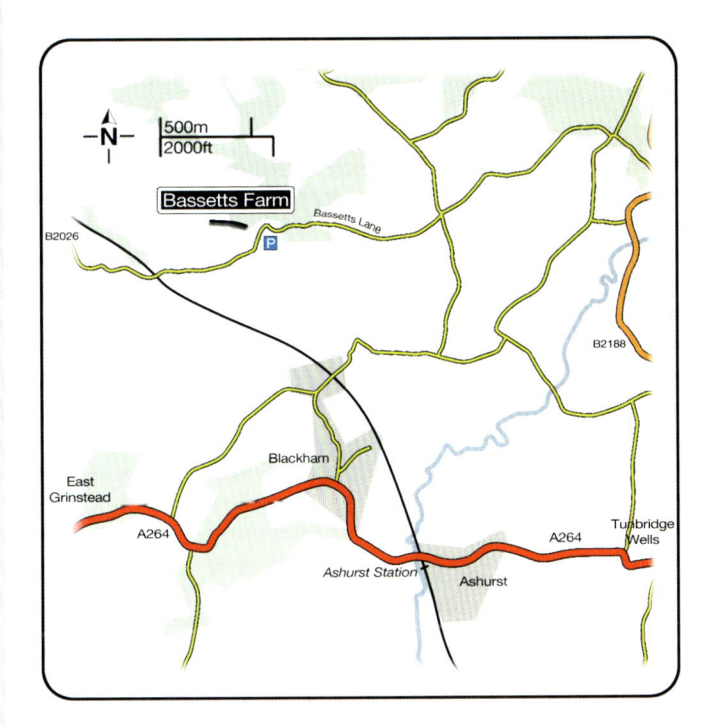

B2026

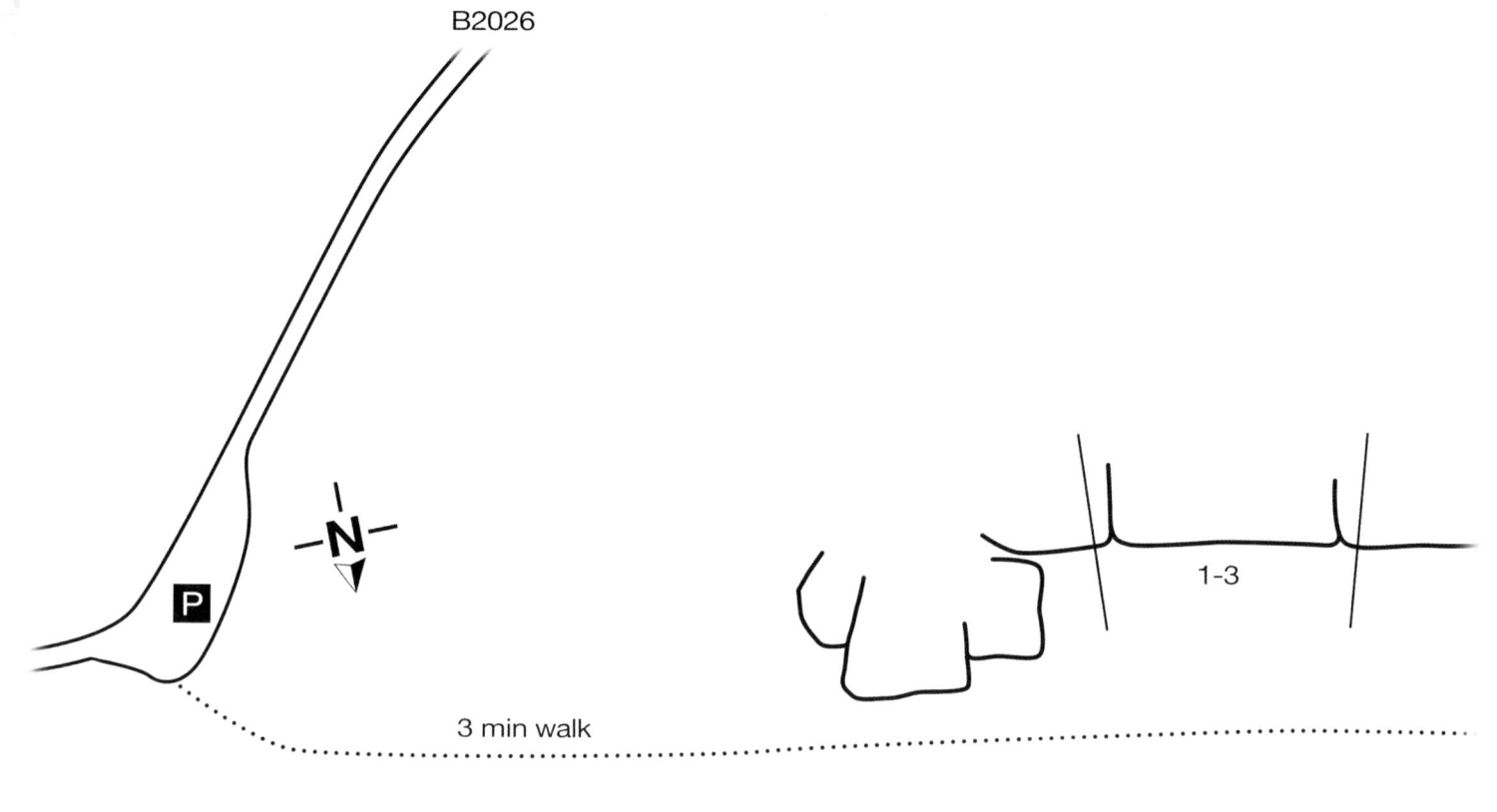

P

N

3 min walk

1-3

41 *Bassett's Farm*

1. **6B+** *Good Boy*
   This is a great traverse on positive holds and poor feet. Can be done both ways at no change to the grade.

2. **7A+** *Pirelli*
   The middle break line gives this hard traverse on small edges. It can be done both ways, but left to right is the easier line. From right to left is 7B.

3. **6A+**
   The highest break line of the three. This is an enjoyable traverse that takes the highest line of holds. Can be done both ways at no change to the grade.

James O'Neil | Route 3 | 6A+

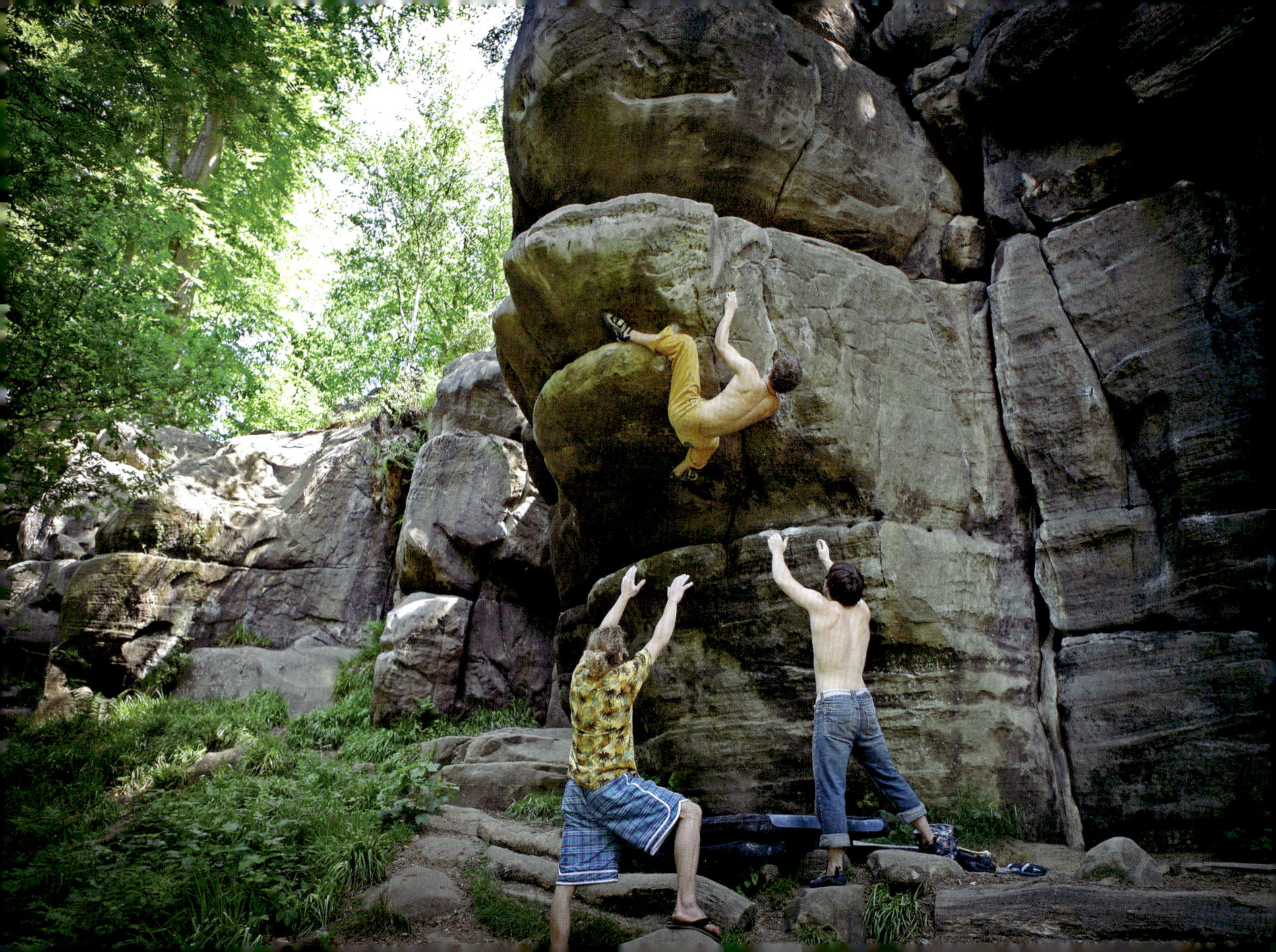

HARRISONS

INTRODUCTION

This is the largest crag of the area and has some classic boulder problems. The North boulder provides some great lines and will keep you busy for quite some time with something for everyone. This is one of the most well known areas in the sandstone and can get very busy during the summer months. This shouldn't put you off though as there are some great problems all the way along.

ACCESS AND APPROACH

From Groombridge village head towards Eridge up and over the railway bridge. Then take a right hand fork signposted for Eridge Station. About 200m on the right is the turning for Harrisons rocks that should be signposted. Follow this down to the car park and please park sensibly to allow room for other visitors.

Harrisons also offers a few facilities such as toilets, drinking water and camping. Please make sure you check the camping rules and pitch correctly. This is not a free car park or campsite and money will be collected or please use the honour box on the way out.

CONDITIONS

The majority of the climbs are kept wet during the colder months due to the crag being quite sheltered because of its surroundings. However lots of work is being done to open the area up so that it will dry out quicker. The North boulder is normally the first bit to dry out but this does still require a week of good weather for it to become fully climbable. This crag is steeped with history so please do not risk ruining any of these problems by climbing on the damp rock.

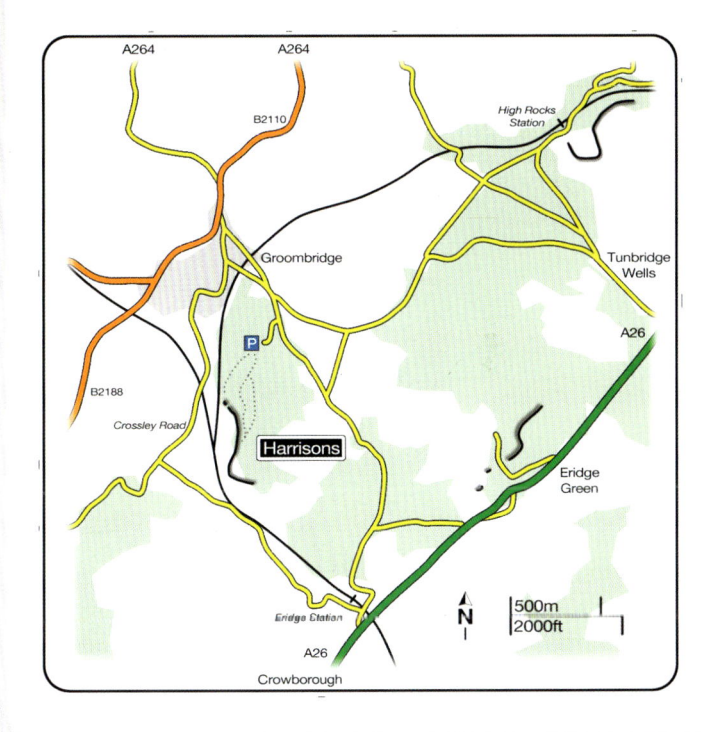

Dan Moore | Route 104 | 6A+

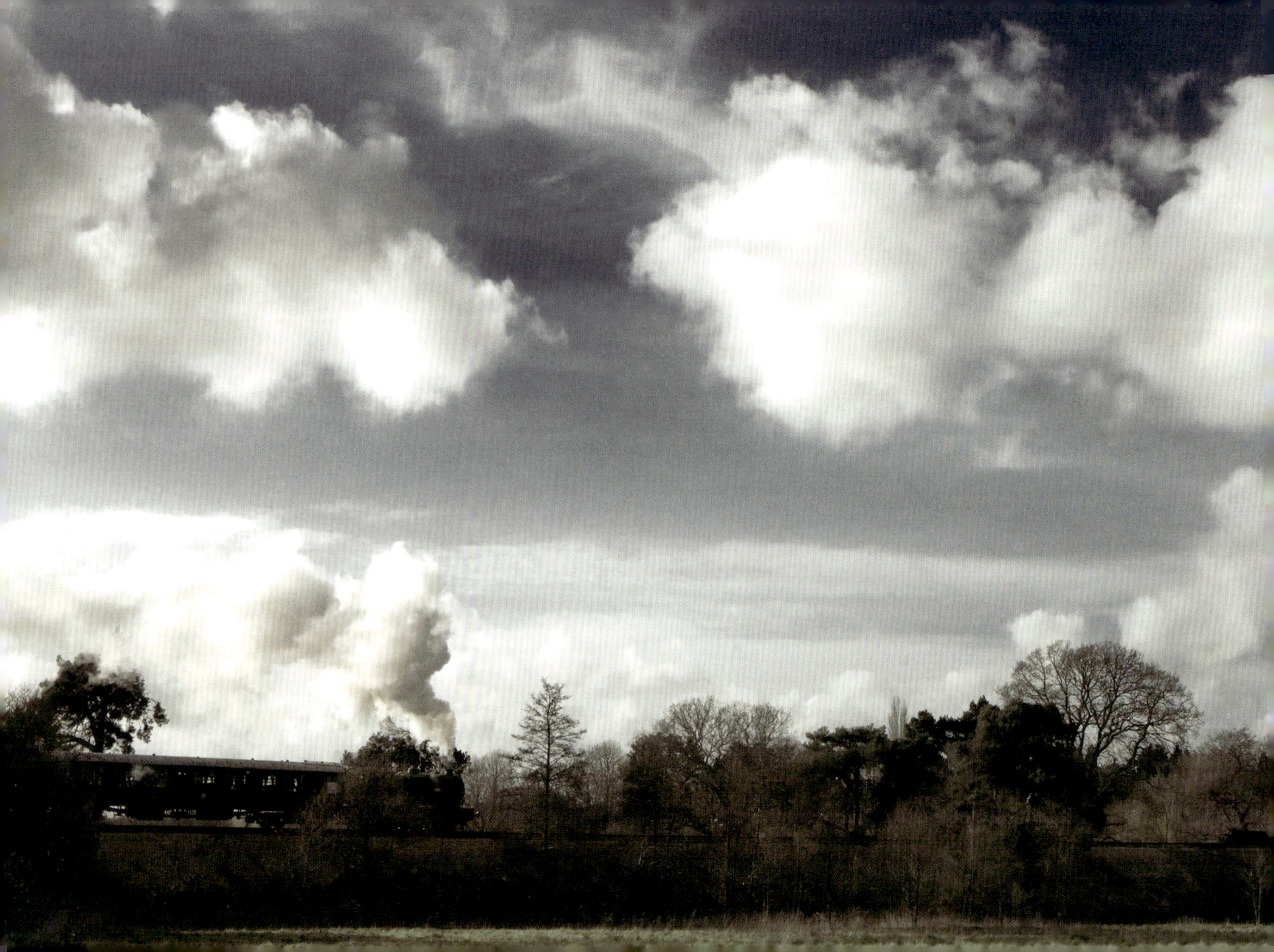

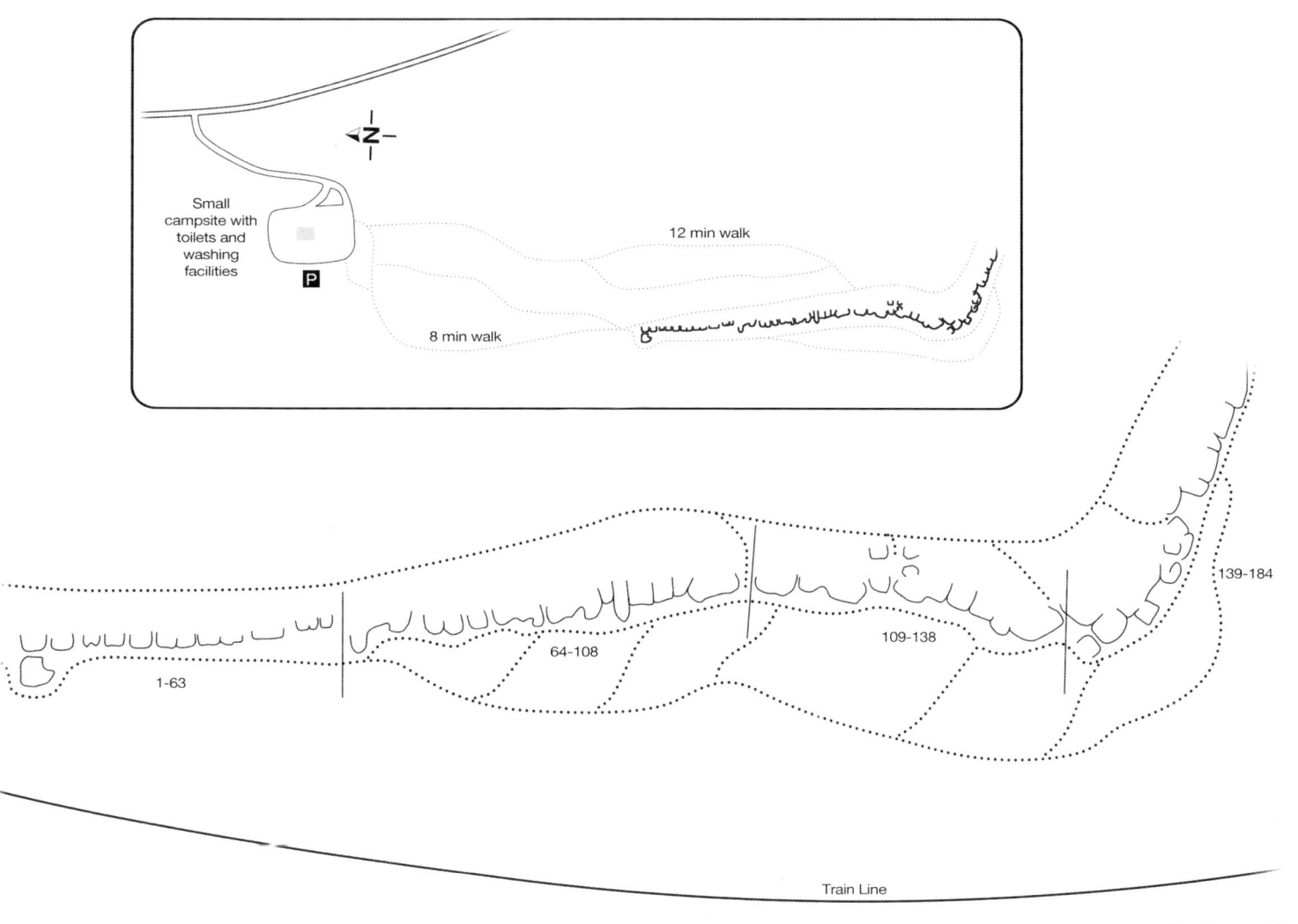

Small campsite with toilets and washing facilities

N

12 min walk

8 min walk

1-63

64-108

109-138

139-184

Train Line

Harrisons 46

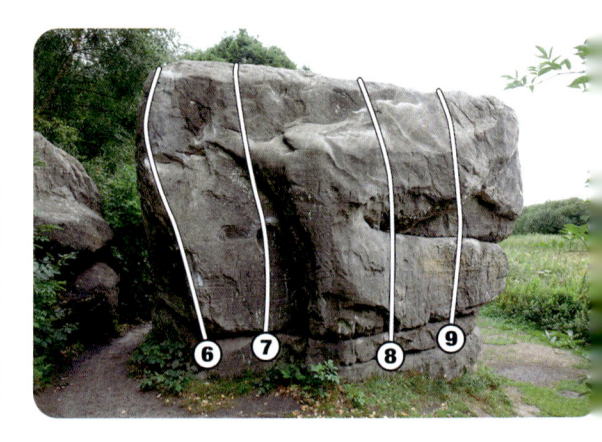

1. 3+
   The short wall on the left hand side as you walk in.

2. 2+
   Up on to the ledge and then onwards to the top.

3. 4+
   The arête climbed mainly on the left.

4. 6B
   Straight up the blank face.

5. 6B
   A crimpy wall with a flick to the top.

6. 6B *ss*
   A fun little climb up the arête that greets you as you enter Harrisons.

7. 4
   Climb up to the ledge and use this to top out.

8. 4+
   From the ledge climb up and over.

9. 5
   Climb up the face via the undercut feature.

The Castle Climbing Centre

Great Route Setting

Climbing Shop & Organic Cafe

www.Castle-climbing.co.uk

Carbon Neutral, Water Neutral, Zero Waste by 2015

Find us on Facebook

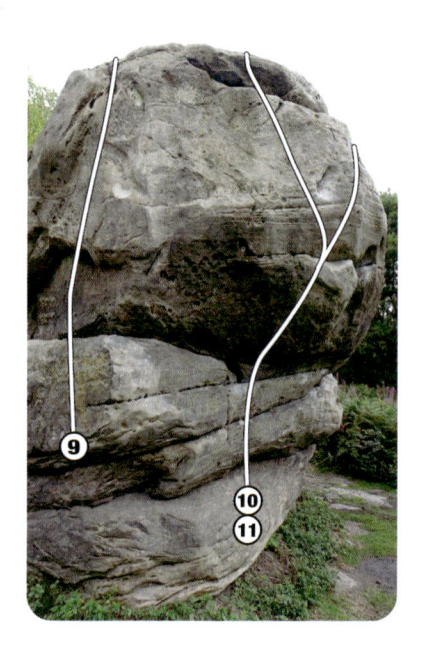

10. 6A+ *Torque Wrench left*
A classic of the boulder, climb up via the finger slot.

11. 6A+ *Torque Wrench right*
Climb up using the finger slot with the left hand.

12. 7A *Finger Flow*
Climb up to the right of the thin layaways. The hardest straight up on this boulder.

13. 5+
Follow the line of good holds up the groove.

14. 6C *Strong Struggle*
Climb straight up the middle of the face.

15. 6B
From the good flake climb either direct up or exit off right at the same grade.

16. 6B+
Climb up to the tricky slopey exit.

17. 6B *The Sheriff*
The blunt nose is a classic little climb with a tricky top out. No sneaking off round the right.

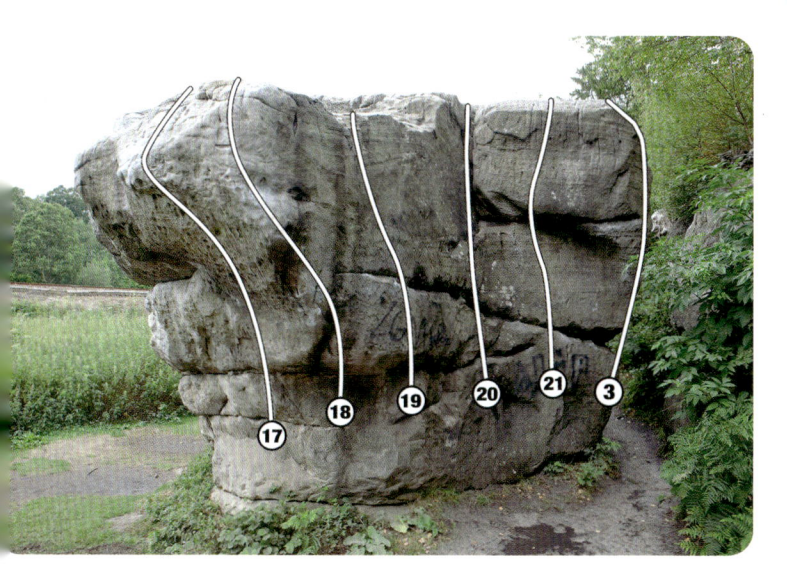

18. 6A
The wall just right of the nose.

19. 3+
Up the wall starting on the break.

20. 2+
Climb up the corner via breaks and the flake to exit.

21. 5+
Climb up the wall just in between the corner and the arête.

*You can also traverse around the whole boulder for a pumpy 6C.

Jan Grove | The Sheriff | 6B

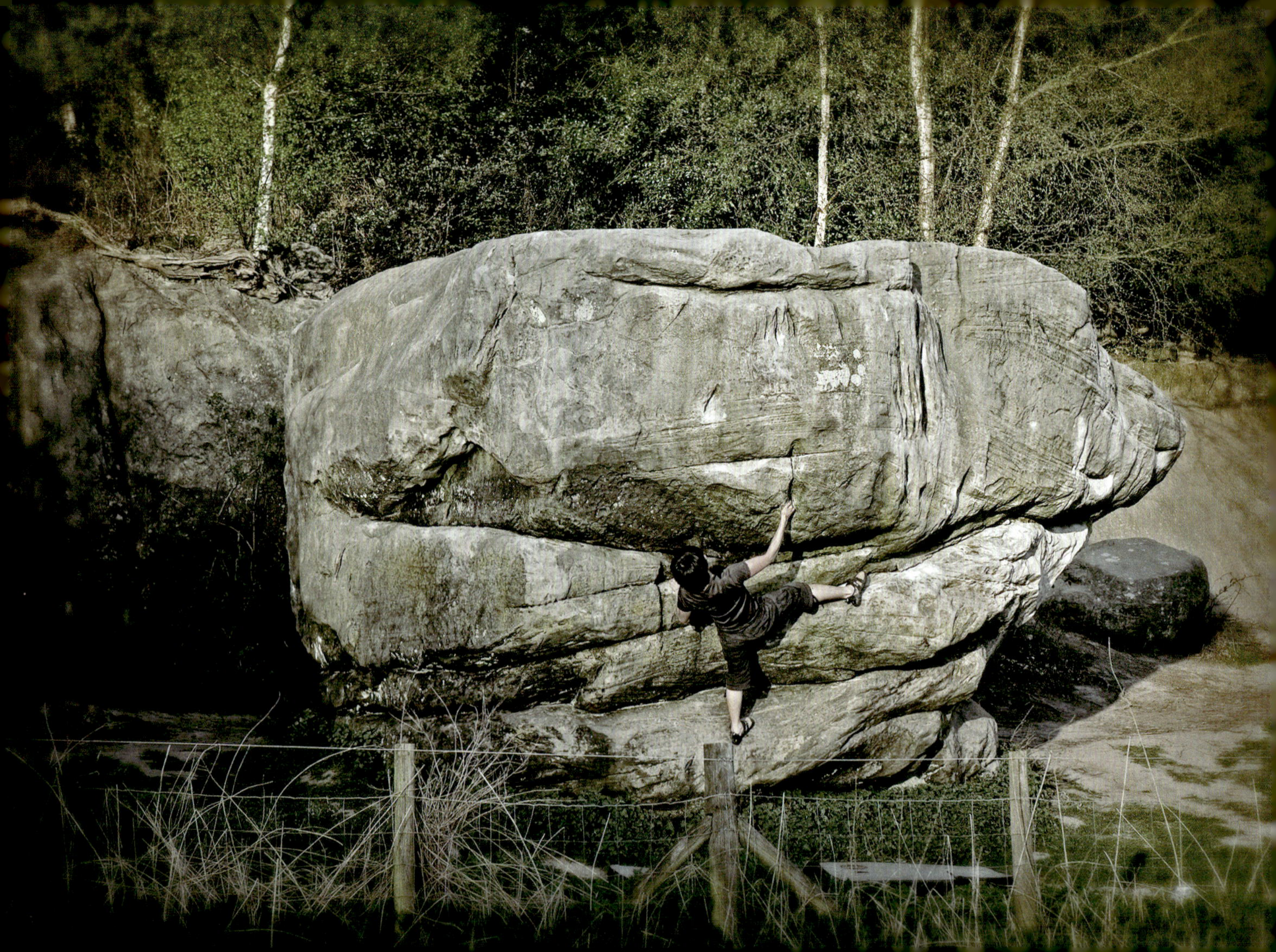

22. 1
   The left hand end of the slab.

23. 1
   Straight up the middle of the face.

24. 1
   The right hand end of the slab.

Andrew Tong | Torque Wrench Right | 6A+   Joshua Crouch | Route 24 | 1

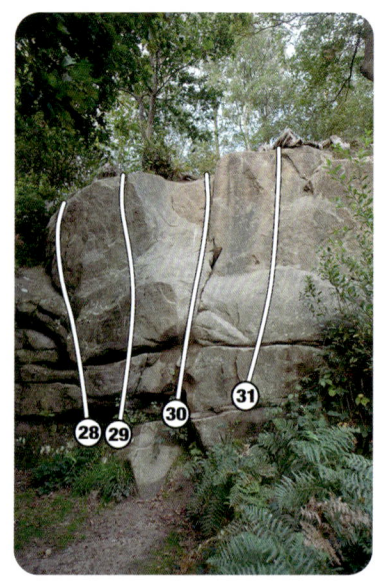

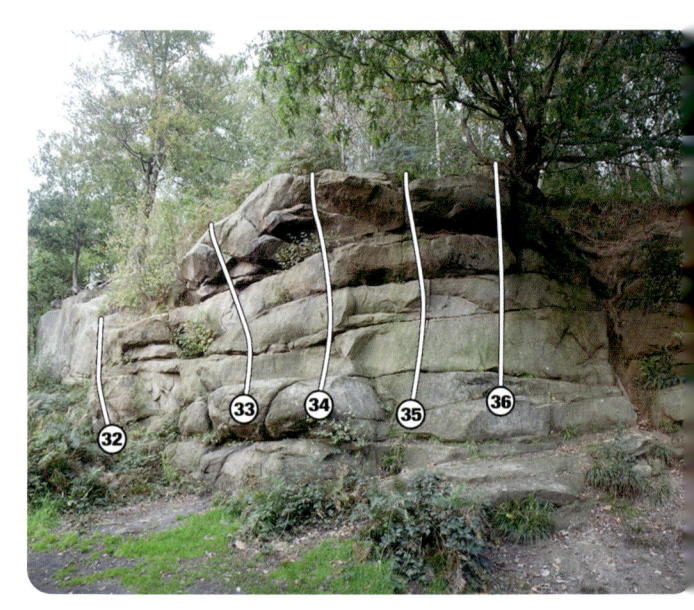

25. 2
Climb up the wall just left of the crack.

26. 2
Climb the corner crack line.

27. 3
Climb the wall to the right of the crack line.

28. 2
Climb up the diagonal crack and ramp.

29. 5+
Up on to the ledge and then up the crimps on the face to a slopey top out.

30. 2+
A hard start leads to an easier finish up the corner.

31. 3
Climb up the right hand wall using the tree root at the top.

32. 2
The short easy wall on the left hand end.

33. 2
Climb up the series of ledges.

34. 3
Up the ledges to the small roof which provides the hardest moves.

35. 3
Another easy climb up the right hand side.

36. 3
Climb up to the tree and use the roots to top out.

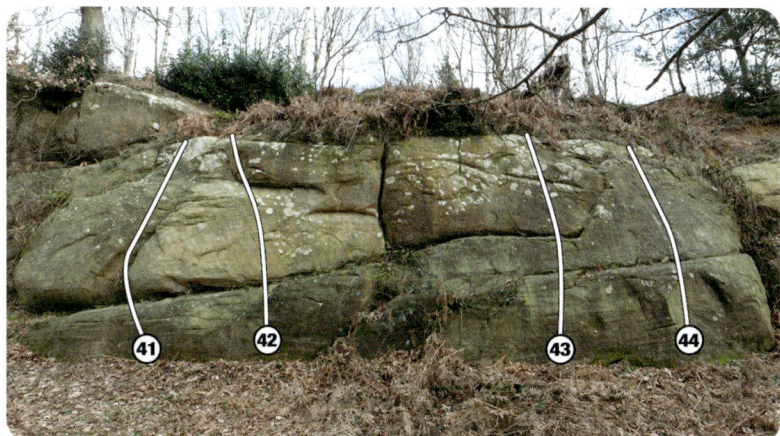

37. 1
A short easy climb.

38. 1
Climb up the blocky holds.

39. 1
Another easy climb.

40. 2
A hard start leads to a much easier top.

41. 3
Up on to the ledge then follow the crack.

42. 3
Climb up via the smooth undercut feature.

43. 2
The often green wall with the bush to top out in.

44. 3+
The balancy slab on the right.

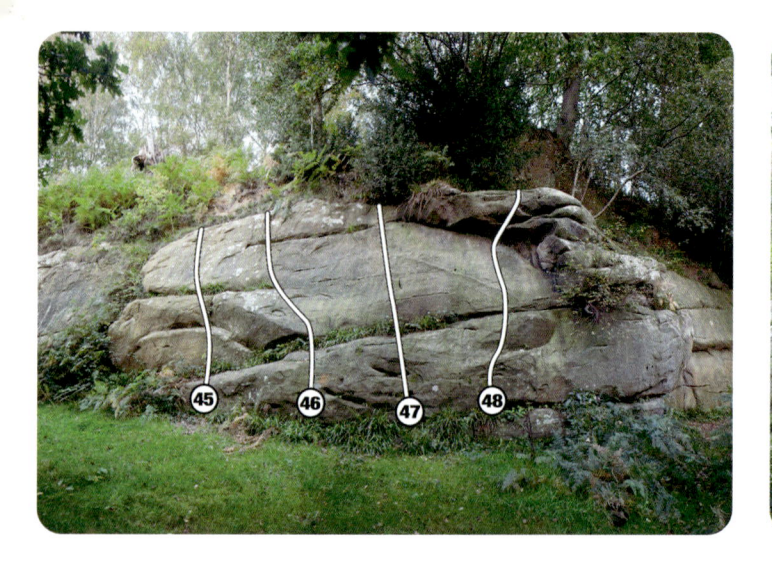

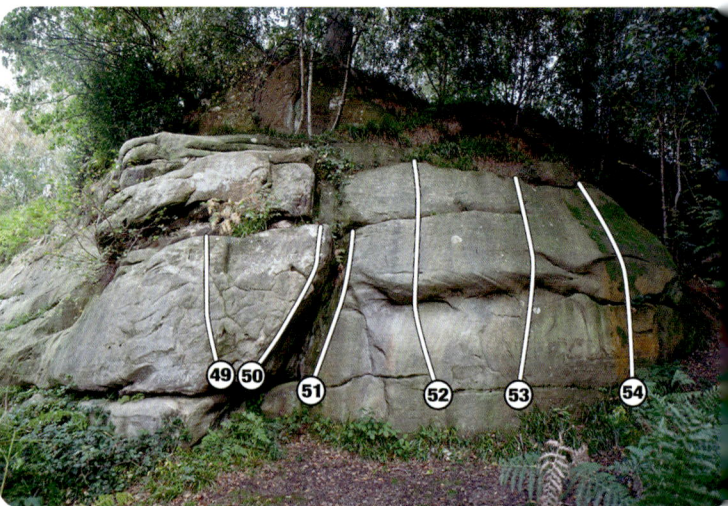

45. 2+
The large ledge to start and then up the wall.

46. 2
Climb up and then left up the slab.

47. 2+
Up the slab making use of the good sidepull.

48. 3
Up the slab and then exit off right over the small roof.

49. 4+
The short wall is more of a one move wonder. Can be done as a very bunched sit start at 6A+.

50. 6A+ ss
The small overhang has some great moves on it.

51. 3
Layback up the corner crack.

52. 5
Climb the small roof using a left hand undercut to start.

53. 5
The wall with some very rounded holds.

54. 4
Climb the right hand end of this wall. Often mossy and green.

55. 6C
The long traverse of the middle break. Start by the tree roots on the left and then work your way along with very poor footholds. Finish up the crack above number **56** or jump down.

56. 4
The large flat holds to start and then up via the pockets.

57. 5
Climb the wall via the layback hold.

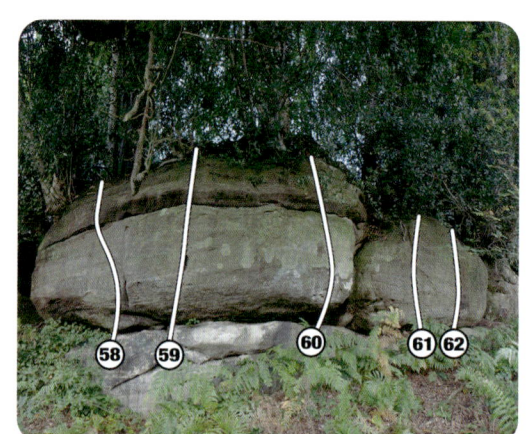

58. 6A
Using the slopey sidepull to start and then a flick to the break.

59. 6B
Using the hole and sidepull climb straight up with poor foot holds.

60. 6B
The arête and holds on the face.

61. 6A+
The short wall with a hard move to start.

62. 5+
Starting on the jug in the crack climb straight up.

63. 6B+ *ss*
Start on the side pulls and then up to a gaston in the groove and topping out in to the little wood.

Paul Houston | Route 69 | 6A

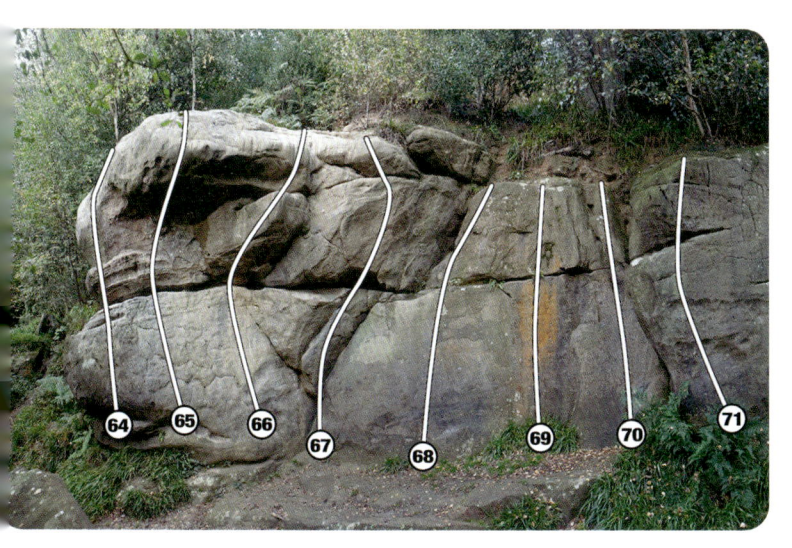

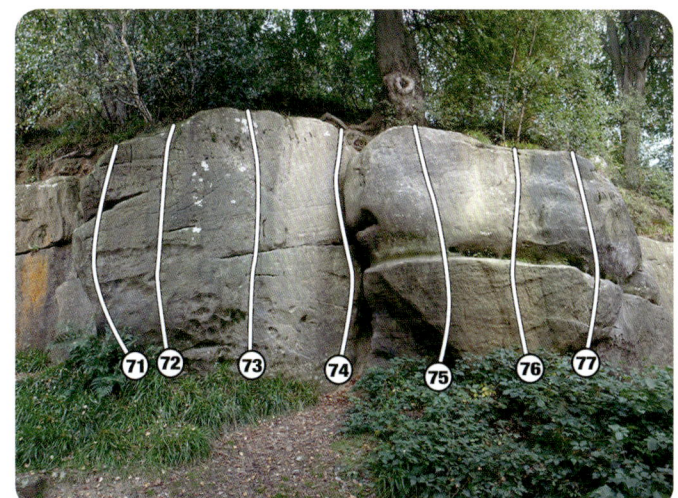

64. 6B
Tackle the bulge and roof with hidden pockets. A very bad landing.

65. 6A+
The roof with a slopey exit.

66. 5+
The easiest line through this wall.

67. 6A
The flakes and then up through steeper ground.

68. 2
An easy line up the corner.

69. 6A
A long reach or dyno between the breaks with poor foot holds.

70. 2+
The easy crack on the right.

71. 5+
The arête has some great moves up it on both sides.

72. 5
Climb up the face on slots and bad foot holds.

73. 5
The wall just to the right on good holds and big moves.

74. 3
A lovely little chimney.

75. 6B
A mantle to gain the ledge and then the shallow scoop to finish.

76. 5+
Another mantle but easier to gain ledge with aid of sloping incut holds.

77. 6A+
Straight up the steep bulge.

Harrisons 58

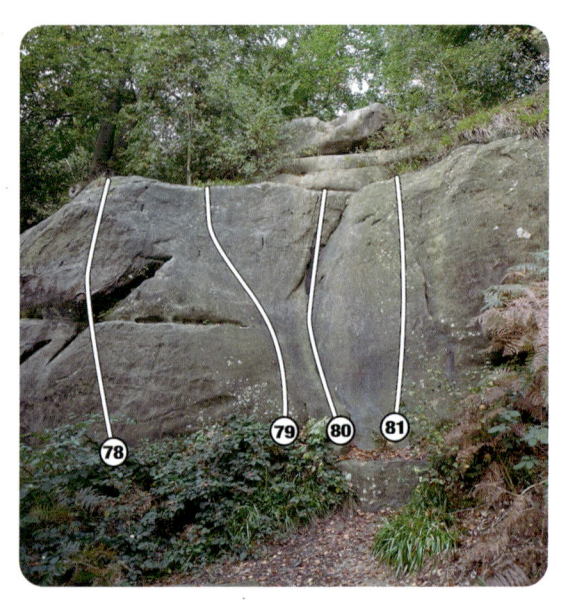

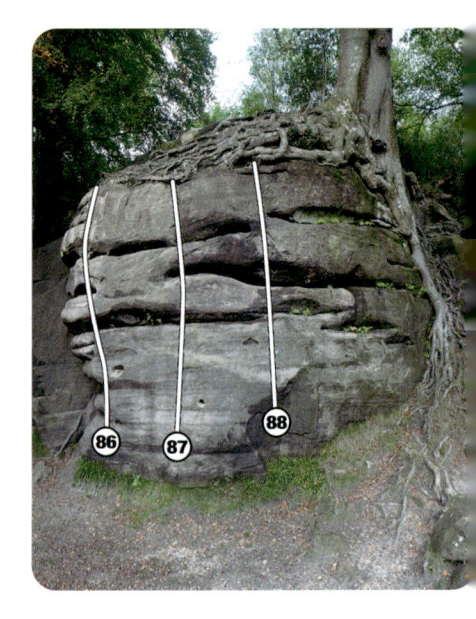

78. 6A+
The diagonal crack and bulge.

79. 3+
The smooth ramp and sidepull is a great little climb. Without use of the good sidepull makes this an interesting 5.

80. 4+
Climb up the slippery corner and crack.

81. 5+
Direct up the flake with poor foot holds.

82. 6A+
This climb has a slopey mantle to finish.

83. 6A *ss*
The undercut crack to start and harsh topout to finish.

84. 5+
Balance your way up the blunt arête.

85. 3+
Climb up the corner crack.

86. 5+
Climb up the large breaks which hold hidden holds.

87. 6A
The centre line of slopey breaks using the tree roots at the top.

88. 5
Good holds up the wall and use of the tree roots is allowed.

59 *Harrisons*

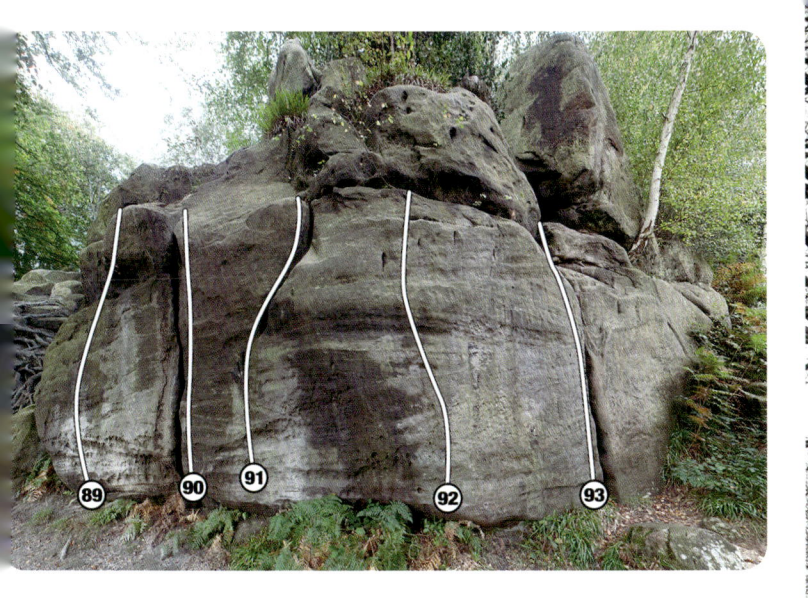

89. 6C+ *Soft Rock*
The blank looking wall has some very technical climbing on it up the thin pockets.

90. 5
Layback up the crack.

91. 5
Some great moves moving form flake to flake.

92. 6A
An interesting little route that is both balancy and powerful.

93. 4+
Layback all the way up the crack.

James O'Neil | Route 90 | 5

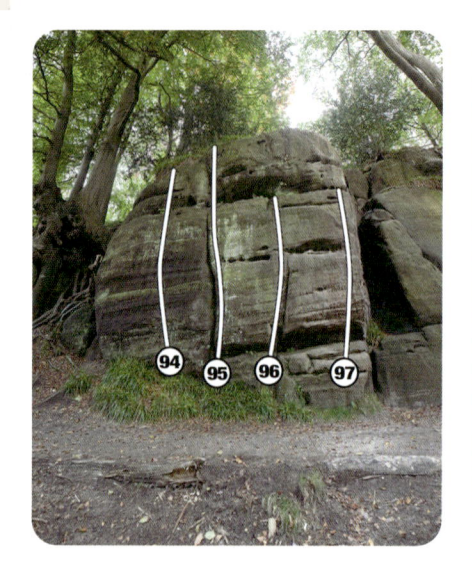

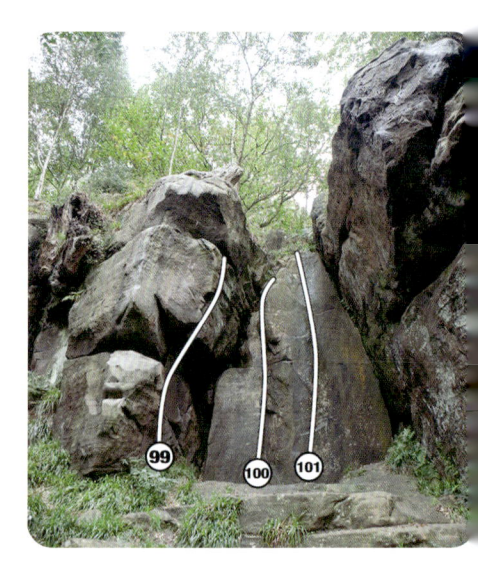

94. 6B+
The blank wall via some thin moves.

95. 6A
The rounded crack that forces some barn doors. With use of side holds drops this down to a 5.

96. 5
Layback to the hole and then up.

97. 5+
The blunt arête to the break.

98. 2
The short crack line on the slab.

Project.
The blank slab is a project for those with very delicate foot work.

99. 6B
Climb up to the high break via the flakey crack.

100. 3+
The corner crack via the blocky holds.

101. 5 *Slab Direct*
The pleasant slab with good edges.

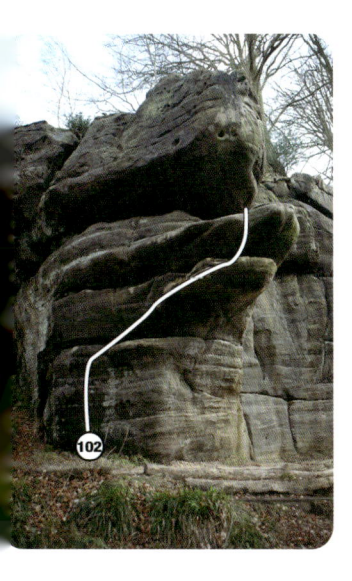

102. 6A+
Up the side of the large roof and then traverse the lip to the jug on the far end. Be careful of the drop when you finish though.

103. 6B
The impressive route up the roof. Starting on good holds under the roof and then moving out to the lip and finishing on the top break will make all your mates bow down to you in awe.

104. 6A+
Starting in the same place as the **103** but continuing straight up.

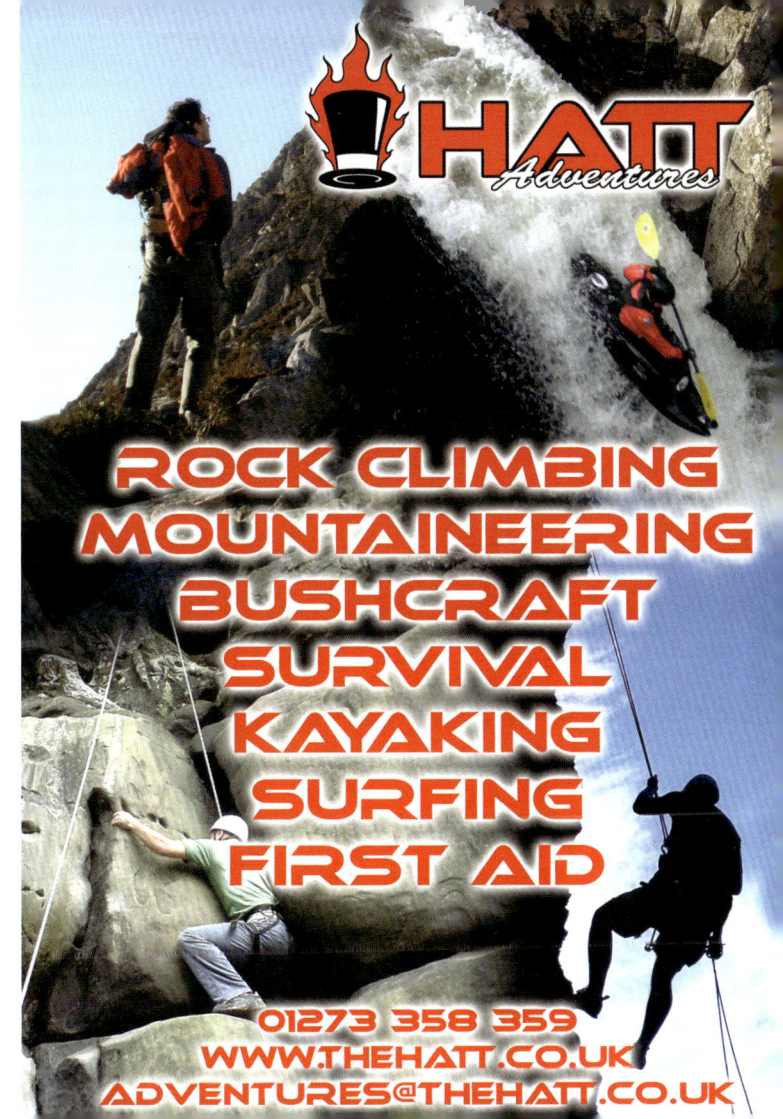

HATT Adventures

ROCK CLIMBING
MOUNTAINEERING
BUSHCRAFT
SURVIVAL
KAYAKING
SURFING
FIRST AID

01273 358 359
WWW.THEHATT.CO.UK
ADVENTURES@THEHATT.CO.UK

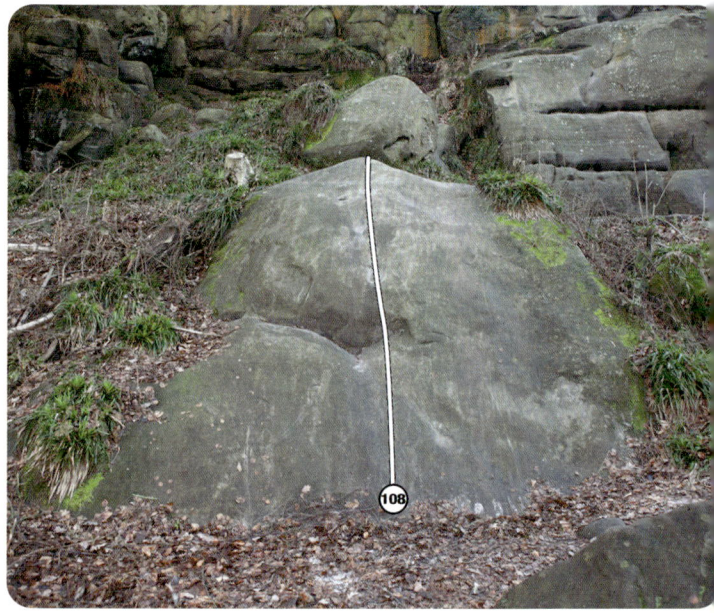

105. 6B+ *Icarus*
A dyno or running jump to the good iron ore jug. The grade is very height dependent.

106. 6B *Nut Tree*
The frustrating blunt arête, takes a while to crack normally.

107. 5+
Climb the flake to the break.

108. 1
The easy slab is great for kids.

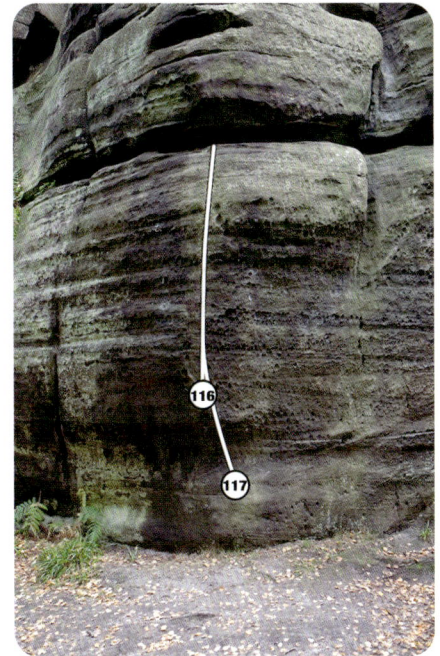

109. 3+
   Climb the large chipped holds at the left hand end.

110. 3+
   Just right again is a similar style climb.

111. 5
   Up the ledge and the rounded slab.

112. 4
   Climb up the large crack.

113. 5+
   Straight up and over the blocky bulge.

114. 4+
   The giant flake is hard to get into, start on the ledge.

115. 6A
   From the large ledge, then ascend the face with the possibility of a band landing back on to the ledge.

116. 6C+ *A killing Joke*
   The arête has some very thin moves on it where a number of options are possible.

117. 7B+ *Supply and Demand* ss
   One of the hardest lines of the crag. Some very thin moves on delicate holds to get into the start of *A Killing Joke*.

Harrisons 64

118. 6B ss
A low start on a good side pull and then upwards and onwards on crimps.

119. 6A
Climb up the awkward arête.

120. 3 ss
Mantle over the short nose at the back.

121. 4 ss
Climb the arête on the right hand side.

122. 5 ss
From the crack upwards, the holds get a bit thinner towards the top.

123. 5 ss
Layback to start and then exit off right.

124. 4+ ss
Climb up the flaky crack.

125. 5 ss
A crouched start on a large flat hold and then up the arête.

126. 3
Up to the ledge and then straight up the wall.

127 2+
Up on to the ledge and then follow the ramp to the top.

128. 4+
A mantle on to the ledge and then up the wall above.

129. 6A *Goats Do Roam* ss
Starting under the low roof make some weird contortions to get on top.

Dan Moore | Highline

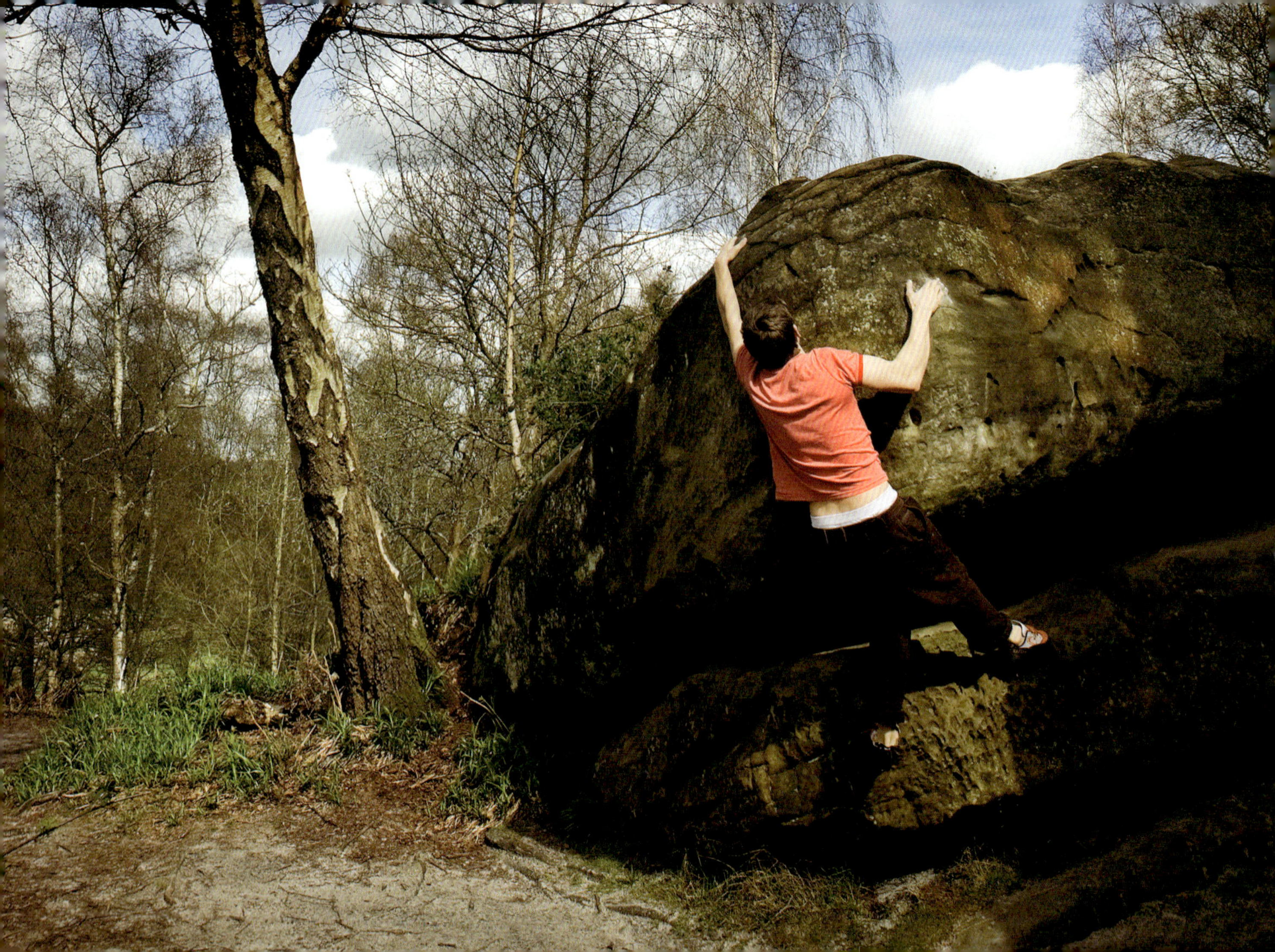

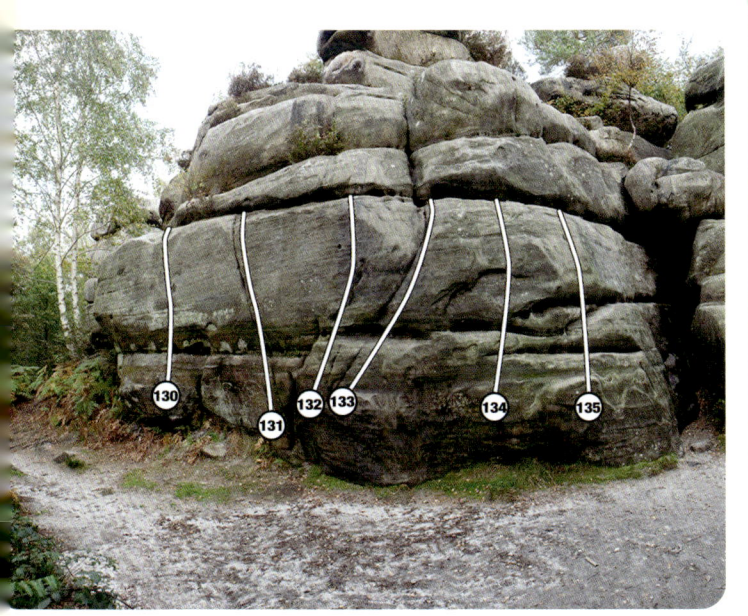

130. 5
Climb the face via the rounded pocket.

131. 5+
Scale the crack line with a hard start.

132. 4
Climb using the good holds on the face.

133. 4+
The rounded slippery crack line.

134. 4
Climb up the front of the rounded bulge.

135. 3
Climb up the slabby right hand wall.

evolution
INDOOR CLIMBING

The Centre of Sandstone Climbing

Equipment
Free Advice
New Routes Info
and
The best indoor bouldering

01892 862924

www.evolutionindoorclimbing.co.uk

Lye Green, Crowborough, TN3 1UX

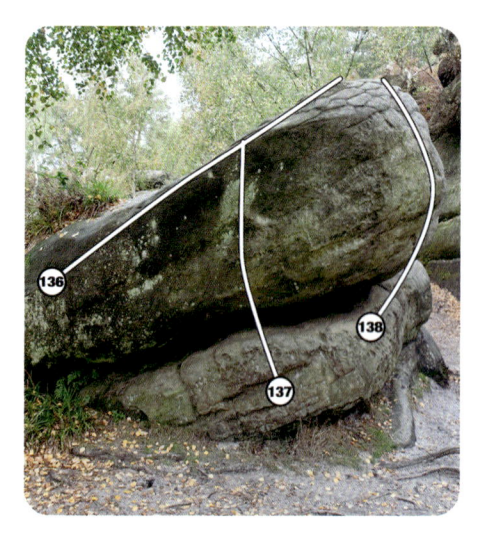

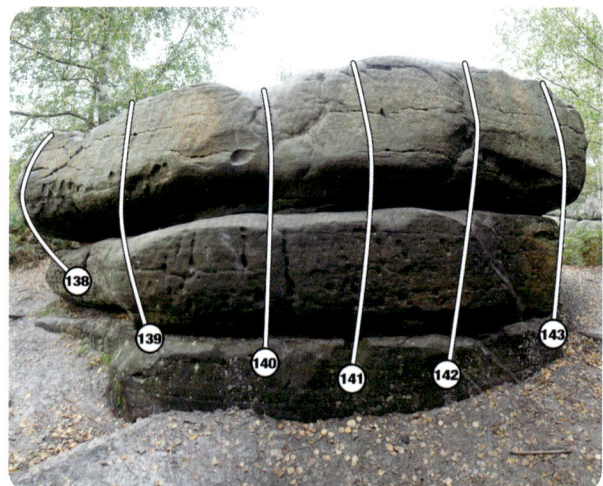

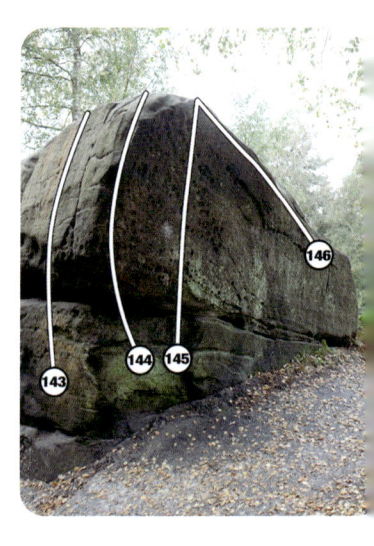

136. 5
Climb the left edge of rising slopers with a tricky start.

137. 4 *ss*
Climb up the face with a mantle, use of a heel aids the top moves.

138. 6A+ *ss*
A low start on the break and then power up the nose.

139. 5+
Climb up the left hand end on good side pulls.

140. 5
Ascend up the rounded groove.

141. 3
Climb up using the small slot.

142. 3+
Straight up using the good hole.

143. 5+
Climb up the slabby face without use of the arête.

144. 4+ *ss*
Up the arête on either side with use of surrounding holds.

145. 5 *ss*
Climb up the pocketed face without any holds on the arête.

146. 5
Starting as far right as you can, follow the line of rising holds up the side.

147. 5
Up the sloping ramp using the good slot.

148. 6A+
The thin blank bulge using the hidden undercuts.

149. 5
Up the rounded crack line.

150. 6B
Up the similar wall using more hidden undercuts.

151. 1
The left hand line of chipped holds.

152. 1
The central line of chipped holds is popular for kids.

153. 1
The right hand line is equally as good.

154. 6A
Up and over the often mossy face.

155. 5
Start on the ring hold and then up to the iron ore holds.

156. 3+
The front face up to the tree, using this to top out.

157. 4+
  An awkward start to get established on the flake.

158. 6A ss
  Climb the small roof off to the left on sideways sloping holds.

159. 6A ss
  Starting in the same place as **158** climb straight up trending right.

160. 6A
  In the cave is this thin hidden wall.

161. 6C ss
  From a low start in the ledge underneath, power out the low arête and then up the face.

162. 5 ss
  A low start on the iron ore edges.

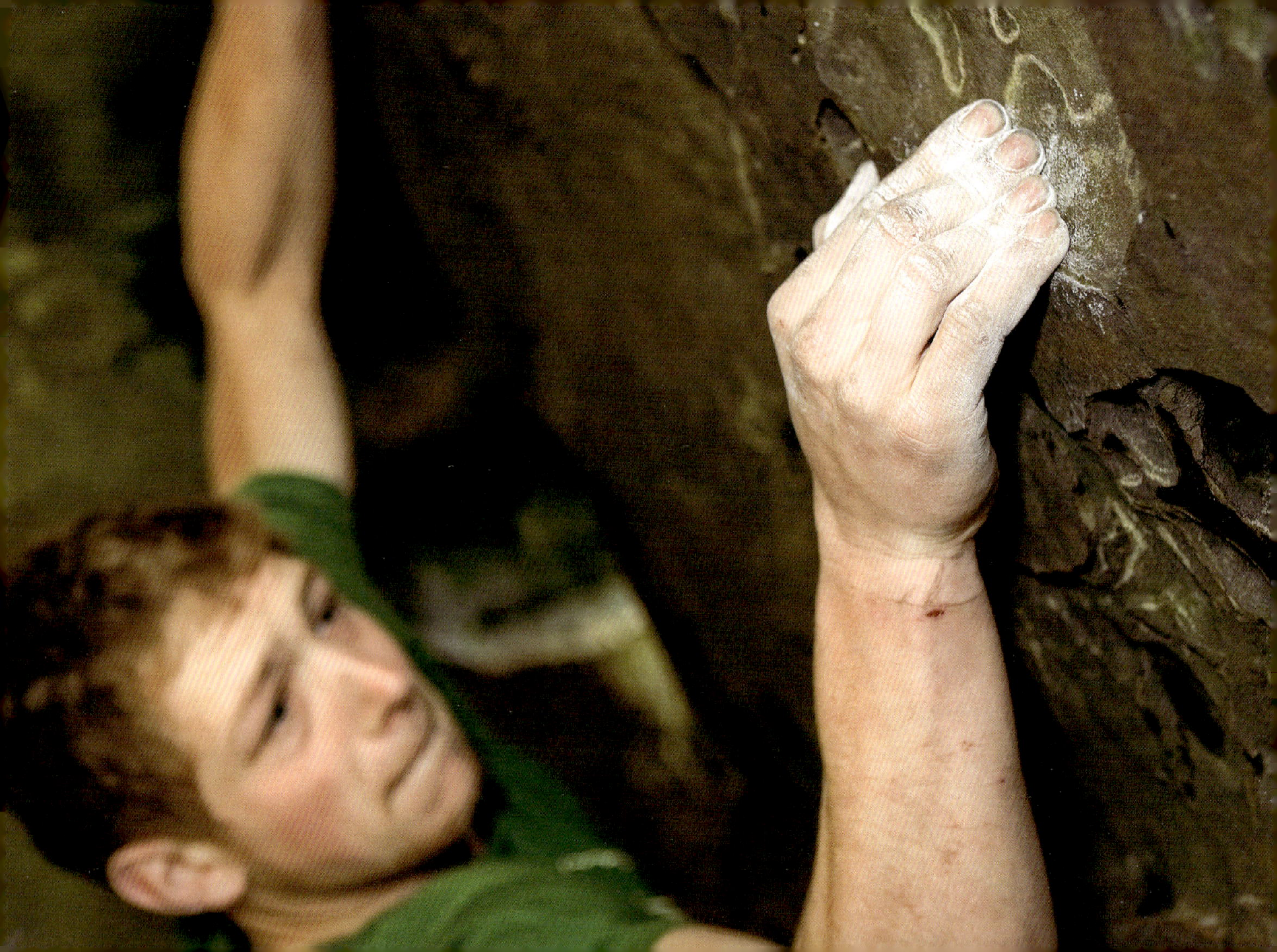

163. 4+
Climb the face to the break, using the flake.

164. 5+
From a low start on the break climb up the crack line.

165. 5
Climb up the good pockets on fragile holds.

166. 5+
Straight up the centre of the wall without use of the large holds off to the left.

167. 4
Climb up the wall using all holds you can get you hands on!

168. 4
The rounded arête to the break starting with a good right hand pinch.

*Still want more? Why not traverse across the face from the start of **168** to the finish of **164** and reward yourself with a lovely 6B+.

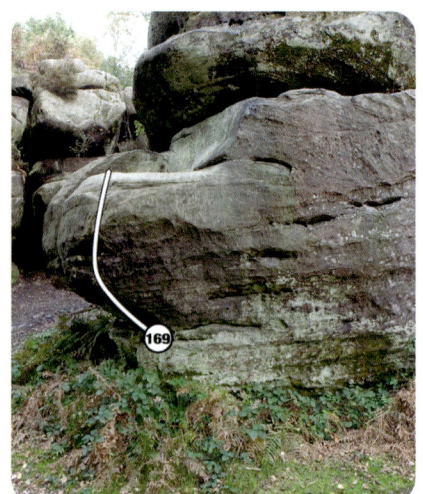

169. 5+
Mantle up the small nose on to the ledge.

170. 6B
Dyno from break to break. Using everything is 4+. There is an awkward sit start to the right that comes in at 6C.

171. 6B
A weird start to gain the ledge and then up and over the bulge.

172. 4
 The fun time crack line.

173. 5+
 Straight up the wall to the right of the crack.

174. 5
 Balancy climbing up the wall in between breaks.

175. 5
 The middle of the wall on good holds.

176. 4
 The ledgy right hand end of this wall.

James Wilmshurst | Route 182 | 6A

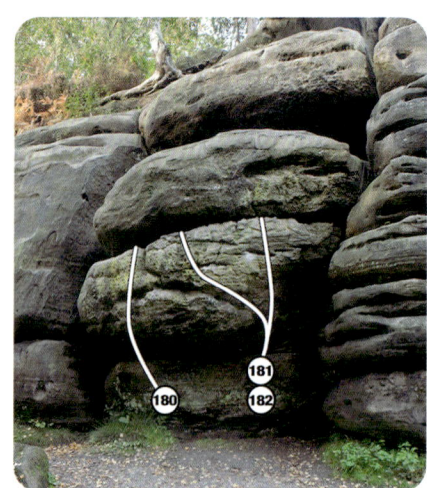

177. 5+
Climb up the left hand side wall via some spaced holds.

178. 5
Climb up the centre line and then veer towards the left.

179. 5+
Start in the same place as number **178**, but this time move up and to the right.

180. 4+ *ss*
Climb up the front of the overhanging wall.

181. 6A *ss*
Starting on the break at the back of the cave, climb out and round to the front on small but positive holds that get bigger as you continue.

182. 6A *ss*
Starting in the same place as **181**, climb straight out and up via the left hand gaston.

183. 6B
A long traverse all the way along the break. Some sections have some very poor footholds. Finish on the tree covered ramp at the end.

184. 6C *The Powerband*
A low level traverse from right to left is rarely in condition but is a pumpy little number if you ever get the chance to climb it.

The route back home after a successful days bouldering

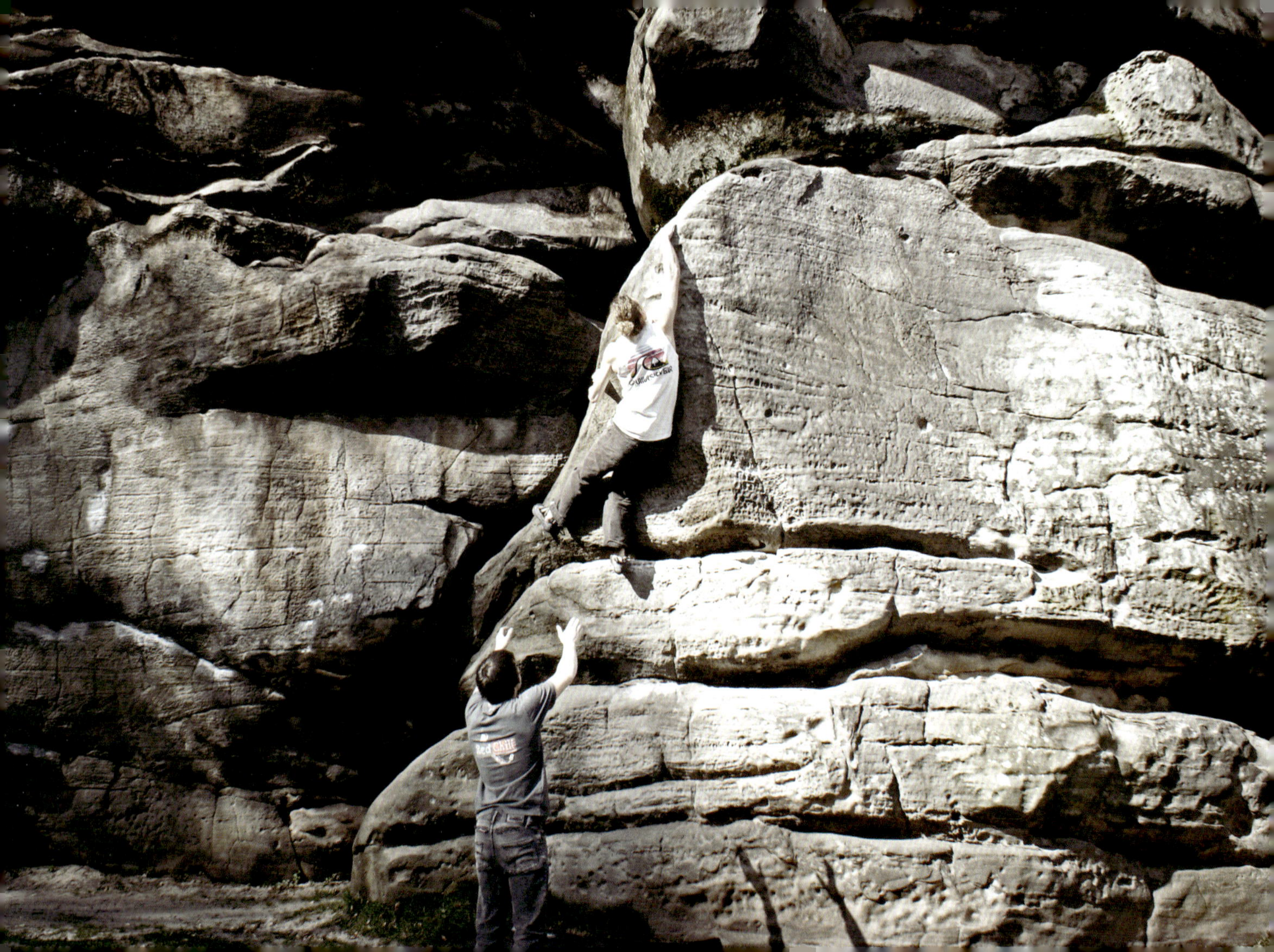

BOWLES

INTRODUCTION

Bowles has a great selection of problems with extra bonuses such as open space and a few facilities. It has a wide selection of grades and a nice friendly atmosphere making it very popular with families.

Fandango wall provides some of the best climbing here and there are countless number of eliminates that can be made up on it. Most sections of this crag offer some great problems and with all the sections linked together it is possible to do a full length traverse of the crag.

ACCESS AND APPROACH

From the A26 Bowles is signposted by a brown sign with a ski slope on it. Follow these signs down to the large car park. There are toilets and drinking taps also available.

This is not a free crag and at time of writing Bowles do charge for climbing here. Please visit the office before you head up to the crag to pay the relevant amount. They do have people checking throughout the day so please don't try and sneak in!

CONDITIONS

The south facing crag is one of the quickest to dry and it is possible to climb here all year round, weather dependant. Providing there has been a couple of good days weather then sections of this crag such as Fandango wall should be dry.

Please be careful climbing here in the winter though as if there has been frost and ice then this can still make the rock very fragile and can lead to holds snapping.

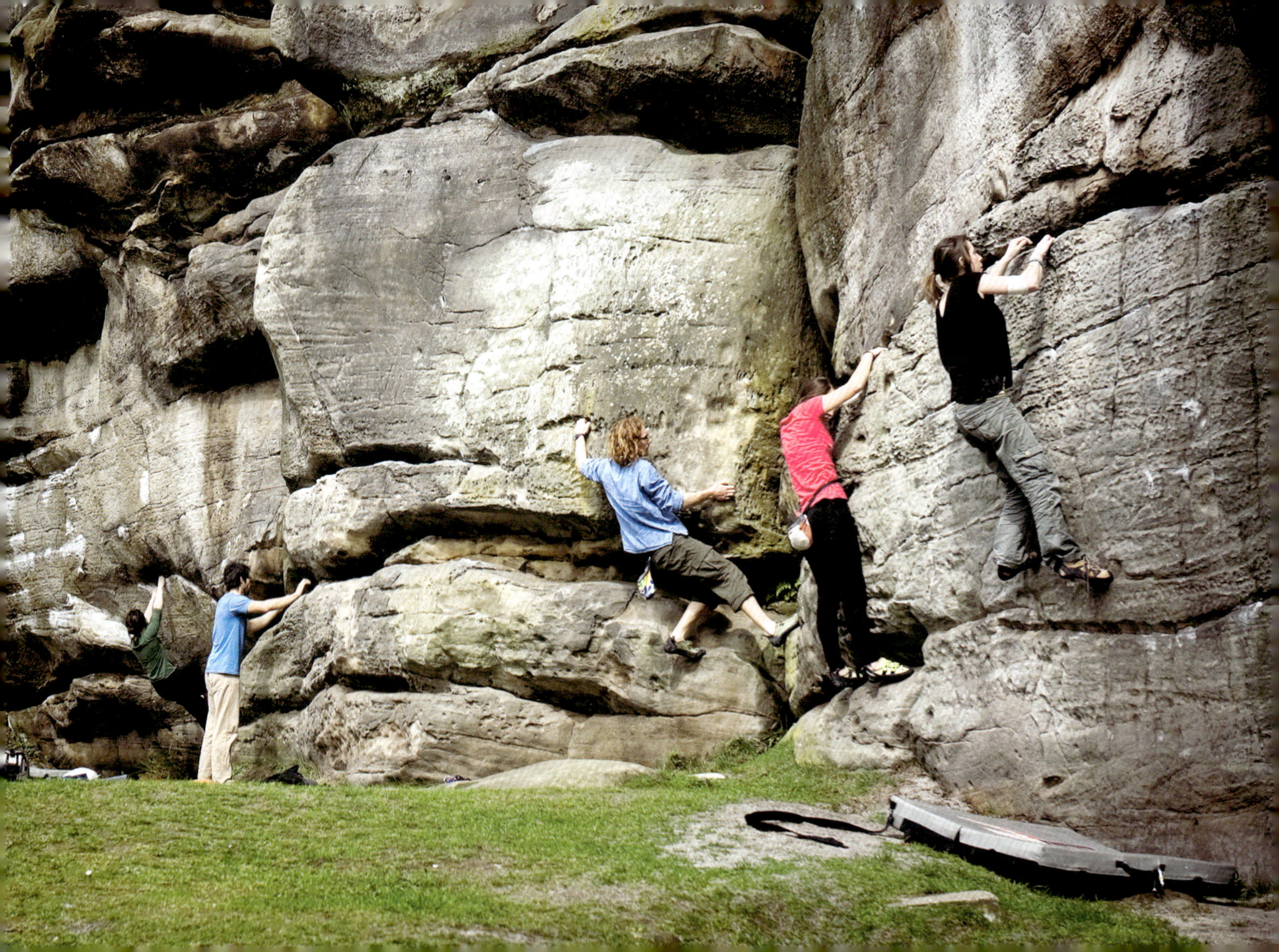

1-12   13-69   70-78   79-112 w/c   113-125

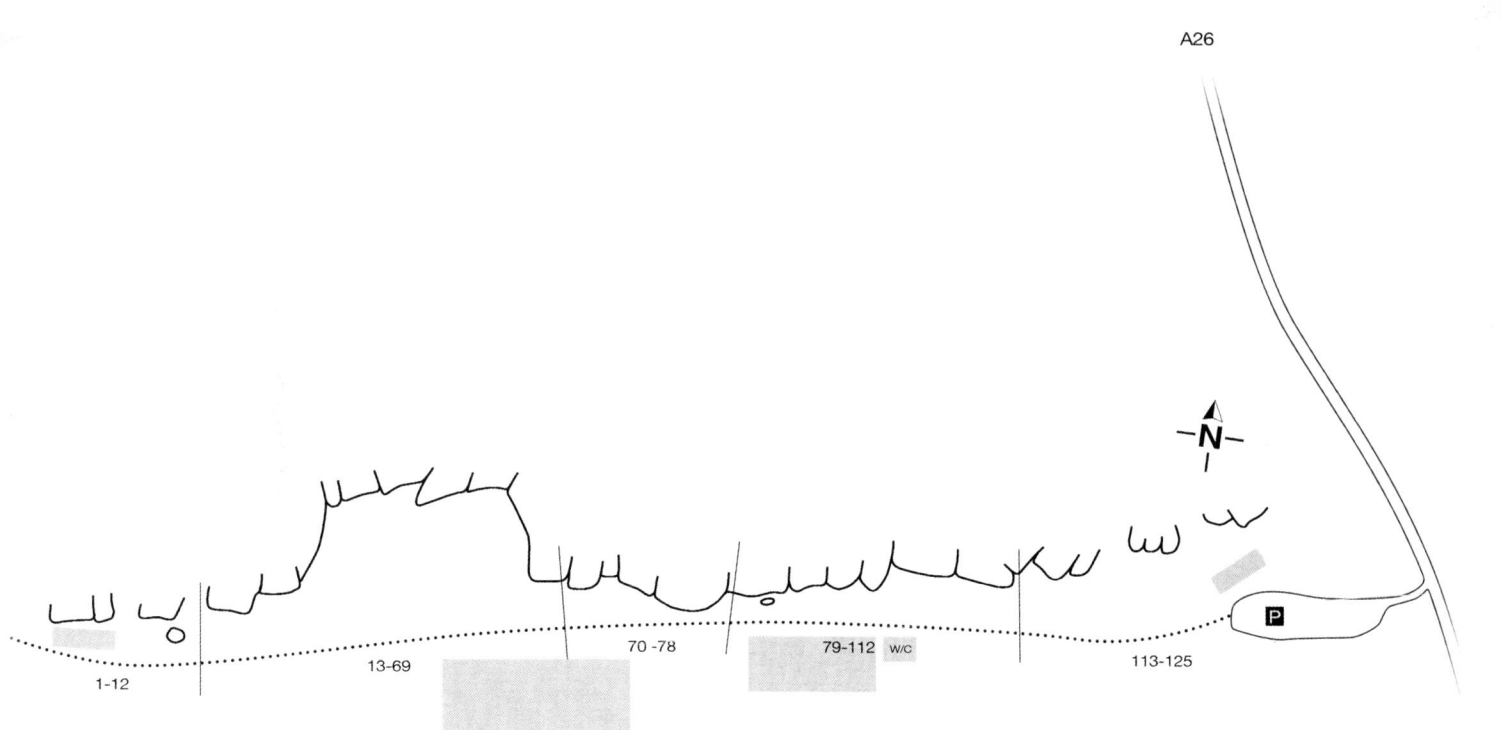

A26

Bowles 82

1. **3**
   The easiest line up the slab. Delicate foot placements to start help gain the large break.

2. **3+**
   Using the Iron ore holds climb all the way to the top and escape off left.

3. **4**
   Climb up the centre scoop.

4. **4+**
   A technical line up the right side off layaways with a spicy top out.

Kat Assersohn | Route 4 | 4+

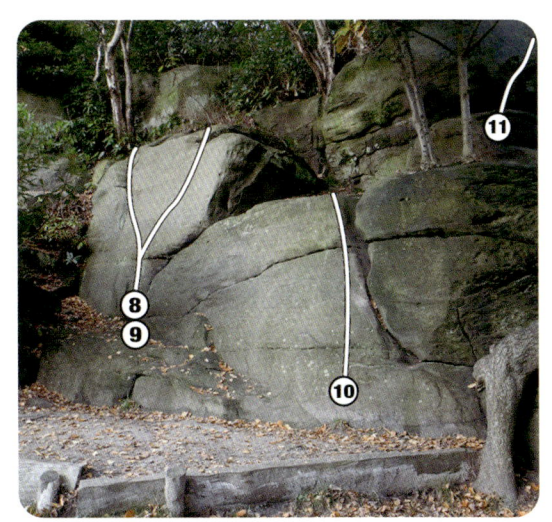

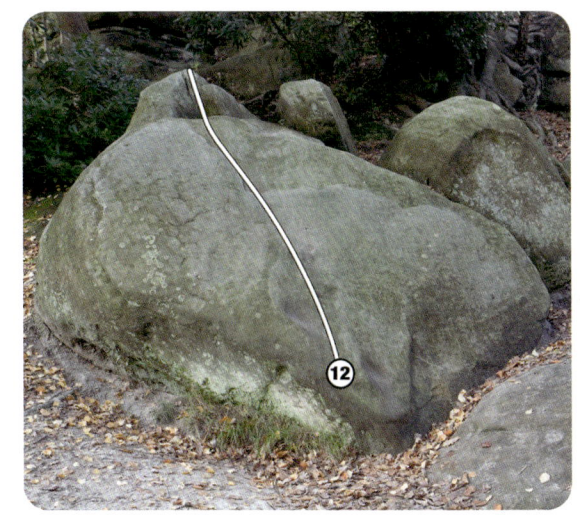

5. **6A** 🔴
A pleasant climb up the front face of this boulder. A tricky highball finish means spotters are advised.

6. **6A+** *ss*
A sit start up the middle of this boulder via some painful pockets.

7. **6B** *ss*
Start under the small overhang on the right hand side. A tricky start to get established on the face and finish on the break.

8. **1**
The left hand line up this small slab using the tree root as a starting foot hold.

9. **1**
The right hand line also provides a nice variation, still using the tree root as a starting foot hold.

10. **1**
An easy crack line which is great for kids to scramble up.

11. **4+**
An interesting climb up the curved ramped boulder.

12. **1**
A very easy slab line and a good introduction to bouldering for the little ones.

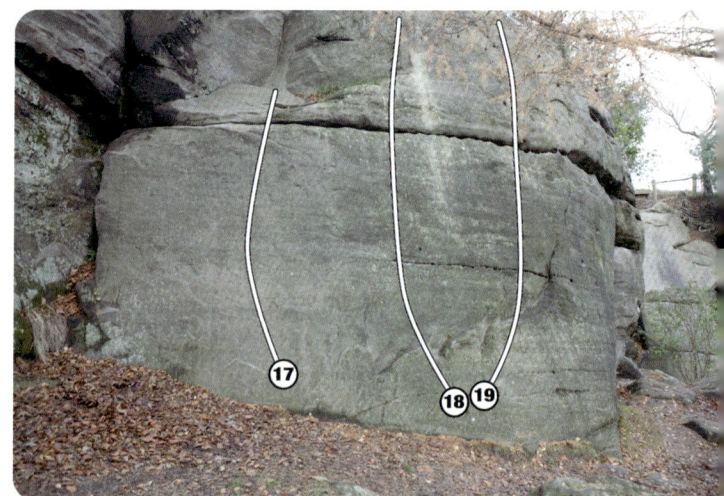

13. 6A+
Pull on the obvious ledge them make a powerful flick to a slopey jug of victory, finishing just under the bulge.

14. 6B
Starting just left of the nose on poor holds work your way up to a hard finish.

15. 6B+
A hard mantle on the front of the nose with slopers and bad footholds. Top out for the real tick.

16. 6B
Just right again is another tricky mantle on poor quality holds.

17. 3+
A one move wonder up the blank face and then a tricky mantle to top.

18. 3+
An easy wall climb with good feet and bad hand holds the top is easy but feels harder because of the height.

19. 4+
Another great climb following the line of the faint ramp for your feet and then the chipped holds on the top face.

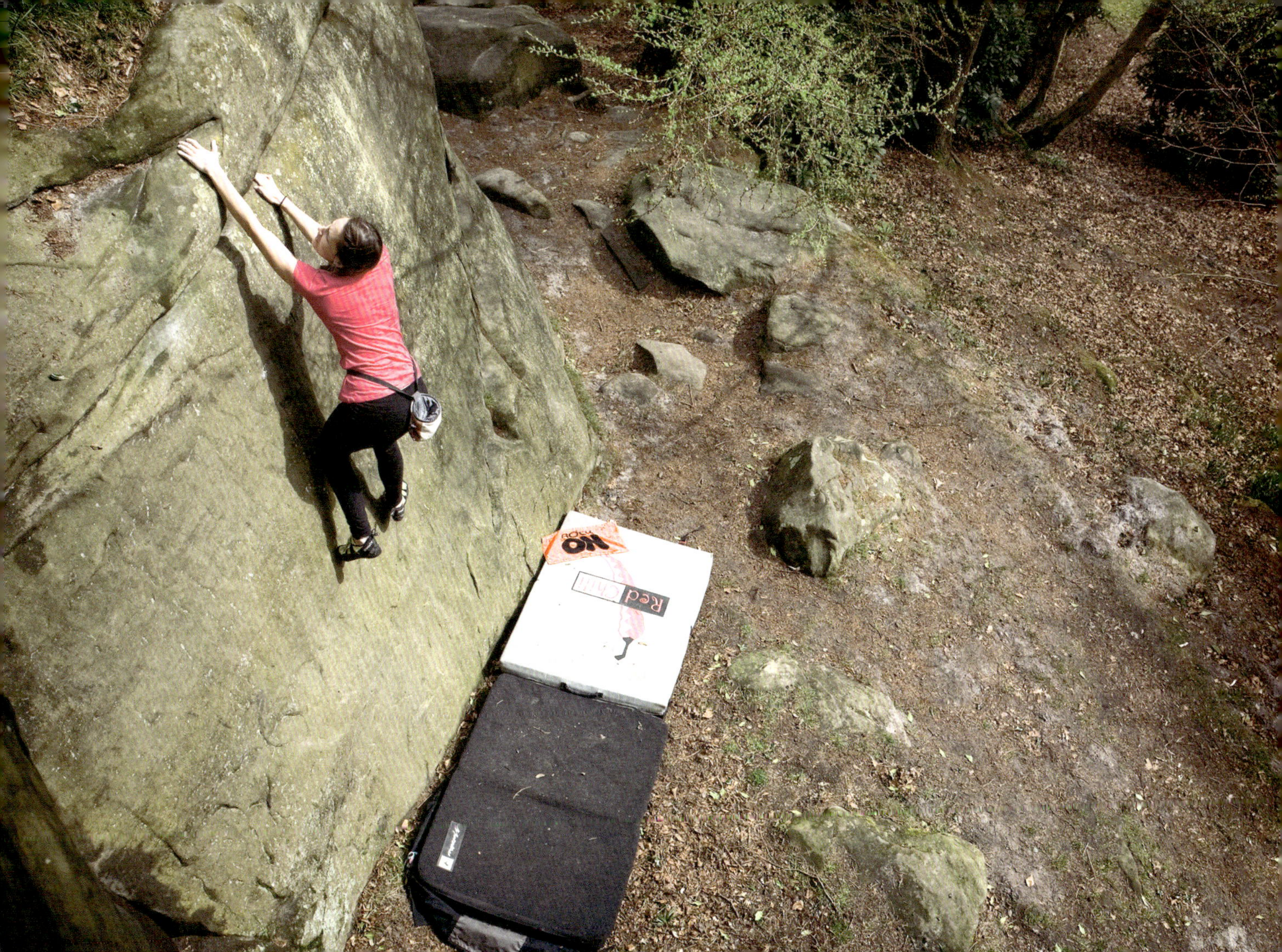
Red Chili

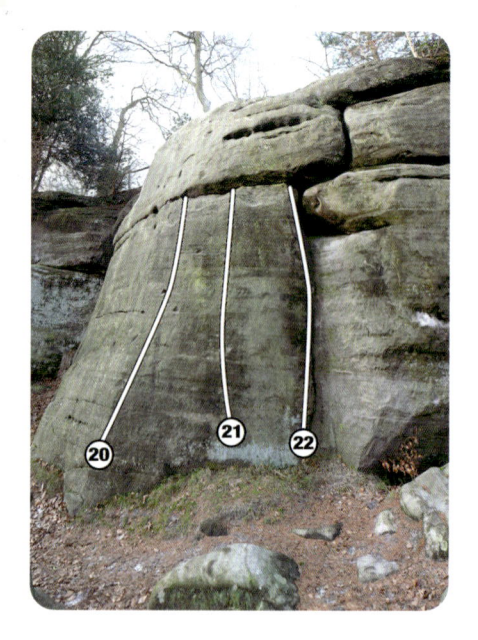

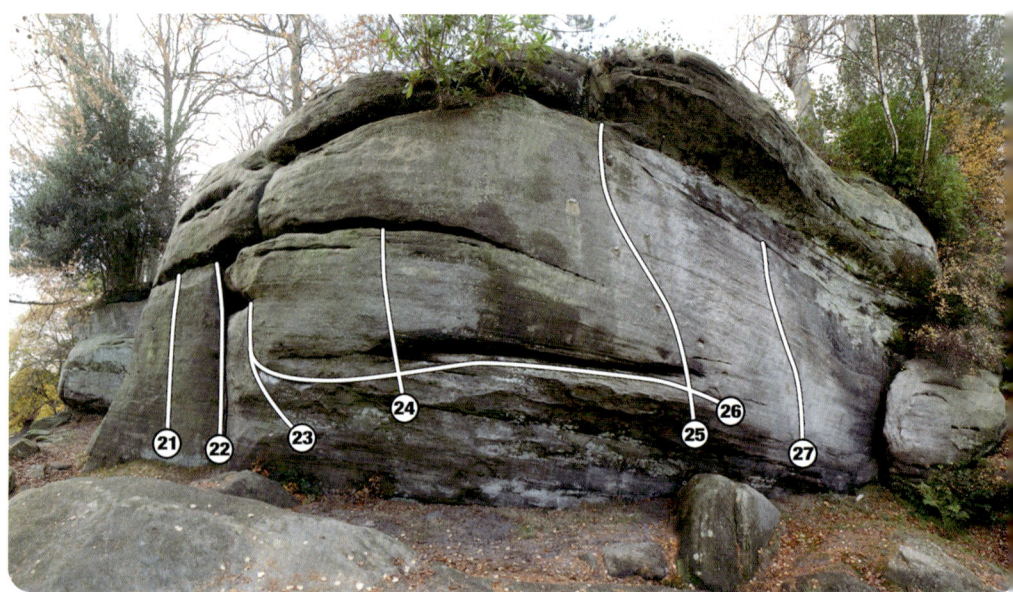

20. 3
An artificial climb up the chipped holds. A top out is possible but is a bit high to boulder.

21. 7B
An eliminate, using the right most chipped hold and a sharp mono to start. Gain the large sloper before finishing on the break.

22. 5 ss
The corner crack line. Can be done with a sit start at 6A+.

23. 6B+ ss
Power up the blunt arête to finish on the break.

24. 6B
A large reach or a dyno up the front face of this boulder.

25. 4
An artificial climb up the glued on jugs.

26. 7B *Maybe When You're Older* ss
From sitting on the large boulder, climb from right to left along the break to finish up number **23**.

27. 6C *Knucklebones*
The line of drilled monos provides an interesting little climb, if not very artificial.

87 **Bowles**

28. 2
The left hand line of the slab gives a short problem finishing on the second break.

29. 2
Another easy line up the middle using chipped side pulls.

30. 1
An artificial climb up the right hand side on chipped holds. Difficult to protect with mats.

Barnaby Ventham | Maybe When You're Older | 7B

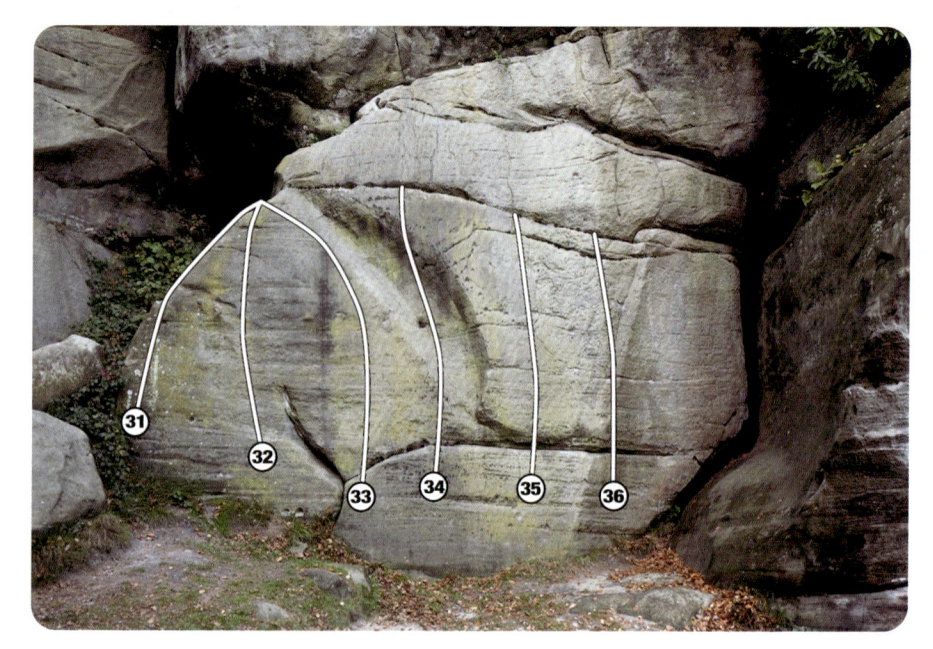

31. 4+
The left arête of the banana wall gives an easier way to the break.

32. 6C+
A dyno from the centre of the wall to the good hold on the arête.

33. 6C *Banana Hammock*
Finishing in the same place as **32** but use the rather fruity slopers of the banana, and other small holds on the face, to gain a rewarding finish.

34. 4+ *Banana*
Climb the start of the banana finishing on the break up to the right.

35. 4+
Climb the wall to the right of the banana on good holds. Finish on the break.

36. 5
The far right hand wall with some fairly tasty edges finishing on the break.

37. 6A
The centre line of the slab is often green but when it does dry out is a nice little climb.

38. 5+
The right hand side of the slab using the good holds from the arête. Finish on the obvious break.

ROCK ON

If (like this 80's throwback) you find yourself in need of rock shoes, bouldering mat or some slightly more up to date clothing (or just more clothing!!) for your next evening/day/week/month out...

Come to Rock On for the best advice and a massive choice of gear, whether it's a bouldering trip to the sandstone or something somewhat further away.

Many shops claim to be climbing specialists. At Rock On we sell climbing & mountaineering equipment, books & dvds and absolutely nothing else. NOTHING ELSE.
Now that's specialist.

Mile End Climbing Wall
Haverfield Road
Bow
London
E3 5BE
Tel: 020 8981 5066

Craggy Island Climbing Centre
9 Cobbett Park
Slyfield Estate
Moorfield Road
Guildford
GU1 1RU
Tel: 01483 565635

Redpoint Climbing Centre
77 Cecil Street
Birmingham
B19 3ST
Tel: 0121 359 8709

www.rockonclimbing.co.uk

BLOC ON *Everything for the dedicated boulderer*

91 *Bowles*

39. 6A
Climb the arête using holds on both sides. Finish in the large juggy flake. Can also be done with a sit start at 6B.

40. 6C *ss*
Using sidepulls and gastons up the right hand crease, to finish on the large flat jug. No holds from the arête are allowed.

41. 7A+ *ss*
An eliminate up the left hand end missing out the good line of holds from Nicotine alley. From a sit start power up the wall finishing on the juggy break. Using everything is 6C.

42. 6B *ss*
Starting under the overhanging middle section, make a hard pull to gain the pocket and finish on good edges to the break.

43. 6A+ *ss*
The line of good holds up the centre of the wall.

44. 7B *Sonic Blue*
Starting on the good finger edge break, take the left hand finger lock and power up to a right hand sidepull. Finish on the large flat jug.

45. 7C *Phasis*
Starting the same as *Sonic Blue* but going straight up to the flake/sidepull missing out the finger lock. Finish out right. There have been many variations of this problem in the past, some rumoured to be as easy as 7A. Can also be done with a dyno sit start from directly beneath the starting holds.

46. 7B *ss*
A great line up the right hand bulge using very small crimps and finishing on the break.

93 *Bowles*

47. 6B+
Starting low on slopers traverse to the middle of the wall and finish direct up the centre on good holds.

48. 7A *Nicotine Alley*
The classic traverse that starts on the furthest right hand end and traverses the whole wall on the middle line of holds. Originally this line finished round the corner on the slab but is now more commonly finished on the large obvious jug.

49. 7A+ *Nicotine Alley Variation*
Take the line of *Nicotine Alley* but stay low at the middle point crossing some very small holds.

50. 6B+ *Tobacco Road*
Follow *Nicotine Alley* to the middle but then take the central line of holds to the juggy break to finish.

51. 6B+
Take the line of *Tobacco Road* but continue along the juggy break to finish at the large obvious jug at the left hand end of the wall.

* This wall has hundreds if not thousands of eliminates that can be done on it. Countless summer days can be spent pottering about on this wall. It would be impossible to list all of these climbs and would also take the fun out of making up your own. The best advice we can give is jump on and get exploring!

Peter Wycislik | Phasis | 7C

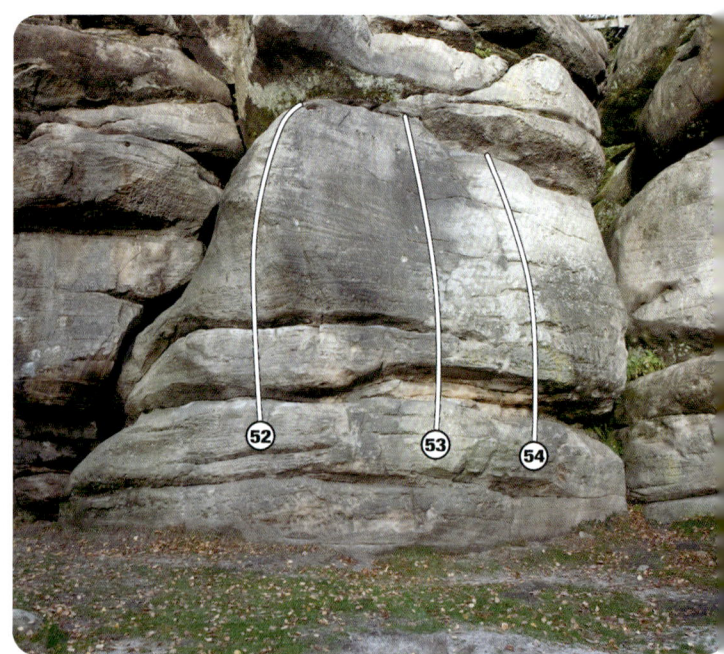

52. **6B+** *Mick's Wall Arête*
Slap your way up the arête finishing on the break.

53. 5
Climb up the centre of the wall on small but positive hand holds.

54. 5
Just right is an easier variation on better holds. A harder start leads to an easier finish on the break.

Bryan Stevens | Full Bowles Traverse

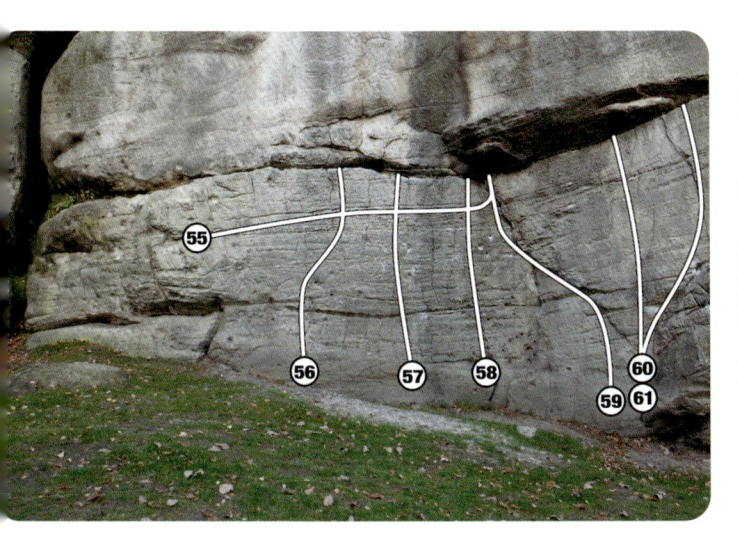

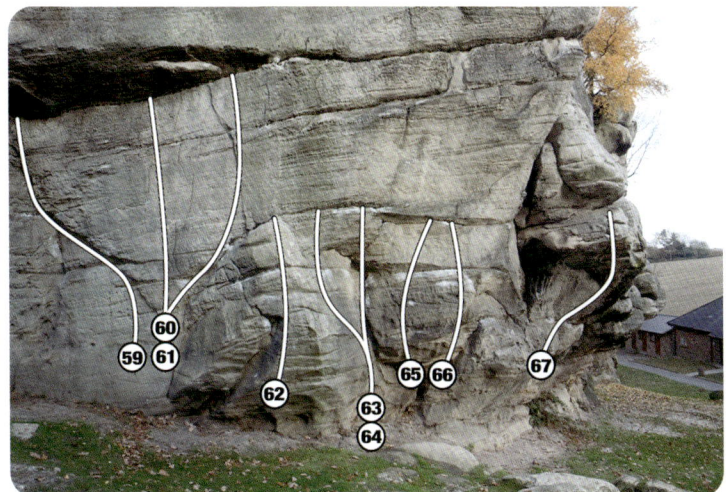

55. 6A+
Traverse the wall on positive crimps and edges just under the break. Without the break of footholds makes this harder at 6B.

56. 6B ss
A tricky finish with poor foot holds leads to some better edges. Finish on the break.

57. 6A+ ss
A nice straight up problem that requires some strong fingers.

58. 5+ ss
Just left of the corner is another straight up problem.

59. 3
An easy problem following the undercut flake up to a good finishing jug.

60. 4
Straight up the wall on good holds finishing on the juggy break.

61. 4
Starting the same as **60**, venture out right onto small crimps.

62. 6A+ ss
Climb the small nose using holds on either side, finishing on the break.

63. 6B ss
Climb just the left hand face without any holds to the right. Eliminating the right hand pocket makes this a lot harder at 7A+.

64. 4
Climb the corner using all holds to finish on the large jug.

65. 5 ss
The wall to the right of the corner gives an ok problem on poor rock.

66. 4+ ss
Climb the overhanging arête to finish in the same place as **65**.

67. 4+
The fierce overhang on good holds to a tricky finish on a large sloper.

Bowles 96

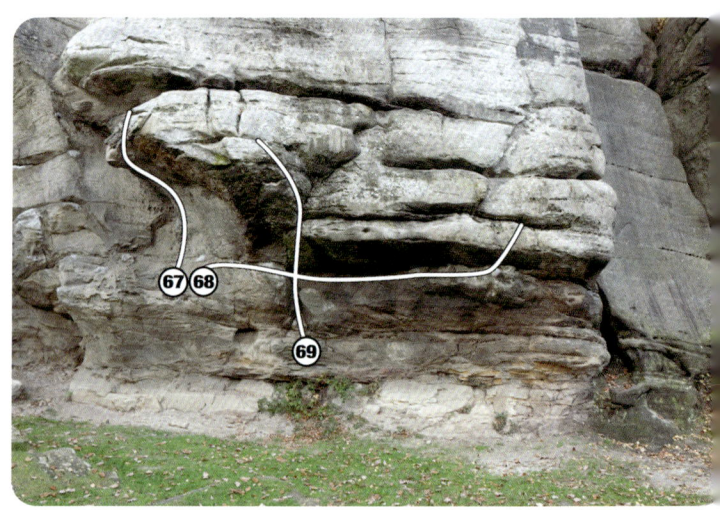

68. 6C
Traverse from left to right underneath the overhang. Finishing just before the arête upwards on good hold in the break.

69. 6A
Vaguely follow the crack line to finish on a poor hold in the break.

*There is an eliminate boulder problem just to the left of **69** called *The Fridge* which goes at 6C+ that is definitely worth a try or two.

Jake White | Route 67 | 4+

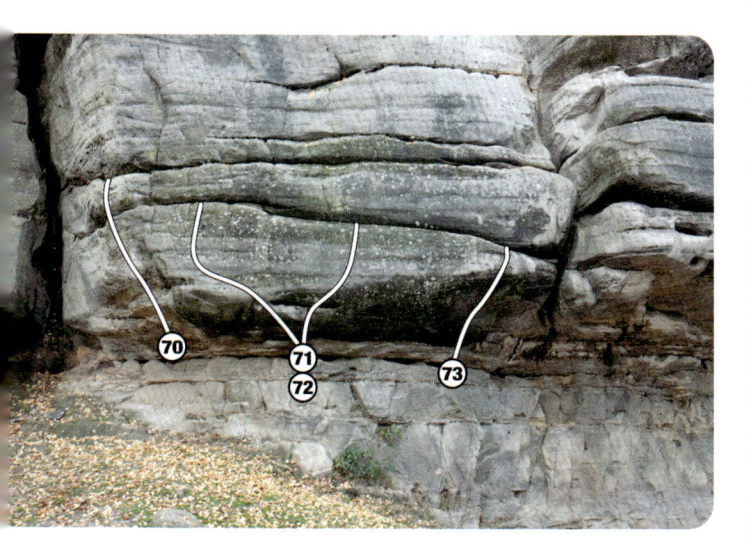

70. 4
Climb the left hand end on good holds finishing on the second break.

71. 6A
Starting in the large flat jug take the left hand line up towards the break.

72. 6A+
Starting again in the large flat jug, this time take the right hand line to finish on the break.

73. 6B+
The small overhang on the right is harder than it looks. After some blind slaps around the lip finish on the flat break.

Barnaby Ventham | Route 71 | 6A

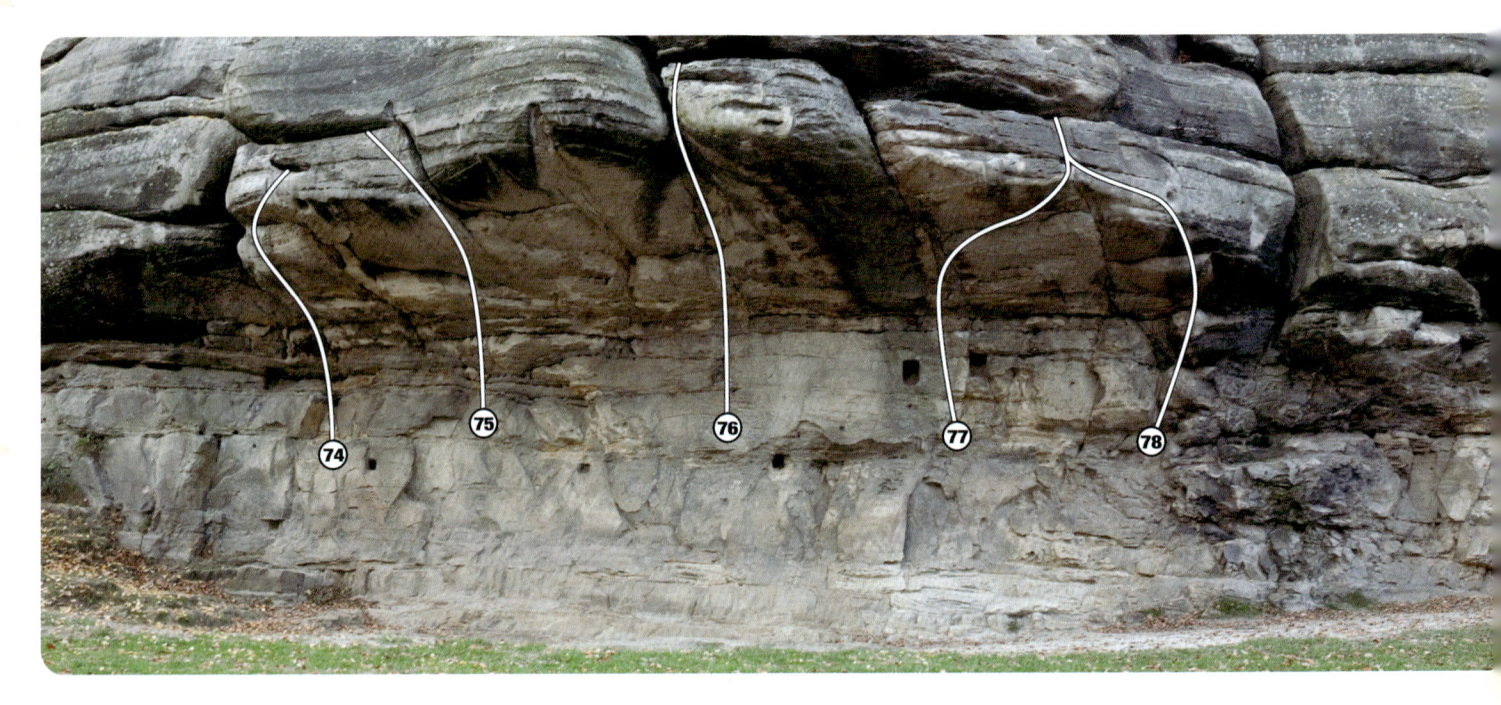

74. 6A
A fun line up the large overhang. Climb up using good holds past the square to finish in the big jug, that looks a lot better than it actually is!

75. 6B+
The start to the route *Them Monkey Things* Climb the crack to finish on the break before the hard climbing starts. If you were to continue you would end up climbing a very highball 7B.

76. 7A+ *Carbide Finger*
Climb the crack line and large square cut holes to gain the break. Turning the lip proves the hardest bit for most people. There are a number of ways to do this, some more successful than others.

77. 6B+ *Cardboard Box*
A great little roof climb on holds that look worse than they actually are. Follow the large flake to a dynamic finish to a reasonably good hold.

78. 6A
A right hand variation to *Cardboard Box* using better holds to start with and traversing along the lip to finish in the same place as the previous route.

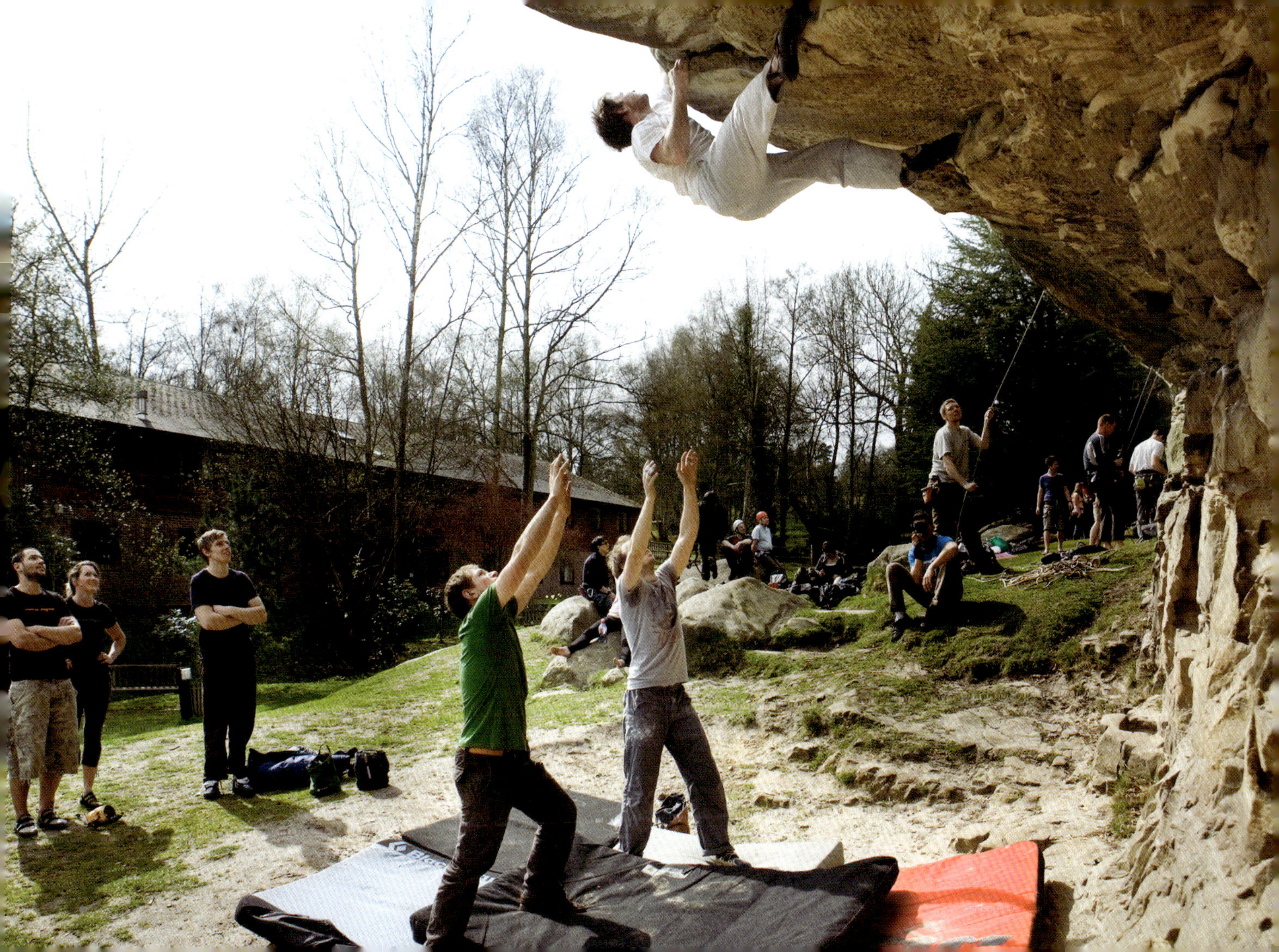

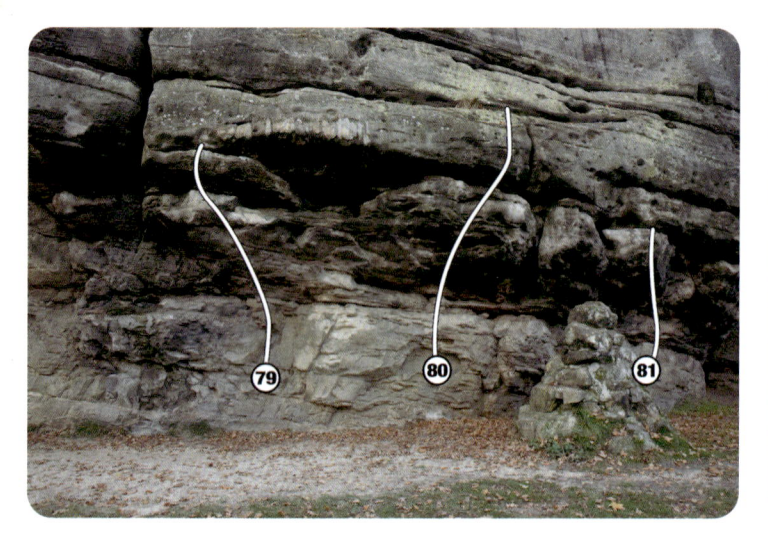

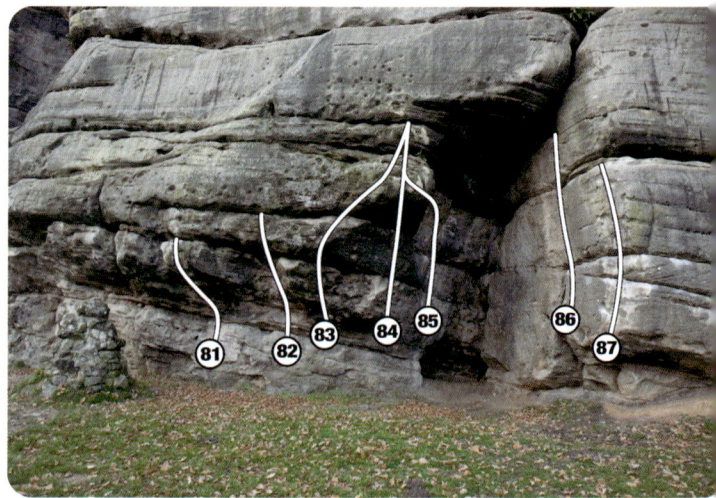

79. 6A
The short over hang is climbed just right of its most overhanging point.

80. 6A
Just to the right of the cairn, climb up the small overhang finishing on the high break.

81. 6B
A dyno from break to break.

82. 5+
Climb up the small crease on reasonably good holds.

83. 6B
Starting just to the left of the large overhanging arête climb up around the side finishing on a good hold at the top.

84. 6B+
Straight up through the middle of the overhang is a tough little challenge.

85. 6A+
Starting to the right and just round the corner follow a line of good holds.

86. 6C+
A large dyno from the low break to the jug up in the corner. Using everything is 5+.

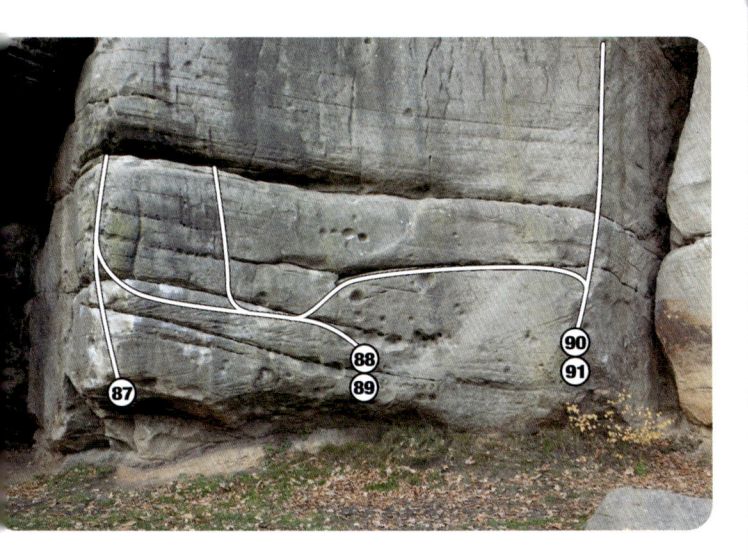

87. 6B
A sit start on arête makes this an interesting little climb.

88. 6A
Traverse from the centre of this boulder to the arête and finish up **87**.

89. 6B
Start the same as **88** but take an earlier finish.

90. 6B+
Traverse from the start of *Sandman* making a hard drop down to continue into either **88** or **89**.

91. 6C *Sandman* ⊙
A highball arête to the break that is easier for the tall. To finish either top it out, escape down the crack to the right or jump off if you have enough mats.

Graeme Harwood | Route 81 | 6B

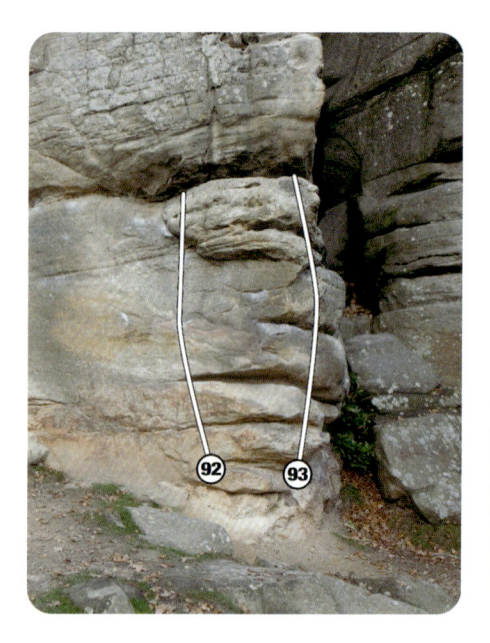

92. 4+
   The wall just left of the arête finishing on the break.

93. 3+
   Climb the arête on large positive holds.

94. 4
   Climb up the centre of the wall, finishing on a good hold up and left.

95. 3+
   The large juggy holds up the right hand end. Can be done with a sit start at 5+.

96. 4
   Starting just round the corner on some good holds, climb this face.

97. 4
A line of good holds up the left hand end.

98. 4+
A tricky start leads to large flat holds. Finish on the break.

99. 6A ss
A sit start under the slopey ledge just left of the crack.

100. 6A+ ss
A sit start on the right hand end on large flat slopers. Some heel hook work may be needed.

101. 6B+
A long traverse on slopers. Starting on the right hand work your way along the obvious line to finish either up **97** or at the last hold.

Bowles 104

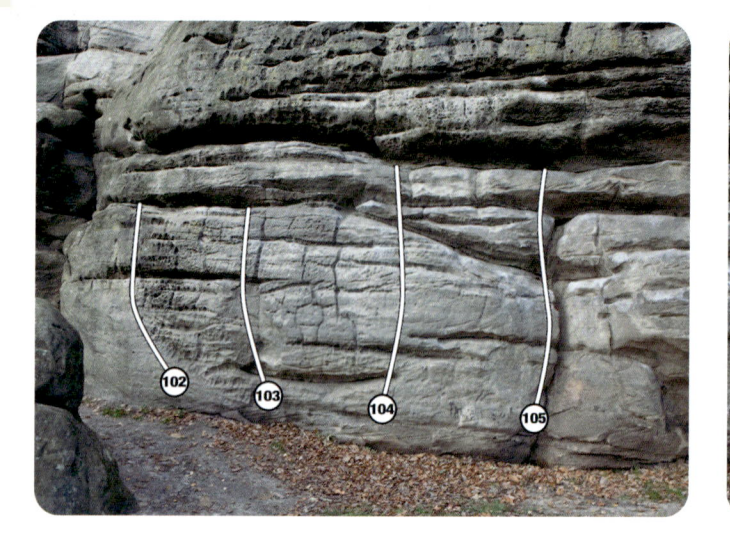

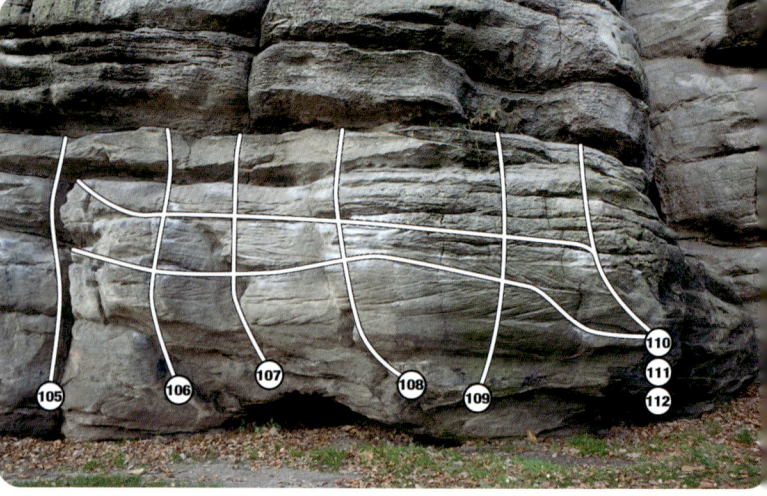

102. *5 ss*
The left hand line of good holds with a tricky sit start.

103. *5 ss*
Another tricky start leads to better holds. Finish on the break.

104. *4+ ss*
A line of good holds to finish on the break.

105. *5 ss*
A great problem up the crack line.

106. *5+ ss*
A sweet little climb up the left side of this bloc.

107. *6A ss*
A sit start on the large obvious feature.

108. *6A ss*
Make large pulls to sloping edges then power to the rewarding jugs.

109. *6A+ ss*
Starting on the small but positive crimps, power up to gain better holds.

110. *6B+ ss*
Starting on the right hand side, using the small sideways crimps and thinner edges below the low break.

111. *6A+ ss*
Starting in the same place as **111** but work your way along the lower break to reach the crack.

112. *5+ ss*
A sit start on the low obvious jugs and then climb up the right hand side finish on the break.

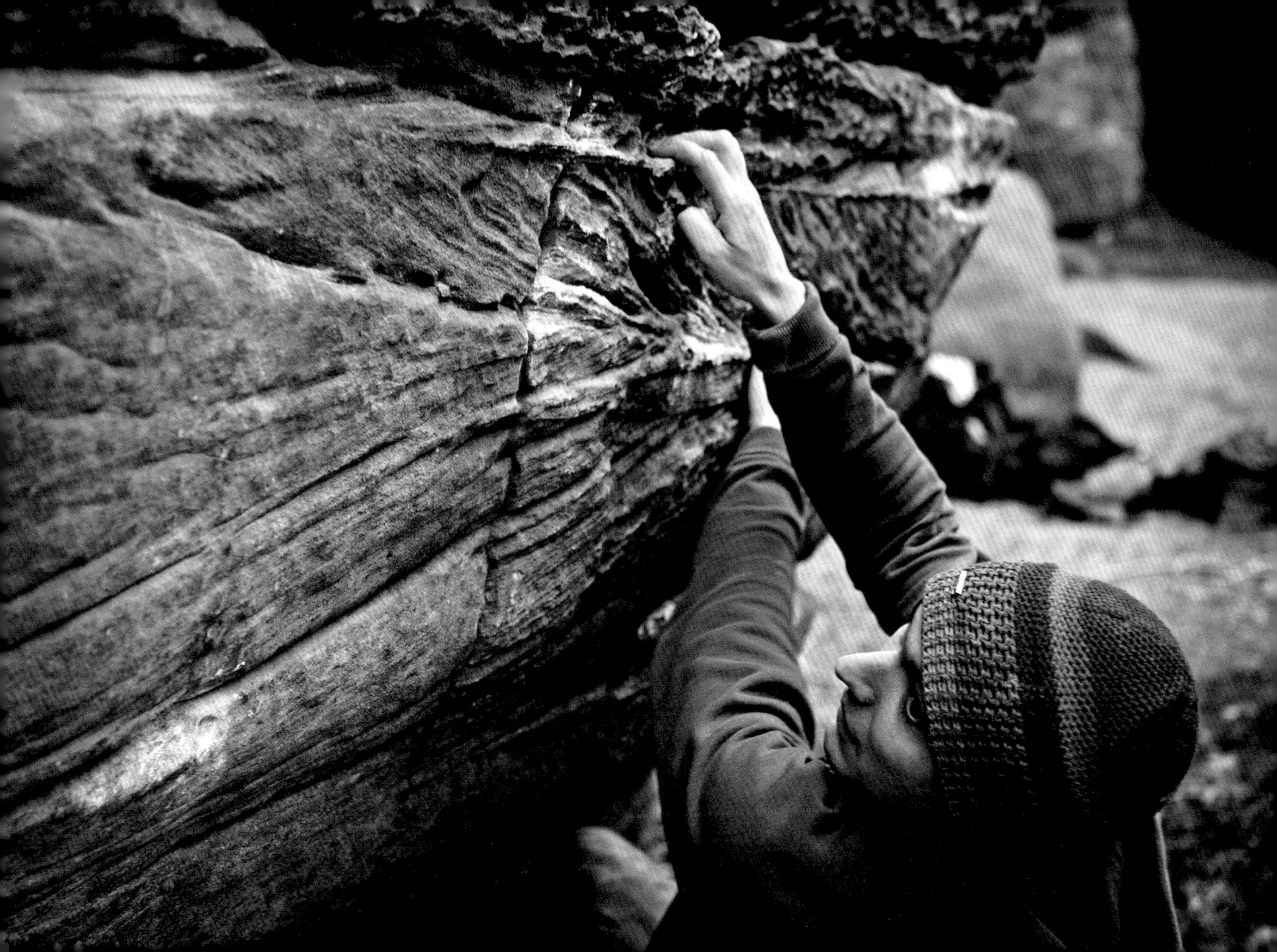

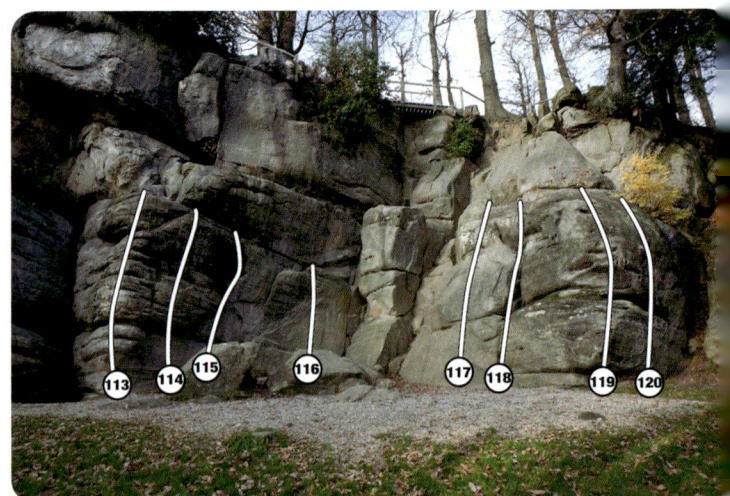

113. 3
Climb the juggy rounded arête.

114. 5
The slightly overhanging face just to the right of the arête.

115. 5
To the right again is another short problem to the break.

116. 5+
The short wall via some crimps to the juggy break.

117. 4+
Climb up the slab to the right of the easy gully. There are many fun eliminates to be had up this wall.

118. 4
The large crack all the way to the obvious break.

Charlotte Latter | Route 113 | 3

119. 4+
Climb the blunt arête to the slab above where good holds are found.

120. 5
The face to the right of the arête is climbable a number of ways.

121. 6C ss
From a sit start on the right under the arête, move out left to a small collection of holds including a mono and then make a big move up the face to the slopey break.

122. 5+ ss
From the same sit start as **121** climb straight up on the right hand side of the arête.

123. 5+
Straight up the high face via some good holds. Either finish on the top break or go for the highball top out.

mountain-trips
.co.uk

Mountain-Trips runs a range of instructional courses in rock climbing, scrambling and mountain walking within the U.K.

Contact:
07793355948
www.mountain-trips.co.uk
laurence@mountain-trips.co.uk

124. 4+
This climb is short lived but still fun. Up to the right Gaston and then out to the top.

125. 6A
The nose of the arête up in the woods is a hidden classic. There are other climbs in this surrounding area but none of which are of great quality.

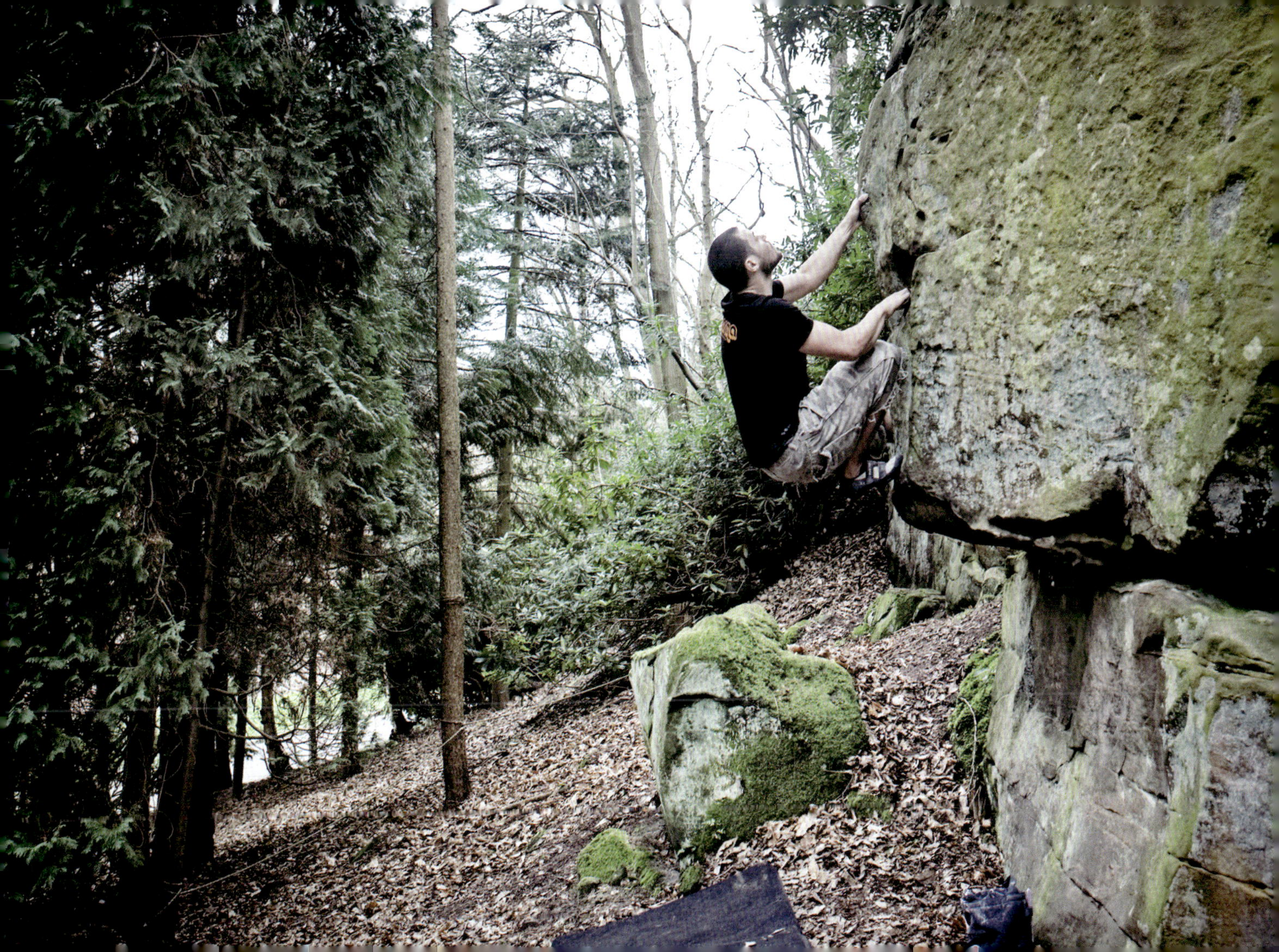

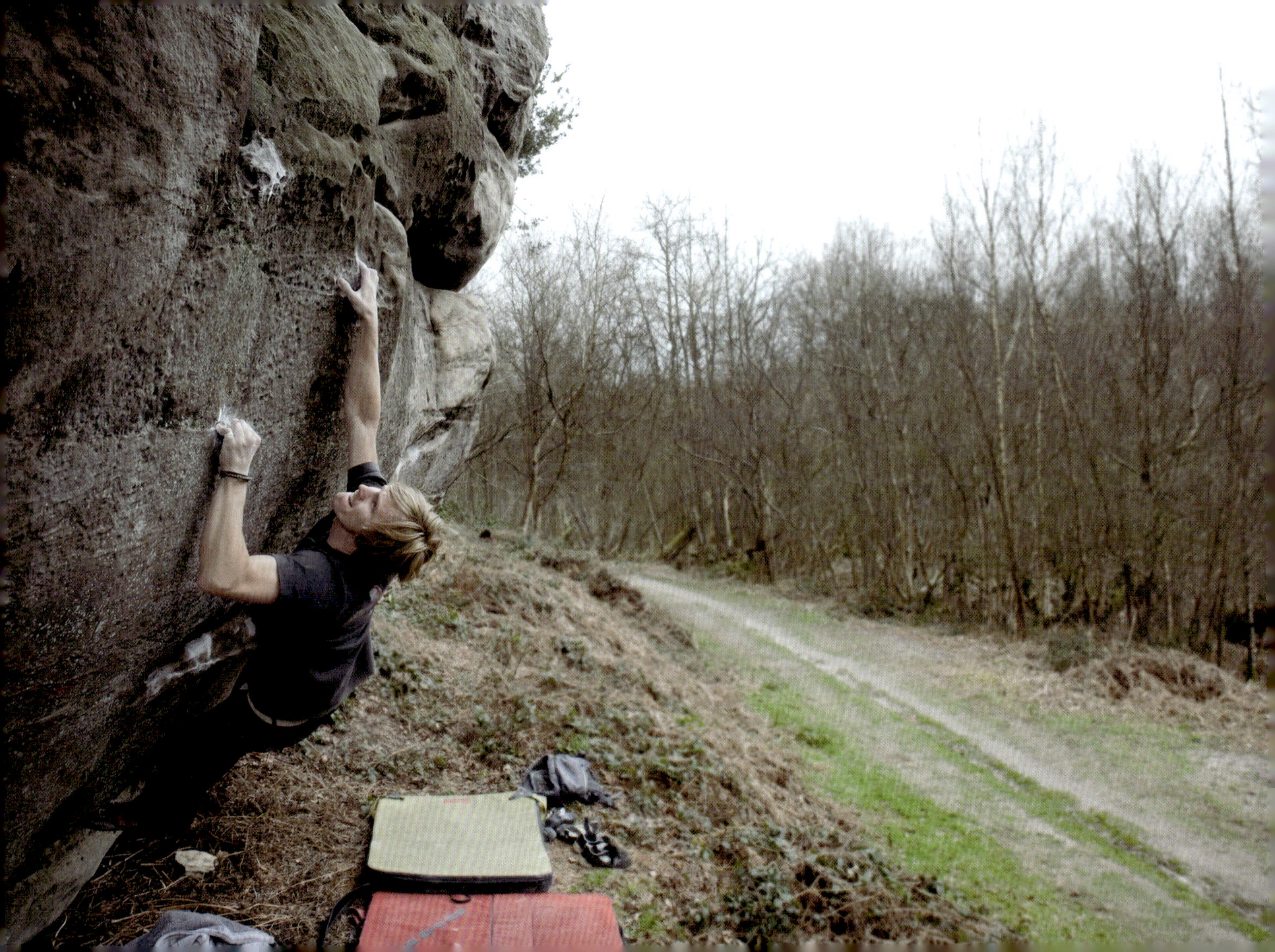

ERIDGE GREEN

INTRODUCTION

This has had a lot of development recently and is now one of the best bouldering areas in the South. The crag is an untouched haven in quiet and relaxed setting giving it a really unique atmosphere. Set in large woodland you really get to go back to nature.

For those hunting out quality climbs the must do climbs here are 'Parisian Affair' and 'The Leaf'. For those wishing to push themselves then Eridge provides, classic lines such as 'Nightfall' and 'Judamondo' which require some top end climbing and there is still plenty of room for some harder lines!

ACCESS AND APPROACH

From the A26 heading away from Tunbridge Wells looking out for the pub on the right-hand side called The Nevils Crest and Gun. Just after this take a small road after the church. This then leads down to the small car park of Eridge.

If heading from the south towards Tunbridge Wells then the turning is just after a left hand bend at the top of a hill. Look out for the church again and you should be fine.

The crag has several areas that climbing is banned from so please be aware of these and do not climb here. These are marked out on the map in the grey areas. This is a popular area for walkers and excessive amounts of chalk, finger tape, tick marks etc are not acceptable (all should be kept to an absolute minimum).

The area is managed by the British Wildlife Trust who do an amazing job in maintaining this crag. Please do your bit to respect this area to keep climbing permitted and not jeopardize its future.

CONDITIONS

Eridge as some great but very fragile rock so please take extra care here. As with most other crags this will require a long spell of good weather to dry out the majority of the crag. Different parts of the crag are sheltered in different ways and so some sections may dry out quicker than others.

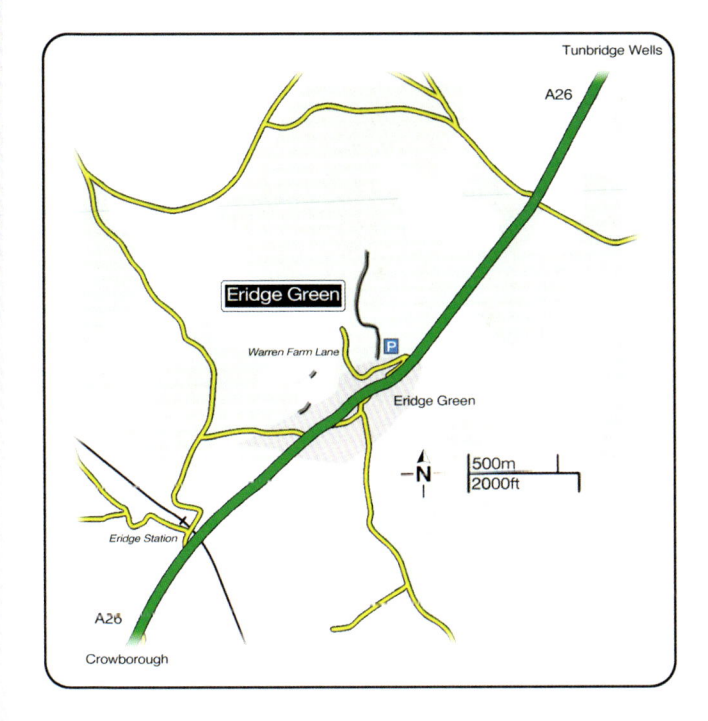

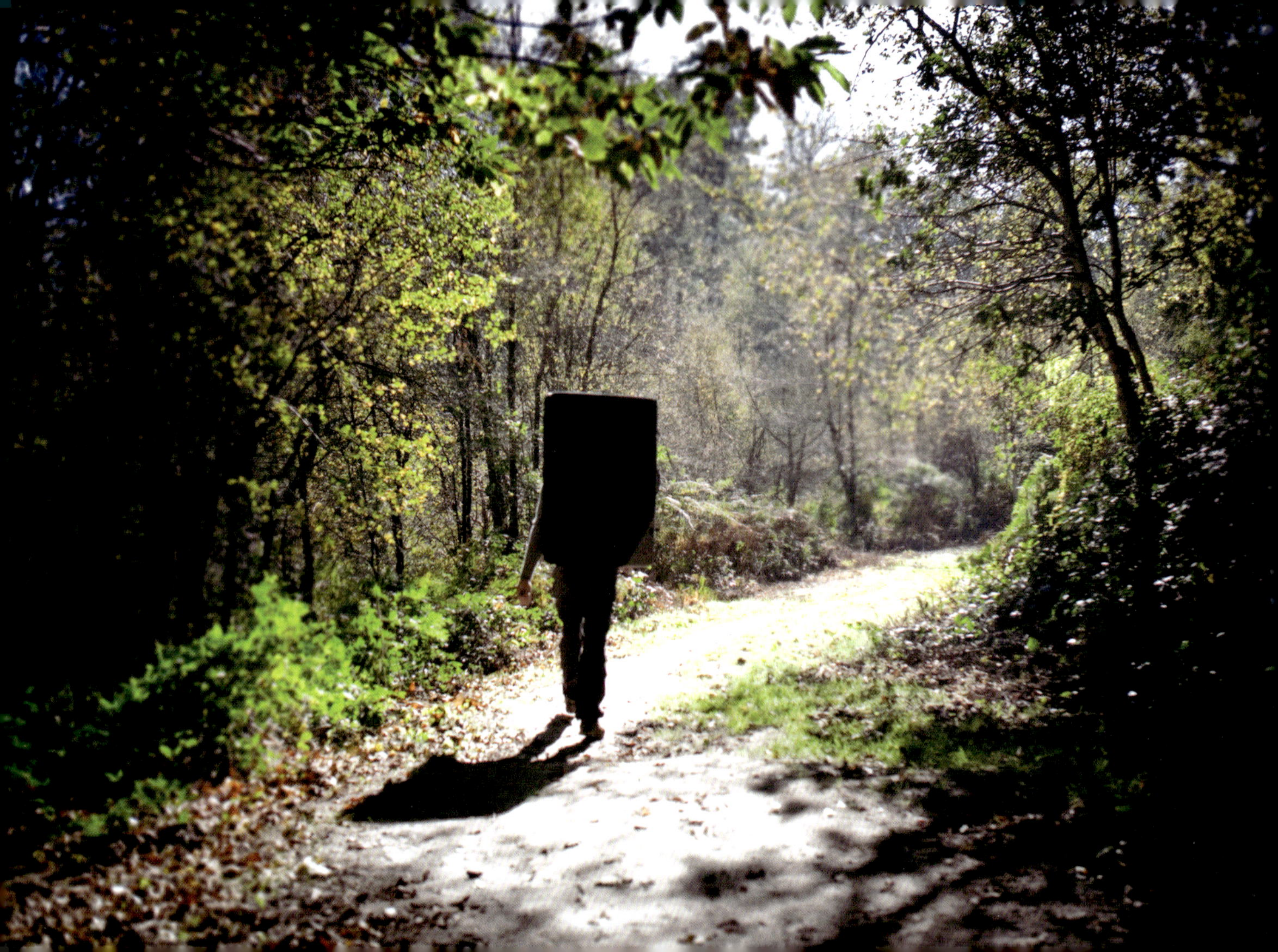

SSSI, Please don't climb in these grey areas.

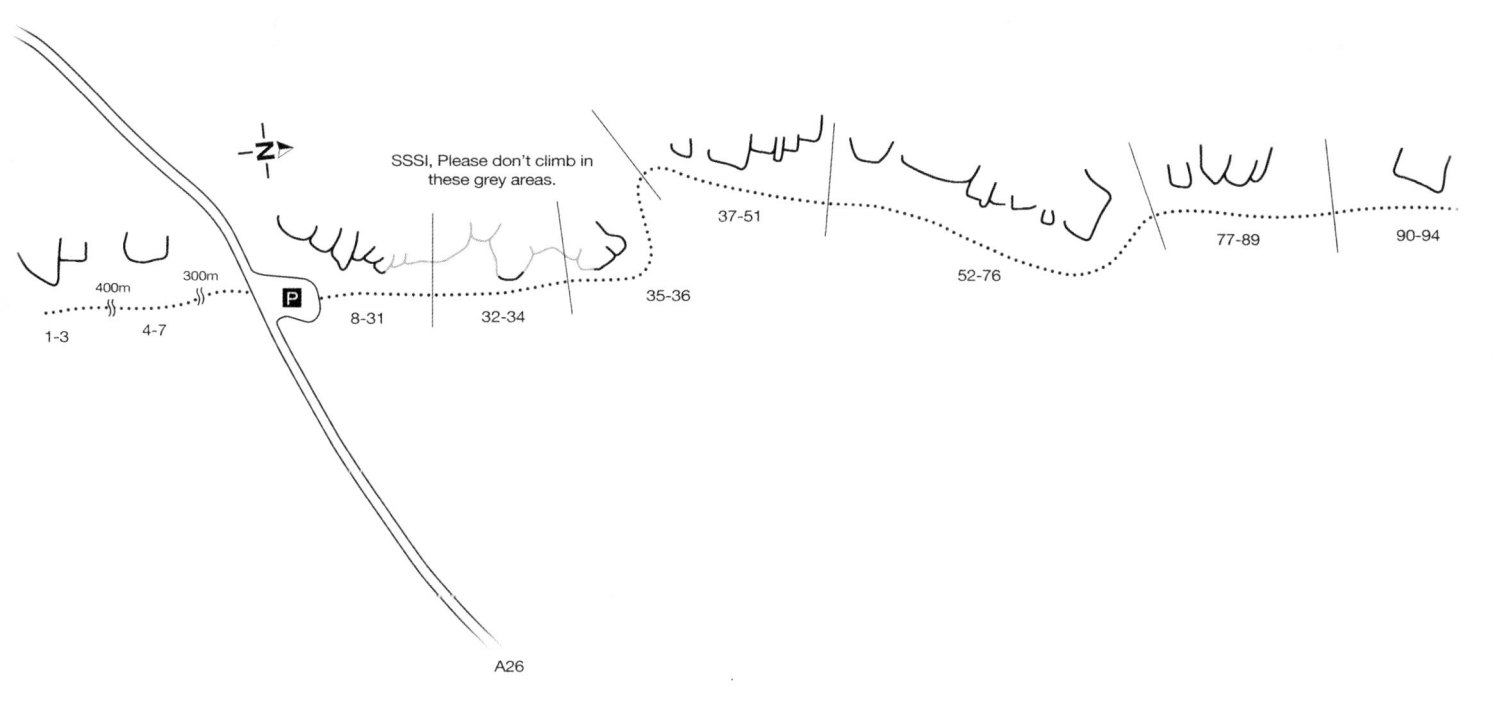

1-3 4-7 400m 300m **P** 8-31 32-34 35-36 37-51 52-76 77-89 90-94

A26

Eridge Green 114

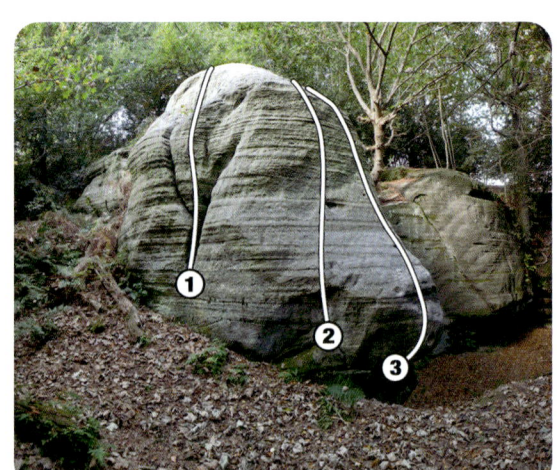

1. 4
The easiest line up this boulder provides a pleasant little climb.

2. 5
Easy start leads to a scary slabby top out.

3. 6B *Elephant's Chode* ss
The low nose of this boulder provides a strenuous start and then a mantle into a slab! What more could you ask for?

Project.
A highball project up the widely spaced holds. Has been attempted on both rope and highball but neither has gone yet.

Eridge Green car park

4. 6B
Using the large sandy holds to start gain the sloping ramp which at first glance seems completely blank.

5. 4
Follow the line of good holds up the central crease.

6. 4+
A great climb on large holds up the layback, going into a sandy top out so treat with care.

7. 6A+
Direct up the right hand face on good layaways and gastons leads to a tricky top out.

Ben Read | Route 6 | 4+

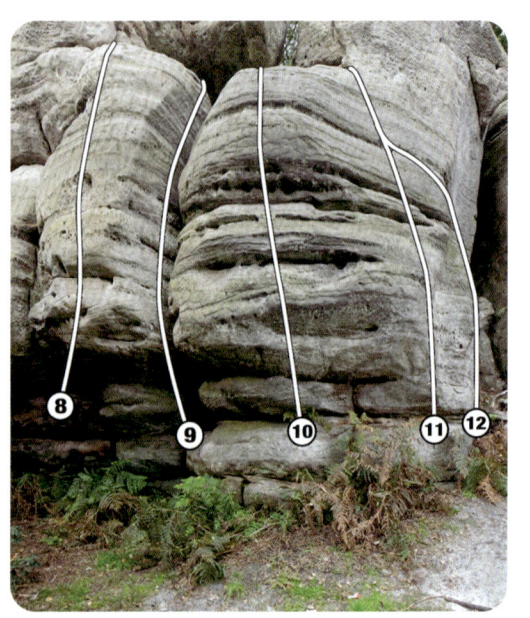

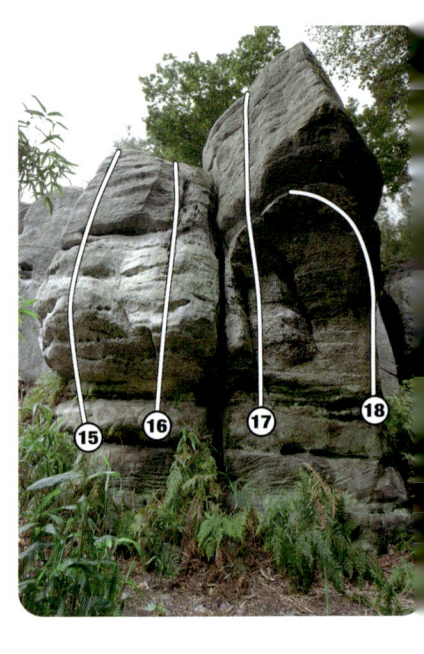

8. 6A
Just left of the crack is a blunt arête with a steep start.

9. 4
Follow the crack line to the break and then either top out or climb back down.

10. 5+
Take the line of breaks up the front face.

11. 5
Just right again is another climb on similar holds. Finish at the break or top out.

12. 5+
Starting just right of number **11,** climb up on good holds to traverse back into **11**.

13. 5+
Climb up the front scoop that faces the car park. Great climbing with a spicy top out.

14. 6A
A hard start and a hard finish with an easy section in between.

15. 6A+
Starting under the low roof, use good holds to get established and then cruise to the top.

Eridge Green

16. 6B 🅗

Another steep start just left of the crack leads to easier terrain.

17. 7B *The Watchtower* 🅗

The highball line just left of the prow has some great moves on it. Large moves between positive holds makes this photogenic route a must do at Eridge.

18. 6A

The direct start to the route *Prowess*. Use good holds to gain the jug under the large roof. This can also be extended out into the *Watchtower* at 7B.

James O'Neil | The Watchtower | 7B

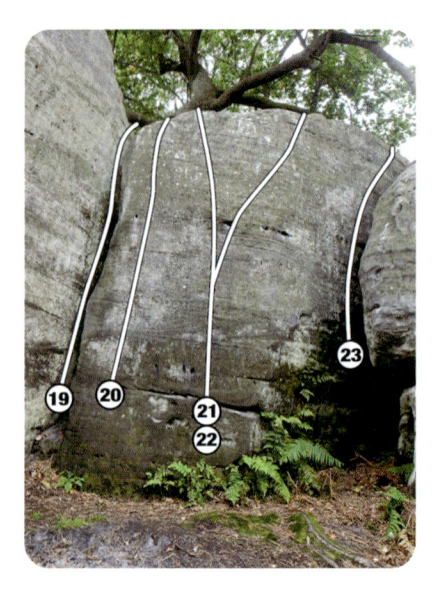

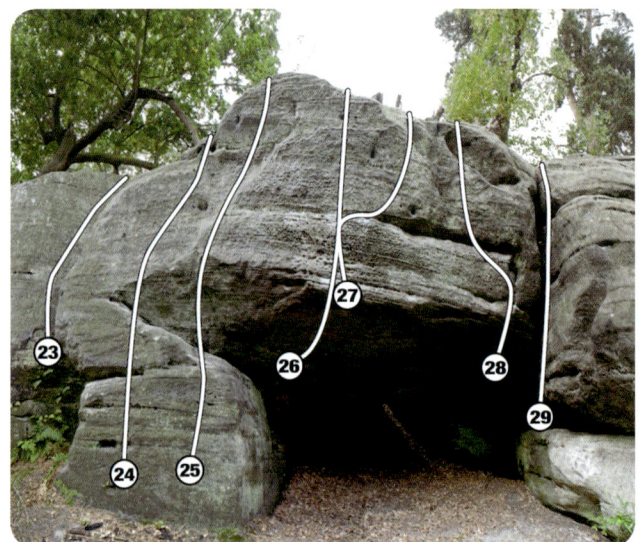

19. 3
Climb up the crack to the top using both sides.

20. 5
Climb up the left hand side of the boulder using the arête as a layback.

21. 7A *Sansara*
A hard slab that has gained the reputation as the hardest 7A on the sandstone. The tempting arête unfortunately is not in.

22. 7A
A right hand variation to *Sansara* is very reachy.

23. 4
The large crack line just right of *Sansara*.

24. 3
Follow the ramp upwards on good holds for both hands and feet.

25. 3+
Starting just right of the cave climb up on good holds.

26. 7A+ *Yankee Affair*
Starting on good holds in the cave dyno out to the jugs just past the lip. No left hand wall allowed for the true line.

27. 6A+ *Parisian Affair*
A long reach (or jump start for the vertically challenged) to the good holds on the lip and then direct up the face.

Eridge Green

28. 6A
Starting on the right hand side of the cave climb up to the break and then follow the holds leftwards and up to finish.

29. 4
Climb awkwardly up the crack line just right of the cave.

30. 6A+
The blunt nose provides a great boulder problem all the way to the top.

31. 5+
Starting just right of the nose climb up using good hidden holds to the top.

The next section of climbs are banned for climbing, please respect this and do not attempt to climb any of the rock here, no matter how good it looks!

Julia Cartwright | Route 24 | 3+

*Climbing is allowed on this small section but chalk is banned due to the harmful reaction it has to the plant species growing here. Please respect this!

32. 6A+
The low green overhang climbed direct gives this nice little number.

33. 6B
A fun little traverse that joins up with route **32** at the end.

34. 6B+
A long low level traverse that leads into **33** for a fun time pumpy experience.

*The next section of climbs are banned for climbing, please respect this and do not attempt to climb any of the rock here, no matter how good it looks!

Ben Read | Judamondo | 7C

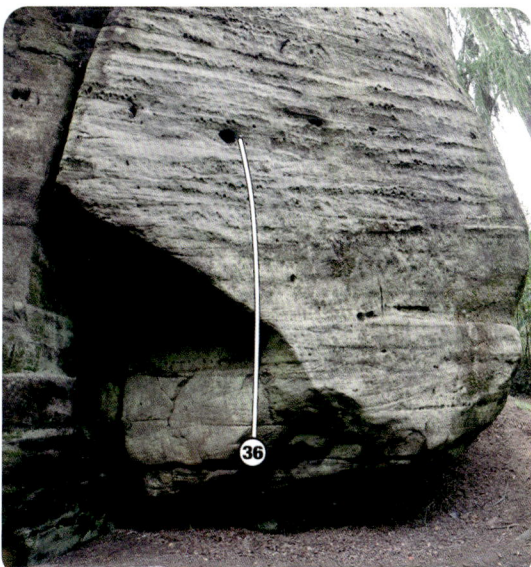

35. 7C *Judamondo* 🔵
Wide moves up the face on pockets and side pulls makes up one of Eridge's hardest lines. Finish in the large sloping hole.

36. 6B ss
A sit start on the right hand side of the undercut feature and finish in the large hole.

37. 7B+ *Velcro Wall*
Climb the front face of this wall making reachy moves to get established onto a stomach churning mantle.

38. 6C+ *Krafty Undercutz* ss
Traverse rightwards into *Velcro Arête* and finish up this.

39. 6C *Velcro Arête* ss
One of the best mid grade problems at Eridge if not the whole sandstone. Great moves climbing the arête on both sides with a sting in its tail.

Eridge Green

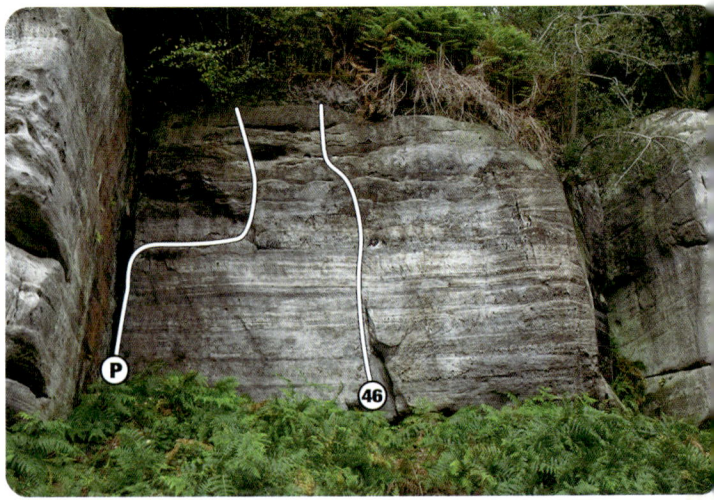

40. 6B+ *The Leaf* ss
The left hand end of the boulder has some great moves. Start on the large undercut and finish at the break.

41. 7B+ *Jack Strong*
A direct line up the middle of the wall via the tiny crimp. Start on the good holds and then power your way up! Once completed why not try the extension?

42. 6B ss
Starting on poor holds gain the good hold in the break and then make a large flick to a good flat hold.

43. 6A ss
Climb the right hand arête from a sitting start.

44. 7B *Turning The Leaf* ss
Climb the low line of holds across the whole boulder to finish up the left hand side.

45. 7C *Jack Strong Extension* ss
Start as for turning the leaf but take an early but much harder finish up Jack Strong.

Project.
A project line up this face. Used to be tried direct but due to holds snapping off this has become near impossible. It is now attempted by traversing in from the crack on the left.

46. 7B *Hypersonic*
A superb line up the centre of the face. From the large hole in the middle make some big moves out to good holds up left and then top out. Recent ascents have used a knotted rope to top out the problem due the increasing shrubbery at the top.

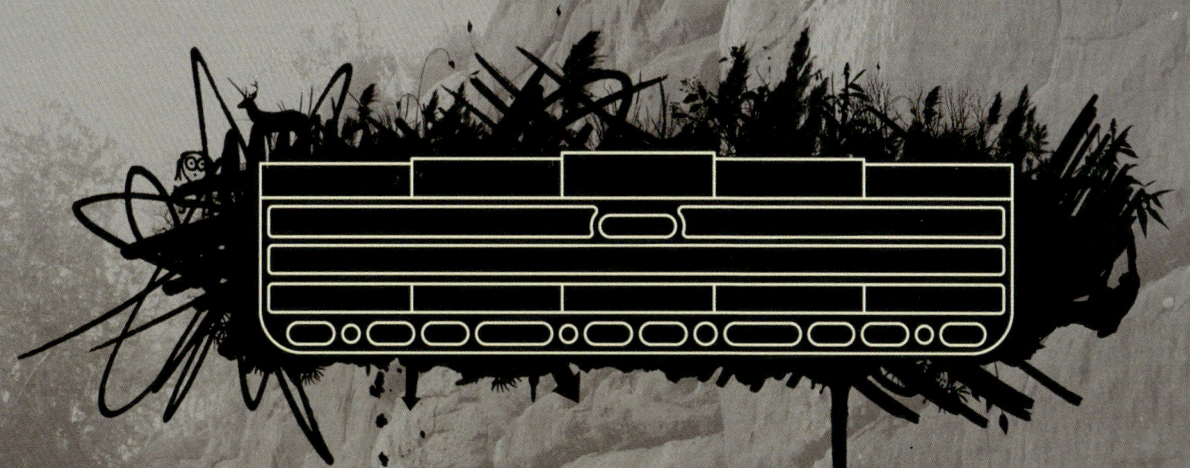

train hard, climb harder, respect your playground

www.karmaclimbing.com

karma

custom fingerboards | campus rungs | climbing walls | clothing

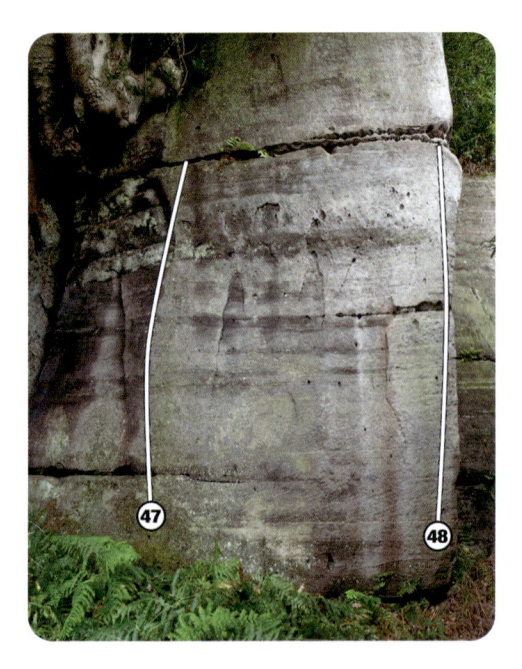

47. 6B
Climb the flake to break.

48. 6A *ss*
From a sit start the left hand side of the arête, climb all the way to the second break.

49. 5+ *ss*
From the sit, climb the right hand side of the arête finishing at the second Break.

50. 5+
A short wall with pockets. Finish at the break.

51. 5+
Climb the short wall to the break using both the arête and the crack. Eliminate either to make this one more of a challenge!

52. 6A ss
Starting on the low break, climb up the nose on good holds to the break.

53. 7B+ *Tusky* ss
Starting in the same place as **52**, climb rightwards finishing in *Nightfall*.

54. 7C *Nightfall* ss
From a sitting start, power up the arête with some hard moves finishing on the large sideways flake.

Ben Read | Nightfall | 7C

55. 5 ss
Starting on the large flat hold climb up using the crack and surrounding holds.

56. 6B ss
From the same start as **55** climb rightwards using a finger lock and edges to the break.

57. 7A *Azazel* ss
Starting in the large slot make a powerful move up to the line of good edges and then continue up to finish on the break. Use of the large feature out right for feet brings the grade down to 6C.

58. 6A+ ss
Climb the crack line using an unusual sidepull on the right hand side to gain the large finger slot.

59. 6A ss
From a sit start on the line of small holds. Finish on the large flat holds of the break.

60. 6A ss
Use painful and fragile pockets to gain the large flat holds to finish.

Eridge Green

MOON
100% CLIMBING

CLOTHING AND HARD GOODS
VISIT: WWW.MOONCLIMBING.COM

BEN MOON
VOYAGER (V14)
BURBAGE NORTH

"IT HAS BEEN QUITE A BATTLE, I MUST SAY, AND I'VE LOST TRACK OF THE NUMBER OF DAYS I HAVE SPENT ON THIS PARTICULAR CLIMB... I FELT SO UNMOTIVATED OVER THE SUMMER AND WONDERED IF I WOULD EVER START THE BATTLE AGAIN... IT'S AMAZING HOW A FEW COLD DAYS CAN TURN YOUR MOOD AROUND!"

BEN WRITES ON THE MOON BLOG ABOUT HIS ASCENT OF VOYAGER (V14), BURBAGE NORTH, PEAK DISTRICT.

PHOTO: WWW.ADAMLONG.CO.UK

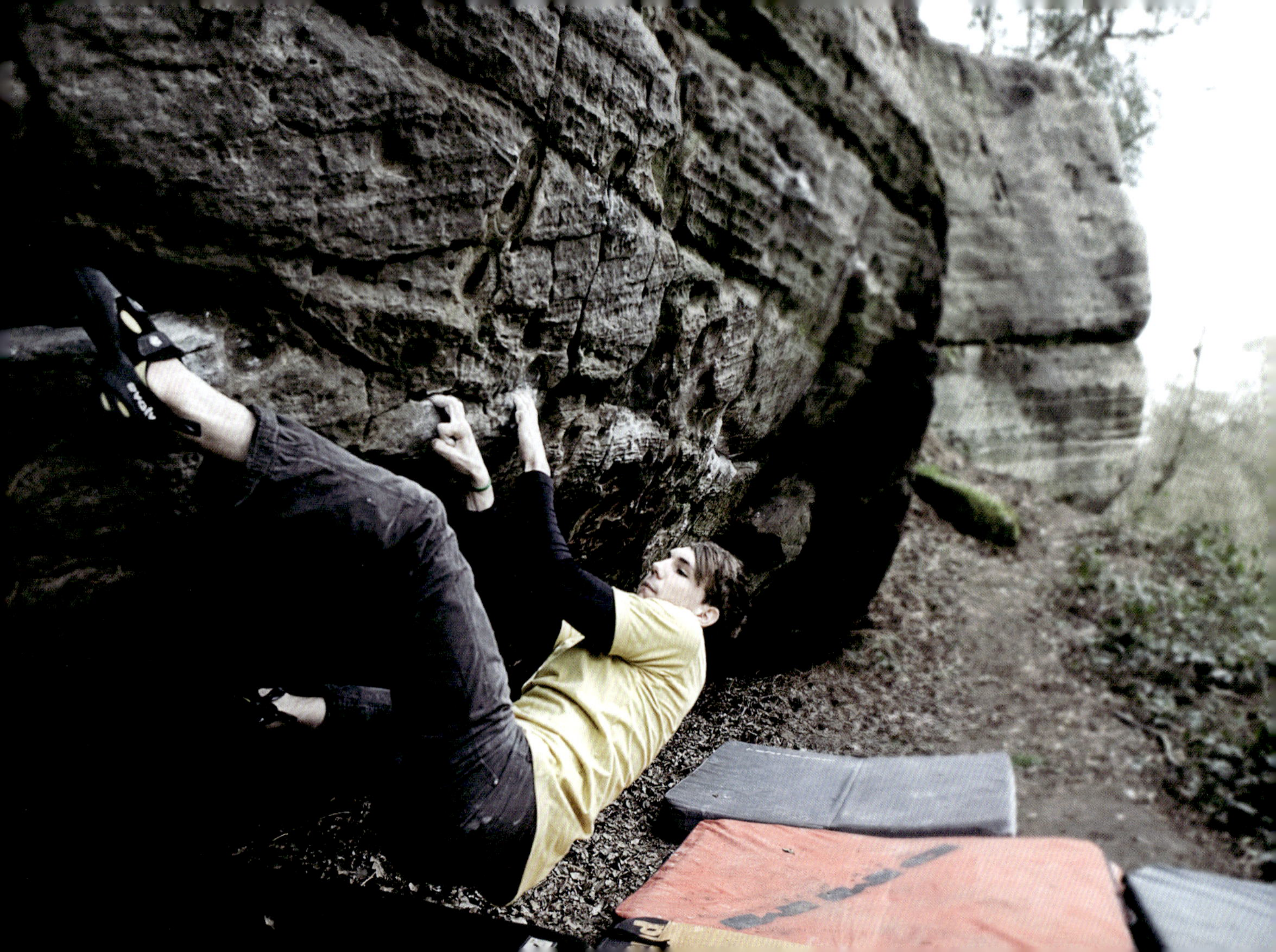
evolv

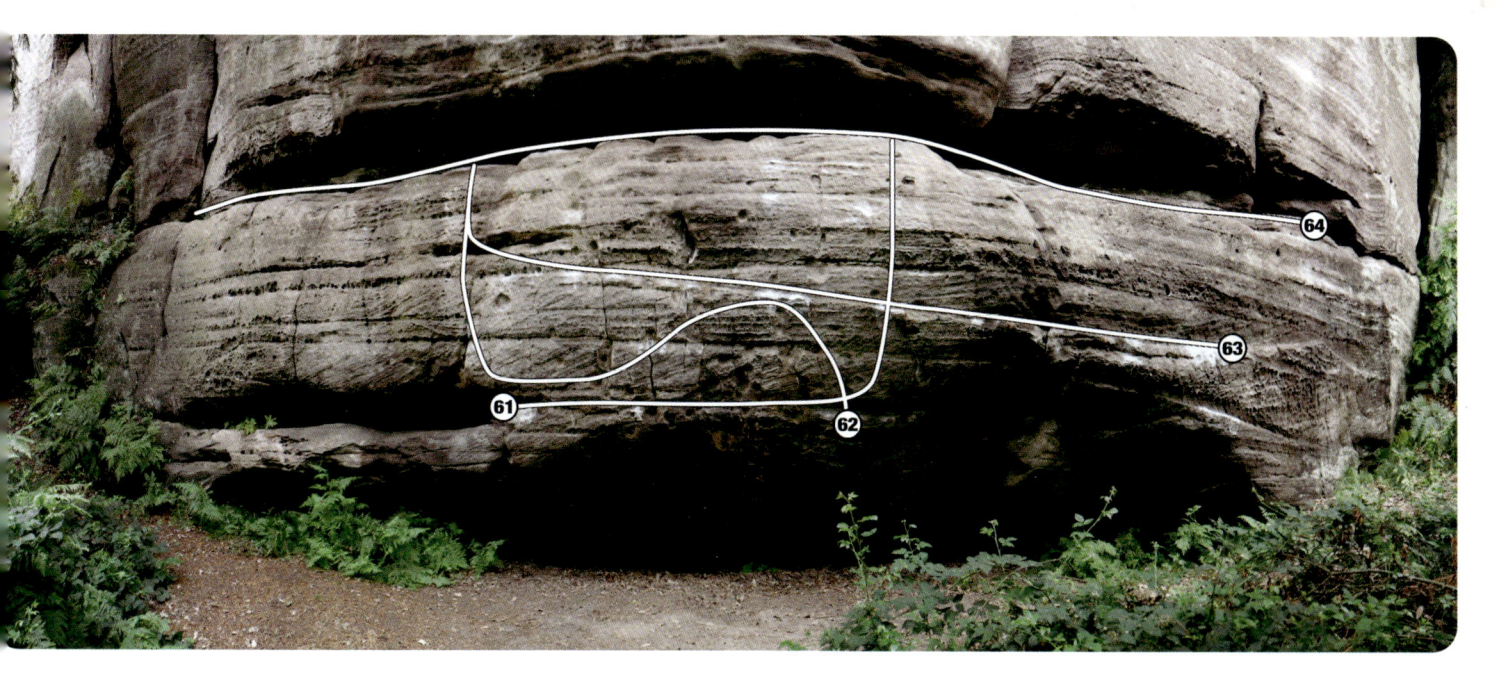

61. 7C *Goat Rage* ss
Starting on the large flat hold follow the line of pockets all the way to the start of *Azazel*, and then finishes this line up to the break.

62. 7A *Indian Traverse* ss
Start as for *Azazel* and then traverse left along the line of good edges after the first few moves. Then move down to the start of *Goat Rage* by a slot and pocket to then finish up the crack line.

63. 7C *The Read Line*
Follow the line of crimps and edges along the obvious break line. No holds allowed above or below this line. Finish up the crack line to the break.

64. 6B *Daylight Throbbery*
Starting on the right hand side follow the break of slopers all the way to the left hand side of the wall.

65. 6A *ss*
Climb the arête from a sit start finishing on the juggy break.

66. 4+
Follow the flake to the rewarding break.

67. 6B
Climb to the good hold on the lip of the overhang.

68. 4+
Climb up the left face of this wall on good holds all the way.

69. 5+
Climb up the right hand side of the wall using good holds on the face and the arête.

70. 6B
Climb the triangular arête, this boulder gets mossy very quickly so does require a little bit of cleaning from time to time.

Eridge Green

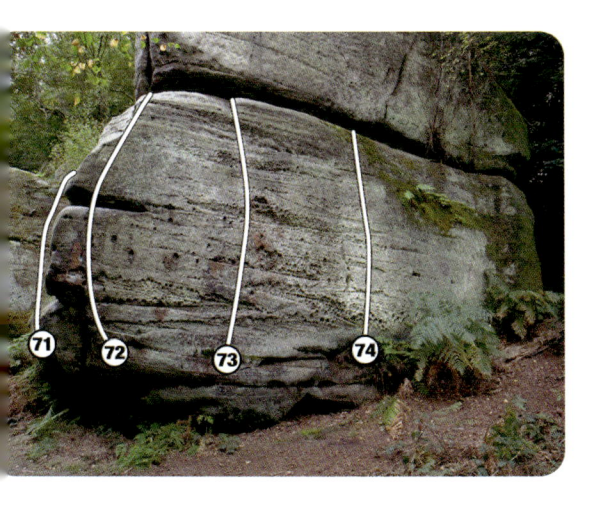

71. 6A *ss*
From a low start on slopers, power up to finish on the break via some undercuts.

72. 5+ *ss*
Climb the arête using good holds on both sides.

73. 5
Climb straight up the centre of the wall on the red tinted pockets. Finish on the break.

74. 6A
Climb up the left hand side of this wall using small put positive holds.

75. 4
Follow a line of good holds up to the large undercut feature which is then used to gain the top.

76. 4+
Climb the right hand side on good holds.

Mike Hadcocks | Route 72 | 5+

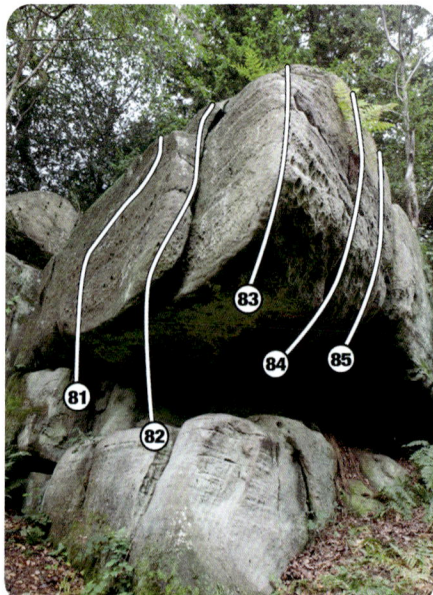

77. 5
Spaced pockets make up this short but pleasant little climb.

78. 4
Climb the crack line up the centre of this wall.

79. 5+
Just right of the crack is another short climb up positive holds.

80. 6A
Climb the wall just right of the arête.

81. 5+
Starting on the boulder make a hard pull, followed by easier moves.

82. 6A+
Get established on the large flake, then layback up this to finish.

83. 6C *Black Cadilac*
Climb the blunt nose direct to the top.

84. 6B+
A line up the right hand face using good holds either side of the crack.

85. 6C *White Lincoln*
Climb up the right side of this bloc, using just the right hand side of the crack and the arête. Without the rock underneath for your feet, goes at 7A.

86. 6B
Climb up the front face of the large rounded boulder.

87. 6A+
An interesting little climb up the heavily featured wall.

Eridge Green

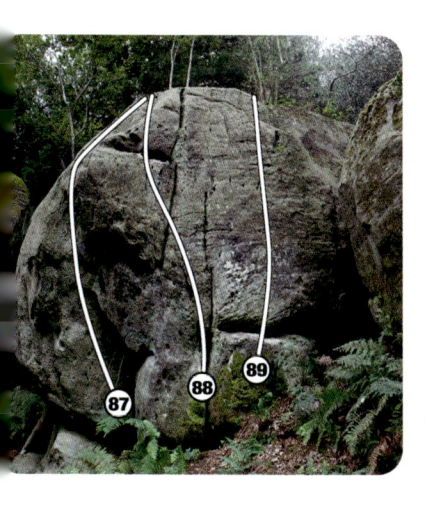

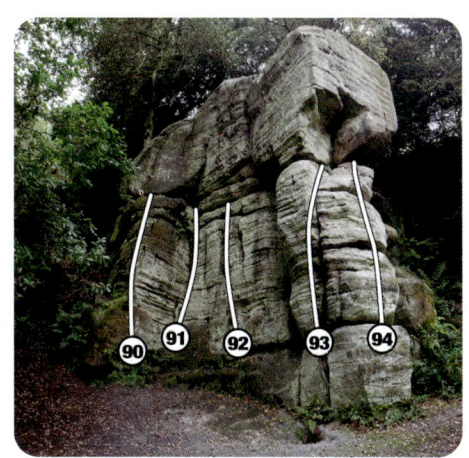

88. 5
A great little climb up the hidden face of this boulder using the short series of cracks.

89. 6A+
The blank looking wall just right of the previous climb.

90. 3+
Climb the blunt arête on the left side of this wall.

91. 3
The corner crack line gives a short but sweet little boulder problem.

92. 4
Climb directly up the face of the central wall to finish on the break.

93. 4+
Follow the vague crack line to the break.

94. 4
The last climb of Eridge up the far right end.

* The rest of the boulders and climbs along from this point are banned from climbing. Please respect this and do not attempt to climb any of these.

James O'Neil | Route 93 | 4+

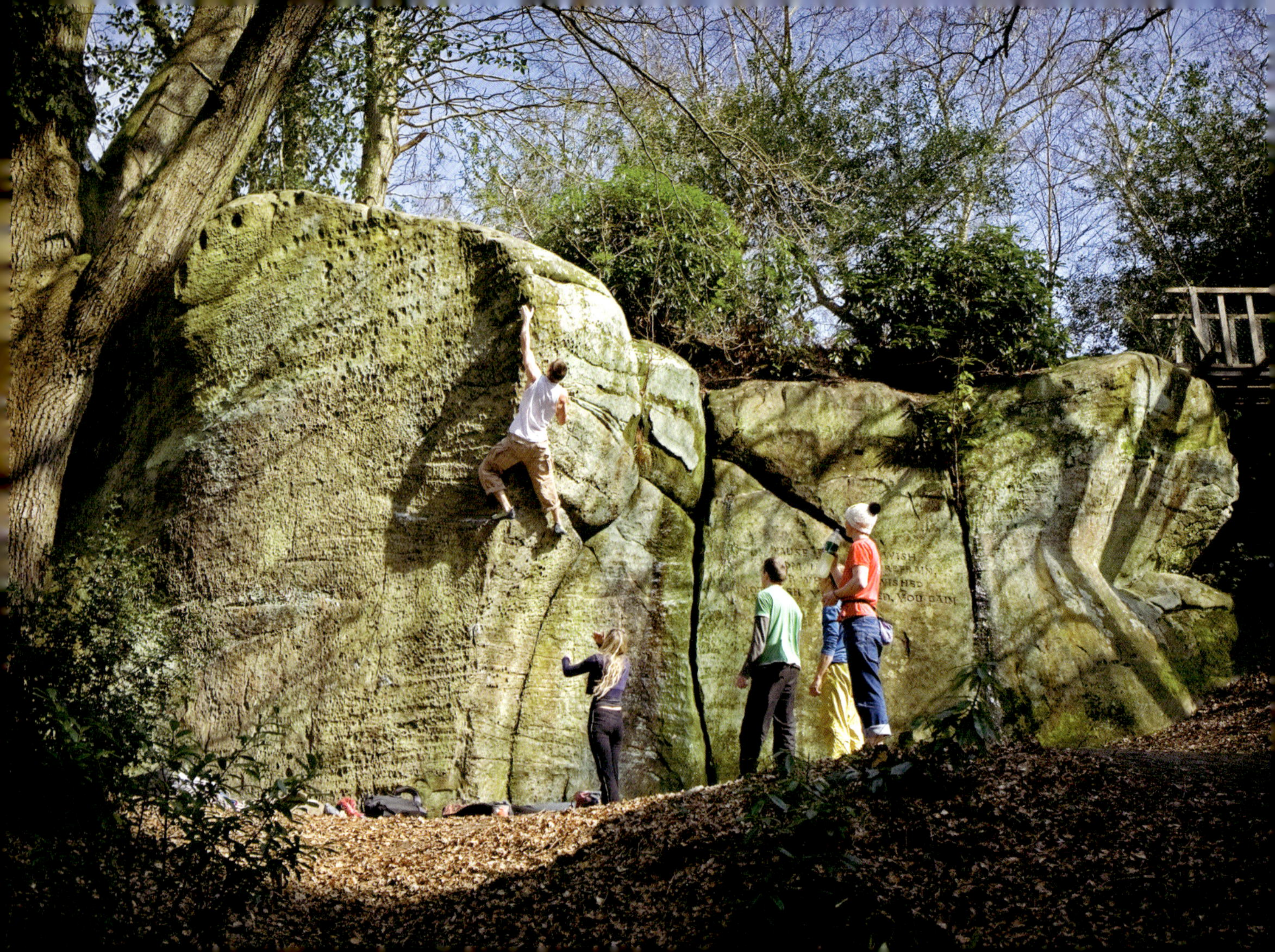

HIGH ROCKS

INTRODUCTION

High Rocks is without doubt *the* place for hard bouldering in the South East. The sheer number of lines here matches that of some of the big bouldering areas elsewhere in the country. The quality of these problems are evident to anyone who climbs them.

It has a wide variety of grades but a lot of the best climbs fall in the 7a and above bracket. High Rocks also provide us with the hardest climbs in the area- 'Don't Pierdol' is at the top of the list at 8a+ but there are numerous projects that could well push this off the top spot.

It is a popular destination for walkers and is also a wedding venue so please respect others that may be using the rocks and make sure that you are considerate to their needs.

ACCESS AND APPROACH

Being a popular venue for tourists it is well signposted from Tunbridge Wells off the A264. There are a number of approaches that all lead to the main car park by the High Rocks Inn. The car park is free but the rocks are not.

High Rocks is privately owned, so please ensure that you pay the relevant fee to enter the premises. Access is a privilege so please respect the owner's decision and do not put this into jeopardy by breaking in. Boulderers have had a bad press at this crag as many people have snuck in and put all the hard work that has been put into allowing climbers to continue to use the rock at risk.

Payment is taken in the Inn itself and there are regular checks by High Rocks staff who wander round the rock. If you don't want to pay, then don't climb here. At time of writing season passes are also available for the more dedicated boulderer.

CONDITIONS

High Rocks takes nearly the longest to dry out and so is not climbable until the late spring and summer months of the year. The Matterhorn boulder and surrounding areas are normally the first to dry out but still need to be treated with caution.

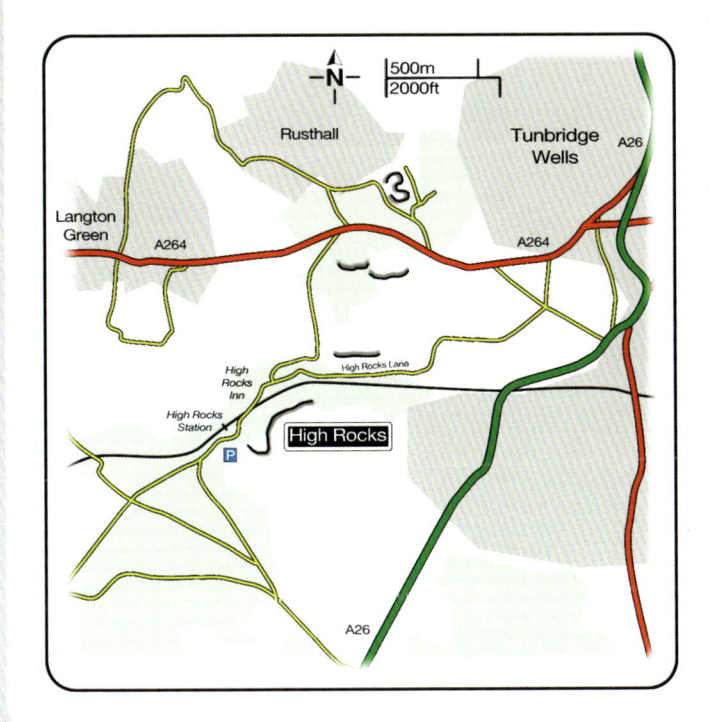

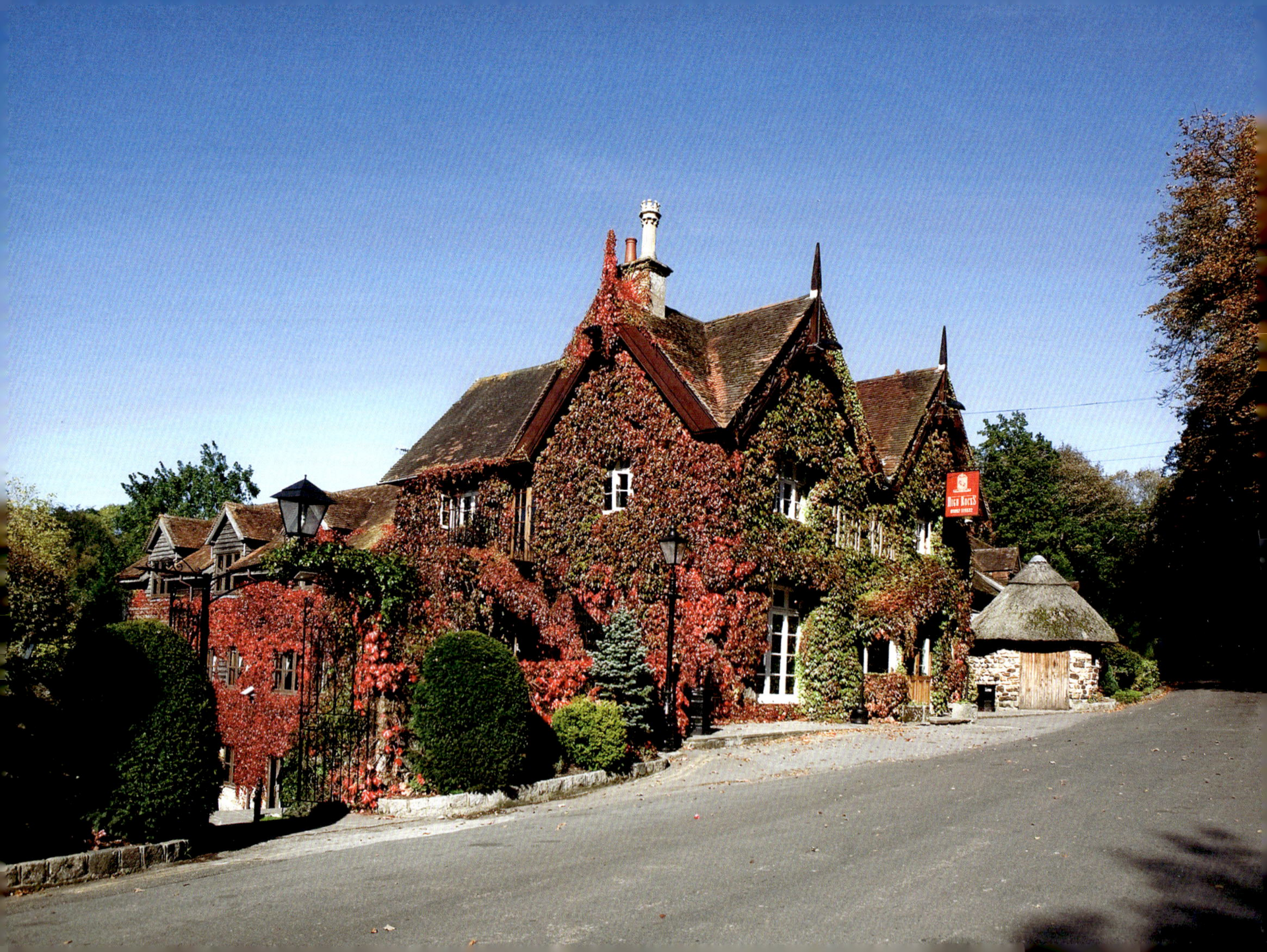
HIGH ROCKS

1-11

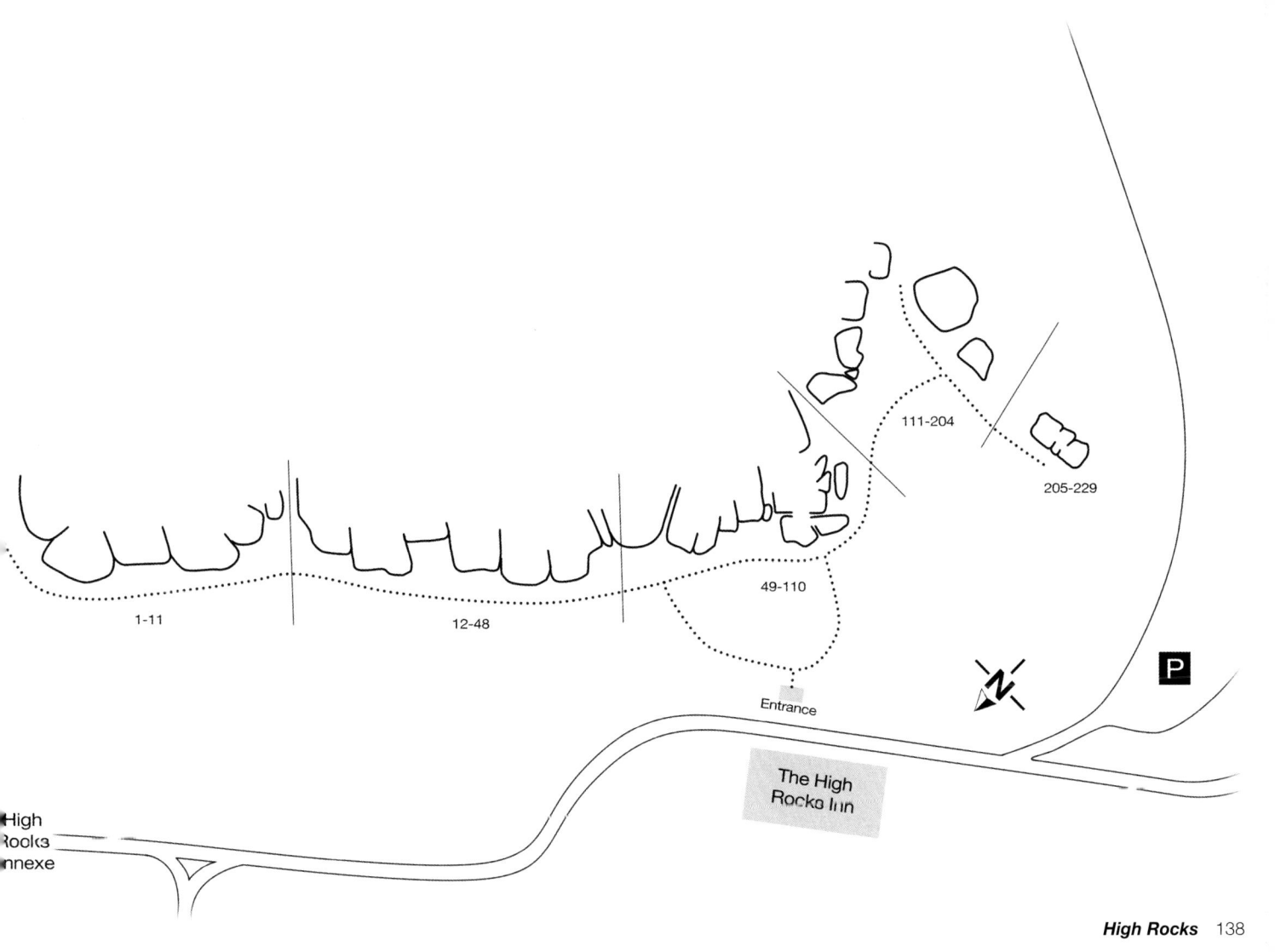

12-48

49-110

111-204

205-229

Entrance

The High
Rocks Inn

High
Rocks
Annexe

P

High Rocks 138

1. 7B *Clowns Pocket*
The large dyno from the side pulls to the large jug.

2. 6B+
Climb the right hand end of this wall up the crack like feature finishing on the break.

Seb Crump | Route 10 | 6B+

3. 6B+ *Bolt Route*
The line of mono's up the middle of the face. Finish on the break.

4. 7B
The next line of mono's is a tricky little number where smaller fingers are definitely an advantage.

Project.
A project line up the face on widely spaced holds.

5. 6B
Starting in the large flake follow good holds to the big hole like feature.

6. 6A
The corner crack line finishing on the break.

7. 6B
The start of the route *Second Generation* a nice little problem on its own though.

8. 7A *Pammy* ss
Climb the blunt rounded arête with some hard moves on small holds.

9. 7C
A traverse line into *Resurrection*, does not change the grade but does make it harder.

10. 6B+
There are many eliminates that can be made up on this wall but using everything gives this grade.

11. 7C *Resurrection*
A hard line up the arête, all holds are in but a purer line is to not use any of the chipped holds. A great problem either way though. A sit start can be added but is not really worth it.

Project.
The direct start to the famous route *Chimera* has been attempted by many people before but with not much success.

12. 5+
The line of massive jugs up the over hang finishing on the break.

13. 6A+
Starting in the same place as **12** but taking a right hand finish to the large ledge.

High Rocks

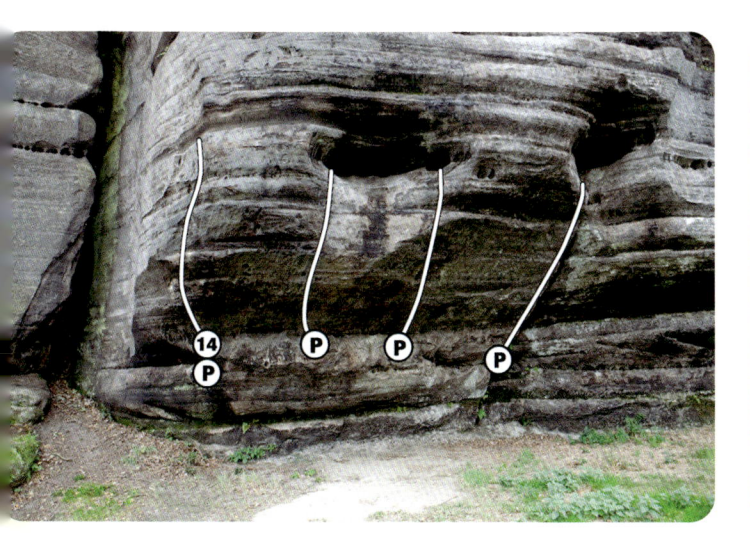

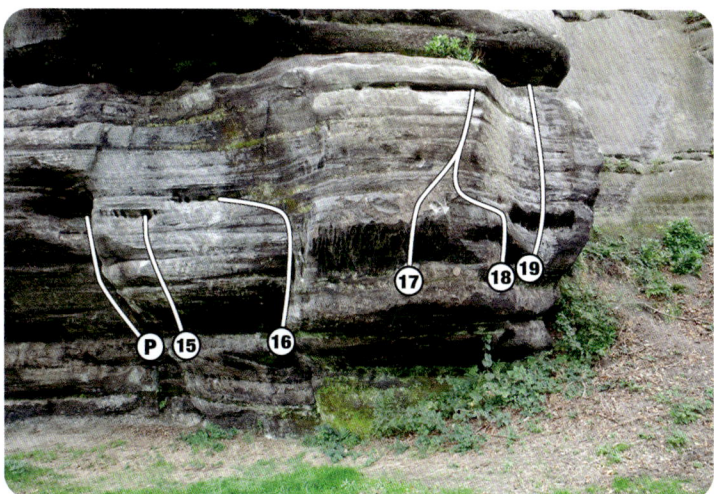

14. 7A+ *Vandal*
Starting on large jugs climb the arête to a sideways pocket. Finish here for the original tick or venture onwards to new ground.

Project.
There is a project problem of the vandal extension. All the moves have been done but not yet as a highball from the ground. Some very large committing moves makes this a daunting challenge.

Project.
Another project roof that may or may not go but either way does require a bit of work.

Project.
Surprise surprise, another project roof. Some wild big moves on barely holdable holds will make this one of High Rocks hardest additions if it ever goes.

Project.
A project crack line for those who are a bit sick and twisted!

15. 7A *Superman*
A poor route where the first move is the hardest. A jump start to the rail and then continue up to the break. There is the possibility of a proper start being added but it is yet to be done.

16. 6A+
The start to the route *Judy* start up the corner crack and move left to finish on the large juggy break. A direct finish to the break is 6C+.

17. 7B+ *Shadow Of The Wind*
A great route up the front face of this wall. Finish on the break.

18. 7A
A variation start on the previous route, starting on the right and traversing in at mid height.

19. 6A
Climb up the shallow groove with some interesting positions.

High Rocks 142

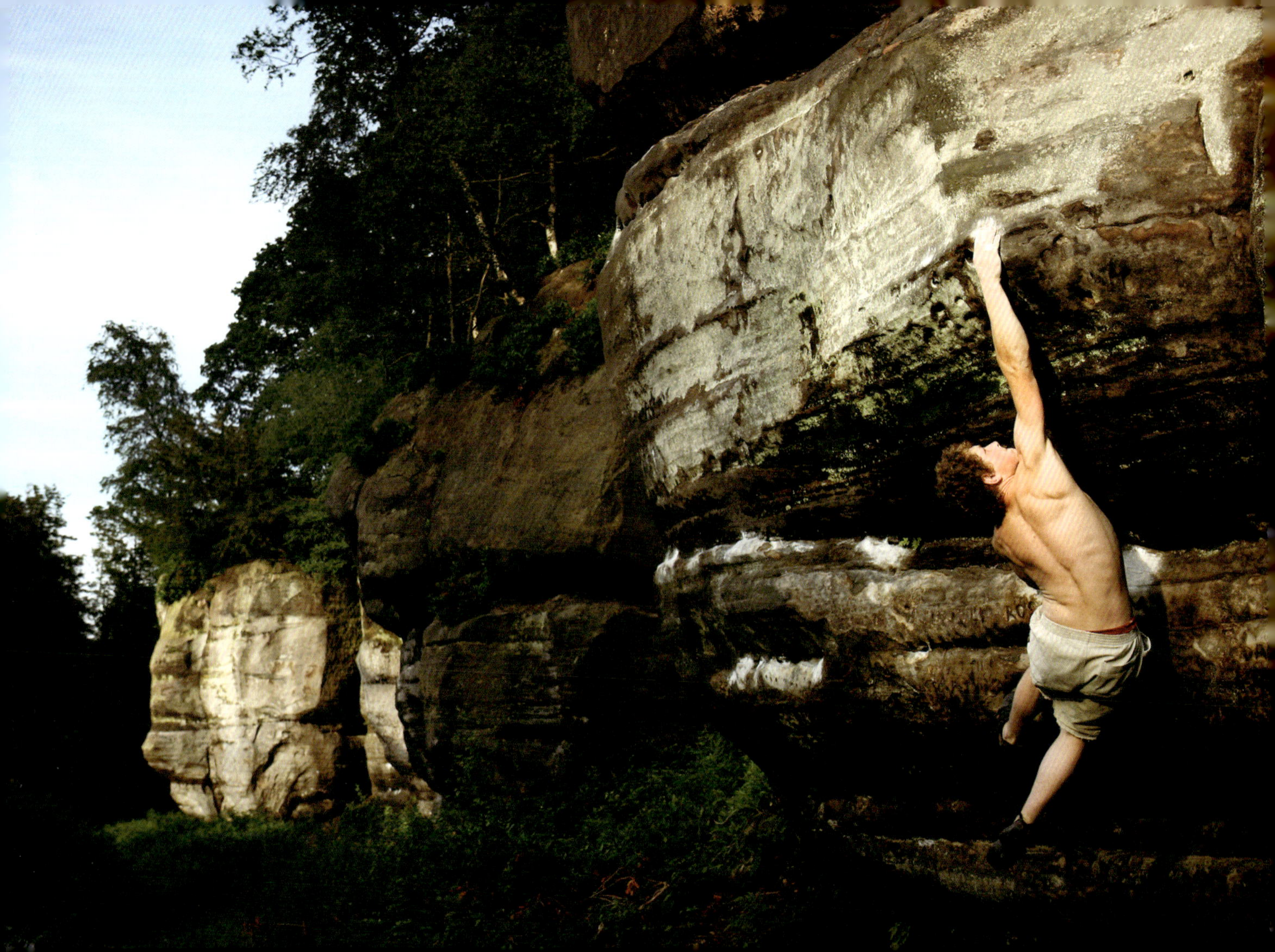

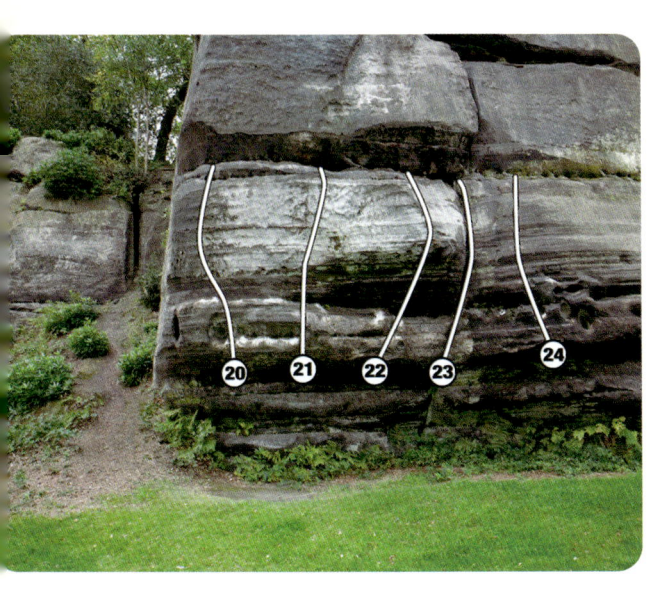

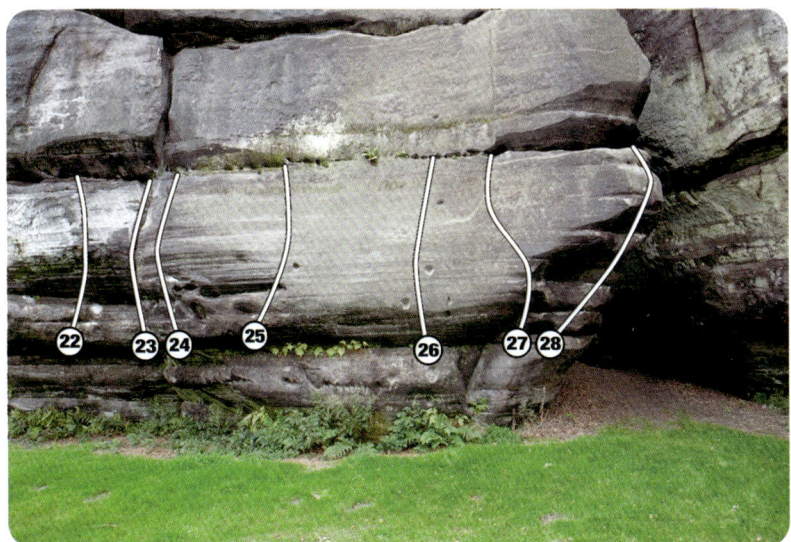

20. 6C *Salad Days*
Climb up the arête with aid of undercuts and sidepulls finishing on the break.

21. 7C *Dogtown*
The direct line up the centre of the face. May now be harder due to the loss of an undercut.

22. 7B *Pet Cemetery*
Starting on the large jugs on the right hand side make a large move to a pinch and then finish up on the break.

23. 5
The crack line in between the two walls is of poor quality.

24. 7A *The Real Slim Shady*
A tough little number that has a number of ways to complete it all at about the same grade. Finish on the break above the sloper.

25. 6A+
A nice little climb using the undercut pocket to reach up to the break.

26. 6A
Follow the second line of chipped pockets to the break, these look much better than they actually are.

27. 7A+ *Atomic Mushroom*
Starting under the roof on good holds make a large pull or flick to the sloping feature and then work your way up to the break.

28. 6A+
Climb straight up the underside of the small overhang.

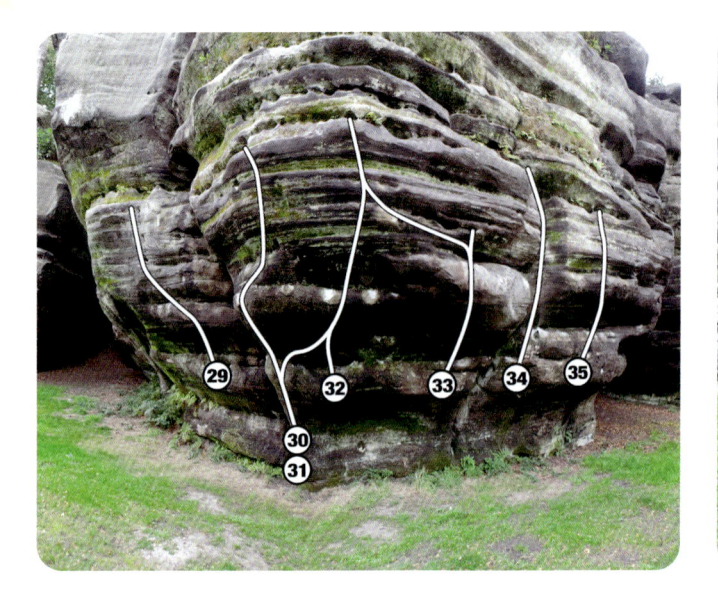

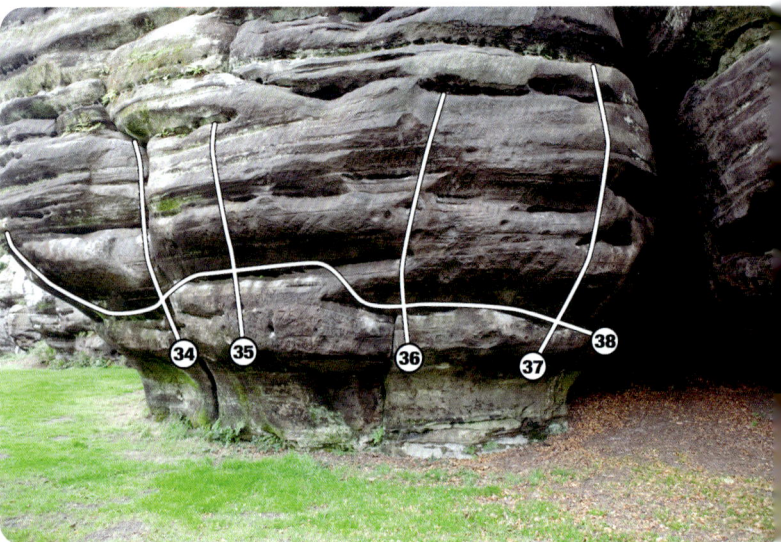

29. 6B
Starting on positive holds make some large moves upwards and left to a good jug on the lip of the overhang.

30. 6C *Spanked* ss
From a sit start at the bottom of the prow make some large moves between goodish holds to finish on the large obvious jug.

31. 7A *Superfly* ss
Starting in the same place as Spanked move up right at the break and then follow this line of holds. The true line does not use the large flat ledge out right for your heel on the higher moves.

32. 6C
Starting on the break and using the ledge is the original problem before *Superfly* was added.

33. 6C
Starting on the break to the right make a big move to the ledge and either finish here or continue up Superfly which comes in at 7A.

34. 5
Climb up the crack line in the corner.

35. 6B+
A controversial route that climbs up this section of the wall. Using all the holds comes in at the above grade but there have been many variations and eliminates on here, some rumoured to be up to 8A.

36. 6A
Take the line of widely spaced pockets and ledges to finish on the break.

37. 6A+
Climb the right hand end via some big moves.

145 *High Rocks*

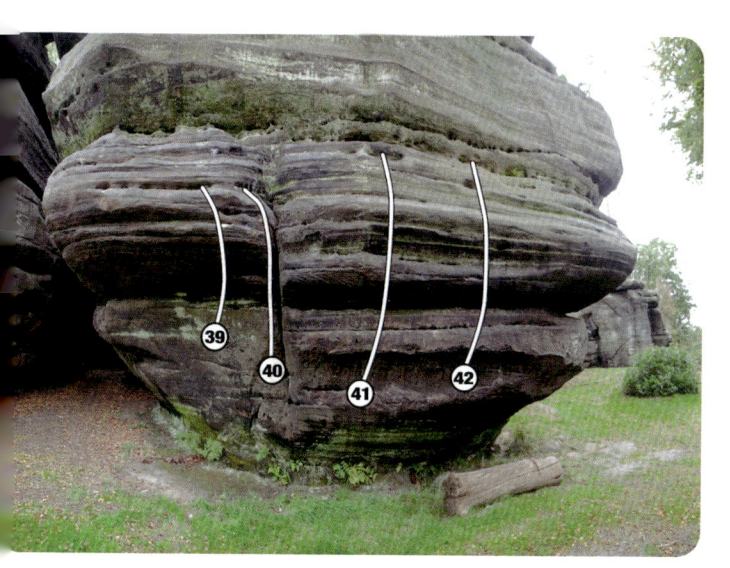

38. **6C**
Traverse all the way along the break line to the start of *Spanked* and *Superfly*. This route makes a great extended start to other problems and can be used as a great training route for those working on stamina. Legend tells it has been repeated up to 8 times back and forth.

39. **6C**
The large roof has very little to offer apart from this line on the right. A dyno from the break to the obvious hold.

40. **6A**
The corner crack line to the obvious break finish.

41. **6B+**
Stick the slopey breaks to a good jug.

42. **6C**
Climb the slopey breaks to the high break with good holds on it.

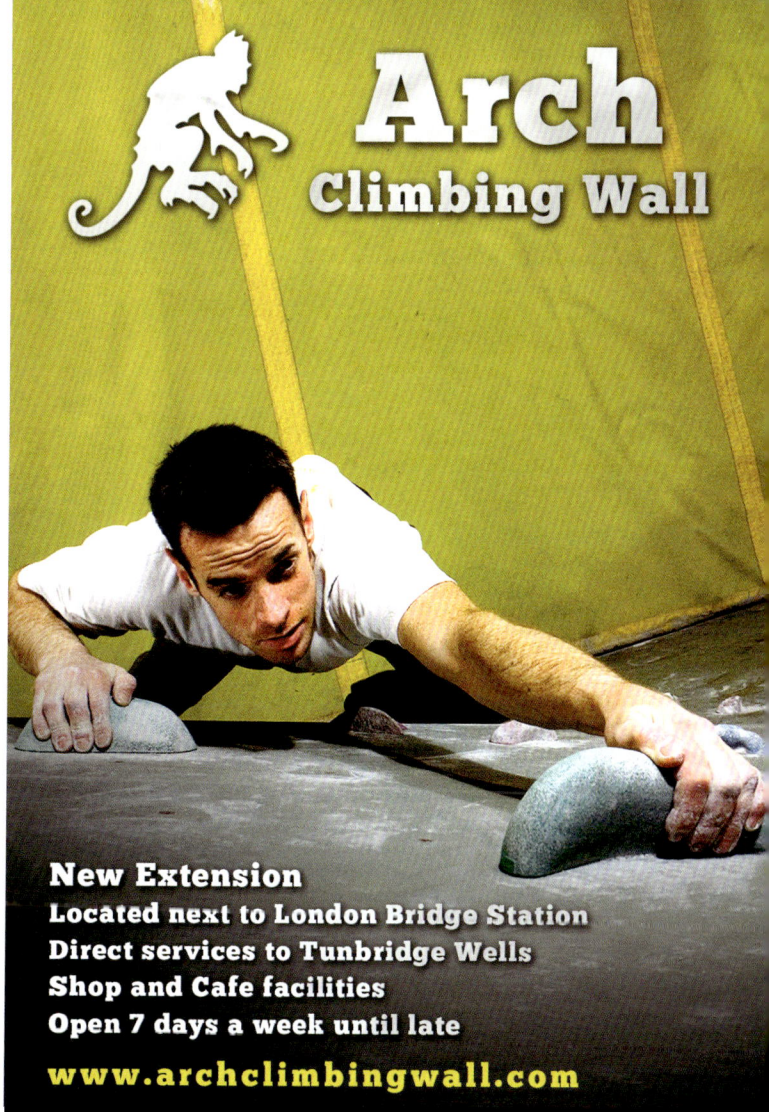

Arch
Climbing Wall

New Extension
Located next to London Bridge Station
Direct services to Tunbridge Wells
Shop and Cafe facilities
Open 7 days a week until late

www.archclimbingwall.com

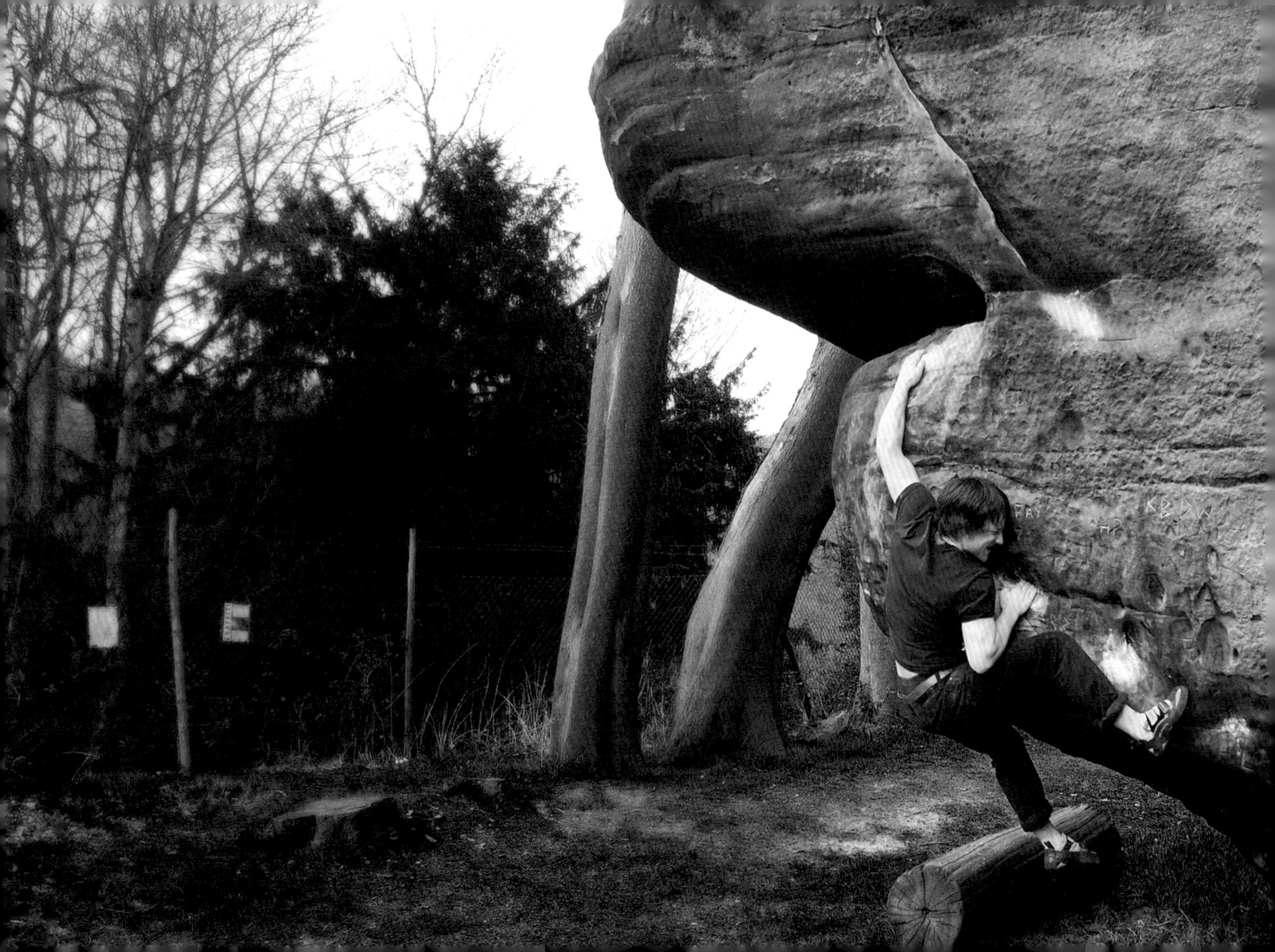

43. 7A *Magnetic* ss
A great little route that starts underneath the over hang and powers up with big moves in between good holds. Finish up the large flake to the break.

44. 4
Climb the corner and crack slab with the large footholds to start.

45. 4+
Just right again is another short line up the undercut feature to the break.

46. 4+
Climb the arête on the right hand side using good holds.

47. 6B+
Climb up the overhanging nose using both sides. Start underneath the overhang and make some big moves to get established on the front. Finish on the break line.

48. 6C
Starting in the same place as **47** branch off right and climb up this face. Finish again on the break.

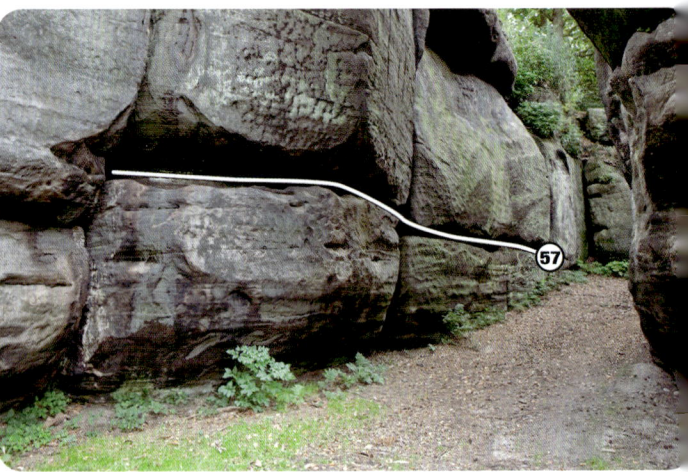

49. 4
Climb the crack line on the face.

50. 6A *ss*
A sit start on good holds and then climbing all the way up to positive holds on the top break.

51. 6A+ *ss*
A hard sit start leads to easier climbing up the face.

52. 5+
Climb the front of this wall on large holds finishing at the break.

53. 5+
Another short climb up the wall just left of the crack.

54. 5
The crack line gives a short layback climb. Finish on the break.

55. 5+
The direct start to the above crack line has some big moves on poor holds.

56. 5+
Climb the wall up to the large pocketed slots. Finish as high as you wish to go.

57. 6C
A long sloping traverse from a low start deep in the gully. Finish at the second crack line.

*There are several green slabs to the right of the start of **57** that have been bouldered before. However, they rarely dry out due to lack of sunshine and because of this have a good layer of slime on them most of the year. There is a tricky problem up the blank wall at the far end called *Orcanyon* which goes at around 7A if you're ever interested.

149 *High Rocks*

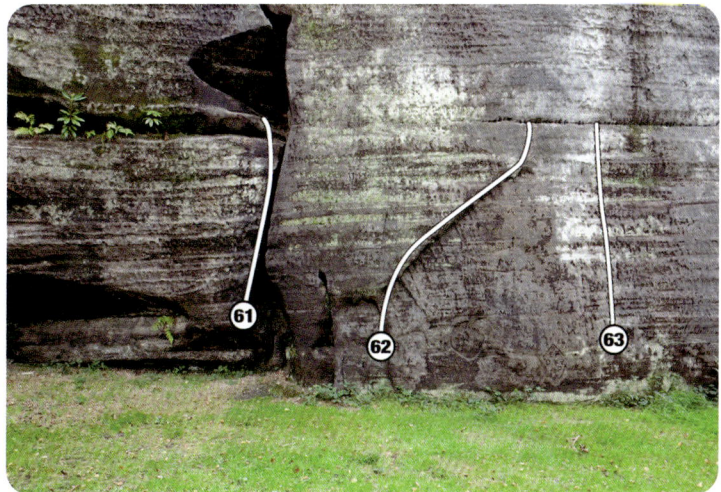

58. 6B
A traverse along the break line from the crack. Finish on the large jugs from route **59**.

59. 6C *Ben's a Woofter* ss
The sit start of the crack line finishing on the large obvious jug.

Project.
A line up the front face of this wall has been attempted but to no success so far.

60. 6A
Starting in the same slot as the previous routes traverse round the corner to finish on a good hold in the next break.

61. 6A ss
Climb the crack line from a sit start finishing on the break.

62. 6C
Follow the line of undercut holds up diagonally right finishing on the small break line.

63. 6C+
The blank wall that has a good left hand slot on it. Some delicate moves to gain this and then finish on the break line.

*To the left of these boulder problems are more green slabs down the gully. They rarely dry out due to lack of sunshine and because of this have a good layer of slime on them most year round. The short slab to the left of the arête at the bottom is called *Growing Pairs* and is 6C+.

High Rocks 150

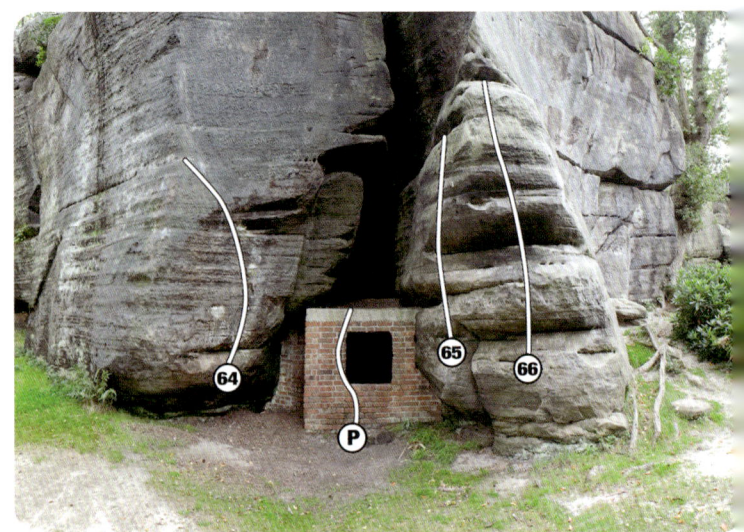

64. 6A+ ss
Climb the wall just left of the brick house, finishing with pinches on the obvious feature. This has been highballed all the way to the top and is a very serious challenge at 6C!

Project.
One of the hardest project lines on the sandstone. The tough red brick wall has a sitting start leading to a tricky layback section and then a horrible mantle of doom to finish off with. Who knows what superstar will make the first ascent?

65. 6A
Climb the wall just to the right of the shelter.

66. 6A
The blunt nose has good holds hidden on it.

Superstars try, superstars fail.

67. 5
Climb up the easy slab to the break.

68. 5
To the right of the previous route is a slightly harder variation on thinner holds.

69. 5+
Climb up using the large under cut to make progress to the break.

70. 4
Use the crack and surrounding holds to climb to the break. This has a bad landing so be careful when climbing here.

71. 5+ *ss*
A short climb up the crack.

72. 5+
Starting just right of the crack climb up the pocketed wall diagonally right up to the break.

High Rocks

73. 7B+
Difficult technical climbing up the left hands set of layaways.

74. 7B *Porgs Progress*
More technical climbing on layaways with a tricky top out.

75. 3+
Layback up the crack, topping out with aid of the tree roots.

76. 3+
Wriggle up the crack to victory.

77. 6C *Look Sharp*
Make a difficult start to a sustained balancy layback, finishing at the break.

78. 2+
Another wonderful High Rocks chimney to play in.

79. 4+
Nice climbing on positive holds finishing on the obvious flake.

80. 7C *Yoda Assis* ss
Hard climbing from the sit, leads to a desperate mantle. The wall to the left is unfortunately not in.

81. 7A+ *Yoda*
Hard mantle this is, young Skywalker.

82. 5
The blank slab is easier than it looks.

83. 6B
This tricky line takes a while to master.

84. 6A
Climb up the corner of the boulder to a slopey top out.

85. 6A+
The back side of this boulder gives a great little roof with a tricky top.

86. 6C+
A dyno or a very big reach form pocket to pocket.

High Rocks 154

87. *7C Kinda Lingers* ss
The left hand variation from a sit start traversing into the arête and finishing up this to the break.

88. *7A+ Kinda Lingers Stand*
The stand start is a feisty little climb, a ground jump start is not the true send.

89. *6C*
The long move from the pockets to the sharp pocket out left.

90. *6C+*
A dyno or weird contortion of moves from the pockets to the break.

91. *7A*
A traverse from the right arête into either of the previous routes.

Mike Hadcocks | Kinda Lingers Stand | 7A+

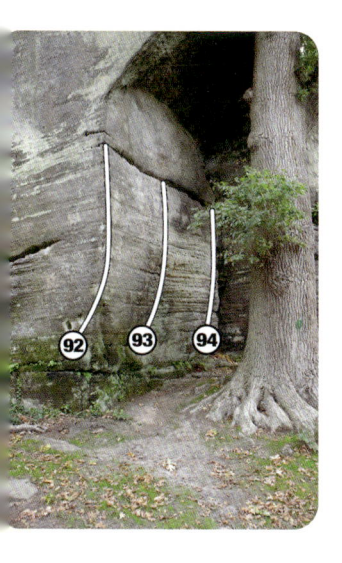

92. **7A+** *Darth Vader* ss
   The high arête under the large roof is climbed form a sit start in the big pocket.

93. **5**
   Climb up the face under the big roof on the honeycomb looking wall.

94. **5+**
   Climb the arête on the spaced breaks.

95. **6A+**
   The arête is harder than it looks and uses mainly holds from the right hand face.

96. **5+**
   Climb up the crack using surrounding holds.

97. **5+**
   Climb up the breaks and slots.

Mike Langley | Yoda | 7A+

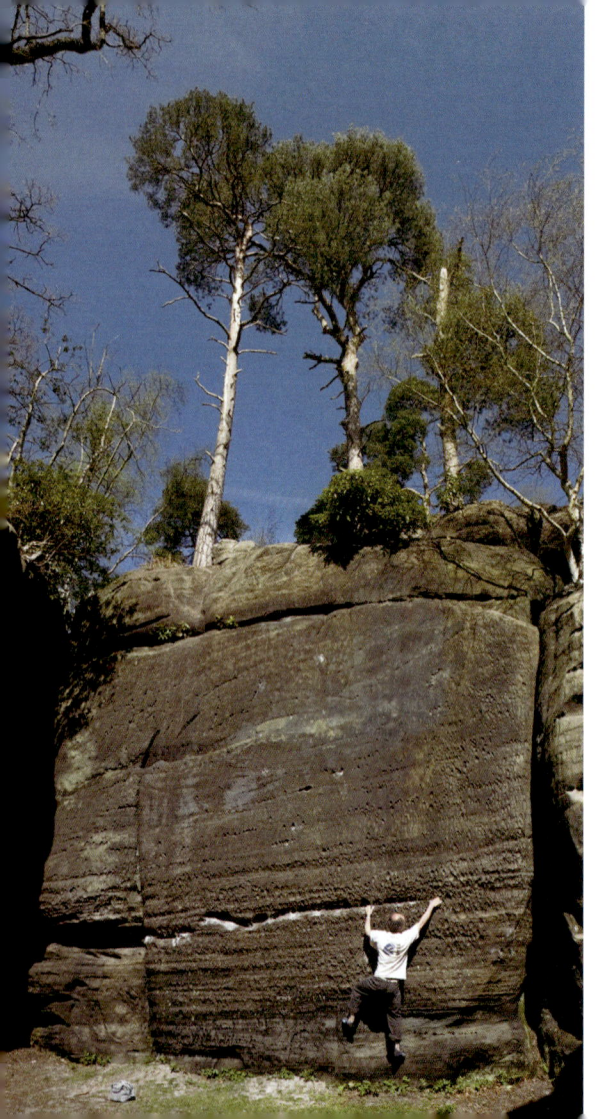

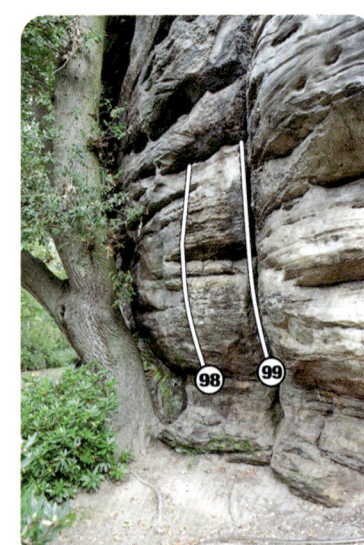

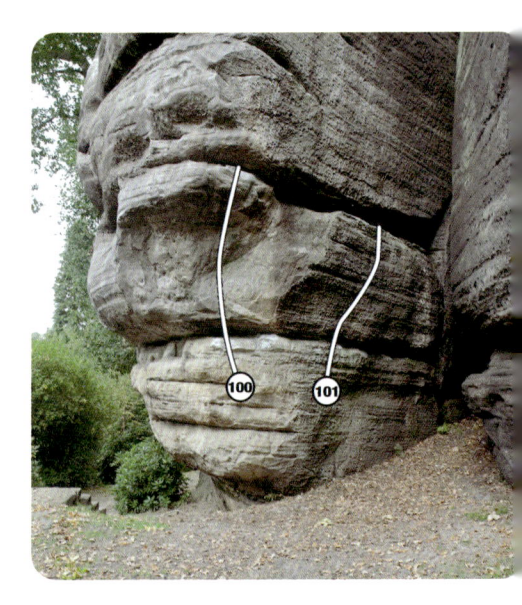

98. 6A+
Climb the front face to the left of the crack line.

99. 6A
An amazing crack line that is full of wonder and joy. Be careful of the steps.

100. 7B *Chez's Dyno*
The large dyno from the jugs to the obvious break. Using everything gives a nice yet contorted 6B+.

101. 6A+
The wall to the right gives a small overhanging route on crimps. This can also be done as a dyno at 6B+.

Ian Bull | Lord | 6A+

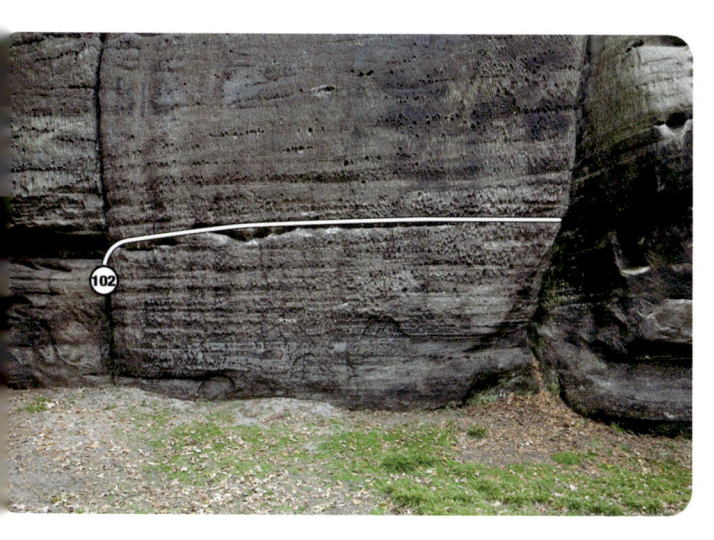

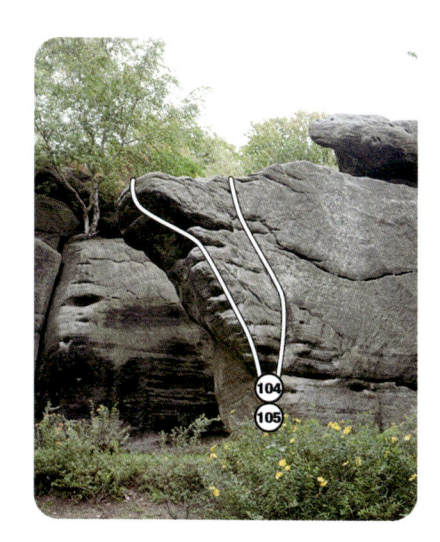

102. 6A+ *Lord*
The traverse along the line of obvious holds.

103. 6B+ *Shattered*
The rounded arête which is hard in the middle but leads to easier ground.

104. 6B+ *Roofus* 🎱
The large roof is a daunting challenge and a serious highball especially with the concrete floor! The descent route is by down climbing an easy crack line over to the right.

105. 6A 🎱
The wall to the right is just about shorter enough to get away with some mats as it has good holds most of the way up. The descent route is by down climbing an easy crack line over to the right.

High Rocks 158

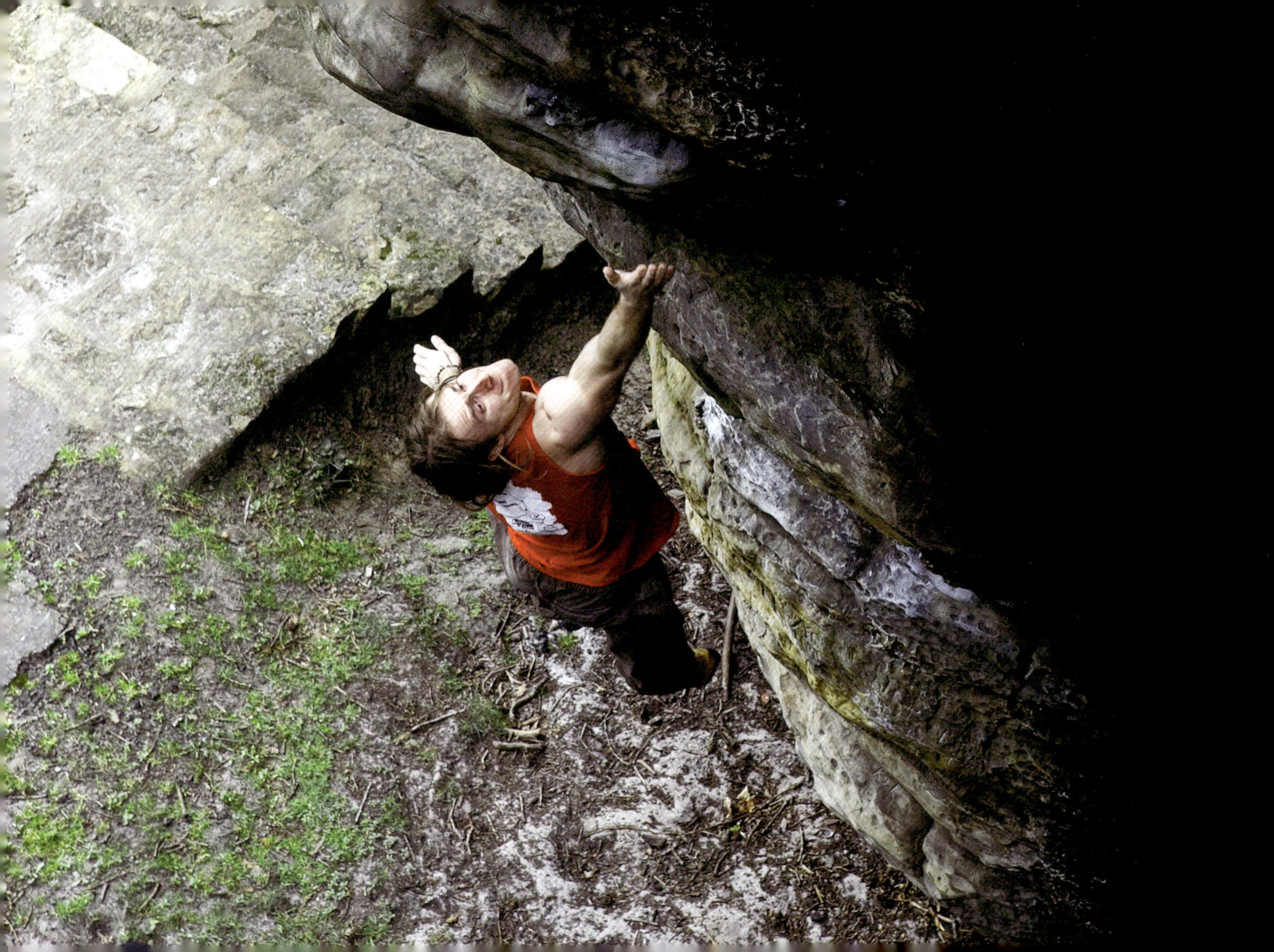

106. *5+*
A short overhang welcomes you with some delightful edges to pull on.

107. *6A Unfinished Business* ss
The short corner wall has some good moves if not very short lived. There is also a project sit start not using the right wall.

Mike Hadcocks | Chez's Dyno | 7B   Ben Read and Barnaby Ventham | Easy sunset solo

108. 6B+
The short green slab has a tricky climb up the left hand side.

109. 7B
A very hard mantle up the centre of the slab.

110. 6A
A balancy climb up the right hand side.

*This wall is often very green and often very wet, but in the peak of summer after many days of being dried in the sun it is transformed into a tricky little gem stone that'll have you coming back for seconds.

111. 4+
Climb the left hand side up the flake.

112. 5
Follow the crack line to the break.

113. 5
Climb up the right hand side of the pocketed wall.

114. 6A
The arête is easy low down with a sketchy top out.

115. 6A+ *Odin's Wall*
Climb straight up the pocketed wall.

116. 6A+
Follow the crack line to the top of the wall.

High Rocks

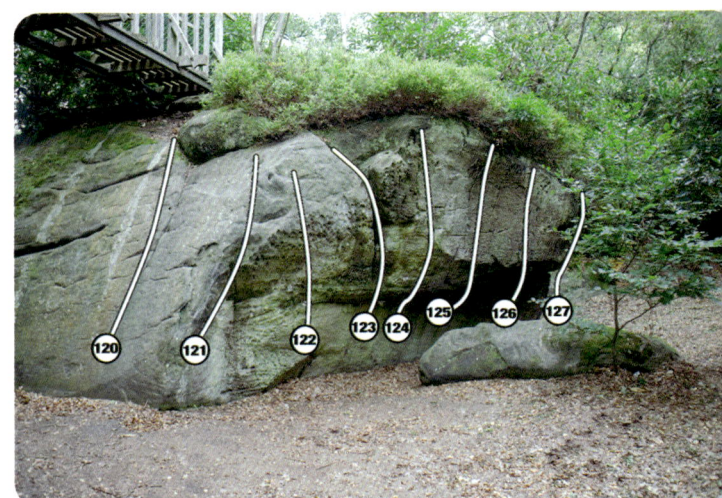

117. 5+
Climb the arête to the very green top out where some secateurs maybe necessary.

118. 6A ss
The centre crack line from a sitting start.

119. 6A ss
Starting in the low flake at the bottom of the crack follow this to the top.

120. 3
The slab line on the far left of the wall under the bridge.

121. 4
The next line along is a short but fun climb.

122. 5+ ss
Straight up the wall via the curved featured hold.

123. 6C+ ss
The crack line from a sit start using none of the surrounding holds.

124. 6C ss
The wall to the right of the crack has some big moves on positive crimps and pockets. Finish on the final holds or top out in the bushes.

125. 6C+ ss
Straight up the centre of the wall on thin sharp layaways.

126. 6B ss
To the right end of this heavily featured wall is another sharp climb but on slightly better holds.

127. 5
The right end of this wall from a stand start.

163 *High Rocks*

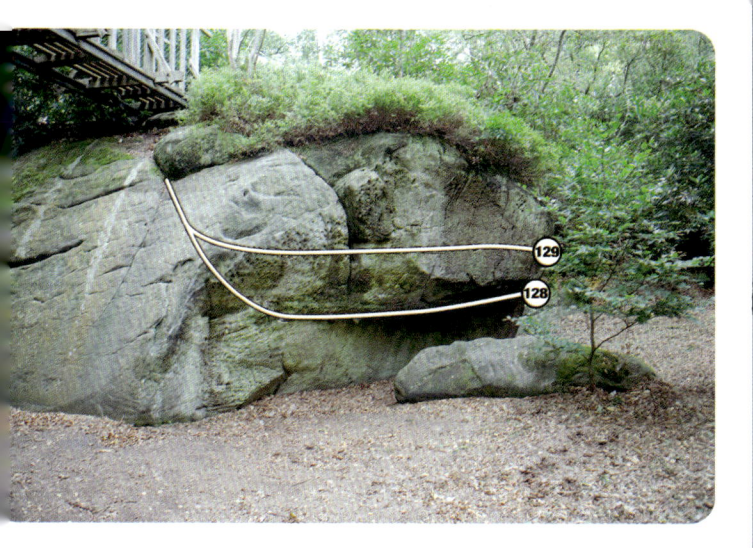

128. 7C *Bum Dragon*
The low level traverse on the bottom break. The name gives a lot away!

129. 7C *Crosstown Traffic*
A traverse across the face of the wall using the layaways and positive but sharp crimps. An early finish just right of the crack goes at 7B.

Jon Partridge | Crosstown Traffic | 7C

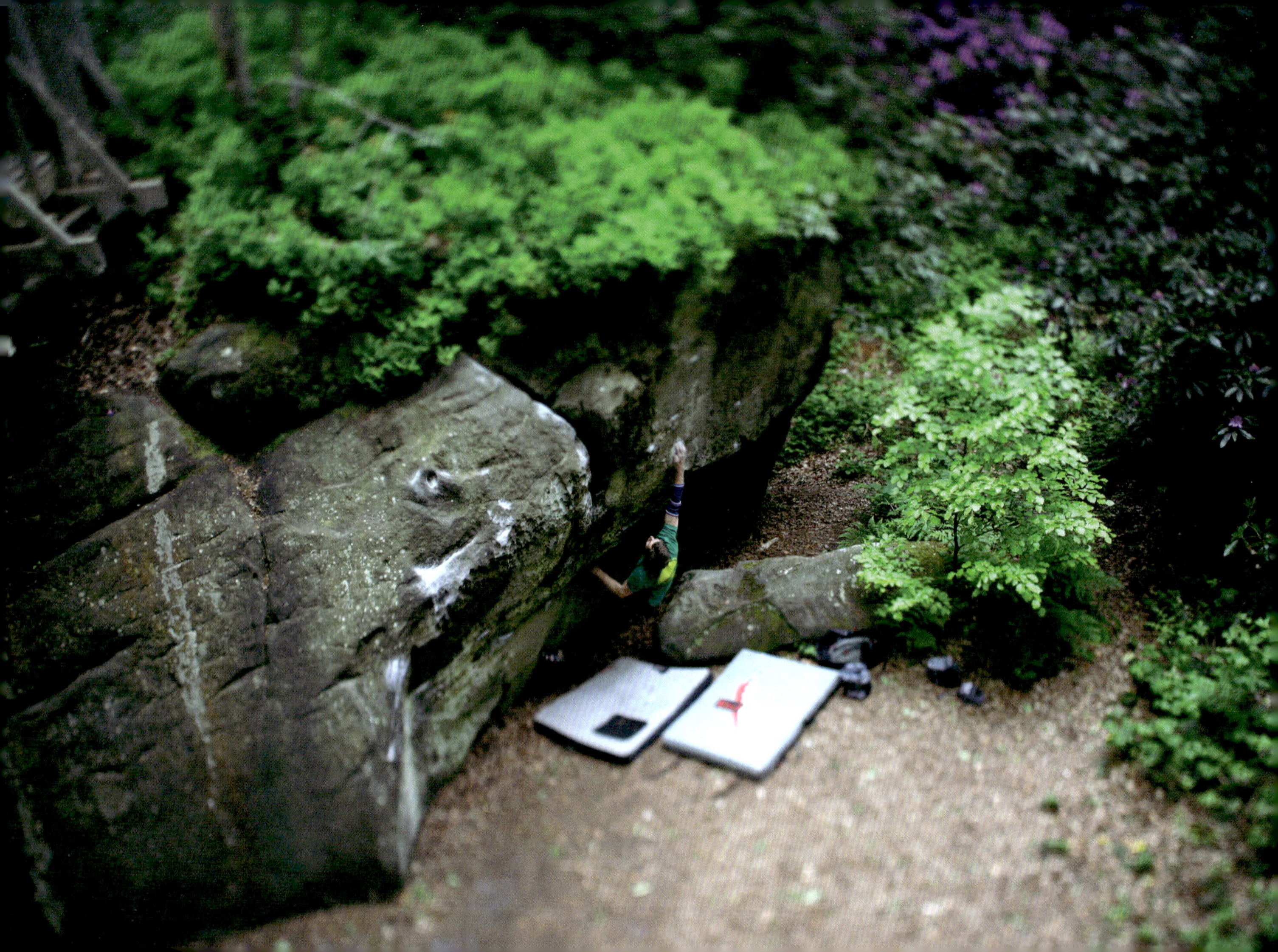

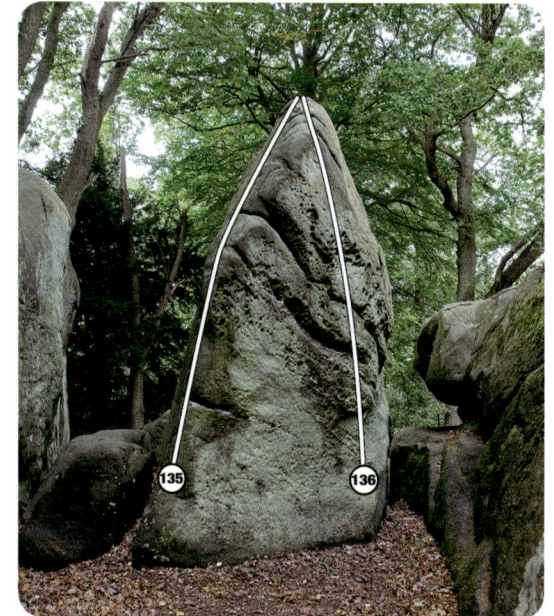

130. 3
The left hand end of the slab up the obvious ledge feature. Also quite fun trying this with out hands.

131. 5
The middle of the slab provides a delicate little climb.

132. 6B+
The delicate slab climb that is difficult and a little bit awkward. There is also a novel little route dynoing to the bridge from the large flat hold. this goes at 6B.

133. 4+
Just to the right of the bridge is a short little climb.

134. 6C+
The wall to the left of the arête is a tough climb with a sketchy landing.

135. 4+
The left hand side of the triangular wall.

136. 4+
The right hand side of the triangular wall.

High Rocks

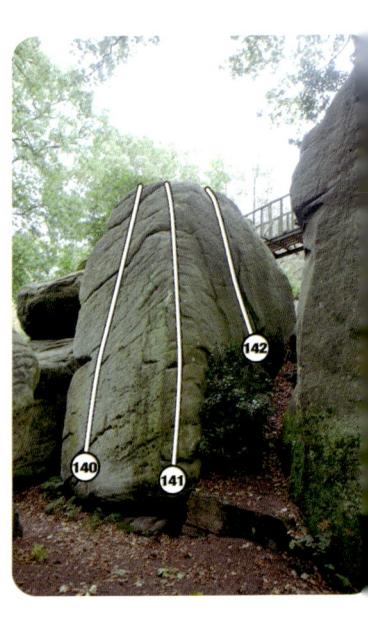

137. 6A+
The mantle up the front face of this wall.

138. 7A *ss*
From a sit start power up on burley slopers.

139. 6A
Just to the right is another mantle up the face.

140. 5
Climb up the centre face of this wall.

141. 4
The arête is one of the few easy climbs in this area, good for a warm up.

142. 6A+
The obvious line in the gully.

Yann Genoux | Honeycomb | 6B+

143. 6B+ *Honeycomb*
The original line up the pocketed wall starts on the left and works right to the good holds.

144. 6B+ *Honeycomb Direct*
The direct line up the front face is a great climb but a little committing.

145. 6B *Craig-Y-Blanco*
Straight up the arête is a pleasant climb until the top out.

146. 5+
The short crack line to the sideways break.

147. 4+
The crack line to the break.

148. 6A+ *Wishful Thinking*
The front of this wall up the letters. Jumping is not permitted for the grade. Please do not brush or use too much chalk.

149. 6A
The green wet crack, great!

150. 6A+
Climb the overhang up the left had side.

151. 7C *Final Destination*
The large dyno from the sideways slots to the hard to stick sloping top.

152. 6A+
Climb the usually mossy overhang.

High Rocks 168

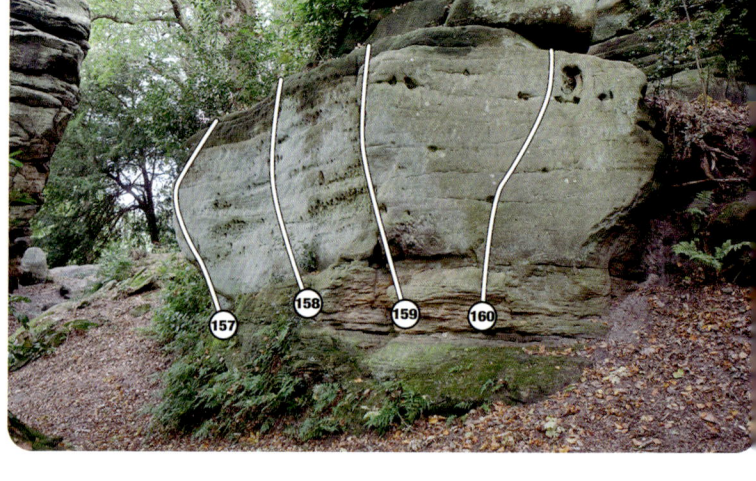

153. 6A
   The left hand end of the overhang climbed on the side.

154. 6B
   Starting on the round ball like feature climb up the front face on good holds with a slopey top out.

155. 6A+
   Starting on the large jug like break climb straight up the over hang.

156. 6B
   The tricky right hand end of the overhang.

157. 4
   The left hand side of the short wall.

158. 3+
   Starting on the ledge climb up on good holds.

159. 4
   Climb straight up the blunt nose in the centre of the wall.

160. 3
   Follow the line of pockets and good holds up to the right.

High Rocks

161. 6B+ *Return Of The Mojo* ss
The left hand side from a sit start.

162. 7B ss
Traverse across the line of sloping breaks to finish up number **164**.

163. 7B *Mojo* ss
Starting from small undercuts make some big moves out on slopers.

164. 7A ss
Starting on crimps, move out to a side pull and then climb up using just the sloper on the face and pop to the break eliminating all other holds.
Using everything is 6B+.

165. 6A ss
Climb straight up the crack line.

166. 6A ss
Another short roof that finishes on the break.

Kornelija Howick | Route 168 | 6A

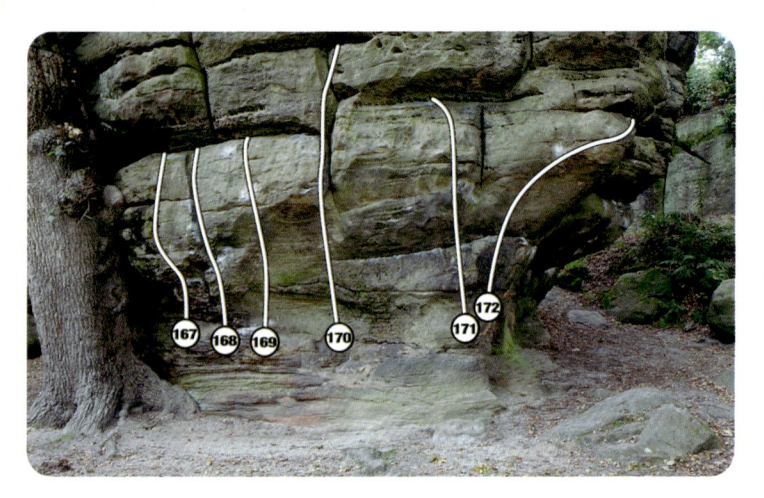

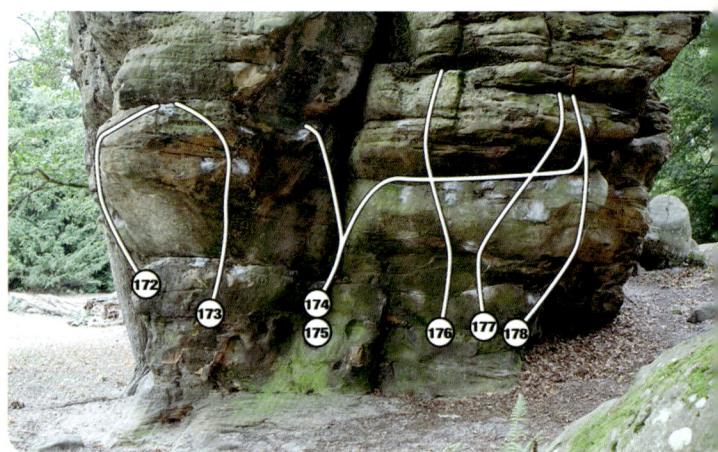

167. 6B
There are many eliminates that can be made up on this wall but just to the left of the crack is a short climb eliminating the crack.

168. 6A *ss*
Straight up the short crack line and surrounding holds.

169. 6A+ *ss*
The wall in between the two crack lines.

170. 5+
Straight up the crack to the break.

171. 6A+
Using slopers, pinches, cracks and crimps make your way to the break.

172. 6A+
Starting on good holds in the break make some long moves on the left side of the overhang to finish on the break.

173. 6B
The big reach or jump from the holds on the break to the two obvious holds and then to the break.

174. 6A
Starting at the bottom of the crack climb up to the left.

175. 6A
Starting in the crack traverse off right to the arête and up the jugs.

176. 7A *Happy Days ss*
From a low start on the break, lean back and engage the thumbs. Then make a strange flick to the jugs and continue up. This can also be done as a dyno, ignoring the thumbs which is called *The Fonz*.

177. 6C *Happy Days Variation ss*
Starting slightly right of the original route using just the right hand hold and then finish up to the right.

178. 6A+ *ss*
The arête climbed from the sit all the way round to the break. Using just the slopers is a nice little problem boosting the grade to 6B+.

171 *High Rocks*

… # world class
bouldering

1. always dry
2. 200 graded routes in one spot
3. open day AND night
4. bar next door

see you there

craggy island 2

t: 0844 8808866
e: sutton@craggy-island.com
www.craggy-island.com

Craggy Island   Oaks Park Sports Centre
Woodmansterne Road   Carshalton   Surrey   SM5 4AN

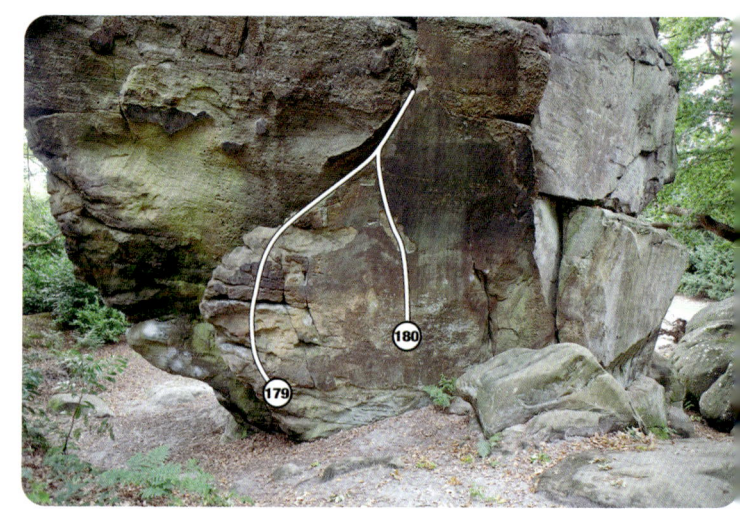

179. 4
Follow the ramp of good holds to the break.

180. 6B
A direct line up the small crimps on the face.

Charlotte Steel | Route 171 | 6A+

181. 7A+
Using sharp edges and a big dynamic move, reaching the break will be a highly rewarding achievement.

Barnaby Ventham | Happy Days | 7A

175 *High Rocks*

182. 6A
The direct line up the face just right of the arête. From a sit start this is 6A+.

183. 6B
Straight up the face with a tricky mantle to finish.

184. 6A
Up past the large flake and then top it out.

185. 5
Start up the middle of the boulder and then follow the flake to the right to good holds.

186. 6B+
Using all holds up the crimp covered face.

187. 7A+
Climb up using only the small crimps up this wall and the left hand hold of the two crimps on the face. Eliminate but worth doing.

188. 7C+ *The wish*
From the small undercut holds make a strenuous pull to the two crimps on the face and finish direct. Starting on the two crimps with stacked pads is 7C.

189. 8A+ *Don't Pierdol* ss
The sit start to *The Wish* is the hardest problem on the southern sandstone to date. All you have to do is a couple of hard moves to get established into the start holds of *The Wish* then continue to levitate to the top........simple!

190. 6A *Brenva* 🔴
A couple of hard moves or a little jump to better ones and then straight up the arête on good holds and flowing moves.

191. 7A *Brenva Assis* ss 🔴
The sit start of the arête on sidepulls and a heel hook. Has had several grades over the years but this one seems to have settled for now.

Peter Wycislik | Don't Pierdol | 8A+

177 *High Rocks*

192. 7A *Old Kent Road* ss
   Traverse across obvious line of holds and up the arête. Using the large flake brings this down to a 6B.

193. 7B *Neil's Eliminate Traverse* ss
   Climb the line of *Old Kent Road* but when you reach the arête climb round the corner and climb up the hanging slab of **204**.

194. 7C *The Slow Pull* ss
   Starting as for *Brenva Assis* traverse across the bottom of this boulder to join into *Old Kent Road* and finish up this.

195. 7C+ *The Public Footpath* ss
   Climb the line of the *Slow Pull* but instead of finishing up the arête climb round the corner and climb up the hanging slab face of **204**.

Project.
   This project traverse line crossing the two obvious crimps on the blank face and then into *Old Kent Road*.

196. 6A+
   Climb up *Brenva* and then follow the line of good holds at mid height to join up with the flake and then finishing up number **182**.

Mateusz Ligas | The Slow Pull | 7C

197. 7B+ ss
Starting as for *Brenva Assis* and then traverse right with some hard thin moves into the next route.

198. 6B
The great slab line up the green face and a line that requires a lot of delicacy and technique.

199. 6A ss
From a low start climb the very font like wall up to a mantle.

200. 6B+
The blunt nose has a tricky little mantle to finish.

201. 2+
Climb up the ramped wall to a standing position.

202. 6B+
Climb up the line of holds just left of the main face.

203. 7A
Start the same as the previous route and traverse into the next route.

204. 7A *Neil's Eliminate* ss
From an awkward sit start climb up to the hanging slab and then to the top. By eliminating the arête makes a great 7B from the same start.

Mateusz Loskot | Route 199 | 6A

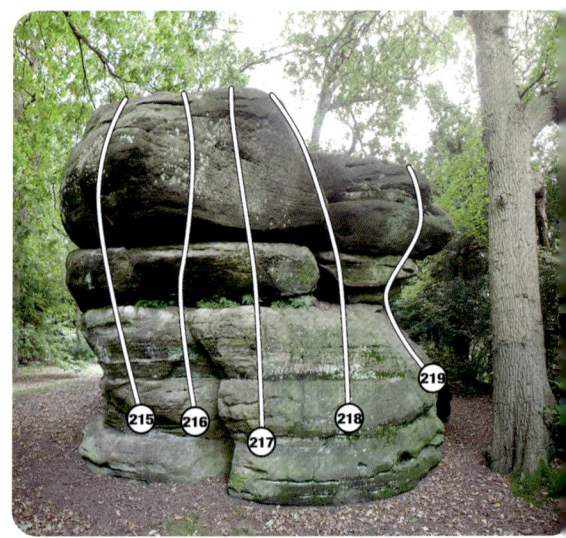

205. 3+
The arête on the far left side.

206. 4
Straight up the face on good but slopey holds.

207. 5
The line just left of the crack.

208. 3+
Climb up the line just right of the crack.

209. 6C
A dyno from the break to the top of the wall.

210. 4
Straight up the middle of the wall.

211. 5
The slopey right hand end of this section.

212. 6A
Starting on the right hand wall under the roof climb up and over the bulge on the left end of this.

213. 6A
The blunt arête just right of the chimney gap.

214. 7A *Oak Tree Corner*
The line of bad holds up the middle of the face.

215. 6C *Chez's Arête*
The blunt arête is a great little climb.

216. 7A+ *Greenside Boulder*
The line just right of the arête.

217. 6B
An easier line up the middle of the face with a tricky mantle.

218. 3
Climb up the crack line and ramp.

219. 6A
The ramp and then up and over the short roof.

High Rocks

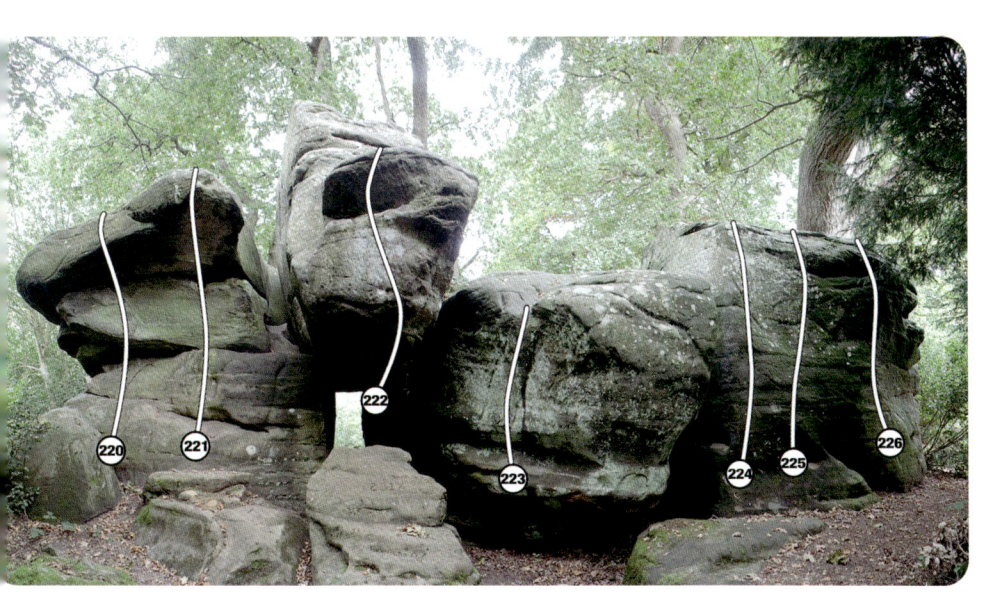

220. 6A
Straight up the left end of the face.

221. 6B+
Up on to the ledge and then a quick little excursion over the roof with a tough mantle to end.

222. 7B+ *The Lemur*
The prow above the chimney is a great little problem. Do not use any of the surrounding boulders or walls for the true tick.

223. 4+
The line up the crack and then mantle.

224. 5+
The rounded line just right of the crack.

225. 5+
Just right again is this short line.

226. 5+
A ramp to a tasty mantle.

227. 3+
Climb straight up the arête.

228. 4
The left hand side of the face from break to break.

229. 3
Up the right hand side on good holds.

High Rocks 182

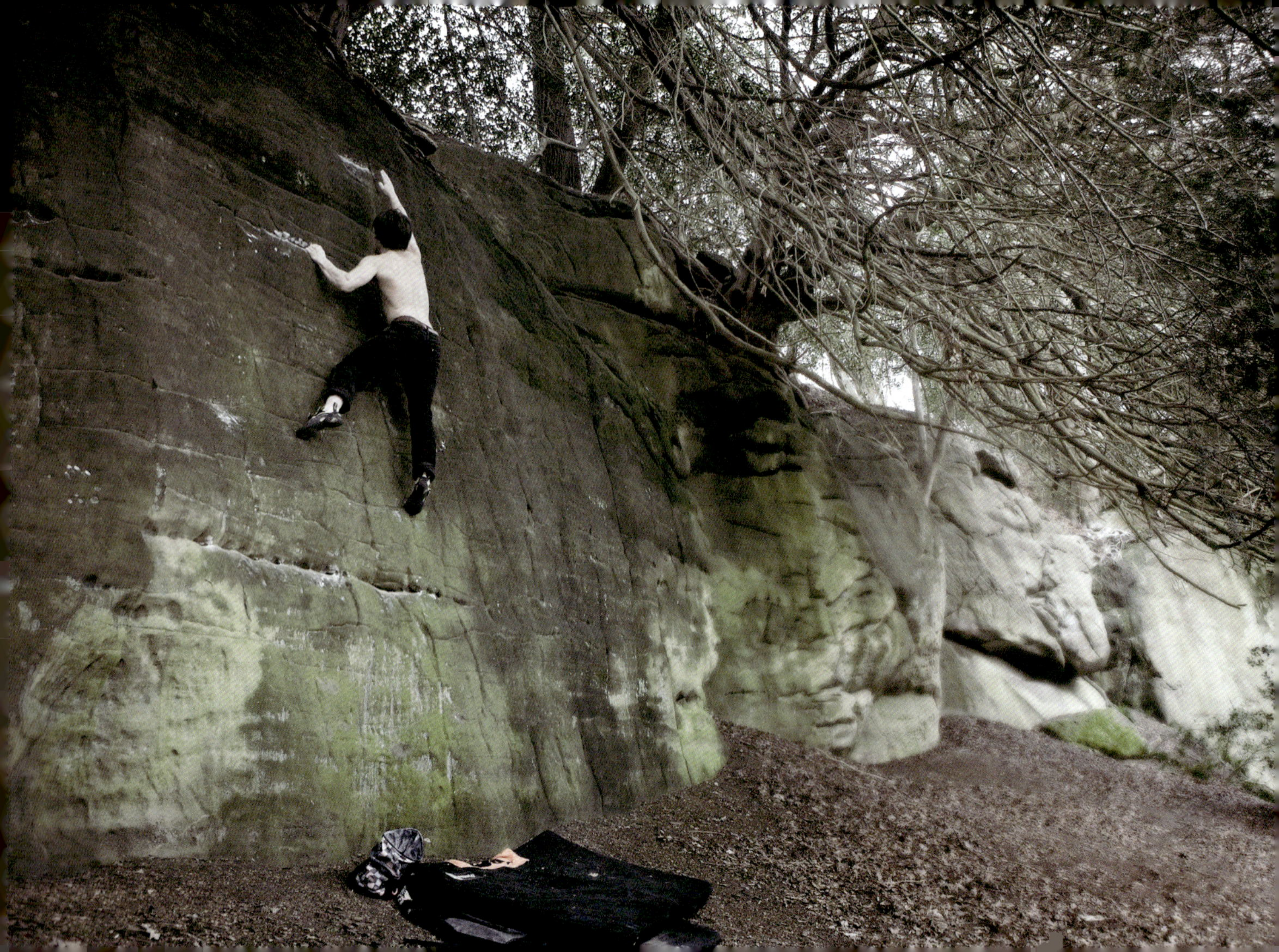

HIGH ROCKS ANNEXE

INTRODUCTION

This small outcrop lies on the opposite side of the road to the main High Rocks crag. It is a strange but peaceful place that is known for its hard slab lines. Protecting these climbs with boulder pads can be quite tricky as the floor slopes away and with that so do your mats! A couple of spotters to catch you and to stop your boulder pads escaping down the hill are advised.

ACCESS AND APPROACH

From the High Rocks Inn head back up towards Tunbridge Wells so the main part of High Rocks is on your right hand side. Go down a slight hill crossing the railway bridge and you will then come to a triangular T-junction. Parking up on the grass verge here is normally the best option and then continue past the turning up the road parallel to the train line. About 200m on your left will be a small woodland that holds the crag, there are several paths leading up to the base of the rock.

This crag is on private land, but the owners do allow climbers access providing they go and ask first at the bungalow around the corner. This is located just up from the parking on the grass verge towards Happy Valley. Please make sure you check current access information which can be found on the BMC's website.

CONDITIONS

The rock stays green looking nearly all year round due to the dense trees surrounding the crag. Don't let this put you off straight away though as it is always worth investigating to see if the rock is dry. This crag is best tackled in the summer months and normally in the evening when the temperature is cool and friction is on your side.

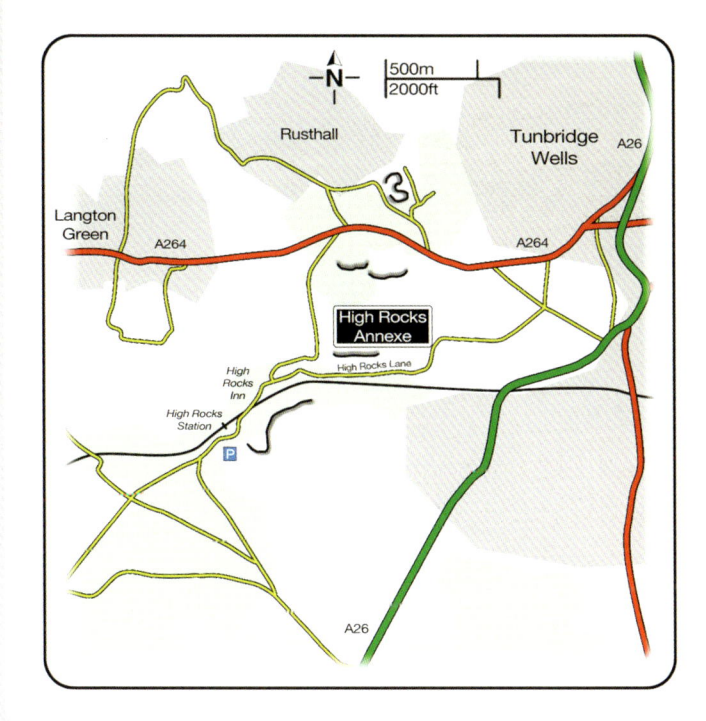

ames O'Neil | Change In The Weather Direct | 6C+

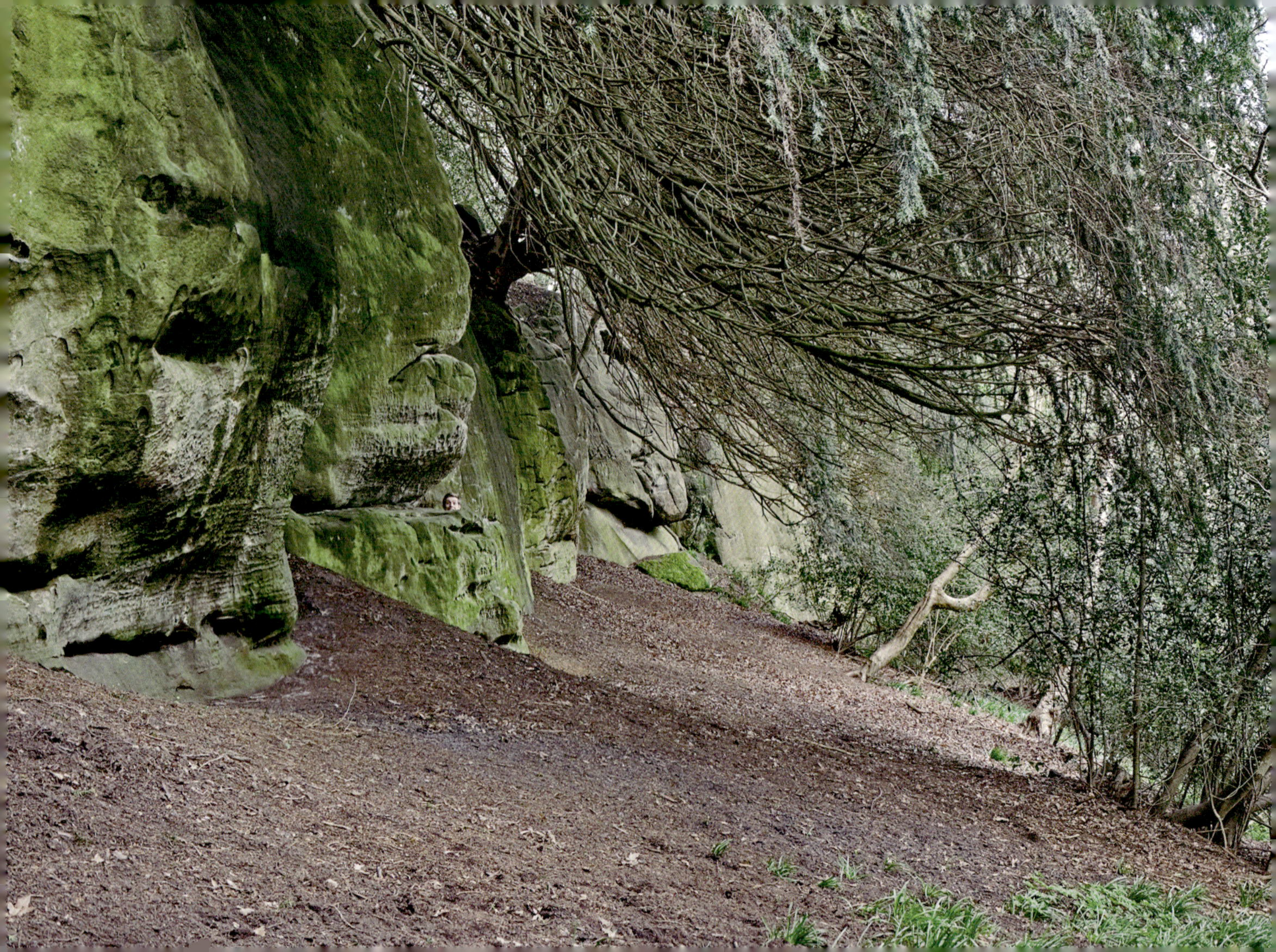

1-6 7-11 12-17 18-24

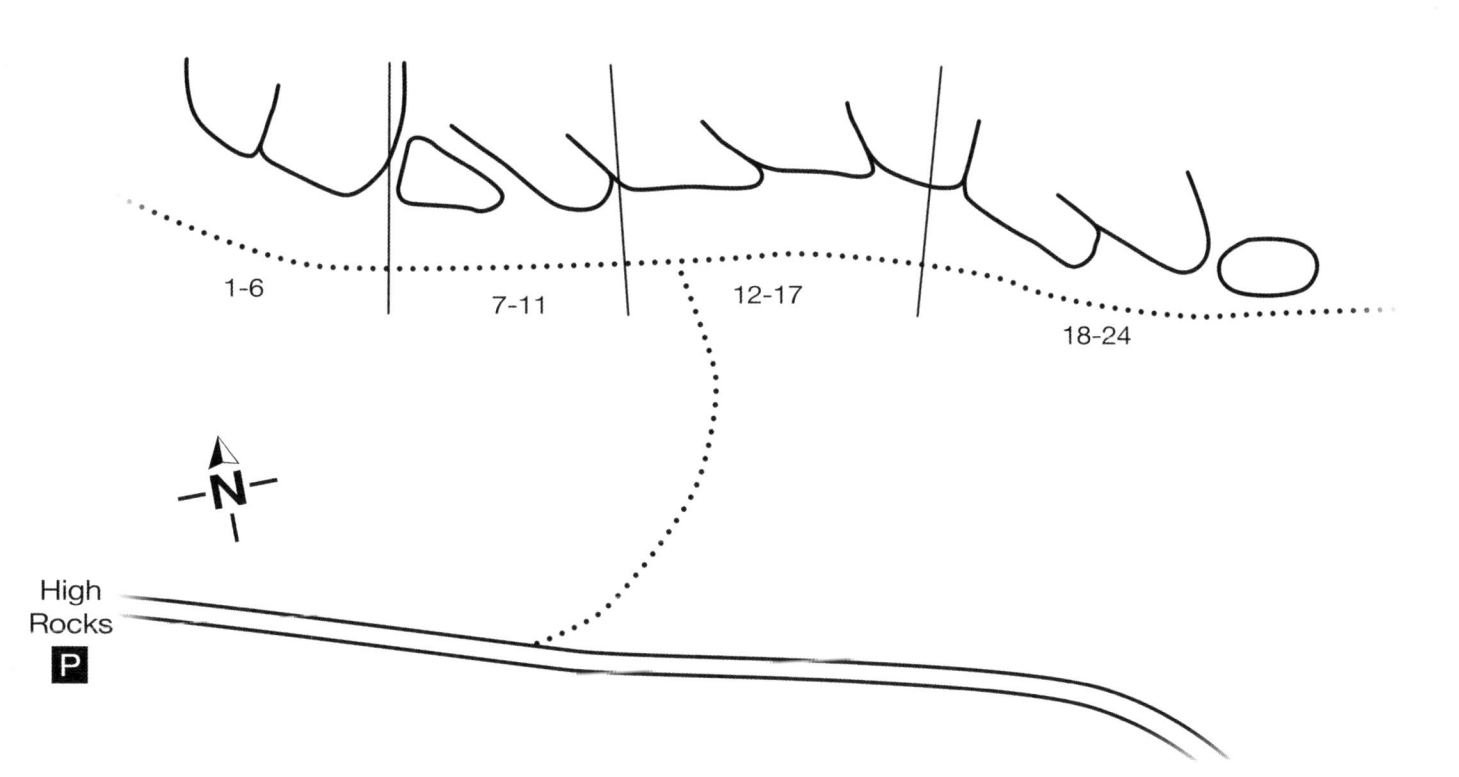

N

High Rocks
P

High Rocks Annexe 186

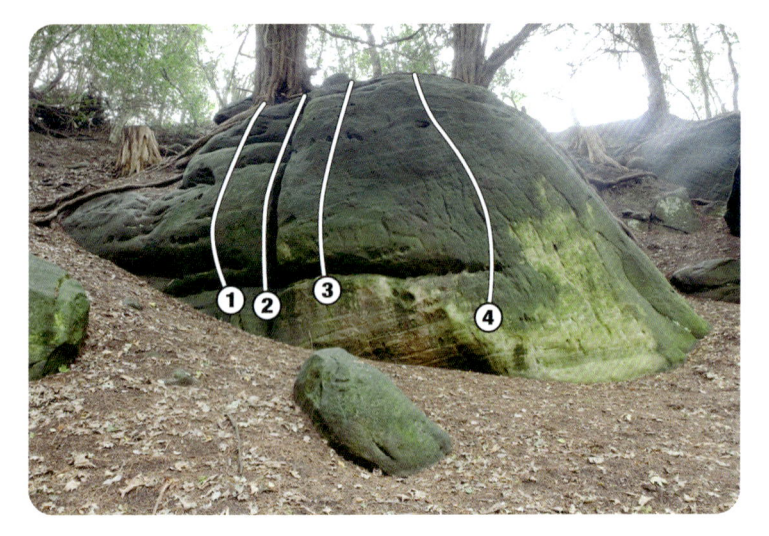

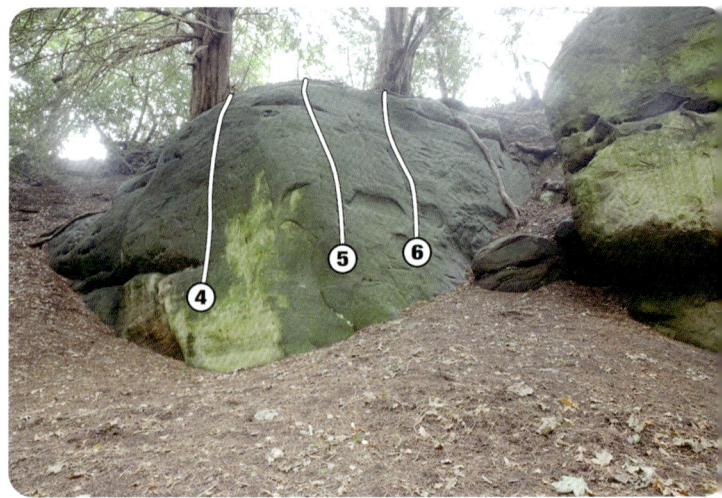

1. 4
   Climb the wall left of the crack

2. 4+
   Follow the crack line all the way to the top

3. 6A
   The balancy but powerful wall to the right of the crack is a good tick but has a spicy top out. The arête is allowed for this climb.

4. 7A *Southern Softie*
   A great slab route up the right hand side of this wall. This route is much harder for those who are a bit vertically challenged.

5. 6A+
   The steep slab on the rounded arête has an interesting finish.

6. 4
   A nice pleasant slab on good holds using tree routes to finish.

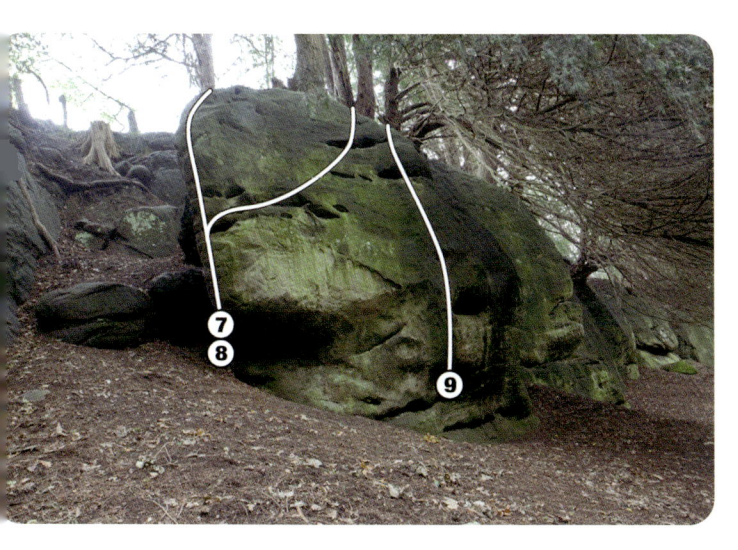

7. 6A+
   A poor climb up the arête.

8. 5+
   Follow the line of large slots and pockets across the front face of this boulder. Top out to finish.

9. 6B+
   A hard start leads to the larger holds of number **8**, follow these then to the top.

Project.
   A hard line up the centre of this face remains a tough project.

10. 6B
   Slap your way up this corner to a hidden hold over the top.

11. 7B *Boogie Woogie Walk*
   A technical little number up this open groove can be finished either off left or direct at the same grade.

High Rocks Annexe

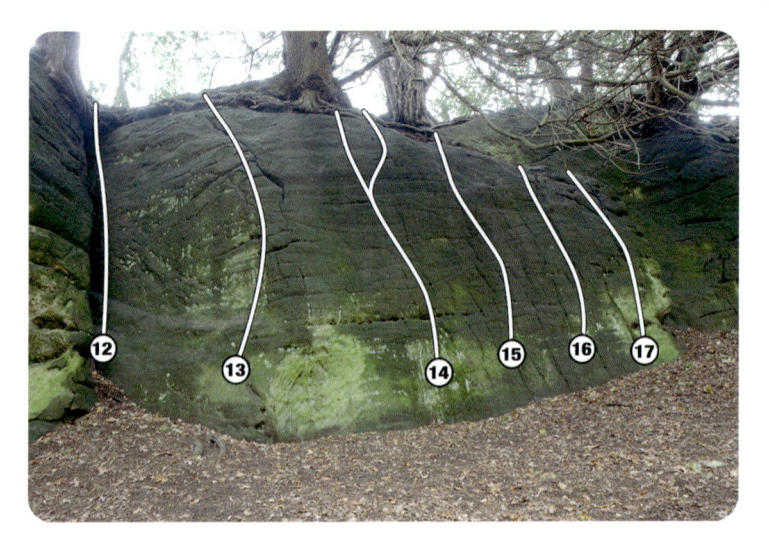

12. 3
The horrible dark crack that is often wet and very often boring.

13. 4+
A great climb up the positive holds using the tree root to top out.

14. 6C *Change In The Weather*
The classic slab line up the face which looks a lot easier than it actually is. A direct finish gets you an extra + on the grade.

15. 6B
An easier version of the previous climb on good holds with some interesting moves.

16. 5
A pleasant little climb up the shallow crack line and surrounding holds.

17. 4
Short, green and not very nice. Can't you just wait to get on this?

18. 5+
The small overhang provides a short little boulder problem that makes a change to all the slabs.

19. 5+
Big holds to start that get smaller as you get higher.

20. 6A
Climb up the right hand side of this wall not using the ramp to the side to start.

High Rocks Annexe

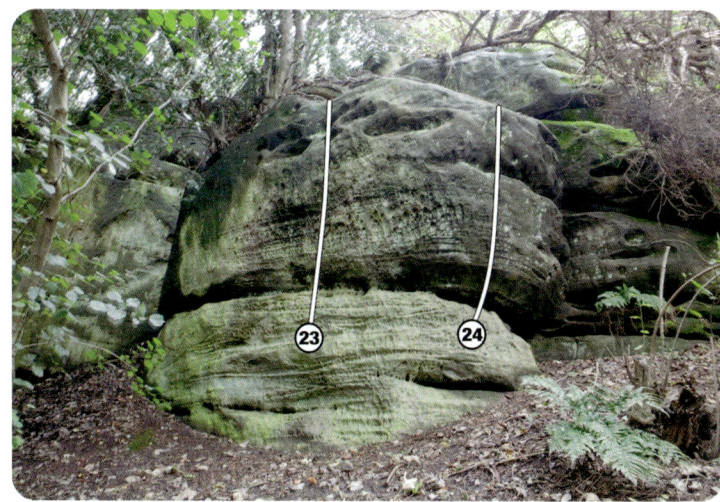

21. 6B+ *The Entertainer* 🕒
A tricky slab line up the blank face. Start on the right hand side moving across the slab following the line of small holds. May be a little too high to boulder for most, but it is there for the brave!

22. 4+ 🕒
Climb the line just around the corner of the arête.

23. 5+
The central line up this rounded wall is not really worth doing.

24. 5+
Another climb of similar quality up the right hand side. Here for those who want it though!

High Rocks Annexe

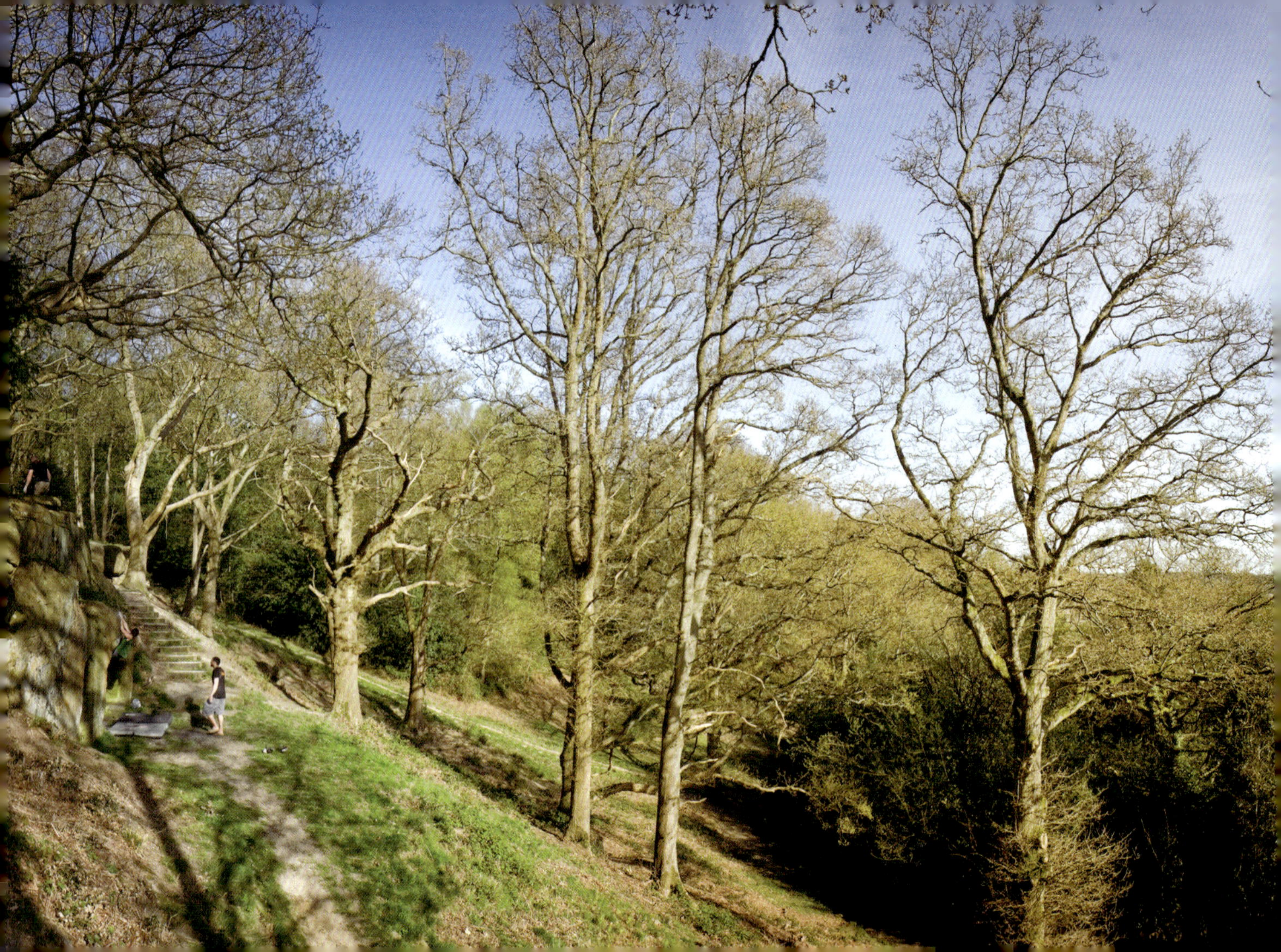

HAPPY VALLEY

INTRODUCTION

Set back in woodland this small selection of rock has a nice choice of easy to mid range climbs. It is an ideal place for those starting out and can be quite a fun place to go if you are looking for a chilled day. There are some great problems here including 'Red Snapper' which is one of the best overhangs on the sandstone.

ACCESS AND APPROACH

From Tunbridge Wells take the A264 away from town heading towards East Grinstead and Groombridge. Look out for signs pointing towards The Beacon hotel and restaurant down Tea Garden Lane. Parking is on small lay-bys just before The Beacon itself. Opposite the parking is a footpath which leads along to an opening with a long line of steps leading down the bank. The first set of climbs are in this large open area and the rest of the climbs are down the steps and along the path at the bottom.

This is a popular spot for dog walkers so do not be surprised to be greeted by a large black nose as you top out the climbs!

CONDITIONS

The rock tends to dry reasonably quickly as it is all fairly open which allows the wind to pass through easily. Although this crag does not see as much attention as other areas so be warned that it is still possible to come off sandy and fragile holds due to the minimal traffic that is seen here. Please make sure that you clean off any dirt or sand gently with a rag or towel and do not use brushes to clean up holds.

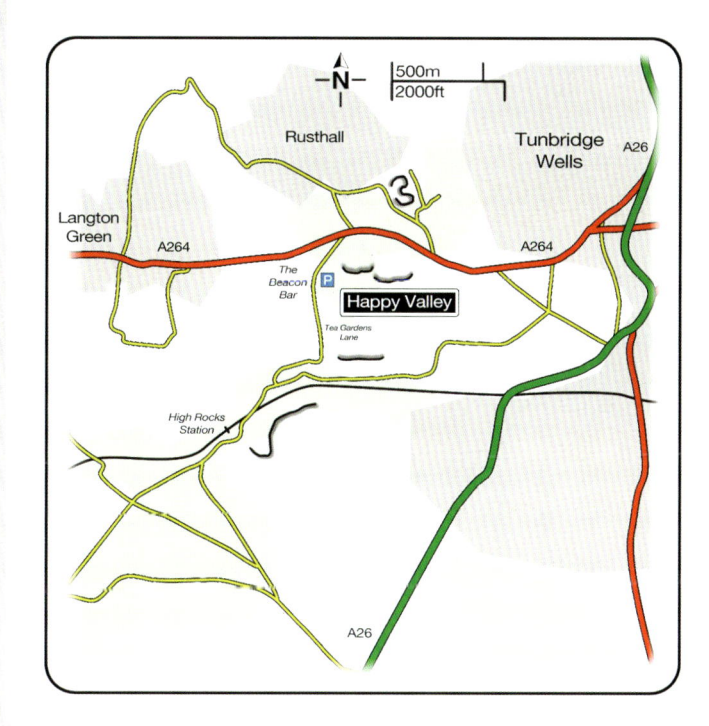

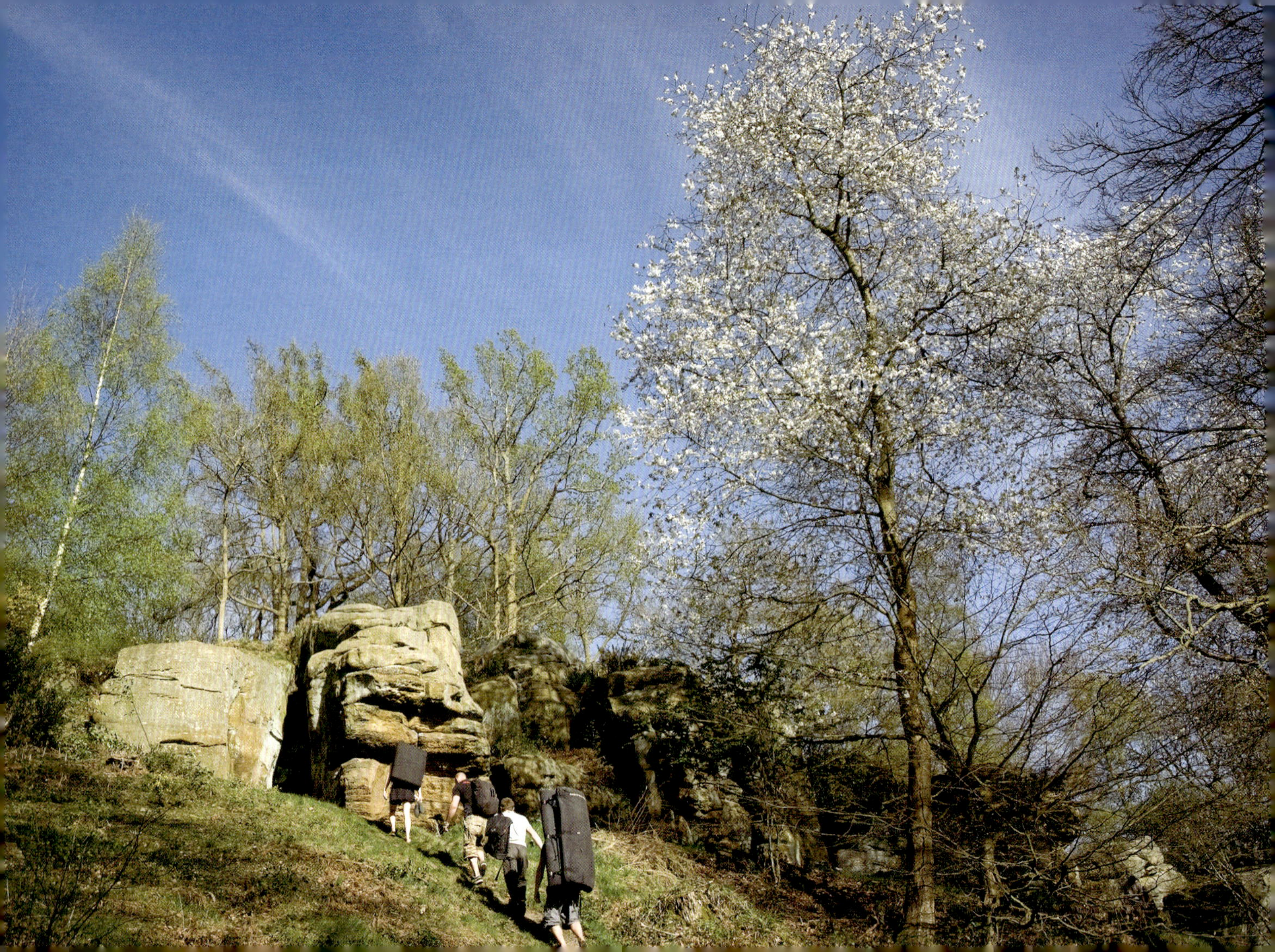

The Beacon Hotel
P

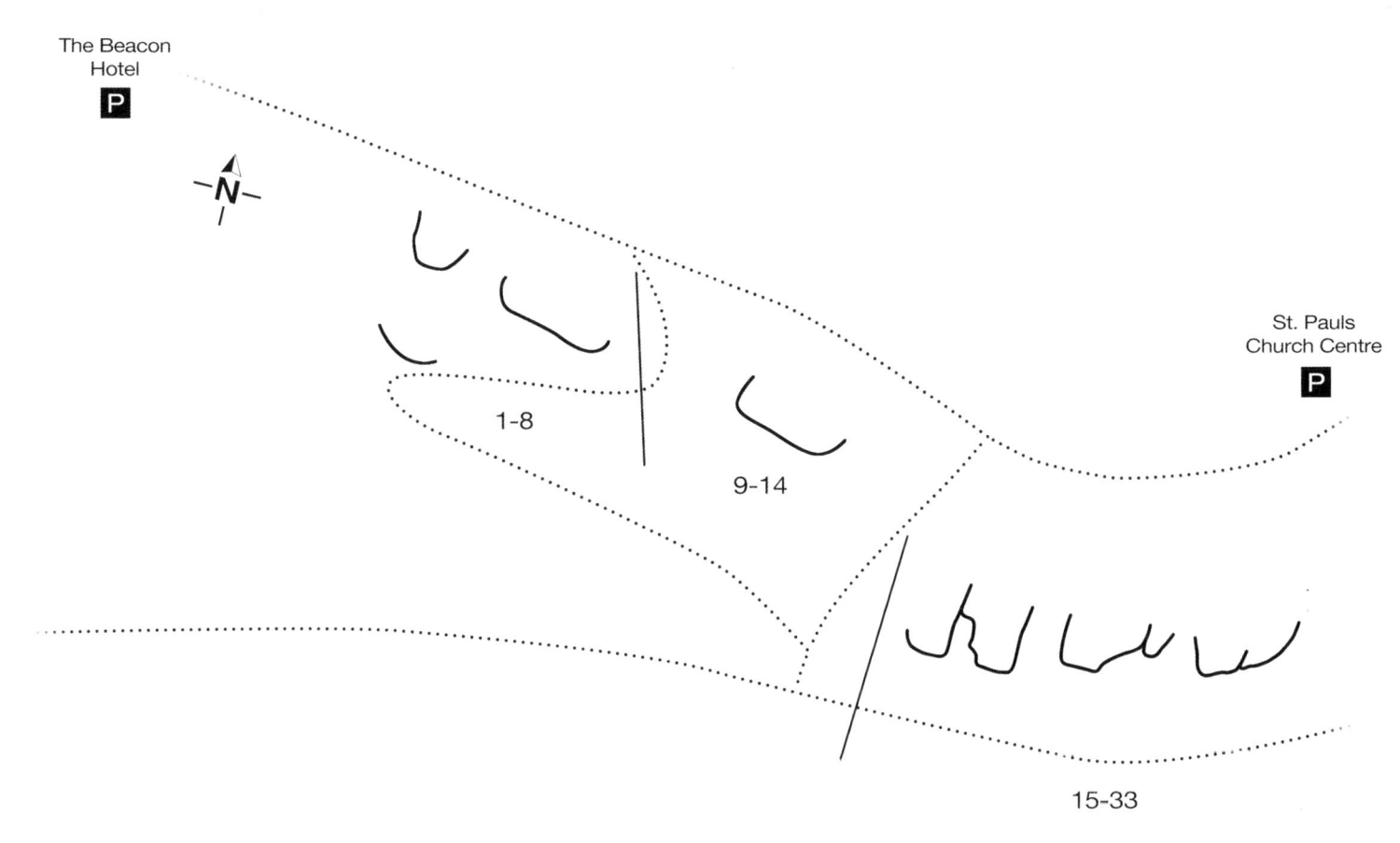

N

1-8

9-14

St. Pauls Church Centre
P

15-33

Happy Valley 194

1. 4
 The scoop of this bottom slab provides a nice little climb.

2. 3+
 Starting on the good breaks out left and traverse rightwards and up following the good holds.

Tom Murrell | Route 5 | 5

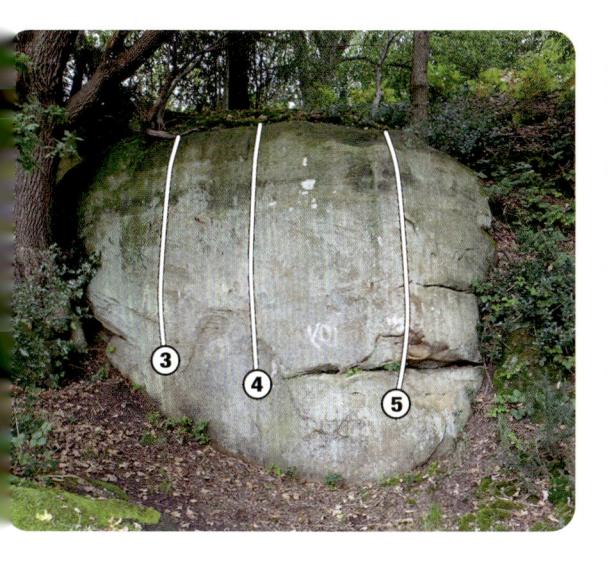

3. 6A+
The left hand side of the face using good layaways to start. Use the tree root to top out.

4. 7A
The blank wall using the furthest right pocket from the previous route. A slopey top out greets you after the lack of holds on the face! The sit start still remains a project.

5. 5
A nice little climb up the right hand side of the arête with a tricky mantle to finish.

*The next section of rock has a couple of climbs up it but is of poor quality and soft rock so we have decided not to include it

6. 6A+
Bridge up the door way to start and then reach round to the break and then a hard mantle to finish.

7. 6B
Starting on the two pockets on the back wall make a big move out to the lip of the overhang and mantle up to glory. The ledge and wall to the left are out.

8. 6B+
Starting on the pocket at the back of the cave, make a big move out to the lip and then mantle to finish. The wall and ledge to the right is not in.

Happy Valley

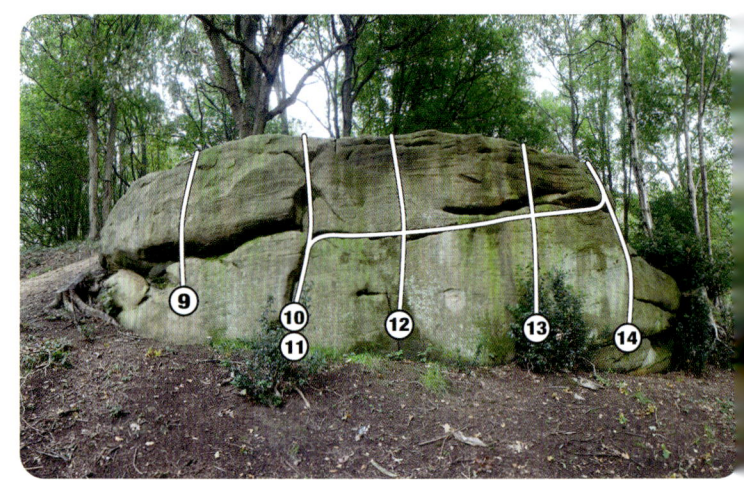

9. 5
Using the good edge to start and then make some big moves to a slopey top out.

10. 3+
Climb up the set of good layaways.

11. 5
Starting in the same place as number **10** follow the break of slopey holds all the way across the face and up the end route.

12. 4
The scoop in the middle has this great little climb up it.

13. 6A
A blank start leads to the break and then a tricky finish. Be wary of the large tree stump below.

14. 2
Start on the front face and then step round to the right up the scooped ramp.

Ben Read | Happy Valley rope swing   Toby Leckie | Route 12

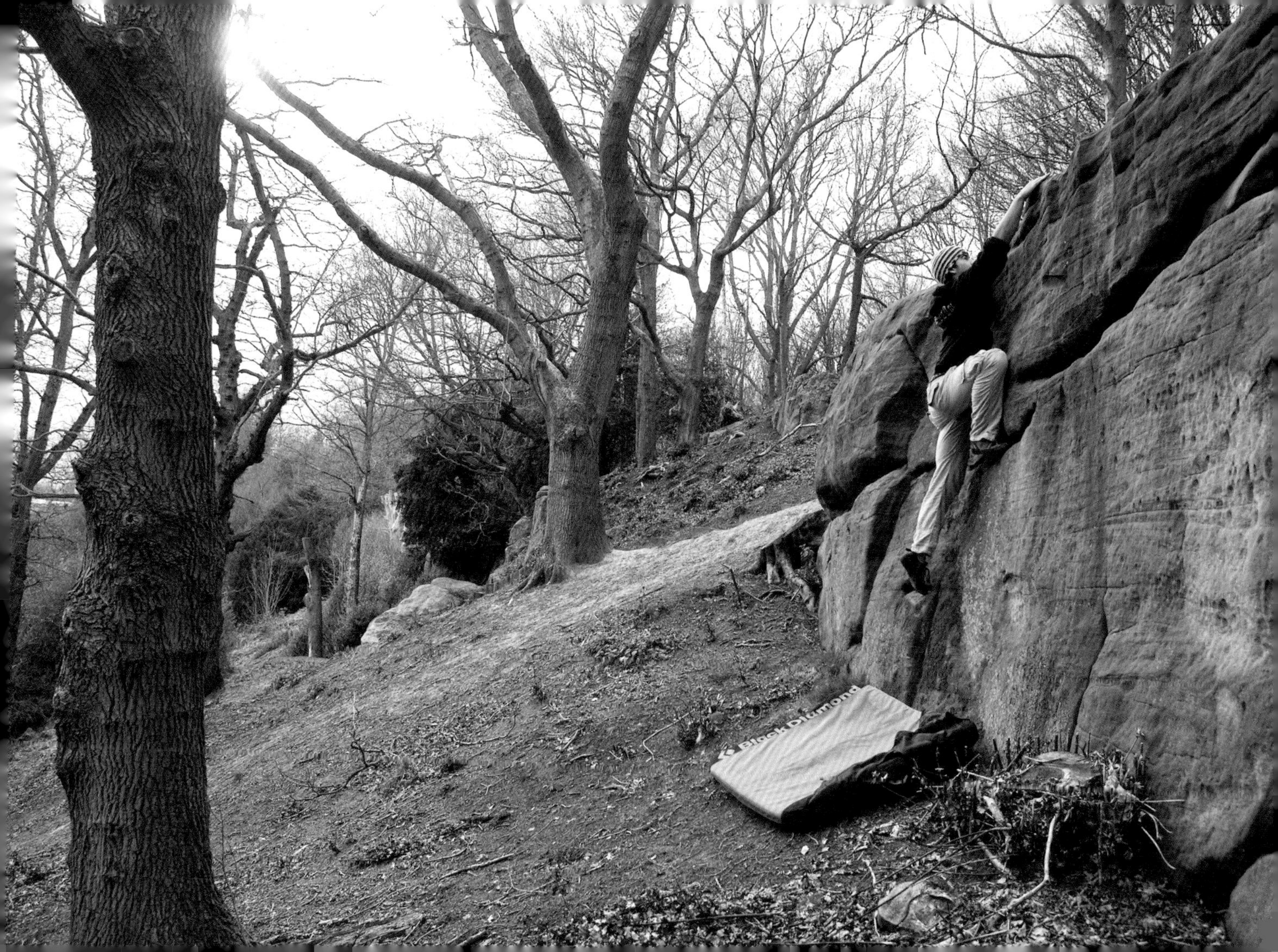
Black Diamond

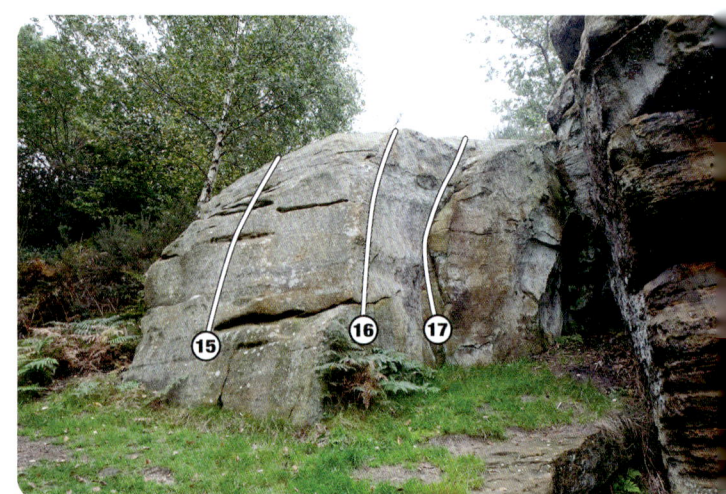

15. 3+
Straight up the left hand end with a slopey top.

16. 6A
Climb the arête on the right which includes a high step. The ledge to the right is not in.

17. 4+
Follow the line of diagonal holds to the top.

Charlotte Latter | Red Snapper | 6A

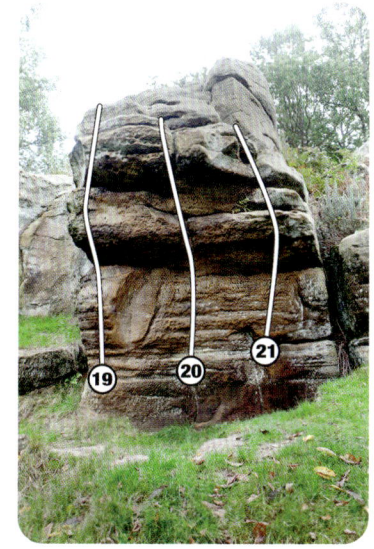

18. 5
The side face on the iron ore holds is a great little climb.

19. 5
Climb the juggy arête all the way up and over, a fun little number!

20. 6A *Red Snapper*
An easy start up the massive red jugs in the centre of the face. This does lead to a harder finish though. One of the best climbs at Happy Valley.

21. 6A
A harder start than *Red Snapper* but with an easier finish

Adur Outdoor Activities Centre

Brighton Road
Shoreham-by-sea
West Sussex
BN43 5LT

Tel: 01273 462928
Fax: 01273 441990
Email: adur.outdoor@westsussex.gov.uk

CLIMBING WALL FACILITY
- 10 Metre High Wall
- Covers 300+ sq. metres
- 50+ Top Rope & Lead Climbs
- Separate Bouldering Room
- Individual and Group Access
- Monthly Route Setting

OPEN EVERY DAY
(Except Bank Holidays)

ALSO AVAILABLE AT AOAC
Kayaking/Canoeing
Mountain Biking
Low Ropes Course
Team Building
Orienteering
Raft Building
Residential Facilities

www.aoac.org.uk

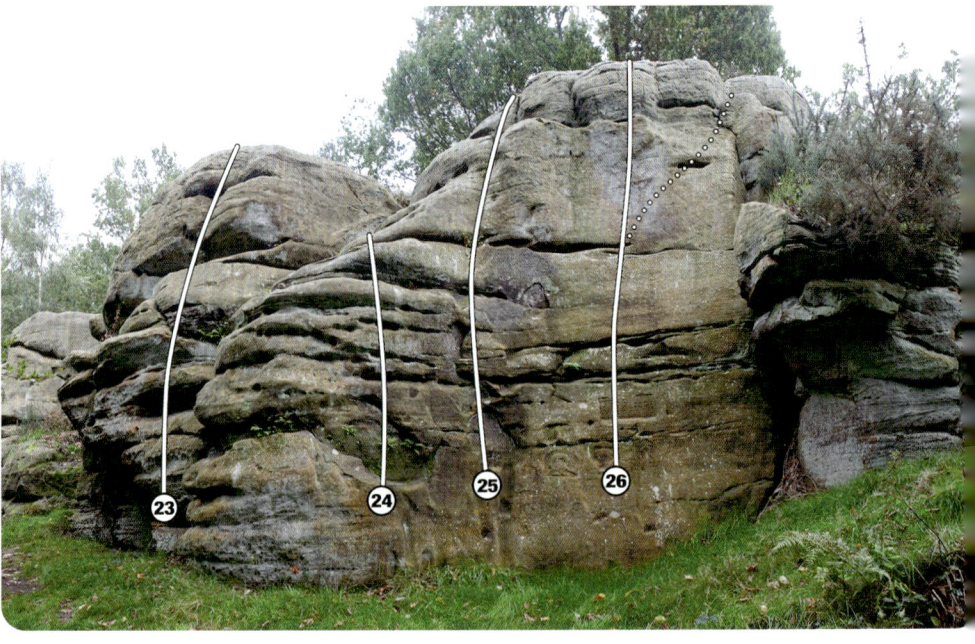

22. 4+ ss
The sit start is the hardest move on this short little juggy arête.

23. 5 ss
Another pleasant little climb up the face of this wall.

24. 3+
Follow the line of rounded breaks up the short wall.

25. 4 ⓑ
A nice little route up the flakes and layaways.

26. 5+ ⓑ
A centre slab is a great route that requires some delicate climbing. An easier finish off right is also worth doing for those not willing to battle with the slopey top.

27. 4
Just left of the crack is a short climb with a slopey top out.

28. 4+
Very similar to the previous climb this follows the line of good holds to the right of the crack.

201   *Happy Valley*

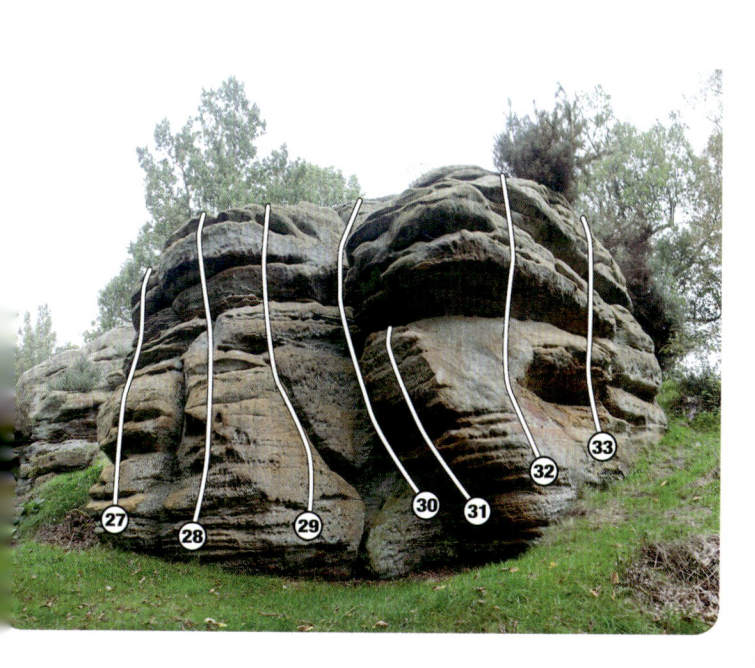

29. 5+
The skull guards this route of death, Climb if you dare!

30. 4
Climb up the corner crack line of good holds.

31. 6B ss
An eliminate up the overhanging face using only the holds on the face, the arête and side wall are out. Using everything is 6A.

32. 3+
The short slab route finishes to the left of the shrub.

33. 3+
This short slab route finishes to the right of the shrub.

Stuart Read | Route 26 | 5+

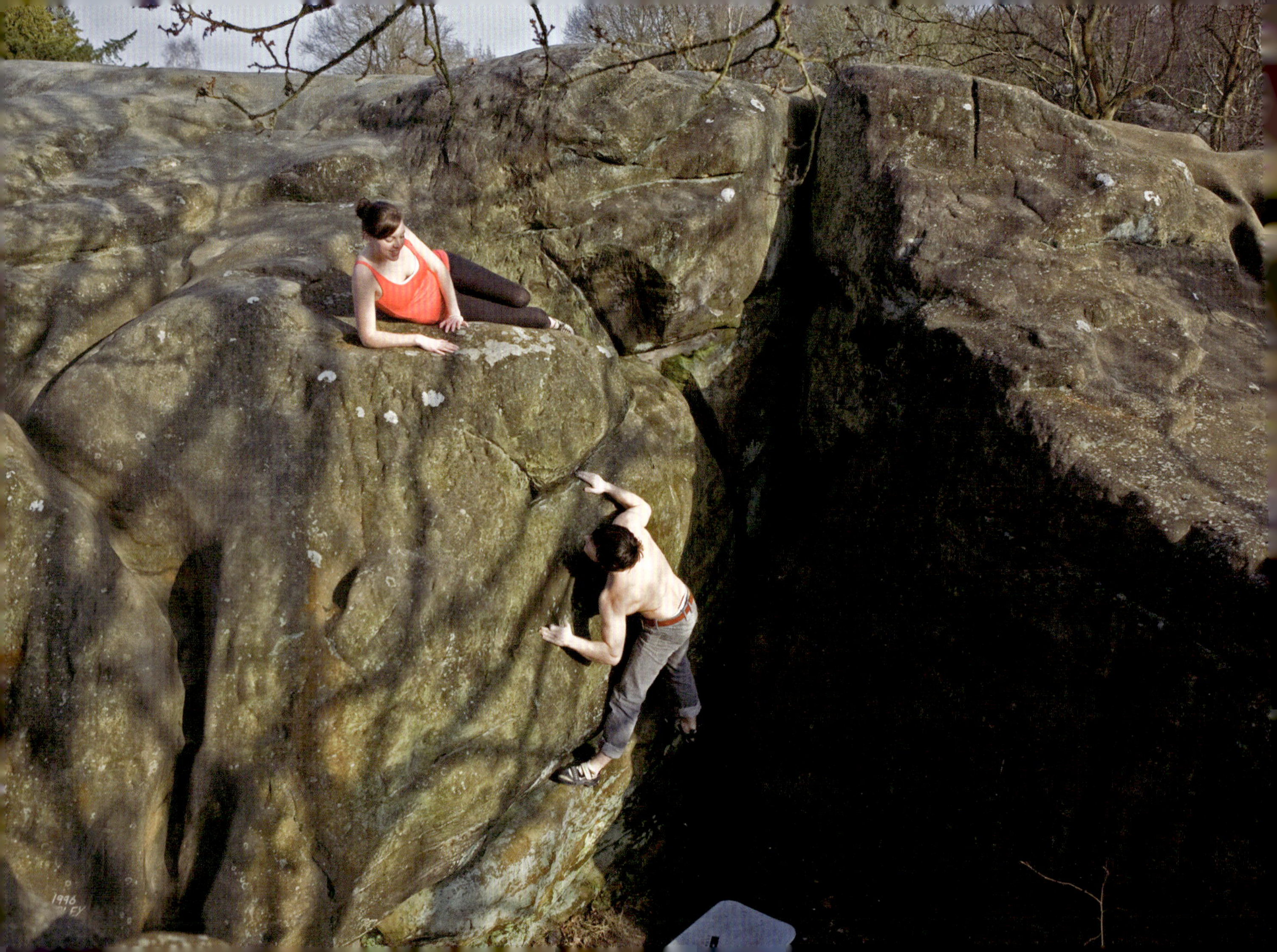

TOAD ROCKS

INTRODUCTION

This unusual collection of rocks provides some great fun in a relaxed and laid back area. The large sandy area and proximity to the Toad Rock Retreat pub means it will be popular for both kids and adults alike! There are tons of rocks to explore with various passageways and tunnels leading all over the place meaning that hours can be spent pottering around. Due to the high number of routes and complexity of all the boulders it is not really feasible to list and grade all of the problems. We have therefore decided to mention this crag and showcase a few pictures to hopefully capture the fun vibe that Toad Rocks holds and suggest you go and explore for yourself.

We have decided not to list every problem at Toad Rocks unlike the other crags. This is because it has so many different boulders and passageways that it would be near impossible to map all of these out in a clear way. Also the low grades of most of these problems mean that it is very hard to distinguish between the grades. Toad Rocks is best enjoyed by jumping around and climbing whatever you may find, a fantastic chilled venue!

ACCESS AND APPROACH

From Tunbridge Wells take the A264 towards East Grinstead and Groombridge and head along this for about 1 mile. You will then be looking out for a road called Rusthall Road on your right hand side. Take this turning and then the next right hand turn signposted for the Toad Rock Retreat. Follow this down and then park along the side of road in front of the rocks.

There are several collections of rocks all around this area so make sure you give yourself time to explore properly but just don't get lost!

CONDITIONS

These rocks are best visited during the summer months due to the large amount of passage ways and cracks that take time to dry out. Also the large sandy area works well as a beach type sandpit and no one likes visiting the beach on a cloudy day do they?

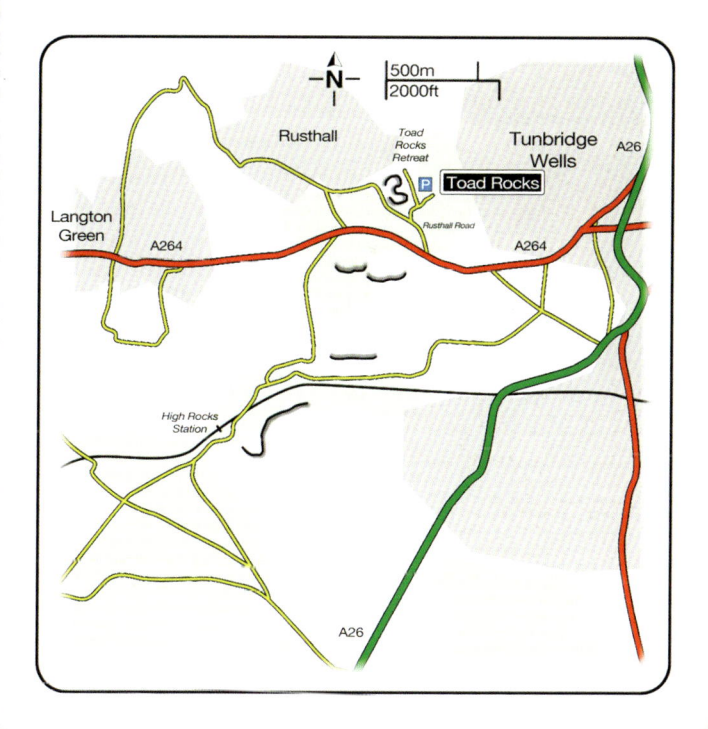

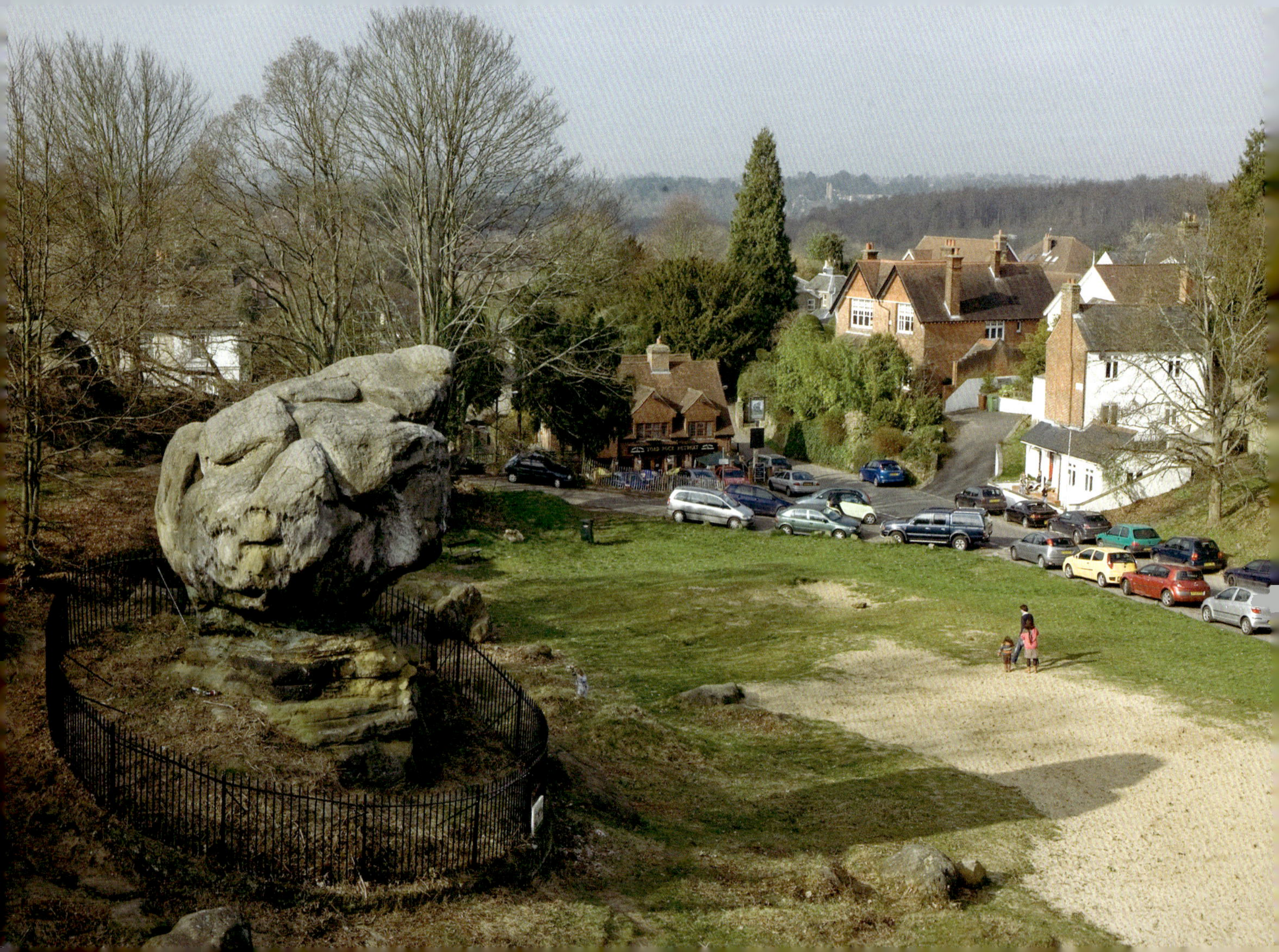

A264

P Parking on road

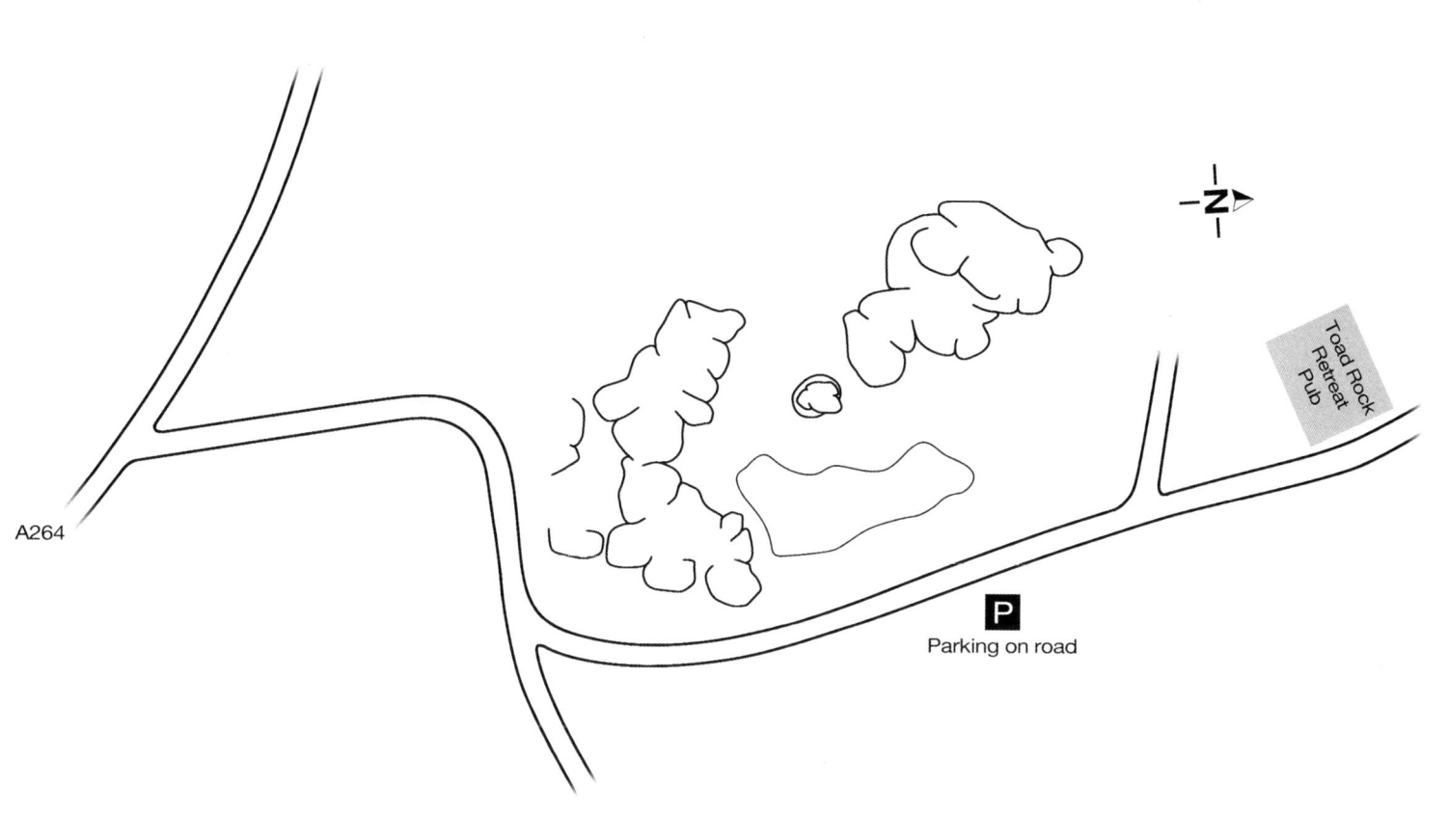

Toad Rock Retreat Pub

N

Toad Rocks 206

207 *Toad Rocks*

Toad Rocks 208

ELIMINATION WALLS

There are many places at the sandstone where you can make up endless eliminates to keep you entertained. We have listed the walls that we think are best for eliminates and here and have left the pictures blank for you to draw on your favourite routes to save you forgetting them.

FANDANGO WALL - BOWLES

Probably the most famous wall on the sandstone bouldering scene due to it staying dry most of the year round and its gradual overhanging face covered in holds.

ASHDOWN WALL - STONE FARM

This wall has a large variety of holds including slopers, crimps and cracks. There is also a good selection of large positive holds making this a fun wall for everyone.

Elimination Walls 210

THE MATTERHORN – HIGH ROCKS

The stiff face of the Matterhorn boulder provides many hard eliminates from straight ups to desperate traverses. The holds are generally small and painful but that has not stopped people pulling on them!

BARREL WALL – ERIDGE GREEN

The short barrel like wall has a good selection of crimps and pockets covering it. A lot of the existing lines here can be linked in to each other which mean that there are several very hard problems to be had as well as endless eliminations you can make up for yourself.

Elimination Walls 212

TOP 5's

SLABS

Change In The Weather – High Rocks Annexe p.189

Southern Softie – High Rocks Annexe p.187

Sansara – Eridge green p.119

Biometric Slab – Stone Farm p.25

Route 3 – Bowles p.83

OVERHANGS

Mojo – High Rocks p.170

The Sherriff – Bowles p.49

Stinging Nettle – Stone Farm p.38

Superfly – High Rocks p.145

Red Snapper – Happy Valley p.200

Barnaby Ventham | Red Snapper | 6A

There are many great problems on the sandstone and to highlight some of these we have come up with our top 5 dynos, slabs, traverses and overhangs. This does not mean that these are the only good problems of this type but in out eyes are definitely worth a look at.

DYNOS

Final Destination – High Rocks p.168

Chez's Dyno – High Rocks p.157

Yankee Affair – Eridge Green p.119

Banana Hammock Dyno – Bowles p.89

Route 101 – Stone Farm p.37

TRAVERSES

Maybe When You're Older – Bowles p.87

The Read Line – Eridge Green p.130

The Slow Pull – High Rocks p.177

Nicotine Alley – Bowles p.93

Old Kent Road – High Rocks p.177

Mike Hadcocks | Yankee Affair | 7A+

NOTES

NOTES

NOTES